FEB - - 2007

ALSO BY BERNARD CLAYTON

THE COMPLETE BOOK OF

SOUPS
and STEWS

UPDATED

BERNARD CLAYTON, JR.

Drawings by John Burgoyne

SIMON & SCHUSTER

New York   London   Toronto   Sydney

SIMON & SCHUSTER
Rockefeller Center
1230 Avenue of the Americas
New York, NY 10020

For information about special discounts for bulk purchases,
please contact Simon & Schuster Special Sales:
1-800-456-6798 or business@simonandschuster.com.

Designed by Katy Riegel

Manufactured in the United States of America

1   3   5   7   9   10   8   6   4   2

Library of Congress Cataloging-in-Publication Data
Clayton, Bernard.
The complete book of soups and stews / Bernard Clayton, Jr. ;
drawings by John Burgoyne.—Updated
p.   cm.
1. Soups.   2. Stews.   I. Title.
TX757.C57   2006
641.8'13—dc22   2006045023
ISBN-13: 978-0-7432-7715-0
ISBN-10:   0-7432-7715-5

Acknowledgments

I AM INDEBTED to hundreds of people across the United States, the Pacific, and Europe for helping me with this book. There is a responsive chord among people about food—soup in particular—and it made writing the book an exciting and rewarding experience. We spoke the same language. Throughout the text of the book I have given credit to several who have been helpful and whose recipes I have used or adapted.

Cookbook authors, like cooks, collect cookbooks. I surround myself with several hundred volumes, and their places on the shelves around the room have become so familiar to me that I can reach for them in the dark. When this book began, the books on baking were moved across to shelves over the firewood box, and the volumes on meats, vegetables, fruits, spices, herbs, stocks, stews, and many other topics were brought center stage where I could reach for them with ease.

Here are some of those books to which I turned time and again to find a technique, check a fact, spell a word, uncover an obscure recipe, find a contemporary one, or confirm a judgment. These authors and their books have made my kitchen a richer and more enjoyable place in which to cook and write. You may feel they can do the same for your kitchen. Other important volumes not listed here are given credit in the text of several recipes when it seemed appropriate to do so.

Elizabeth Andoh	*At Home with Japanese Cooking* (Knopf)
James Beard	*American Cookery* (Little, Brown); *The Theory and Practice of Good Cooking* (Knopf)
Jane Brody	*Jane Brody's Nutrition Book* (Norton)
Penelope Casas	*The Foods and Wines of Spain* (Knopf)
Samuel Chamberlain	*British Bouquet* and *Bouquet de France* (Gourmet Books)
Julia Child	*Mastering the Art of French Cooking,* I and II (Knopf); *Julia Child and Company* (Knopf)
Craig Claiborne	*Craig Claiborne's Gourmet Diet* (Times Books); *A Feast Made for Laughter* (Doubleday); *The Chinese Cookbook* (Lippincott)
Pierre Franey	*60-Minute Gourmet* (Ballantine Books)
Marcella Hazan	*The Classic Italian Cookbook* (Knopf)
Ken Hom	*Chinese Technique* (Simon & Schuster)
Mollie Katzen	*Moosewood Cookbook* (Ten Speed Press)
Diana Kennedy	*The Cuisines of Mexico* (Harper & Row)
Albert Levie	*Meat Handbook* (Avi Publishing)
Florence Lin	*Chinese Regional Cookbook* (Hawthorn)
Dione Lucas	*The Dione Lucas Book of French Cooking* (Little, Brown)
Thomas Mario	*Quantity Cooking* (Avi Publishing)
Lillian B. Marshall	*Cooking Across the South* (Oxmoor House)
Richard Olney	*The French Menu Cookbook* (Simon & Schuster)
Jacques Pepin	*La Technique* (Pocket Books)
Reader's Digest Association, Ltd., London	*Farmhouse Cookery*
Irma S. Rombauer and Marion Rombauer Becker	*The Joy of Cooking* (Bobbs-Merrill)
Ann Seranne, editor	*The Southern Junior League Cookbook* (Ballantine Books)
Yeh Ching-Huei	*Chinese Cuisine II (Huang Su-Huei)*

These reference volumes will enrich any kitchen library:

	Larousse Gastronomique (Crown)
	The Escoffier Cook Book (Crown)
	Foods of the World series (Time-Life Books)
Culinary Institute of America	*The Professional Chef* (CBI Publishing Company, Inc.)
	The Cook's Catalogue (Harper & Row)

A dedication . . . then and now.

To the 126 friends and neighbors who volunteered at the begin
ning of this book to taste, test, and comment on these soups and
stews. They said the job was not arduous.

I called on them twenty-five years later to taste new recipes in
this revised edition. They not only liked the recipes but asked to be
called anytime in the future for other tastings and other books.

B. C., Jr.

Contents

A Word from Bernard

DURING MY EARLY DAYS MAKING, baking, and writing about breads, it became clear that I should treat their longtime companion, soup, with equal zest. Hence, *The Complete Book of Soups and Stews*.

The two—soup and bread—have been table companions for centuries, to the point where it is difficult to think of one without the other. In travels throughout North America and Europe I have found them inseparably entwined. And it is hard to think of any accomplishment more satisfying to a home cook than a well-made loaf or a well-made bowl of soup.

Writing this book proved to be a happy experience filled with pleasure and discovery. The concerns and techniques in baking are considerably different from those involved in making soups, but I found the easy-to-follow, step-by-step presentation I had developed for the bread and pastry books to be equally effective.

Soups and stews are easier to make than baked goods. Unlike breads and pastries, where there is a note of finality when the oven door closes on your creation, soups and stews can be added to and taken from during the entire cooking process, right up to the moment they are ladled into a tureen or soup bowl. Even then, a final adjustment can be made before the first spoonful is eaten: some soups are finished with special sauces and garnishes at the whim and the taste of each guest.

All the recipes in the book have been taken apart, tested, tasted, judged, and adapted, where need be, to make them wholly compatible with the contemporary American kitchen.

The steps in each recipe are timed so that you know exactly how to schedule preparation, in part or in total.

The recipes have been chosen not only for the experienced cook but for the beginner as well. At no time will the new cook be left wondering what is expected next. The directions move easily through all the steps, leaving nothing to chance.

If you are a cook skilled in the kitchen, you will find new ways to enhance your skills, as well as new recipes to explore. The book will offer many points of departure from which you can sally forth to develop your own recipes based on tested procedures.

Introduction

D IETS COME AND GO, but soup goes on forever.
And for the best of reasons.

Soup is delicious. Soup is nutritious. Soup can light the inner fires. Soup can be hot or cold, thick or thin. Soup is healthy, light, and stimulating; it agrees with almost everyone.

A light soup served as a first course can excite the appetite for the courses to follow, and at the same time dampen the craving for too much food. Medical studies have disclosed that a dieter can lose a pound a week thanks to soup's unique role at the table.

To make soup or stew one needs fresh ingredients, a modicum of confidence, and readable, accessible recipes. This book is such a collection, and confidence, if lacking in the beginning, will grow as you turn more and more of the pages that follow.

The Complete Book of Soups and Stews, Updated is not complete in the literal sense, for it would take volumes to embrace onion soups alone; however, the range is complete—from chicken soups and chili to jambalaya and billi-bi.

The recipes include one or more of almost every kind of soup and stew, traditional as well as contemporary.

The book departs from the way in which most cookbooks usually categorize soups. *Larousse Gastronomique,* for instance, puts everything into two broad areas—clear soups and thick soups. *The Joy of Cooking* has nine divisions—bouillon, consommé, broths, jellied soups, vegetable soups, purees, cream soups, bisques, and chowders.

In this book, priority is given in most instances to the chief ingredient, whether it be vegetable or seafood or a meat or a grain, not whether a soup is hot or cold, thick or thin. For example, the fourteen chicken soups are placed together under *chicken*.

One hungers for a special flavor or taste such as tomato or mushroom or oyster. This is the primary inspiration of soup making, while the preparation, though important, is secondary.

STOCK

Considerable attention is given to stock because this rich broth is so important to the taste of good soup and stews. Not all recipes call for stock. Some generate their own stock while they cook, and even these are richer and more flavorful if stock, rather than water, is used.

TO LOSE WEIGHT

Soup can help you lose weight, and once it is off, soup will help keep it off. The reason is surprisingly simple. A bowl of soup takes more time to eat than a hamburger or a slice of pie or a baked potato. You are eating more slowly, and you are eating less.

Soup served at one meal a day, usually at lunch, can result in a weight loss of more than one pound a week. The time of day when the soup is eaten is important. Soup at lunchtime is more effective than soup at dinner because the diners tend to be less hungry at the evening meal for having had soup earlier.

Doctors have long known that caloric intake can be substantially reduced by such behavioral changes as putting cutlery down between bites, taking smaller mouthfuls, chewing more deliberately, and pausing between bites. Certain foods can force the eater to slow down. It takes longer to pull off artichoke leaves than it does to eat a dish of green beans. French fries go down faster than a baked potato. More time is spent munching a hard roll then eating soft bread.

Soup, by its very nature, is the foremost slow-down dish. Coupled with great nutritional benefits, soup makes an ideal component of a diet.

SALT AND SALT-FREE

There are many good reasons to make soup at home, and one of them is the control it gives over sodium intake, an important factor in a family's good health.

A quarter of Americans are genetically prone to developing high blood pressure if their diet is rich in sodium. The average American consumes 10 to 12 grams (2 to 4 teaspoons) of salt a day, or about 15 pounds a year.

Most vegetables—important ingredients in almost all soups—are low in sodium and can be consumed in unlimited quantities in a low-sodium diet. There are a few that are naturally higher in sodium—beet greens, celery, and spinach—but their contribution is considerably less when they are used fresh, not canned.

Homemade soup allows the cook complete mastery over the ingredients, including sodium. More often than not, a few drops of lemon juice can replace salt. Lemon juice and freshly ground black pepper can be more exciting than ordinary salt and pepper.

Canned soups, on the other hand, are notorious for their saltiness. The hidden salt and sodium-containing additives in canned soups and stews contain at least twice as much sodium as the average amount of salt used when soups and stews are homemade.

Why so much salt in processed foods? It enhances the flavor and preserves the product; in baked products salt restrains the yeast from working too enthusiastically and reduces water absorption. Salt is added to butter as a preservative and to cheese to control ripening. Pickles and sauerkraut are heavily salted to preserve them.

On the other hand, flavor bases (page 14), used by professional cooks to make stocks, soups, and stews, contain some salt, but most are accompanied with a caution *not* to add more salt until all the ingredients have been added and the flavors have had a chance to blend. Then, if necessary, salt is added to taste.

FAT-FREE

It is possible to make soup virtually free of fat. The fat molecules can be blotted off the surface of a hot soup with a paper towel or poured off in a special cup that decants the soup through a spout at the bottom.

But even these methods may leave a trace of fat. The surest way to remove fat is first to refrigerate the soup or stock. As it chills, the fat congeals on the surface, where it can then be easily taken off and discarded.

CREAM SOUPS

Many cream soups are spoiled because they are too thick—they go beyond creaminess to resemble something like paste. Very distasteful. A potato soup, for example, continues to thicken not only during the cooking process but while it is kept warm for serving. A cook should continually check for thickness, and test before serving. A tip of a spoon drawn across the surface should not leave a furrow. If it does, thin the soup with stock, water, or cream, whichever is most appropriate. Don't serve a soup if it comes off the ladle in globs.

HOT AND COLD

Hot soup should be served hot. Cold soup should be served cold.

To give hot soup the send-off it deserves, pour steaming hot water into the individual bowls and tureen 10 minutes before they are to be filled. Allow the hot water to remain in the vessels until the moment the soup is to be ladled. Discard the hot water and pour in the soup. Served in this fashion, soup is usually so hot—and remains so—that you may wish to caution your guests that your soup is served *hot!*

For cold soup, place the bowls and tureen in the refrigerator for at least 1 hour beforehand. Metal vessels can become attractively frosty after a thorough chilling in the refrigerator, or even the freezer.

TO SIMMER AND BOIL

Simmering is one of the most important (and misunderstood) words in the kitchen. A *simmer* is the languid movement of heated water and other liquids just before the bubbles break the surface. While a thermometer is useful in determining the simmer (190°F in my kitchen, 600 feet above sea level), that temperature varies if the simmering is done at sea level, where water boils at 212°F, or in mile-high Denver, where the boiling point is 203°F.

There is far less risk if you learn to judge simmering visually.

The purpose of simmering is to cook the ingredients for a long period in order to extract the flavor without allowing them to break into particles that would cloud a clear soup to the point where it could not be clarified afterward because the fat and other particles had been emulsified into the broth.

A *gentle boil* is just beyond a simmer. The bubbles form in the bottom of the pot and slowly make their way to the top, barely breaking the surface. Sound can aid in determining how fast a boil is developing. In a quiet kitchen the bubbles can be heard moving in the bottom of the pot several minutes before they begin to surface. Most of the time a gentle boil is as effective as a simmer and faster. Be watchful. Without your attention, a gentle boil can turn into a raging boil as the pot becomes saturated with heat.

A *gentle boil* is followed by a *boil* and then a *hard boil,* the last a vigorous volcano capable of breaking ingredients apart. While all stages have their place in soup making, proceed to each cautiously.

Stock, made initially over low heat, can be reduced with rapid boiling to concentrate and enhance the flavor, but this reduction is done after the solid ingredients have been discarded and the fat particles removed. To reduce before straining would irrevocably cloud the liquid.

BACK OF THE BOOK

Traditionally, in most cookbooks, the glossary—a compendium of spices, herbs, and seasonings, and charts of weights and measurements—as well as the index are printed in the back of the book. Not hidden, precisely, but not pushed forward, either. So early on, get familiar with these terms and techniques. They are so important that they must be mentioned here at the beginning.

Enjoy.

Equipment Important to Making Stocks, Soups, and Stews

THE *BATTERIE DE CUISINE* OF even the most humble kitchen can produce the tools to make a soup. A knife . . . a pot . . . a stove. But to make the full range of stocks, soups, and stews in this book calls for something more. These are suggestions for equipment to help—not absolutely necessary but definitely desirable.

KNIFE

It is always possible to substitute this pot for that one, or borrow a pot from a neighbor, but there is one tool that is essential to every kitchen—a sharp knife! One knife in particular—the French or cook's or chef's knife—is a necessity in the kitchen to transform stalks, roots, and leaves into all the different shapes and sizes appropriate for soups and stews.

All knives cut, but no knife cuts and chops as well as this. A French knife usually has a blade 8 to 10 inches long. Volumes have been written about this one knife, and a cook's apprentice learns early on to protect the blade with the same fierce devotion that a samurai shows for his sword. It is a cutting tool with a shape that has been honed and refined to near perfection by generations of cooks; the French knife is to the cook what the chisel is to the sculptor—a hand instrument without which a professional or a serious amateur cook can hardly function.

The ability to use the French knife does not come overnight, however; it is acquired gradually with each onion chopped, each carrot diced, and each stalk of celery sliced.

Two kinds of steel are used in the French knife as well as other knives used in the kitchen—carbon and stainless. The carbon knives have been admired for years because they hold a keen cutting edge—but they are easily tarnished by acidic fruits and vegetables. Until recently most stainless steel blades were difficult to sharpen and they held their edges poorly. This changed in recent years with the introduction of new high-carbon stainless steel blades, especially those from Solingen, Germany. They now equal the best of carbon steel knives. I have only stainless knives in my kitchen now, and they are a joy to use because they are rust- and stain-free.

The classic French knife has a triangular blade, the cutting edge turned to a gentle curve toward the tip. When selecting a French knife, make certain the tang (the obverse end of the steel) is thick and runs the whole length of the handle and is visible on top and bottom. Wooden handles that have been impregnated with plastic can withstand frequent washings in hot water. Choose a handle that allows your fingers to grip firmly without the knuckles hitting the cutting board when you are dicing or slicing. Make sure that the knife you choose is comfortable for you.

The drawings on pages 7 and 8 illustrate the proper way to hold the knife. In the beginning it may seem easier to let the index finger rest on the top of the blade. Don't do it—it makes chopping difficult and tiring.

When guiding vegetables under the blade, do so with the knuckles of the other hand held curved against the blade to protect fingertips!

Also important to the care of a knife are a sharpening stone and a steel—a length of tapered rod to restore the edge of the knife each time before it is used.

Two other knives recommended for a kitchen in which a lot of soups are made are a 4-inch paring knife and a 6½-inch utility knife.

STOCKPOT

The stockpot is designed especially for its job—tall and narrow, so that the liquid bubbles up through the layers of meat, bones, vegetables, and aromatics to create a rich flavorsome stock. At the same time, the narrowness of the stockpot reduces evaporation and conserves the liquid.

A stockpot is great to have, but good stock can be made almost as well in pots and kettles designed for other jobs.

If you are in the market for a stockpot, what size should you choose? Buy the largest you think you will need—and then double it. Stockpots for the home kitchen range in size from a small 4-quart pot upward to 20- and 22-quart vessels. Some of the larger ones are made with a spigot to drain off the stock or consommé without disturbing materials floating on the top or resting on the bottom. But these pots with spigots are expensive and their use in the home kitchen probably does not warrant their cost.

I have a medium-weight black aluminum-alloy stockpot in which I made all the stocks and consommés in the book, with a yield generally of about 6 to 8 quarts. This always gave me enough stock for the soup preparation at hand as well as a supply to freeze and use later.

If you are puzzled about the relationship of the pot size to the amount of stock produced, keep in mind that much of the bulk is caused by the bones and vegetables that are discarded after they have given up their flavors. The stock itself is only part of the volume.

SAUCEPAN AND SAUCEPOT

A saucepan is more than the small vessel in which to warm the baby's bottle. It and its larger companion, the saucepot, are two of the most important utensils in the kitchen.

The saucepan, the smaller of the two, has a long handle with which it is moved around on the stove or lifted off. It may also have a loop handle on the other side to hold if the pan is especially heavy. The saucepan comes in a range of sizes from 2 cups to 15 quarts.

The saucepot is identical in use but for larger quantities. It has two loop handles, rather than a long one, for lifting truly heavy loads. Saucepots come in sizes ranging from 8 quarts to 15 gallons.

Both the saucepan and the saucepot have tight-fitting lids.

The saucepot is probably too large for most kitchen stoves, but it is worth considering if guests are many and frequent.

To determine the size of the pot best for your kitchen, figure that a modest serving of soup and stew is about 1½ cups per person. So, to make stew for a party of eight would require a 4-quart pot at the very least. A 6- or 8-quart pot would give a comfortable margin.

In my kitchen I have 12- and 8-quart saucepots with loop handles only. Next in line are the saucepans—1½, 2, 3, 4½, and 6 quarts. The 4½-, 6½-, and 12-quart models are used the most. The ones I like best are of black aluminum alloy with tinned iron handles to retard the passage of heat. Infrequently I use a copper saucepot.

CASSEROLE (METAL)

A vessel of equal utility in the kitchen is the casserole that can be used both in the oven and on top of the stove. It is used for many dishes and comes in many sizes, shapes, and materials. Some casseroles are cast iron; others are of stainless steel, aluminum, and on and on. Some are round; others are oval. Some have stubby handles while others have loop handles.

DOUBLE BOILER

The double boiler is an ideal vessel in which to cook cream soups and other mixtures at temperatures below boiling without the risk of scorching and curdling. The Pyrex glass double boiler holds only 1¼ quarts but allows you to see whether the water in the lower container is boiling or simmering.

CHINOIS OR CHINA CAP

A chinois is a metal strainer, conical in shape and size and reminiscent of an Asian head covering of another era.

Its long, sturdy handle makes the chinois easy to hold or rest over a bowl as stocks or soups are poured through it. It comes in a range of hole and mesh sizes. Solids are pureed by pressing them through the holes with the specially designed wooden roller that usually comes with this utensil.

The chinois alone is usually sufficient to strain most stocks and soups. For a clearer liquid, cheesecloth is draped inside the chinois and the broth goes through both meshes.

An ordinary sieve is good for straining, but most sieves have limited capacity when stock is poured through to separate the liquid from the solids. With care, however, they can be used.

A colander, a less sophisticated piece of equipment, does a valuable job in the kitchen for washing and draining food. In a pinch, the colander can be lined with cheesecloth for more subtle straining, but it is not ideal.

TIMERS

While timing is not as critical in making soups and stews as it is in baking pastries or breads, it is important to go back to the stove at intervals to check progress. It is easy in making soup to go off and forget about the project because of the length of time some soups and stews are on the stove. A timer will remind you that something is cooking.

My favorite is a round 60-minute timer on a cord that I wear around my neck whenever I leave the kitchen. It is made by Terraillon and sold in most gourmet cookware shops and by catalog.

THERMOMETER

Is it a simmer? Is it a hard boil? Which? To make this determination by sight comes with experience (pages xviii–xix) and a thermometer can be of great help in deciding which it is.

The Taylor Bi-Therm Pocket Dial Thermometer (0°F to 220°F) is an accurate instrument to check temperatures of liquids. It is held in the soup only momentarily and then withdrawn. This thermometer is especially helpful in determining the temperature of hot soup before it comes to a simmer.

OTHER EQUIPMENT

Other tools to be found in a well-equipped kitchen would include a food processor, a blender, food mills, a slow cooker, a mixer (with meat grinder), scales, ladles, wooden spoons and spatulas, and a slotted spoon. For the times when it is impossible to get the temperature lower without shutting off the heat, a metal or asbestos heat diffuser placed under the pan is effective.

Perhaps a microwave oven has a place in soup making but I am uncertain where. Of course it is excellent for thawing and heating soups and stews that have been frozen.

How to Prepare the Six Vegetables Most Important to Stocks, Soups, and Stews

CUTTING VEGETABLES IS AN ART. And, after you become accomplished with the French or cook's knife, and appreciate that it is a tool, not a weapon, cutting can be satisfying, even fun. The expertise comes only after many bags of onions and many stalks of celery. But it does come.

There are half a dozen vegetables—onions, celery, carrots, leeks, garlic, and shallots—essential to the preparation of many stocks, soups, and stews, and each is cut in a slightly different way. Parsley, an equally important vegetable in the kitchen, requires no special cutting technique. Rich in vitamins A and C, parsley is used in many recipes in the book. Some call for sprigs of parsley, while others, such as those for the basic stocks, call for the stalks or stems to be tied into a bundle and dropped into the pot to be retrieved later and discarded.

This step-by-step guide is an adaption of one written by Thomas Mario in his fine book *Quantity Cooking* (Avi Publishing), which has been one of my trustworthy guides in the world of soups and stews.

ONIONS

Cut a thin slice from the neck of the onion with a paring knife and remove the skin from the neck to the root end, folding the skin back rather than cutting it. Trim the root end but

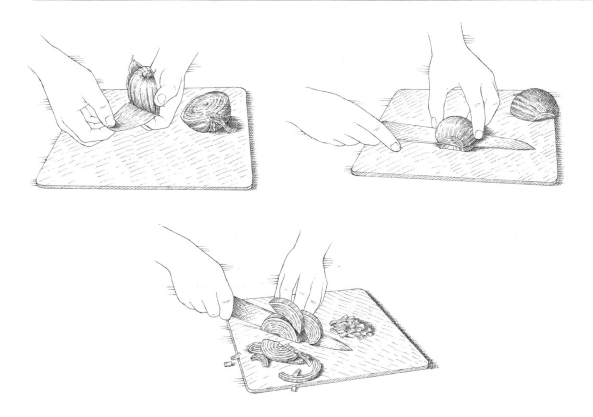

don't cut deeply into it. It is the section to which the onion layers are attached, and the root end holds the onion intact on the cutting board as it is being cut.

Diced

Cut the peeled onion in half from neck to root end. Place flat side of onion on the cutting board with the root end to your left (if you are right-handed). Holding the knife over the onion, make vertical lengthwise cuts from root end to stem end. The thickness of these slices will vary: for small dice, cut ½-inch slices; large dice, ¾-inch slices.

Hold the blade horizontal to the cutting board and cut lateral slices toward the root end of the onion, choosing thickness of dice required. Don't cut into the root end. The onion must stay intact.

Now cut a vertical slice across the onion, choosing the thickness desired.

Dice remaining half of onion in the same manner.

Finely Chopped

Slices should be cut ⅛ inch thick and chopped.

For extremely fine pieces, continue chopping until all particles are no larger than 1⁄16 inch.

Julienne

Cut the peeled onion in half through the root end, and place flat on the cutting board, root end to the left. Beginning at the stem end of the onion, cut vertical slices across the onion—⅛ inch thick. Toss the slices with fingertips to separate slices. The slices will separate into julienne strips when stirred with a spoon.

Sliced

Cut a thin slice off one side of a peeled whole onion so that it will rest flat on the cutting board. Place the onion on its flat side, root end to the left. Make vertical, parallel slices of desired thickness.

CELERY

In most soups and stews only the large outer stalks—or ribs, as they are often called—of celery are used. The small inner stalks are usually served as iced celery hearts or used in salads. Stalks should be separated, washed, and scrubbed with a vegetable brush. Cut off the leaves unless the recipe calls for them. If the stalks are large and tough, peel them with a vegetable peeler with a floating blade to remove the stringy outer portion.

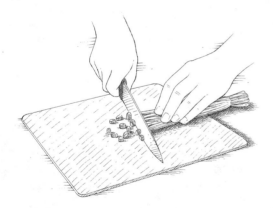

Diced

With the knife point at the narrow end of the stalk, cut celery lengthwise into strips. For small dice, strips should be ¼ inch wide; medium dice, ½ inch wide; and large dice, ¾ inch wide. Hold the celery strips in a bundle in the left hand and cut across strips to make dice of the proper size.

Chopped

Cut the celery into large dice, as above, and chop until celery is reduced to the desired size.

Julienne
Cut the celery stalk laterally into slices no thicker than ⅛ inch. Cut crosswise into 1½-inch pieces. Cut pieces lengthwise no larger than ⅛ inch.

CARROTS

Small, young, tender carrots need not be peeled for most soups, but large carrots are peeled before they are cut into various shapes. Carrots used in making stock needn't be peeled in either case, since they will be discarded with the other vegetables used in making the stock.

Sliced
Cut a thin lengthwise strip off each carrot. The slice should be just thick enough to permit the carrot to rest flat on the cutting board without wobbling. Cut the carrots crosswise into ¼- or ½-inch slices, or diagonally if desired.

Diced
Cut the carrot to rest flat on the cutting board. If the carrots are large, cut into several lengthwise pieces about 3 inches long. Cut slices lengthwise into the desired thickness of the dice. Place strips in a bundle to hold in the left hand while cutting them crosswise into desired dice.

Julienne
Cut as above but instead of into small dice, cut to 1½-inch length. Cut the lengthwise strip into ⅛-inch-thick pieces.

LEEKS

Usually the white and some of the firm part of the green are required. For some soups only the white part of the leek is used, with the top green ends going into the stockpot. For all uses, cut off the stringy root end but leave the solid part intact. After cutting leeks lengthwise (as below), hold them under cold running water and wash away the sand and dirt.

Diced
Cut the leeks lengthwise toward the root end, slicing to within an inch of the end, making halves, quarters, sixths, or eighths depending on the size of the dice required. Separate the layers and wash until completely clean. Place leeks on cutting board, root end to your left. Cut crosswise into size of dice required. When the root end is reached, cut it first lengthwise and then crosswise to make dice.

Chopped

Cut leeks into ½-inch dice and chop with tip of knife.

Julienne

Cut leeks lengthwise as above, and then crosswise into 1½-inch pieces. Cut the 1½-inch pieces lengthwise to make ⅛-inch-thick strips.

GARLIC AND SHALLOTS

Usually these two flavoring vegetables are chopped extremely fine except for a few instances when they are lightly crushed under the flat of a knife or left whole for a sachet or bouquet garni. Garlic comes in a cluster called a bulb or head, which separates into sections called cloves. To separate the cloves, place the whole bulb on the cutting board at an angle. Holding it with the left hand, strike it solid blows with the palm of your right hand until the cloves come apart.

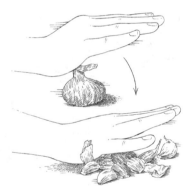

To peel garlic or a shallot place the clove on a cutting board. With the flat side of a French knife against it, strike the blade with a blow of the fist. The clove will be partly crushed and the skin loosened. Remove the skin and discard. Place the partly crushed garlic or shallot on the cutting board and chop with the knife tip on the board.

Stock: The Principal Ingredient

STOCK IS THE LIQUID in which meat or meat bones, fowl or fowl bones, fish or fish bones, and vegetables have been cooked to extract their flavor. While stock is the foundation of nearly all soups, the meatier ingredients of stews create their own delicious broth, which may be enhanced on occasion with the addition of the concentrated flavor of a stock or bouillon.

The basic ingredient of many soups and stews, stock begins with a long, slow simmering of meat and vegetables in slightly salted water. Stock is the exception to almost everything one has learned about cooking. The young and tender are put aside in favor of meat and bones from aged animals and mature vegetables—the most flavorsome. Instead of attempting to trap flavorful juices within the materials being cooked, one makes every effort to *extract* and *exploit* every vestige of flavor from them.

Stock should have a pleasant flavor of the meat, poultry, seafood, or vegetable with a minimum of salt. It should leave a delicate, mild aftertaste.

Stocks are known among cooks as *fonds de cuisine,* the foundations of the kitchen. Escoffier, the great French chef, said, "Stock is everything in cooking. . . . Without it, nothing can be done." An exaggeration perhaps, but it does underline the importance of stocks in the kitchen. They are essential not only to soups and stews but for making sauces, gravies, and braised dishes.

In every kitchen there arises the need for store-bought stocks to supplant or augment the homemade ones. Perhaps there isn't time to make a stock, or the necessary ingredients may not be in the market. The role these commercial stocks have in the home kitchen is outlined in a following section (page 14).

There are five principal stocks.

• WHITE STOCK (FONDS BLANC): For soups and stews that require only light flavoring. Made with meat bones, usually beef, but veal and poultry may be added. The bones are simmered in water with aromatic vegetables.

Cooking time: Simmer 6 to 8 hours.

• BROWN STOCK (FONDS BRUN or ESTOUFFADE): Used in dark soups and stews that have a pronounced beefy flavor. Veal and beef bones are used in combination and are caramelized and browned in the oven to impart flavor and color before the water is added. Vegetables, herbs, and spices are added.

Cooking time: Bake 3¾ hours in the oven; then simmer 5 to 6 hours.

• CHICKEN STOCK (FONDS DE VOLAILLE): Mainly for light and flavorful dishes. Derived from simmered fowl. The most economical pieces are backs, wings, gizzards, and necks. It is simmered with a mirepoix of vegetables and herbs and spices.

Cooking time: Simmer 3 hours.

• FISH STOCK OR FUMET (FONDS DE POISSON): Seafood soups and stews are made with fish fumet, derived from poaching fish and/or fish bones in water. It utilizes a mirepoix of vegetables and wine, vinegar, or lemon juice in its preparation.

Cooking time: Smother 10 to 15 minutes; simmer 45 minutes.

• VEGETABLE STOCK (COURT BOUILLON): Used in the preparation of vegetarian dishes as well as fish, and on occasion used in place of chicken stock. It is obtained from onions, celery and carrots cooked in water and flavored with herbs and, in some instances, garlic.

Cooking time: Gentle boil, 30 minutes.

Most of the soups and stews in this book call for one of these five. Many are made with water and actually make their own stocks as the soups or stews cook. There are also specialty stocks such as dashi, the one made with seaweed for Japanese soups (page 24).

Here are important pointers for making stock:

• Avoid an aluminum pot, if possible, because it will affect the clarity of the stock. Under no condition store stock in such a pot, for this will make the stock bitter as well as stain the pot.

• Meat and bones from older animals are the most flavorsome. Bones contain eight times the amount of gelatin that is in meat, hence the importance of bones in making stock.

• Trim fat off meat and bones to minimize the fat that will cook to the top during the long simmering.

• Bones and meat that have been frozen (most are today) need not be blanched before using. However, if the bones are fresh or smell unnaturally strong, wash, blanch in boiling water, drain, wash again before putting them into the stockpot to simmer, or into the baking pan if making a brown stock.

• Vegetables for a mirepoix are chosen in the ratio of 60-20-20: 60 percent onions and 20 percent each carrots and celery.

• Don't use strong-tasting vegetables such as broccoli and cabbage.

• Vegetables are cut into large pieces rather than finely chopped.

• As all stocks are strained, there is no need to place herbs and spices in a metal or cheesecloth sachet.

• Stock begins with cold water, added to the other ingredients, which is brought to a boil and skimmed often to remove scum that accumulates on the surface.

• Don't salt heavily at the beginning. Reduction of stock and its various subsequent uses make it impossible to judge the amount needed. However, a moderate amount of salt is important in the preparation of stock because it helps draw the albumin from the bones and keeps the stock clear. Kosher salt is preferred because it contains no additives that could cloud the stock.

• The contents of the stockpot should be stirred only two or three times during the first hour. Excessive stirring may cause the stock to become turbid.

• Don't cook beyond a simmer or gentle boil or the stock will become cloudy.

• Be watchful of the stove heat during the long period of cooking the stock. Burners, both gas and electric, can be irrational at times. Temperatures may change as the gas pressure fluctuates or as the stockpot becomes saturated with heat. A stock that is barely simmering one minute may be boiling furiously the next. A tiny adjustment of a burner can throw the stock into panic. In brief, don't stray far away during cooking. It is better to turn off the heat when you must leave the kitchen than to risk returning to a bubbling volcano.

• Stocks can be made with carcasses of previously cooked turkey, duck, goose, and chicken. The quantity of such bones should be double that of uncooked bones for stock of equal strength.

• It is not necessary to pour all stocks through cheesecloth, especially those that will be used in soups and stews that don't demand clarity. Usually a chinois or sieve is sufficient. Allow the stock time to rest; during this time most of the sediment will fall to the bottom. Ladle out carefully.

• To clarify stock beyond what cheesecloth alone will do, strain by the following method and chill the stock. For each quart of stock, add 1 slightly beaten egg white and a crumpled eggshell. Stir them into the stock. Bring the stock to a simmer slowly without stirring. A heavy crust will form on the surface as the soup heats. Simmer for 10 to 15 minutes. Move the pot carefully from the heat and let rest for 30 minutes. Push the crust aside and ladle the stock into a chinois or sieve lined with a triple thickness of moistened cheesecloth.

• Any stock can be concentrated in flavor and volume by boiling it down. The reduction is made after the stock has been cooked and the solid ingredients have been removed. The extreme is meat glaze, or *glace de viande,* a reduction of brown stock to the point that it is a gelatinous mass on the bottom of the vessel, thick enough to coat a spoon.

• When stock is to be refrigerated, there is no need to remove the fat that rises to the top. It will seal off the stock until, just prior to reheating, it can be lifted off with a slotted spoon and discarded. (Some use this discarded fat to make a roux.)

• To prevent spoiling, refrigerated stocks should be brought to a boil every 2 to 3 days and returned to the refrigerator.

• Finally, there is this maxim among chefs that should be posted in each soup maker's kitchen:

> "Keep it hot,
> keep it cold,
> when in doubt
> throw it out!"

HOMEMADE VERSUS STORE-BOUGHT

Stock, as we have seen, is the liquid from boiled meat, poultry, seafood, or vegetables, plus seasonings, that is used as a foundation not only for soups and stews but also for sauces and gravies.

Many recipes in this book call for stocks. They can be homemade or store-bought. The choice is yours. The resulting soups will differ, of course, but that's the fun of tasting and testing until you strike the combination that brings the greatest pleasure to the palate.

Confusingly, stocks are not called stocks on supermarket shelves. They are called consommés, bouillons, and broths, and they come bottled, canned, cubed, and granulated. Some taste good. Many don't. Some are too weak to do the job. Some are too salty, others too flat. There are a few, however, that are robust and full-bodied and these can make things better when used judiciously. Those in granular form, for example, are made of vegetable protein and can enhance stocks when employed in small amounts.

The Food Base
This picture changes dramatically in restaurant, club, and hotel kitchens. While many make their own stocks from scratch, professional kitchens have for their use a *base* of real

food essence. These are high-quality products made for a critical and demanding trade. The beef bases are actually made with beef, the chicken bases are made with chicken, and the fish bases are prepared with fish.

Bases usually come in 1-pound glass or plastic containers, and each, as a rule, will make about 5 gallons of stock. One teaspoon will make 1 cup. Except for those that are dehydrated, such as the French onion soup, bases must be refrigerated and will keep for up to two years. Highly concentrated, they are thick and must be spooned.

One outstanding line of food bases is produced by the L. J. Minor Corporation, Cleveland. They are made with no artificial preservatives or flavors and with a minimum of salt. The Minor list includes beef, chicken, fish, vegetable, ham, garlic, clam, onion, French onion, mushroom, brown sauce, and shrimp.

The staffs of commercial kitchens greatly admire these bases by Minor and others, including LeGout, Swiss Knorr, and Sexton Gold. They save labor in the kitchen, conserve fuel, lower serving costs, and have a natural wholesomeness and homemade flavor that complement quality cooking. Small club and restaurant kitchens depend almost entirely on food bases as stocks, but the larger ones use bases only to supplement their own stocks.

Unfortunately these bases are not readily available to the home cook. They are sold almost exclusively by food wholesalers to commercial kitchens, and it is difficult for the home cook to break into this supply chain unless he or she knows the chef at the country club or the soup cook in the restaurant across town.

The one that is available to the home cook, fortunately, is the best—Minor's. A Michigan firm, The Flavour Base, has the franchise for selling a wide variety of Minor's bases, which are available in small (4-ounce) and large (1-pound) containers. The mushroom base in a small jar, for instance, will make 5 quarts of mushroom soup, a good return on investment.

The Flavour Base has put together a special "professional sampler" for the home cook containing six 4-ounce jars of beef, chicken, brown sauce, mushroom, lobster, and onion base. The address is P.O. Box 2515, Dearborn, MI 48123.

One attempt has been made to produce a base for the home cook of the same high quality as those for the restaurant trade. It is called "Simmerin's"—beef and chicken. It is a concentrated stock in a 3½-ounce bottle and is manufactured by a company famous for its deviled ham spread, the Wm. Underwood Co., One Red Devil Lane, Westwood, MA 02090. These bases are carried in supermarkets.

Consommés, Bouillons, and Broths

Back to the supermarket shelves. The choice of these products is so great and the quality so varied that one must make his or her own judgments by tasting/testing them in the kitchen. Here are some I have tried with varying success—Sweet Sue, College Inn, Swanson, Campbell's, Wyler's, Lite-Line (low-sodium by Borden), Knorr Swiss, Romanoff MBT, Weight Watchers, and Herb-Ox.

Several are "flavored" rather than made with the real essence. Flavored chicken, for example, is made with vegetable protein, to which a bit of chicken fat has been added for flavoring. Some of the canned consommés and bouillons, if not insipid, go too far in the other direction with too much salt.

If you are into serious soup making, sample them all. The total cost for one of each will be no more than $15 and can be the excuse for having a tasting affair where guests vote for their favorites.

In sum, every kitchen should have a supply of some kind of ready-made stock product on hand, whether it be the food bases or cans and packages of consommés, bouillons, and broths.

In fairness I must write that I have used Campbell's canned beef bouillon with considerable success for many years. I have used it to make an outstanding French onion soup. I am aware of its saltiness, so I take that into account when I season the soup.

Store-Bought Soups and Stews

There comes a time in every cook's life when a can of soup (not stock) is the only answer. Some canned soups are very good. These can be made better with an inspired addition of a spice, a cup of wine, a spoonful of vinegar, a squeeze of lemon, a garlic clove, or a handful of rice or pasta. These will take away the factory taste with a creative touch of yourself.

White Stock
Fonds Blanc

Makes approximately 6 quarts

Originally white stock was made primarily with veal bones but today it is made with nearly any combination of beef, veal, or poultry bones. This recipe calls for beef bones, but feel free to make substitutions.

INGREDIENTS
5 pounds meaty beef bones, cut into short lengths
Water to cover, to blanch and discard
Water to cover (about 8 quarts), 4 inches above bones
2 teaspoons salt

Mirepoix
1½ pounds onions, peeled and chopped
½ pound carrots, scrubbed and chopped
½ pound celery, including leaves, chopped

Sachet d'épice

2 cloves

3 cloves garlic, bruised

3 bay leaves

1 teaspoon black peppercorns

½ teaspoon thyme

6 to 8 sprigs parsley, tied together

SPECIAL EQUIPMENT	Large (12- or 16-quart) stockpot or kettle. Chinois or sieve. Cheesecloth, optional.
PREPARATION	Rinse bones under running water and place in the stockpot.
BLANCH	Cover with water and bring to a boil. Immediately pour off the water, which will carry with it scum and bits and pieces of flesh and bone.
BOIL/SIMMER 6–8 hours	Cover bones again with water to a depth of 4 inches above them and add cold water as necessary to maintain liquid at this level during the long simmering. Bring the water to a boil, reduce heat, and simmer for at least 6 to 8 hours. Kitchens in fine restaurants allow it to simmer for up to 12 hours.
	Skim the surface repeatedly as foam collects. Stir the pot once or twice during the first hour so the bones don't stick to the bottom.
	Add the salt as the stock begins to simmer, and stir to blend.
MIREPOIX 2 hours	Prepare the onions, carrots, and celery for the mirepoix. Add to the stock for the final 2 hours. (If the stock is to cook for 6 hours, drop in the mirepoix at the end of 4 hours.)
SACHET 30 mins.	A half hour before the stock is finished, add the sachet d'épice and parsley.
STRAIN	Place the chinois or sieve over a large bowl or pot to receive the stock.
	Although the vegetables, bones, and sachet are to be discarded, since much of their flavor has been extracted, there is considerable good left in the vegetables and scraps of meat to use for pet food.
COOL	If possible arrange a cold-water bath in the sink in which to set the pot of stock to cool rapidly. Stir frequently. If this can't be done, place the pot in the refrigerator. (I have placed stockpots in snowbanks, but these are not always available.)
	Stock will keep refrigerated 2 to 3 days in covered containers but

should be reheated and cooled again if to be kept for several more days. Stock freezes very well for long periods. Pour the stock into convenient 4- to 6-cup plastic freezer boxes. Label with contents, date, and volume. Cover and freeze.

Brown Stock
Fonds Brun

Makes approximately 6 to 8 quarts

Beef bones and vegetables browned and caramelized in the oven before they are simmered in the stockpot give fonds brun *its rich color and pronounced good taste. While brown stock is easy to make, it does take a watchful eye over a long period of time. The effort is worth it. The result will be several quarts of rich stock to use now or freeze to use in the weeks and months ahead.*

The bones and the mirepoix bake in a moderately hot (400°) oven until both are browned. Care must be taken, however. If the oven is too hot or the pan is left in the oven too long, some of the vegetables may burn, giving the stock a scorched taste. When the bones and vegetables are placed in the stockpot, they are cooked at a simmer or gentle boil. Anything more vigorous would make the stock cloudy and limit its use.

INGREDIENTS   3 pounds meaty beef and/or veal bones, fresh or frozen
Cold water to rinse, if fresh bones are used

Mirepoix
1 pound onions, peeled and roughly cut
½ pound *each* celery and carrots, cut into 2-inch pieces
1 tablespoon salt, kosher preferred
3 cups either fresh or canned whole tomatoes or
    1½ cups tomato paste or tomato puree

Sachet d'épice
1 clove
1 clove garlic
2 bay leaves, crumbled
½ teaspoon peppercorns
½ teaspoon thyme

5 or 6 sprigs parsley, tied together

SPECIAL EQUIPMENT	Large roasting pan to fit the oven. Large (12- to 16-quart) stockpot or kettle. Chinois or sieve. Cheesecloth, optional.
PREPARATION	If the bones are fresh, boil them one time in water to cover, and drain. Bones that have been frozen—and today most of them have been—need not be boiled.

PREPARATION — Trim fat from any meat there is, as fat is the biggest enemy of stock and will have to be taken off later if not now.

Preheat oven to 400°.

BAKE
400°
2 hours

Scatter the meat and vegetables over the baking pan. Sprinkle on the kosher salt. Place the pan on the middle or lower rack in the hot oven.

Check the pan frequently and stir the meat and vegetables with a wooden spoon each time. Lower the heat if vegetables are getting too brown and likely to burn—especially those around the edges of the pan.

Remove the pan from the oven.

BOIL/SIMMER
4–6 hours

Scrape everything in the baking pan into the stockpot including the *fonds,* or crusty bits, from the bottom of the pan. To loosen the *fonds,* deglaze with a cup of water poured into the pan. Much of the flavor is in the *fonds,* so be certain you scrape off all you can.

Pour in 8 quarts of cold water and bring to a boil, skimming off sediment as it rises to the surface. Simmer for 4 to 6 hours—the longer the better—to extract all of the flavor from the ingredients.

Stir gently once or twice to free any sediment to rise to the surface.

SACHET
30 mins.

A half hour before the stock is finished, add the sachet d'épice and parsley.

REST
1 hour

When the stock is cooked, turn off the heat and let it rest for 1 hour. Discard the sachet and parsley.

STRAIN

Ladle the stock through a chinois or sieve. For a sediment-free stock, ladle through a double or triple thickness of moistened cheesecloth.

COOL

Cool the stock quickly before storing. Placing the stockpot or kettle in the sink and running cold water around it is perhaps the best way to achieve this. Stir frequently. If a large stockpot is too much for your sink, divide the stock among pint and quart containers to cool and also to store. Putting the stock outside in cold weather (in a sheltered spot) is a good way to cool it.

When the stock has cooled, refrigerate the amount that is to be used in the next day or so and freeze the rest.

Discard the cooked bones and vegetables.

Chicken Stock
Fonds Blanc de Volaille
Makes 6 quarts

In some commercial kitchens, what is called "chicken stock" is made with turkey or duck or pheasant or any bird at hand. In the home kitchen, however, chicken almost always is used—not necessarily the expensive parts, but the necks, wing tips, backs, gizzards, and feet. Or the chicken might be a whole fowl, the term used for old chickens that have labored long and well in egg production. Less expensive than other whole chickens, the old birds make a rich and delicious stock.

Homemade chicken stock has a texture and richness on the tongue that few if any commercial products can equal. It is the principal ingredient in making at least half the soups in this book.

Chicken stock is so easy and economical to make that store-bought stock should be used only because of time constraints. Even that situation is avoidable if a supply of homemade stock is kept in the freezer.

There are two ways to approach the selection of the bird. A stewing hen or other large chicken will provide both stock and meat. Long simmering will draw out most of the flavor; thus cook for less time if the meat is to be used in another dish. Some of the richness may be sacrificed but the stock will still be good, though not as rich. Or you may find that chicken pieces are cheaper—backs, wings, necks, and, if your market has them, feet. Use them in combination, or with a whole chicken if needed to reach the weight called for in the recipe. Wings, backs, and even necks produce some meat that can be used for less-than-special dishes.

It is easy to think of stock quantities in these increments:

> *To make 6 quarts of stock, begin with 8 quarts of cold water.*
> *Add 6 pounds of chicken pieces and/or a whole chicken.*
> *Add 3 pounds of mirepoix—1½ pounds of onions, ¾ pound of carrots, and ¾ pound of celery.*
> *Also add salt, pepper, and sachet d'épice.*

This recipe will make 6 quarts, or 24 cups, of stock. It is time-saving to make at least 6 quarts. If your soup pots are not large, scale down the recipe to fit the vessel at hand. This is no big problem; it simply means you will make stock more often.

INGREDIENTS

6 pounds chicken, whole or in parts
2 teaspoons salt

Mirepoix
1½ pounds onions, peeled and coarsely chopped
¾ pound *each* coarsely chopped carrots and celery

8 quarts water

Sachet d'épice
2 cloves
3 cloves garlic, mashed
3 bay leaves, crumbled
½ teaspoon *each* black peppercorns and thyme

5 or 6 sprigs parsley, tied together

SPECIAL EQUIPMENT

Chinois or sieve. Cheesecloth, optional.

PREPARATION

Wash the chicken or chicken pieces under cold running water. Place in a stockpot and cover with water, about 8 quarts.

BOIL/SIMMER
1 hour

Bring the stock to a gentle boil, reduce heat to a simmer, and cook for 1 hour. Skim frequently as sediment comes to the surface. Do not cover. For a concentrated stock, don't replenish water as it evaporates. Otherwise, add water.

MIREPOIX
2 hours

Add the mirepoix and return to a simmer. Continue cooking for a total of 3 hours.

SACHET
30 mins.

A half hour before the stock is finished, add the sachet d'épice and parsley.

REST
30 mins.

When the stock has finished cooking, remove from the heat and put aside to rest and cool. Of all the primary stocks, chicken stock is the most susceptible to spoiling or souring, and its temperature should be lowered as quickly as possible.

COOL

Cold water flowing around the stockpot will dissipate the heat quickly. If the large stockpot is too large for the sink, divide the stock among small containers to cool. Stir occasionally to move the warm stock at the center out to the cool sides.

STRAIN

Strain the stock by ladling through a chinois or sieve. Straining it a second time through moistened cheesecloth will remove almost all of the sediment. Discard the sachet, parsley, and vegetables. The meat from the chicken bones can be used in other dishes.

CHILL

The stock may be refrigerated 2 or 3 days but it should be brought to a boil if it is to be held longer. Frozen stock can be kept for at least 1 year at 0°.

Fish Stock or Fumet
Fonds de Poisson

Makes about 6 quarts

Fish bones stripped of meat, but with tails and heads attached, seem unlikely ingredients for a fine, light stock that is the foundation for a great many seafood soups, stews, and chowders. However, the skeletal remains of the fish, called the frame, *are just where much of its gelatinous goodness is found.*

Not all fish bones make good stock. The bones and big heads of round fish—cod, red snapper, grouper, striped bass, haddock, and others—do. Flat fish—sole, flounder, and halibut—do not.

Fish stock, like chicken stock, takes considerably less time to make than stocks made with beef bones. The fish will have given up all of its flavor in an hour or less.

A fish frame is one of the cheapest ingredients used in stock preparation. Usually the fish vendor is delighted to get rid of it, and so is the fisherman next door, who may be surprised to find the bones of his catch as worthy of attention as the meat. However, fish bones, heads, and trimmings should be used the same day they are available. Because fish bones are only washed, and not blanched as meat bones are, it is important that they have the characteristic clean smell of fresh-caught fish. Cut the gills from the fish head or they will make the stock bitter.

Although the bones can be put directly into the water to simmer, the stock will have more flavor and take less time to cook if the bones and heads are cooked first in butter or oil in the tightly closed stockpot. A clean light taste also comes from the white mirepoix, *the mix of vegetables without the carrots.*

INGREDIENTS
4 pounds fish bones, heads, and trimmings, coarsely chopped
2 tablespoons butter, margarine, or oil

Mirepoix
1 pound onions, peeled and coarsely chopped
½ pound celery, with tops, chopped
½ pound leeks, with green, chopped
6 sprigs parsley, including stems

1 teaspoon salt
1 teaspoon lemon juice
5 quarts water

Sachet d'épice
1 clove
1 clove garlic, mashed
1 bay leaf, crumbled
¼ teaspoon thyme
½ teaspoon black peppercorns

SPECIAL EQUIPMENT	Chinois or sieve. Cheesecloth, optional.
PREPARATION	Rinse the fish bones and heads in cold running water and chop the bones coarsely into 3- or 4-inch lengths.
SMOTHER 5 mins.	In a large (8- or 10-quart) stockpot or kettle, heat the butter until bubbling. Add the fish pieces, stir into the butter, cover tightly with a lid, and cook over medium heat for 5 minutes.
10 mins.	Mix in the mirepoix, salt, and lemon juice. Cover again and continue cooking for an additional 10 minutes or a total of 15 minutes.
BOIL/SIMMER 45 mins.	Cover with 5 quarts of water and bring to a boil. Lower the heat and simmer uncovered. Skim if necessary.
REST 30 mins.	Take the vessel off the heat and let the stock rest for 30 minutes before straining through a chinois or sieve. Fish stock is also put through cheesecloth to catch any tiny fish eggs, which become as hard as buckshot when cooked.
CHILL	Cool stock in a water bath and then refrigerate or freeze.

Vegetable Stock
Court Bouillon

Makes 4 to 5 quarts

The French words court bouillon *mean a short or quick stock that is made with vegetables and savory herbs. No meat. Unlike other stocks, which are simmered, court bouillon is boiled to extract all the flavor from the vegetables.*

Court bouillon is a light, tasty stock that can be used in fish soups and stews and other delicate soups, which could be overwhelmed by a heavy meat stock. It is widely used in all vegetarian soups and other dishes.

INGREDIENTS	2 tablespoons vegetable oil or butter or margarine
	1 tablespoon salt
	3 ounces white cider vinegar

Mirepoix
2 cups chopped onions
1 cup coarsely chopped carrots, washed but not peeled
1 cup chopped celery, including leaves

6 sprigs parsley
6 sprigs dill, if available
2 bay leaves, crumbled
1 teaspoon black peppercorns
5 quarts water

SPECIAL EQUIPMENT	Chinois or sieve. Cheesecloth.
PREPARATION SMOTHER *10 mins.*	Place the oil or butter in a large (8- or 10-quart) stockpot over medium heat. Put in all of the ingredients except the water, cover tightly, and cook for 10 minutes over medium-low heat until vegetables are limp.
BOIL *45–60 mins.*	Cover with 5 quarts of water, place over medium flame, and bring to a boil. Remove sediment as it rises to the surface. Heat may be reduced slightly, but court bouillon should be kept boiling (rather than simmering) until flavors are pronounced—about 45 minutes to 1 hour.
STRAIN	Strain the court bouillon through a triple thickness of moistened cheesecloth held in a chinois or sieve.
CHILL	Chill, unless it is to be used at once. Refrigerate or freeze until needed.

Dashi (Japanese)

Makes 1½ quarts

The mainstay of soup making in the Japanese kitchen is dashi, a unique stock that has no counterpart in the Western kitchen.

Dashi is a pairing of seaweed and fish in a crystal-clear stock that is smoky in taste, yet sweet. Well-made dashi retains only a hint of its salty background and is not fishy in taste. It is made with kombu (dried cultivated kelp) and katsuo bushi (dried bonito, a member of the tuna family). Dashi gives the Japanese cuisine its characteristic flavor—a mellow sweetness.

I once asked a Japanese cook if she would show me how to make dashi. She looked at me with something bordering on astonishment. "If you can boil water you can make dashi," she said. And so can you.

There are only two ingredients in dashi—a piece of thick kelp leaf and the fine shavings from a block of dried bonito. The shavings are so fine and fluffy that four packets weigh little more than ½ ounce, and it takes but two of them to make this recipe. The Japanese use a special plane to shave the bonito block, but this is unnecessary because of the ready availability of the packets in food stores and specialty shops catering to the Japanese cuisine. Homemade dashi is best. Lacking one or both of the ingredients, use instant dashi. Packets of instant dashi or dashi-no-moto are sold in the international sections of supermarkets and Asian food stores.

There are two kinds of dashi. One is a clear fragrant broth made with this recipe in which the kelp is removed from the water just before it boils, and the bonito flakes are removed immediately after they settle to the bottom of the saucepan.

The second, niban dashi, is a basic seasoning for thick soup as well as a cooking stock for vegetables. It has considerably more strength and is made by further simmering the seaweed and bonito reserved from the milder dashi. See below.

Dashi loses its bouquet quickly and this bouquet is gone altogether if it is not used immediately in a clear soup. As a basic seasoning dashi may be made ahead of time and stored in a tightly covered container for two or three days. While it may be frozen, its delicate flavor and aroma will be lost.

Timing is a most important element in making dashi. The kelp must not be boiled, or the broth will be bitter and cloudy; and if the fish flakes are not strained as soon as they settle to the bottom of the pan, the stock will taste fishy. However, it is a short process, taking no more than 10 minutes after the ingredients are ready.

INGREDIENTS	10 to 12 inches dried kelp (kombu)
	6½ cups cold water
	¾ cup loosely packed bonito (*katsuo*) flakes or 2 packages, 5 grams each, bonito flakes
SPECIAL EQUIPMENT	Sieve, colander, or chinois and cheesecloth, to strain
PREPARATION	Wipe the kelp lightly with a moist cloth or paper towel, but do not wash, because the whitish powder encrusting the surface contains much of the flavor.
BOIL 4–5 mins.	Break or cut the leathery piece of kelp into 3 or 4 pieces that will fit into the saucepan. Cover with 6½ cups of cold water and bring to a boil over high heat. Remove the kelp the moment the water boils. The pieces of

SETTLE *1 min.*	kelp may be reserved for the secondary dashi. Take the saucepan from the heat. Sprinkle the bonito flakes over the surface of the hot liquid and let them settle to the bottom of the pan. This will take no longer than 60 seconds.
STRAIN	Line the sieve, colander, or chinois with moistened cheesecloth. Strain the stock. Gather up the edges of the cheesecloth, scrape the flakes into the pocket, and squeeze out the remaining liquid. Discard the flakes or hold for the secondary dashi.
FINAL STEP	The dashi is now ready to be used in a wide variety of Japanese soups. For two of them see pages 71 and 252.
VARIATION	The kelp and bonito flakes saved from making dashi can be used for making the stronger *niban dashi*. To make 3 to 4 cups, put the kelp and fish flakes in 1½ quarts of cold water. Simmer until the stock has been reduced to 3 or 4 cups, about 20 minutes over medium heat. Add 1 packet of fresh bonito flakes and immediately remove from the heat. When the flakes have settled, strain the liquid through a sieve lined with a double thickness of moistened cheesecloth. Discard the flakes and kelp.

Consommé

Makes 6 to 8 quarts

Consommé, an enriched and crystal-clear broth made with beef or chicken or fish stock, is light, zestful, and appetite-whetting. It was created by the chef to Louis XIV of France in response to a royal command for a perfectly clear soup in which the king might see himself! This consommé may not reflect a royal visage but when it is brought to the table one will be able to clearly see the bottom of the cup or tureen.

Chef Elliott Sharron, whose recipe this is, cautioned, "Think of consommé as feminine . . . soft . . . delicate . . . to be treated like a lady."

Consommé is clarified and strengthened with the addition of lean muscle meat, egg whites, and vegetables. They are cooked together in a stockpot until they congeal to form a raft, which floats to the surface as a signal that the consommé is about done. The clear consommé is carefully taken out of the stockpot without disturbing the raft.

There are a dozen or more classic garnishes for consommé that range from breton (julienne of celery, onions, and leeks) and célestine (julienne of thin pancakes) to Saint-Germain (fresh peas) and rice or barley or pasta.

The recipe below is for beef consommé. Chicken and fish variations as well as Consommé Madrilène and Jellied Consommé follow this recipe.

INGREDIENTS

Note: The meat should include mostly muscle meat from the tough but inexpensive shin, shank, and shoulder as well as the heart. These are rich in albumin.

2 pounds lean ground beef
2 pounds fresh or canned tomatoes (no puree or paste)

Mirepoix
¾ pound onions, chopped or coarsely ground
½ pound *each* celery, carrots, and leeks, chopped or coarsely ground

6 fresh—not frozen—egg whites
1 cup water
1 tablespoon salt, kosher preferred
8 quarts cold brown stock or 6 quarts brown stock plus 2 quarts chicken
    stock (for a lighter consommé)

Sachet d'épice
1 clove
½ teaspoon black peppercorns
1 clove garlic, bruised
½ teaspoon thyme

1 bunch parsley, including stems

Note: All ingredients must be raw and cold.

SPECIAL
EQUIPMENT

The amount of stock should be 5 times the depth of the ingredients when resting on the bottom, so choose an appropriate size of stockpot or kettle. Usually a 12- or 16-quart vessel is adequate. Chinois or sieve.

PREPARATION

Put the ground beef, tomatoes, and mirepoix in the stockpot and mix everything together with hands or heavy wooden spoons. All should be thoroughly blended. In a small bowl mix the egg whites and water. Add this and salt to the stockpot. Stir.
    Pour in the cold stock. Stir to mix.

BOIL
APPROXIMATELY
40 mins.

Place the stockpot over *high* heat. Stir frequently while the solids cook and begin to form the raft. As the raft begins to form, drop in the sachet. When it comes together in a mass, foam will begin to form on the surface. This is the signal that it will shortly come to a gentle boil. *Stop stir-*

ring and reduce heat so that the consommé simmers or gently boils through a hole that will form in the raft.

CAUTION

If it should come to a vigorous full boil, the procedure is ruined. Pour off the stock and start over again with new ingredients.

SIMMER
100 mins.

From the time the material has solidified into a raft, simmer for exactly 100 minutes.

Watch the raft closely. When it sinks slightly and a pool of clear consommé an inch or so deep forms above the raft, the consommé is done. Turn off the heat.

STRAIN

Bubbles coming to the surface will have created a hole in the raft through which the consommé is ladled. Do it with great care so that none of the raft material is disturbed. The consommé can also be siphoned off. Pour the consommé through four thicknesses of moistened cheesecloth lining a chinois or sieve. (In a big restaurant kitchen, the consommé will be drained through a spigot near the bottom of the pot.) Discard raft and sachet.

CHILL

Cool the vessel of consommé in cold running water, as for stock. Stir every 15 minutes to hasten cooling. When it has lowered to approximately room temperature, store in the refrigerator.

Permit fat that solidifies on the top to remain there to seal the consommé. Lift off the fat before using the consommé, of course.

Consommé freezes well and can be kept for a year at 0°.

VARIATIONS

Chicken Consommé: Substitute chicken stock for beef and omit tomatoes. Use 2 ounces lemon juice or vinegar for acid in place of tomatoes.

Fish Consommé: Instead of lean beef, use an equal amount of ground fish fillets, chicken necks, backs, etc. Use fish stock plus 2 ounces lemon juice and vinegar in place of tomatoes.

Consommé Madrilène: Same ingredients as for beef consommé but substitute 6 pounds (approximately 12 cups) tomato for 2 pounds tomato. If it is to be jellied, add gelatin at the rate of 1¼ ounces per quart of consommé to offset the acidity of tomatoes. See below.

Jellied Consommé: After clarification, add 1 ounce of unflavored gelatin for each quart. Dissolve gelatin in water in a small bowl before adding to the consommé. Consommé made with a stock having a high percentage of gelatinous veal bones will jell without the gelatin.

Beef

BEEF IS CONSIDERED by many to be the most fortifying and nourishing of all butcher's meats. So are the soups and stews with beef as their chief ingredients. The popularity of beef spans continents—Swedish *kalops* with sour cream, and Greek *stefato* with feta cheese, America's Super Bowl Sunday Stew, Kansas City Steak Soup, and Philadelphia Pepper Pot.

A Three-Meat Stew

Serves 6 to 8

For nearly four decades we have eaten Jerry Pincetich's delicious food in places all over the world but chiefly in Hawaii, California, and Oregon.

"Elegant" was the name given to this stew by Jerry, and while she is very much the elegant woman, her stew has more earthy qualities than that word implies.

It has three kinds of meat—beef, veal, and lamb—as well as vegetables, a blend of wild and domestic rices, red wine, and a faint hint of cumin.

INGREDIENTS

2 pounds lean beef ⎫
½ pound veal ⎬ cut into 1-inch chunks
½ pound lamb ⎭
2 cloves garlic
2 tablespoons cooking oil
2 tablespoons butter
2 large onions, sliced (about 4 cups)

Sachet d'épice
¼ teaspoon thyme
½ teaspoon oregano
2 bay leaves, crumbled
8 peppercorns

1½ cups water
2 to 3 cups dry red wine (Burgundy is fine)
½ cup finely chopped parsley
1 tablespoon cornstarch, optional, with 3 tablespoons cold water
20 to 24 tiny white pearl onions, peeled
2 cups shelled fresh peas, or 1 10-ounce package frozen
3 carrots, thinly sliced (about 1½ cups)
¾ pound mushrooms, brushed and quartered
1 teaspoon cumin seed, roasted in a small skillet and crushed
1 cup tomato paste
1 tablespoon butter
Salt, to taste (about 1 tablespoon, usually)
¾ cup wild rice or Uncle Ben's mixed wild and white rice

SPECIAL
EQUIPMENT

None

PREPARATION

Cut the meats into 1-inch chunks and discard fat and connective tissue. Rub the sides of a large (4½-quart) stew pot with the garlic cloves. Pour cooking oil into the pot and bring it to smoking over medium-high heat.

SAUTÉ

Drop in just enough pieces of meat to barely cover the bottom of the pan. Don't crowd. Stir with wooden spoon, turning the pieces to cook all sides a deep brown. Remove each batch with a slotted spoon and set aside. Drain off any fat in the pan.

SWEAT
8 mins.

Add butter to the hot stew pot and sweat the sliced onions in it over medium heat, covered, until they are soft and translucent, about 8 minutes.

Assemble the sachet d'épice (in a metal ball or cheesecloth sachet) and place with the onions when they are cooked.

Return the meat to the stew pot. Pour in the water and red wine. More water or wine may be added as needed as the stew cooks down. It should be wet but not soupy when it is done.

BOIL/SIMMER
1½–2 hours

Bring to a simmer, cover and hold at a simmer over low heat. Cook until tender, about 1½ to 2 hours, depending on the meat.

To thicken stew, if desired, stir the cornstarch and cold water in a small bowl to dissolve. Add to the stew.

While the stew is cooking, blanch the pearl onions in a small saucepan half filled with cold water. Cover and bring to a boil. Immediately remove from heat and drain.

20 mins.

When meat is almost fork-tender, add pearl onions, peas, carrots, mushrooms, cumin, tomato paste, and butter. Taste for seasoning, especially salt. Bring to a simmer and cook for 20 minutes.

Add the wild rice or rice blend, cover, and cook over low heat for 30 minutes more.

10 mins.

Uncover and cook for 10 additional minutes. If stew has cooked down too much at this point, add water or wine.

FINAL STEP

Serve in cooking vessel for a family meal, for a tailgate party, or after skiing—or in something fancier for the president of the company or the minister.

Greek Beef Stew
Stefato

Serves 4

Bits of the Greek cheese feta and walnuts sprinkled over the top distinguish this beef stew from all the others. Stefato also includes not only a half cup of red wine but also red wine vinegar, a touch of brown sugar, and a cinnamon stick.

Stefato is often the pièce de résistance of the large noonday meal in Greece.

INGREDIENTS	2 pounds lean beef, cut in 1-inch cubes
	1 tablespoon olive oil or cooking oil
	24 small white pearl onions, peeled
	2 tablespoons butter
	1 teaspoon sugar
	½ cup red wine
	2 cups water (or beef stock for richer flavor)
	1 tablespoon red wine vinegar
	¾ cup tomato paste
	Sachet d'épice
	2 bay leaves, crumbled
	8 peppercorns
	1 2-inch stick cinnamon
	1 clove garlic, mashed
	1 tablespoon brown sugar
	Salt to taste
	½ cup coarsely broken walnuts
	¼ pound feta, coarsely crumbled (Muenster or Monterey Jack may be substituted.)
SPECIAL EQUIPMENT	None
PREPARATION	Cut beef into cubes and trim off fat and connective tissue.
SAUTÉ *4 mins. in batches*	In a medium (3½-quart) saucepan, with lid, heat olive oil over medium-high heat until it smokes. Drop in some of the beef cubes and spread over the bottom. Don't crowd. Stir with a wooden spoon until all sides are brown, about 4 minutes. Remove with a slotted spoon and set aside. Repeat with the balance of the meat.
BLANCH *4 mins.*	While the meat is sautéing, place onions in a small saucepan of cold water. Bring to a boil and drain immediately.
SAUTÉ	When all the meat is sautéed, drop the butter into the saucepan and add onions. Sprinkle with sugar (to caramelize) and sauté to a light golden color over medium heat. Stir onions to color uniformly. Lift out onions with a slotted spoon and set aside. They will be added to the stew after it has cooked for an hour or so. (All cooking is done on the stove top.)

BOIL/SIMMER *1–1½ hours*	Return the meat to the saucepan and add wine, water, vinegar, tomato paste, sachet, and brown sugar. The liquid should barely cover the meat. Add water if necessary. It may also be necessary to add small amounts of water from time to time during the cooking to maintain that level. Bring the liquid to a boil, reduce heat, and simmer with the lid on for 1 to 1½ hours or until the meat is tender when pierced with the point of a sharp knife or fork, or to the bite.
30 mins.	Remove sachet. Taste for seasoning, especially salt. Carefully spoon onions into the stew and mix throughout. Replace cover and simmer for an additional 30 minutes.
FINAL STEP	The nuts and feta cheese may be sprinkled generously over the stew in a tureen or passed at the table, to be added by each person as desired.

Super Bowl Sunday Stew

Serves 6 to 8

Super Bowl Sunday has moved alongside Labor Day, Valentine's Day, and the Fourth of July as a national event and has carried with it a growing tradition of special dishes to be served before, during, and after the football game. None is more representative or more delicious than this serve-it-anytime stew created by Royce Haiman, a talented woman both in and out of the kitchen.

Made early in the morning, the stew simmers quietly for hours until the guests are ready to eat.

It is a mélange of a dozen fresh and canned ingredients that produces a stew worthy of the game it honors. It is so good that it deserves to be served at a tailgate party, a basketball game, soccer, baseball, cricket, or a game of jacks. A universal dish.

It is ideal for making in a slow cooker.

INGREDIENTS	1 pound beef stew cut into 1-inch chunks Salt and freshly ground black pepper to season the meat 3 tablespoons butter 1 30-ounce (large) can tomato juice 1 30-ounce (large) can tomatoes, coarsely chopped 5 stalks celery, leaves included, chopped small 2 carrots, peeled and cut into thin rounds or quarters 2 onions, peeled and thinly sliced 3 cloves garlic, pressed or chopped 1 potato, peeled and cut into small chunks

(continued)

1 10-ounce package frozen cut okra
3 to 4 tablespoons barley
3 beef bouillon cubes
1 16-ounce can corn or 10-ounce package frozen corn
3 tablespoons Worcestershire sauce
2 teaspoons salt, if desired and needed

Sachet d'épice
12 black peppercorns
2 bay leaves
½ teaspoon thyme

6 to 8 sprigs parsley, finely chopped
Water, to be added as needed during the long simmering
Pinch of cayenne, if desired

SPECIAL EQUIPMENT	Slow cooker, if available

PREPARATION SAUTÉ *5 mins.*	Cut the beef into 1-inch cubes and season lightly with salt and pepper. In a 4½-quart stew pot sauté the meat pieces in butter over medium-high heat until they are browned on all sides, about 5 minutes.
	    The rest of the ingredients, plus the sachet, are added one by one.
	    Note: The block of frozen okra can be added as is, for it will quickly thaw in the warming liquid. As the stew cooks through the day, water may be added, depending on how thick you want it to be. I usually add about 4 cups for a thick stew.

BOIL/SIMMER *at least 3 hours*	Bring the stew to a boil; lower heat; and simmer, partially covered, for at least 3 hours. Stir the stew frequently during the day. Near the end of the cooking, taste for seasoning. A partial teaspoon of cayenne will give it a hotter bite, but don't overload. It is not meant to be a hot dish, just well seasoned.
FINAL STEP	Serve from the stew pot into heated bowls. A coarse French peasant bread, served in big chunks and with lots of butter, goes well with this.

Steak Soup

Serves 6

Where but Kansas City for the best steak—and the best steak soup? This is from the K.C. restaurant Plaza III. The recipe is for a robust, hearty soup—good in wintertime to feed hockey players, basketball players, or mountain climbers. For young and old alike.

The frozen mixed vegetables in addition to the fresh ones are a little much for me, so I forgo them. But you may like them.

INGREDIENTS	6 tablespoons butter
	⅓ cup flour
	5 cups beef stock
	2 beef bouillon cubes (to make it beefier)
	½ cup diced celery
	½ cup diced carrots
	½ cup chopped onion
	I cup (8 ounces) tomatoes, fresh, frozen, or canned (peeled and seeded if fresh)
	I pound ground round steak
	I 10-ounce package frozen mixed vegetables, if desired
	I teaspoon Ac'cent (MSG), if desired
	I ½ teaspoons freshly ground black pepper
	I ½ teaspoons protein seasoning such as Kitchen Bouquet or Maggi
	I teaspoon salt, if desired
	Chopped parsley, to garnish
SPECIAL EQUIPMENT	None
PREPARATION COOK *3 mins.*	Place butter in soup pot and melt without browning. Add flour and stir constantly to form a smooth paste. Cook over medium heat for 3 minutes.
BOIL/SIMMER	Slowly pour the beef stock into the paste and stir until smooth and lightly thickened. Add the bouillon cubes. Bring to a boil; add fresh vegetables, including tomatoes. Allow soup to regain the boil, reduce heat, cover, and simmer for about 30 minutes or until the vegetables are tender.
SAUTÉ *10 mins.*	While the stock is simmering, sauté the ground beef in a little butter in a large skillet until it is browned, about 10 minutes. Drain and set aside.

SIMMER
15 mins.

When the fresh vegetables are cooked and the meat is browned, add frozen vegetables (if desired) and meat to the soup. Simmer for 15 minutes.

SEASON

While the soup is simmering, add Ac'cent, pepper, Kitchen Bouquet or Maggi, and salt to taste.

FINAL STEP

Serve from heated tureen into bowls. Garnish with chopped parsley.

Ragout of Oxtail

Serves 4

During its long steaming in the pot, ragout of oxtail gives off an appetizing aroma, a prelude to the final steaming bowlful, with its unique, richly concentrated beefy taste.

It is a stew that belies its unpretentious name. Oxtail does not conjure up thoughts of the high culinary achievement usually associated with such words as tenderloin or filet; nevertheless it is a delicious stew that commands respect at any table.

Ragout of oxtail is an earthy farmhouse dish that came about because country people in earlier times used everything the beast could provide, from head to tail. Today there are few oxen to make a contribution to this stew. Beef does nicely.

While oxtail is relatively cheap by the pound, there is considerable bone, but the meat surrounding it is rich and satisfying. The oxtail pieces (seldom is the tail left whole) can be served bone and all, but eating them is a messy business requiring bibs and lots of napkins. A more satisfactory way is to pick the meat from the bones beforehand and return it to the stew before serving.

INGREDIENTS

2 pounds oxtail, cut into 1- to 1½-inch pieces
½ teaspoon vinegar
2 tablespoons butter
2 tablespoons oil
¼ cup flour
2 medium onions, chopped
4 cloves garlic, chopped
2 medium carrots, chopped
2 stalks celery, chopped
3 ounces sliced bacon, cut into 1-inch pieces
1 15-ounce can tomato puree or 4 ripe tomatoes, peeled, seeded, and chopped

6 cups beef stock

I cup dry white wine

Sachet d'épice

I bay leaf, crumbled

½ teaspoon thyme

2 cloves

5 black peppercorns

A few sprigs parsley

½ pound small white onions, fresh, frozen, or canned

¼ pound small carrots, peeled and cut into sticks

Salt, if desired, and freshly ground black pepper to taste

½ cup bacon bits, freshly made or canned, to garnish

SPECIAL EQUIPMENT	4-quart saucepan or casserole with tight-fitting lid, attractive enough to come to the table as a serving dish. Chinois or other medium-fine sieve for straining stock.
PREPARATION *Overnight*	*Beforehand:* Trim excess fat off the oxtails and soak at least 4 hours or overnight in water to cover plus ½ teaspoon vinegar.
DRAIN	Drain the oxtails and pat dry with paper towels while heating butter and oil over medium-high heat in a heavy frying pan.
BROWN *10 mins.*	Dredge oxtails in flour and place in one layer in frying pan over high heat. Cook, turning to brown all sides, until they are a light golden color, about 10 minutes.

Note: The ragout can be cooked either in the oven—at 425°, to begin—or on the top of the stove. If in the oven, preheat oven now.

Lift out the oxtails with a slotted spoon and drain on paper towels, while cooking the onions, garlic, carrots, and celery in the same pan, about 15 minutes, or until they are slightly browned and wilted. At the same time fry the bacon in a small skillet and when almost crisp scrape bacon pieces and drippings into the vegetables.

Place the oxtails and the vegetables in a medium (4-quart) saucepan or casserole with tight-fitting lid.

15 mins.   Cook, uncovered, on a top burner or in the oven until the fat is absorbed, about 15 minutes.

If to be cooked in the oven, reduce heat to 325°.

Stir in tomato, stock, and wine. Plant the sachet of spices in the middle of it all.

LOW BOIL *325° 2–3 hours*	Cover and cook in oven or on top burner from 2 to 3 hours. Inspect the contents of the pot several times to be certain the liquid is not bubbling too hard. Each time give the oxtails a stir. If cooking too rapidly, reduce the heat further—to 250°.
COOK *45 mins.* *15 mins.*	During the cooking period prepare and cook small onions and carrot sticks. Cook the onions in lightly salted water for about 45 minutes; in a separate saucepan simmer carrots for about 15 minutes. Drain and set aside. When the oxtail meat is fork-tender and can easily be pulled from the bone, remove from the heat. Lift oxtails out of the stock, let them cool a bit, and pick, pull, and cut meat from the bones. A sharp knife with a point will aid in picking the meat off the bones. Cut the meat into bite-size pieces and set aside.
STRAIN	Strain stock and discard the vegetables and sachet that have been cooked with it. Skim off excess fat. Taste and adjust seasonings. Place the meat back in the saucepan or casserole and gently mix it together with the small onions and carrot sticks. Add the strained stock.
REHEAT *5 mins.*	Set the vessel on a top burner and reheat gently, just to the boiling point.
FINAL STEP	Serve at once in heated shallow bowls or deep plates. Sprinkle bacon bits over each portion.

Clear Oxtail Soup

Serves 8

Clear oxtail soup is both eye- and taste-appealing, a lovely deep bronze with a dice of carrots, celery, and turnips and grains of barley suspended just beneath the surface. Or it can include eggs mollet (oeufs mollets)—whole soft-cooked eggs—a delightful variation in the presentation of this soup.

* I was first served this soup with duck eggs by Monsieur Gaston Bichet, whose recipes for breads are some of the best in my book* The Breads of France. *He gave up his restaurant, the two-star Le Relais, hard by the great forest of Chambord, for the life of a country squire in Veigne. M. Bichet served eggs laid by his own ducks. I have since used chicken eggs, which are far more readily available, but if you are lucky enough to come by fresh duck eggs, by all means use them.*

When serving the oxtail soup with eggs mollet, I dispense with the addition of the diced vegetables, barley, and diced meat, and use an absolutely clear broth.

INGREDIENTS   **2 to 3 pounds oxtails, disjointed**

Mirepoix
1 large onion, chopped
2 large carrots, chopped
2 ribs celery, chopped

2 quarts beef stock
4 ripe tomatoes, peeled, seeded, and chopped, or 1 15-ounce can tomato puree

Sachet d'épice
1 clove garlic, mashed and diced
1 bay leaf, crumbled
½ teaspoon thyme
6 peppercorns
2 cloves
2 or 3 sprigs parsley

1 teaspoon salt, if desired
½ cup quick-cooking barley
1 cup diced carrots
1 cup diced celery
1 cup diced turnips or additional carrots and/or celery to equal 1 cup

Note: 3 cups frozen mixed vegetables may be substituted for the above three ingredients, if desired

2 egg whites
¼ cup water
Pinch of salt
Dash of vinegar
1 ounce sherry, optional
Dash or two of Worcestershire sauce, to taste
¼ cup finely chopped fresh dill weed or parsley, to garnish

Eggs Mollet *(if desired):*
8 very fresh chicken eggs, at room temperature (see Variation, page 41)

SPECIAL EQUIPMENT	Chinois or other strainer lined with double thickness of cheesecloth. Whisk.
PREPARATION	Preheat oven to 425°, no hotter.
BAKE *425°* *20 mins.* *30 mins.*	Place the oxtails in a pan (preferably black cast iron to better absorb the heat) and bake until the bones are browned, about 20 minutes. Scatter the mirepoix among the oxtail pieces and return to the oven until vegetables are slightly cooked and tender, about 30 minutes.
COOK *2 hours*	Pour the contents of the baking pan into a large (5-quart) pot. Deglaze the pan with a ½ cup of stock, scraping loose the *fonds* with a flat-edge wooden spatula. Reserve 2 cups stock. Pour balance of the stock plus all tomatoes into the pot. Add sachet. Cover, reduce heat, and cook at low heat—a few bubbles rising to the surface, nothing violent—for at least 2 hours. Salt lightly, if desired. The soup will already be seasoned somewhat by the peppercorns in the sachet but more pepper may be added according to taste. If there is much evaporation of the liquid during the long cooking, replace with stock or water.
COOK *20 mins.*	While the oxtails are cooking, (1) prepare the barley according to instructions on the container and set aside; and (2) dice the carrots, celery, and optional turnips, or substitute the frozen vegetables. Cook the vegetables in the reserved 2 cups of stock until they are done, about 20 minutes for fresh or 11 to 12 minutes for frozen (after bringing to a boil). Drain, adding the liquid to the pot. Set diced vegetables aside. Remove oxtails and, when they have cooled sufficiently, pick meat off the bones and cut into dice. Discard bones and set meat aside.
STRAIN	Pour stock through chinois or other medium sieve to remove the particles of cooked vegetables. Discard these. Skim fat from surface of stock.
CLARIFY	To clarify, wet and wring dry the cheesecloth and drape a double thickness in the chinois or sieve.
BEAT *2 mins.*	Beat egg whites and water together, adding a dash of vinegar and a pinch of salt, until the mixture is frothy. Pour into the hot stock, beating rapidly with a large whisk while bringing the stock slowly to a boil, about 3 minutes. Remove from heat and pour the stock through the cheesecloth. If the

cheesecloth becomes coated with fine particles and the stock will not go through, stop the procedure and wash the cloth. Replace and clarify the balance. (It is pleasing to see the amount of residue left behind in the cloth as the clear, sparkling stock passes through it.)

Add sherry, if desired, and Worcestershire sauce.

REHEAT

Pour the stock back into the washed pot and add the diced vegetables, barley, and diced meat. Reheat just to a simmer.

FINAL STEP

Serve in heated tureen and bowls. Sprinkle a bit of fresh dill or parsley over the top. Toasted croutons also make a good garnish.

VARIATION

Eggs Mollet
Preparing eggs *mollet* is a tedious but possible task. The eggs must be strictly fresh and at room temperature.

BOIL/SIMMER
6 mins.

Have the water boiling in a vessel large enough to hold all the eggs at one time. Lower the eggs into the water in a colander (with large holes) or a sieve. Start timing when the water has returned to the boil. Reduce heat to a gentle simmer. Cook 6 minutes.

COOL
2–3 mins.

When the time has elapsed, immediately lift out the eggs and plunge into cold running water to stop the cooking action. Leave for 2 or 3 minutes.

CRACK/PEEL

Crack the shell of each egg all over by gently tapping with the back of a spoon. Don't rush the operation. Be gentle. Pick off the small shell pieces rather than trying to lift the shell off in large pieces as with a hard-cooked egg. The first egg will be the most difficult.

RESERVE

Reserve the shelled eggs in a bowl of lightly salted warm water until the soup is to be served and then place one in each bowl of soup.

FINAL STEP

Serve. The egg is a delicious surprise.

Philadelphia Pepper Pot

Serves 6

Philadelphia Pepper Pot is looked on with disfavor at some tables because its chief ingredient is tripe, the lining of the cow's stomach. Viewed dispassionately, however, honeycomb tripe is a pleasing work of symmetry and form, far more eye-appealing than a turkey wing or a chicken liver. But, more important, tripe makes a major contribution to the good taste of Philadelphia Pepper Pot and gives it its distinctive texture.

Tripe is eaten with gusto in many countries, especially Mexico, where menudo, *a favorite soup, is made with hominy or chickpeas substituting for potato, and a calf's foot or pig's feet instead of veal bone. Make it hotter with more chilies.*

There are several grades of tripe; the best for this soup is the honeycomb (from the second stomach). When purchasing, be certain it is firm and white, not grayish.

INGREDIENTS

1½ pounds honeycomb tripe

Sprinkles of salt, to rub

1 tablespoon salt

3 tablespoons butter

1 cup chopped onions

1 whole onion, studded with 3 cloves

½ cup thinly sliced celery

½ cup peeled, quartered, and thinly sliced carrots

1 leek (about 1 cup), washed and sliced, including tender green part

½ cup diced green pepper

4 cups chicken stock

1 cup water

1 small but meaty veal knuckle

1 clove garlic, diced

2 to 3 teaspoons dried hot red chilies, crushed, or chili powder to taste

1 bay leaf, crushed

1 teaspoon dried marjoram

1 teaspoon basil

½ teaspoon thyme

2 teaspoons salt, or to taste

½ teaspoon freshly ground black pepper

1 tablespoon cornstarch

3 tablespoons water

½ cup chopped parsley

2 cups diced potatoes (½-inch dice)

1 cup evaporated milk or heavy cream

⅓ cup butter, to swirl into soup when served

½ cup snipped parsley, to garnish

SPECIAL EQUIPMENT	None
PREPARATION BOIL *15 mins.*	Wash the tripe under cold running water. Spread the pieces on the counter or cutting board and rub both sides thoroughly with several teaspoons of salt. Rinse off the salt. Place the tripe in a medium (3-quart) saucepan and add salted water to cover by 2 inches. Bring to a gentle boil and cook for 15 minutes. Drain and set aside. When cool cut into ½-inch cubes. Reserve.
SWEAT *10 mins.*	Heat the butter in a deep (4- to 5-quart) kettle or casserole. When the butter begins to foam, add chopped onions, the whole studded onion, celery, carrots, leek, and green pepper. Cover and sweat over medium-low heat for 10 minutes. Do not brown.
BOIL/SIMMER *1½ hours*	Pour the stock and water into the kettle and add the veal bone and reserved tripe cubes. Add the garlic, hot chilies, bay leaf, marjoram, basil, thyme, salt (if desired), and black pepper. Simmer for 1½ hours. At the end of this period, lift out the veal bone and pick off what meat there is. Cut meat into bite-size pieces and return to the soup. Discard the bone and the whole onion.
SIMMER *20–25 mins.*	Mix together the cornstarch and water in a small bowl. Add to the soup and stir to blend. Add the parsley and diced potatoes. Simmer until the potatoes are tender, about 20 to 25 minutes.
MILK	When the soup is cooked, but still keeping it over the heat, add evaporated milk or cream.
FINAL STEP	Swirl the butter into the soup at the moment of ladling it into the heated tureen or individual bowls. Garnish with snipped parsley.
VARIATION	Try the Mexican way: omit the potato but add 1½ cups canned hominy, drained, or chickpeas. Substitute calf's foot or pig's feet for veal bone. *Olé!*

Beef Stew with Sour Cream (Swedish)
Kalops

Serves 4

While Swedes today form a sophisticated urban society, they keep a firm grip on old country ways. They relish such uncomplicated dishes as salt herring and sour cream, baked brown beans, and this delicious beef stew made with sour cream.

In this recipe the chunks of stew meat are not seared over high heat but sweated in a covered vessel, with a bit of water added to make steam, and then are caramelized as the water boils away. It is an alternative method that can be used in many other meat-based stews. The beauty of it is that no oil is used to brown the meat—a saving in calories.

INGREDIENTS	2 pounds lean beef, cut in 1½-inch chunks
	¼ cup water
	2 tablespoons butter
	1 large onion, peeled and thinly sliced
	1 tablespoon flour
	Sachet d'épice
	¼ teaspoon ground allspice
	8 black peppercorns
	1 bay leaf, crumbled
	2 sprigs parsley
	3 cups beef stock
	½ teaspoon salt, if desired
	¼ cup sour cream
SPECIAL EQUIPMENT	None
PREPARATION SWEAT *30 mins.* *15–20 mins.*	Trim beef pieces of fat and connective tissue. Drop the meat into a medium (3½-quart) saucepan or casserole and add the water. Cover and sweat out juices and fat over medium heat for about 30 minutes.
	Uncover and cook away the liquid, leaving the juices and fat to caramelize on the bottom of the pan. The brown essence may stick to the bottom, but it will loosen as the stew cooks.
PREHEAT *350°*	Preheat oven to 350°.

SWEAT *8–10 mins.*	Lift the meat out with a slotted spoon and set aside. Place the butter and onions in the saucepan, cover, and sweat until soft and lightly browned in the essence.

COOK
2–3 mins.
	Uncover, sprinkle the flour over the onions, and stir for 2 or 3 minutes while the flour cooks and loses its raw taste.
	     Prepare the sachet and place among the onions.
	     Pour in the beef stock. Scrape the bottom with a wooden spoon to loosen the residue. Bring the liquid to a boil, add the meat, and return to a simmer. Add salt if needed.

OVEN *30 mins.*	Cover the pan or casserole and place in the lower third of the preheated oven. A long cooking period in the oven is unnecessary because both the beef and the onions have been partially cooked beforehand. The stew should barely simmer, so check after a few minutes. Regulate the heat accordingly (no more than 200° in my ovens). The meat should be tender when pierced with the tip of a sharp knife. Remove the meat with a slotted spoon and set aside.
DEGREASE	Degrease the liquid. This may be done by skimming off the fat with a large spoon or paper towel while the broth is hot, or by placing the broth in the refrigerator for a few hours to congeal the fat.
WHISK	After degreasing, and when the liquid is warm, whisk in the sour cream, a tablespoon at a time. Taste for seasonings.
FINAL STEP	Blend together the meat and sauce, reheat if necessary, and serve in heated shallow bowls. *Note:* This stew is a close cousin to *boeuf bourguignonne* but without vinegar, mushrooms, or wine.

Beef Stew in Red Wine, Burgundy Style
Boeuf Bourguignonne

Serves 6

Boeuf bourguignonne *has been called the king of beef stews, and rightly so. It is a hearty meal and is fit for a king.*

There is one ingredient that raises it above the others—a young, full-bodied red wine. It can be Burgundy or Beaujolais, Côtes du Rhone, Bordeaux-St. Emilion or, to go farther afield, a good Chianti or even a full-bodied California cabernet sauvignon. But whichever, mon Dieu, not a cheap cooking wine. It deserves a good-to-better bottle. In France the stew is prepared by the bottleful of wine, not by the quarter cup.

As part of the stew there is the traditional garnish of little onions, mushrooms, and lardons.

INGREDIENTS

Stew

1½-pound chunk bacon or lean salt pork, cut into lardons
(strips 1½ inches long and ¼ inch thick)
3 pounds lean beef chuck or rump, cut into 1½-inch chunks
2 tablespoons butter
1 carrot, thinly sliced into rounds or quarters
1 onion, thinly sliced
1 tablespoon garlic, minced (about 2 cloves)
3 tablespoons flour or 1 tablespoon potato flour
1 bottle (25 ounces) red wine (see suggestions above)
1 tablespoon tomato paste

Sachet d'épice
½ teaspoon thyme
4 sprigs parsley
1 bay leaf, crumbled
8 black peppercorns

3 cups hot beef stock, if needed to augment wine in order to cover meat

Garnish
18 to 24 small fresh white onions, peeled and left whole, or canned
2 tablespoons butter
1 teaspoon sugar
¾ pound mushrooms, brushed clean and quartered
1 tablespoon butter
1 teaspoon lemon juice
Pinch of salt
½ teaspoon freshly cracked black pepper
¼ cup snipped fresh parsley

SPECIAL
EQUIPMENT

Appropriate casserole or saucepan in which to prepare and serve stew

PREPARATION

Note: The lardons will provide fat in which to sear the beef pieces and will be one of the 3 garnishes.

BLANCH *10 mins.*	Cut bacon or pork into lardons, strips about 1½ inches long and ¼ inch thick. Simmer in 1 quart of water for 10 minutes to blanch. Drain and pat dry.
TRY OUT	Try out the lardons over medium heat in the selected casserole or saucepan until they have rendered their fat and are brown and crisp. Remove lardons with a slotted spoon and set aside. Pour off and reserve the fat, leaving only enough to cover the bottom of the vessel with a thin coating.
SEAR *3–4 mins.* *each batch*	Heat the casserole to smoking over medium-high heat and drop in the first of several batches of meat to brown. Don't crowd them. Stir frequently to sear all sides. Lift out with a slotted spoon and reserve. Repeat with the balance. If the meat is especially lean, it may be necessary to add a spoonful or so of the reserved bacon grease.
PREHEAT	Preheat oven to 375°.
SWEAT *8 mins.*	When all the meat has been removed from the casserole, add butter and heat to foaming. Add the carrots, onions, and garlic; cover and sweat over medium heat for about 8 minutes or until the onions are soft and translucent.
COOK *3 mins.*	Sprinkle the flour over the vegetables and cook together for about 3 minutes until the flour is absorbed and browned, but take care not to burn. With wooden spoon or spatula, scrape the beef essence from the bottom of the casserole and blend in.
BOIL/SIMMER *10 mins.*	Pour the red wine into the casserole, then add tomato paste and sachet. Stir to blend. Bring to a slow boil over medium heat and add the meat pieces. If the wine mixture does not cover the meat, add hot beef stock. Heat until the stew comes to a simmer.
BRAISE *1½–2 hours* *375°*	Place the casserole or saucepan, covered with a lid, in the oven, basting occasionally, for 1½ to 2 hours or until meat is tender when pierced with the point of a sharp knife. Reduce heat if the stew is boiling rapidly—it should be at a gentle boil, just above a simmer. While the meat is cooking, prepare the onion and mushroom garnishes.
BLANCH *5 mins.*	Place the small onions in a small saucepan with cold water and bring to a boil. Immediately remove from heat and drain. Rinse with cold water.

SAUTÉ
5 mins.

In a medium skillet, melt 2 tablespoons butter and add the onions. Sprinkle with sugar and sauté until golden brown, about 5 minutes over medium heat, moving them around occasionally with a wooden spoon. Remove from skillet and set aside.

3 mins.

Melt the tablespoon of butter in the skillet and drop in the mushroom pieces and the lemon juice. Sauté briskly over medium-high heat for about 3 minutes. Stir or shake during the cooking. Set aside with the onions and lardons.

ASSEMBLE

Fifteen minutes before the stew is finished, remove from the oven. Taste for seasoning, especially salt. Remove the sachet and discard. Stir in the lardons and onions. Scatter the mushrooms over the top in an attractive pattern.

SIMMER
15 mins.

Cover and return to the oven to thoroughly heat all the garnishes, about 15 minutes.

FINAL STEP

Serve in the casserole or pot, sprinkled with snippets of fresh parsley. Hot garlic bread is delicious with the stew. Any of the red wines mentioned earlier will be a fine choice to serve with the meal.

Like all beef stew, this one tastes better the next day, not to mention the day after that.

Chicken

A MEASURE OF CHICKEN'S POPULARITY on American tables is the fourteen soups in this chapter as well as its appearance in other chapters, the more than 225 recipes for chicken in Auguste Escoffier's cookbook, and the two dozen pages of recipes in the chef's bible, *Larousse Gastronomique.* The older (and less expensive) bird is ideal for the soup pot. A bird young in years cannot approach a depth of flavor to equal that of a stewing hen recently retired as an egg layer. The slow cooking brings out the bird's delicious flavor and makes its meat as tender as that of a young capon.

Chicken Velvet Soup

Serves 8

This creamy soup comes with the highest recommendation—my mother's. Her favorite destination when she left our small suburban town was the L.S. Ayres store in Indianapolis and, once there, the Ayres Tea Room. For her, it was because of their chicken velvet soup.

Be forewarned that this soup is as rich as it is velvety, but worth every calorie.

The stock can be made using approximately 2½ quarts of water to simmer one 5-pound chicken for 1 hour; this also produces the necessary white meat.

INGREDIENTS	¾ cup butter, room temperature
	¾ cup flour
	2 cups light cream (or half-and-half)
	6 cups chicken stock, heated
	1½ cups finely chopped cooked breast of chicken
	Salt to taste, if desired (about 1 teaspoon, usually)
	Dash of freshly ground black pepper, to taste
	1 cup snipped fresh parsley, to garnish

SPECIAL EQUIPMENT	None

PREPARATION HEAT *5 mins.* *4 mins.*	Blend together the butter and flour in a medium (3-quart) saucepan. Add warmed cream and stir until smooth. The soup will begin to thicken as it is heated.
	Stir in 2 cups of the hot stock. Over low heat, stir and cook until heated and blended, about 4 minutes.
	Add the remaining 4 cups of stock and the chopped chicken. Season to taste with salt, if desired, and pepper.
	Heat to serving temperature—steaming, but not boiling lest the cream break into unattractive particles. Watch the pot closely to keep from coming to a boil.

FINAL STEP	Serve in a heated tureen and ladle into heated bowls. Garnish with snippets of parsley.

Chicken Liver Mousse Soup (Chinese)

Serves 6 to 8

Connoisseurs of chicken livers—and there are many of us—will love this dish presented in bowls of rich chicken stock ladled over spoonfuls of delicious liver mousse.

Uncooked chicken livers are whirled in a blender and then steamed into a lovely salmon-colored, puffy mousse.

This inspired recipe is from Craig Claiborne and Virginia Lee's fine The Chinese Cookbook.

INGREDIENTS	1 pound chicken livers
	2 tablespoons finely minced fresh ginger
	3 tablespoons chopped scallions, including some of the green part
	6 tablespoons water

3 eggs
Salt to taste, if desired
¼ teaspoon MSG, if desired
½ teaspoon freshly ground pepper, preferably white
½ teaspoon sugar
6 cups chicken stock
1 tablespoon dry sherry or *shao hsing* wine
¼ cup finely chopped fresh coriander or parsley

SPECIAL EQUIPMENT	Electric blender or food processor, steamer. Cheesecloth.
PREPARATION *2 mins.*	Pick over the chicken livers and cut or pull away any tough connective materials. Cut the livers into small pieces and drop into the blender container or processor bowl. Blend at high speed 1 to 2 minutes, or until finely pureed. The liver will be a bright red at this stage.
STRAIN	Place double thickness of moistened cheesecloth over a heatproof 1½-quart bowl, push down the center of the cloth to form a pocket, and strain the liver liquid. Lift the edges of the cloth and hold in one hand. With the other hand gently squeeze the liver puree through it.
BLEND *1 min.* **STRAIN**	Combine the ginger, scallions, and water in the blender or processor bowl and blend for about 1 minute. Strain the mixture through a clean cloth into a small bowl. Add 3½ cups of this liquid to the liver.
BLEND	Break the eggs into a separate bowl. Add the salt and MSG, pepper, and sugar. Stir well with a fork, then pour into the liver mixture. Add ¾ cup of the chicken stock and the wine.
STEAM *15–20 mins.*	Place the bowl in the top of a steamer, cover, and steam over gently boiling water until mixture sets, about 15 to 20 minutes. Test by inserting a spoon into the mousse. Don't overcook, because the cooking will continue for several minutes after it is taken off the heat.
30 mins.	Or place the bowl of liver mixture in a pan of hot water that reaches halfway up the sides—and cook over medium-low heat for about 30 minutes. Test as above.
BOIL/SIMMER	Meanwhile, over medium heat, bring the remaining chicken stock to a boil and hold at a simmer until ready to serve.
FINAL STEP	Spoon the liver mousse into a heated tureen and gently pour in the hot soup. Ladle 1 or 2 tablespoons of mousse and the soup into individual bowls. Sprinkle coriander or parsley over the soup.

Chicken Soup with Mushrooms

Serves 6 to 8

This soup is simplicity itself—dice of breast of chicken and sliced mushrooms suspended in a clear, rich chicken stock.

You may wish to use stock on hand rather than start from scratch, but then you probably won't have the strips of white meat with which to garnish the soup.

INGREDIENTS	4- to 5-pound chicken
	2 medium onions, quartered
	2 carrots, coarsely chopped
	I cup chopped celery
	Sachet d'épice
	I bay leaf
	¼ teaspoon thyme
	3 sprigs parsley
	Salt, if desired, to taste
	Freshly ground black pepper, to taste
	I tablespoon butter
	2 teaspoons fresh lemon juice
	¼ pound mushrooms, thinly sliced
	½ cup snipped fresh parsley
SPECIAL EQUIPMENT	Sieve, colander, or chinois and cheesecloth, to strain
PREPARATION	*Stock*

PREPARATION

Stock

In a medium (3-quart) saucepan, combine chicken, onions, carrots, celery, and sachet. Add water to cover, about 4 to 5 cups. Bring to a boil,

BOIL/SIMMER
I hour

skim the surface frequently, and simmer, covered, until the chicken is tender. Remove the chicken, remove the meat from the bones, and cut the white meat only into small dice *(brunoise)*, making 1½ cups. Set aside. (Save the rest of the chicken for another use.)

2 hours

Return the bones to the saucepan and continue to simmer for an additional 2 hours, adding water as needed to maintain the level of liquid throughout the simmering period.

STRAIN

Strain the stock through a sieve lined with a dampened double thickness of cheesecloth.

Season to taste. Keep hot.

COOK In a small skillet melt the butter and add lemon juice and mushrooms. Cook over medium heat for about 3 minutes.

FINAL STEP Combine the chicken and mushrooms in the stock, reheating, if necessary, and ladle into a heated tureen or casserole. Sprinkle parsley over individual servings.

Chicken Broth (Japanese)
Tori-Gara No Dashi

Makes 1 quart of rich stock

While most Japanese soups are based on the sea-flavored stock called dashi, others have as their base a gingery chicken stock which may be more appealing.

The stock is clear, making a perfect lens through which to view the infinite number of artistic arrangements of ingredients possible in Japanese cookery. The stock is surprisingly piquant because of the ginger and scallions or leeks.

The Egg Drop Soup, Tamago Toji (page 71), can be made with this stock rather than dashi, but a more imaginative use of it is Clear Chicken Soup, Tori No Suimono (page 67), with its colorful arrangement of vegetable pieces in the bowls. However, don't hesitate to use this stock in other soups, including favorites from a hemisphere away.

While the stock is usually made with less expensive chicken parts such as necks, wings, and backs, the meatier parts of the chicken will make an equally nice stock and at the same time provide choice meats for other uses—for instance, in Clear Chicken Soup.

INGREDIENTS
6 cups water
1 to 1½ pounds uncooked chicken pieces
6 slices fresh ginger, peeled and cut ¼ inch thick
5 scallions, white and green parts, cut 2 inches long; or 2 or 3 leeks, white and green parts, cut 2 inches long
1 teaspoon salt
3 whole black or green peppercorns
1 raw egg white or 3 to 4 raw eggshells

SPECIAL EQUIPMENT Sieve, colander or chinois and cheesecloth, to strain

PREPARATION Pour the water into a medium (3½-quart) saucepan, with lid, and add the chicken pieces. Add the ginger and scallions or leeks. Bring the water to a rapid boil over high heat. Skim off froth that forms on the surface.

BOIL/SIMMER *I hour*	Add salt and pepper. Reduce heat to a simmer, cover partially, and continue to cook for about 1 hour or until the meat can be taken off the bones with ease.
STRAIN	Place moistened cheesecloth in a sieve. Strain the stock into a clean saucepan. Set the meat aside for the moment and allow to cool. Rinse the cheesecloth.
BOIL *3 mins.*	Heat the broth in the saucepan and bring to a boil. With a spoon swirl in the egg white or shells. Let the broth return to a rapid boil, then quickly remove the saucepan from the heat.
STRAIN	Again strain the broth through the cheesecloth. Refrigerate the broth overnight to allow the fat to congeal. Lift off and discard fat particles or blot with a paper towel. Pick meat from the bones and reserve for another use. Discard bones and vegetables.
FINAL STEP	The stock is now ready to be used in any soup calling for a clear broth. It may be refrigerated for 2 or 3 days or frozen for 4 to 6 months.

Chicken Soup with Matzo Balls

Serves 6 to 8

Matzo balls floating in a golden broth made with a fat hen is a favorite soup reaching far beyond the confines of the Jewish kitchen. How the chicken is cooked varies little, but matzo balls may be hard and chewy or light and fluffy, or someplace in between.

*   This matzo ball, of German descent, is made with nutmeg, ginger, onion, parsley, and paprika in addition to chicken fat, matzo meal, and eggs. Stiffly beaten egg whites are folded into the batterlike mixture to lighten and fluff the balls.*

*   This soup is also delicious served with liver dumplings, noodles, or rice.*

INGREDIENTS	**Soup** I 3½- to 4½-pound chicken, all parts except liver Water to cover (twice) 2 medium onions, peeled and quartered 6 cloves, to stud onions ½ cup sliced carrots ½ cup chopped celery, leaves included I parsnip, sliced 10 peppercorns

I bay leaf, crumbled
I cup coarsely chopped parsley
Salt, if desired (about I teaspoon)

Matzo Balls (about 18 to 20)
½ cup chicken fat or pareve margarine
    (made without dairy products), melted
I cup boiling water
¼ teaspoon nutmeg
¼ teaspoon ginger
3 tablespoons grated onion
2 tablespoons finely chopped parsley
¼ teaspoon paprika
I cup matzo meal
Salt, if desired
½ teaspoon freshly ground black pepper
3 eggs, separated
Water
I tablespoon salt
Snippets of parsley or chives, to garnish

SPECIAL EQUIPMENT

Sieve, colander, or chinois and cheesecloth, to strain

Note: The soup and matzo ball batter may be prepared the day before, as both should be well chilled—the soup to be degreased, and the batter to stiffen.

PREPARATION

BOIL

10 mins. approx.

Soup

Place the chicken and giblets in a large (4½-quart) kettle and cover with cold water. Bring to a boil. Pour off the water. Wash the chicken in running water and rinse the pot to remove all foam and unwanted particles.

SIMMER

30 mins.

30 mins.

Cover the chicken again with cold water, about 12 cups, and simmer, uncovered, over medium heat for 30 minutes. Do not let it boil or the soup will become cloudy.

Stud the onions with the cloves and add to the kettle. Also add the carrots, celery, parsnip, peppercorns, bay leaf, and parsley. Continue simmering. Simmer for an additional 30 minutes—or a total of 1½ hours.

STRAIN	Strain the soup through a chinois or fine sieve. Discard the vegetables and reserve the chicken meat for another use. For an even clearer soup, strain the broth again through a double thickness of moistened cheese-cloth.
Taste for seasoning.
Chill the soup for several hours or overnight so the congealed fat can be lifted off the top.
PREPARATION	*Matzo Balls*
In a small saucepan combine the chicken fat, boiling water, nutmeg, ginger, onion, parsley, paprika, matzo meal, salt, if desired, and pepper.
COOK
4–5 mins.	Blend together and, over medium heat, cook for 4 or 5 minutes, stirring constantly to prevent burning. When ready, the mixture will pull away from the sides of the pan.
COOL	Let the mixture cool for 5 to 10 minutes before adding the egg yolks, one at a time, and blending together with a wooden spoon. Incorporate each yolk before adding the next.
BEAT/FOLD

CHILL | Beat the egg whites until they are stiff. Fold them into the matzo mixture with a spatula and refrigerate for a few hours or overnight. The soft batter will stiffen as it chills through so that it can be worked into balls.
In a large (4½-quart) saucepan, pour water to the depth of about 3 inches and bring it to a boil. Add a tablespoon of salt and reduce heat to a gentle simmer (a hard boil will break the matzo balls apart). |
| SHAPE | The matzo balls should be about 1 inch in diameter, the size of a walnut. Work with wet hands so the dough does not stick.
Take about a tablespoon of the stiff dough and pinch, pat, and roll it into a ball between the palms. Set aside. Continue until all the batter is used up. |
SIMMER	Slip the matzo balls, a few at a time, into the simmering water and cook gently for about 15 to 20 minutes, or until they are fluffy. (Contrary to the advice of some cooks, the balls are not necessarily done when they rise to the surface.)
HEAT	Meantime, remove fat from the chilled soup and bring the soup to a simmer in a saucepan. Discard fat.
FINAL STEP	Remove the matzo balls from the water with a slotted spoon and slip into the hot soup. Sprinkle with snippets of parsley or chives.

FREEZE   The matzo balls may be frozen after they have been cooked. Place them on a cookie sheet in the freezer and when frozen drop them into a plastic bag to store.

Year 1783 Chicken Soup with Pasta

Serves 10 to 12

Year 1783 Chicken Soup is prepared in three easy stages. The first stage is making the stock; next is cooking the vegetables; and finally, the pasta is prepared. While the number of servings may seem large (10 to 12), the recipe makes the most use of the whole bird without leftover bits and pieces. Freezing what is not wanted immediately is an economy.

The date in the soup's name marks the year John Farley, the head cook at the London Tavern, published his book, The London Art of Cookery and Housekeeper's Complete Assistant.

Here, in part, is his 200-year-old recipe in his own words:

Take celery, and endive, and lettuce and an onion; chop them pretty small, and so pass them in brown butter thickened; put in half broth, half gravy, as much as will fill your dish; put in an ounce and a half of vermajelly of two sorts, and stove it up in your soup till tender; stove some of another sort in broth till thick, and tincture it with a little saffron. . . .

Here is how Farley's excellent soup is "stoved" today:

INGREDIENTS   *Stock*
4- to 5-pound chicken, preferably a capon
6 cups water, or enough to cover
1 sprig fresh thyme or ¼ teaspoon dried
1 bay leaf
2 cloves
1 stalk celery, chopped
1 leek, white part only, chopped

Vegetables
2 stalks celery, finely chopped
1 Belgian endive, sliced
1 head iceberg lettuce, coarsely shredded
1 onion, thinly sliced

(continued)

4 tablespoons butter
4 cups water

Pasta
6 cups chicken stock from above (augmented with vegetable broth,
    if needed)
4 ounces macaroni
¼ teaspoon saffron
4 ounces vermicelli
Salt, if desired, to taste (about 2 teaspoons, usually)
2 grinds of fresh black pepper

SPECIAL
EQUIPMENT

Soup tureen for formal presentation at the table, or a presentable casserole

PREPARATION
BOIL/SIMMER
1 hour

Stock
Place the chicken in a medium (3½-quart) saucepan and cover with
water, about 6 cups. Add thyme, bay leaf, cloves, celery, and leek. Bring
to a boil, reduce heat, and simmer for 1 hour or until tender. Remove
chicken from the saucepan and set aside to cool. Strain and reserve the
stock. If there is time, place stock in the refrigerator overnight to congeal the fat. Lift fat off with a slotted spoon and discard or reserve for
another use.

The chicken can be made part of the soup in one of two ways. As in
Farley's time, the chicken may be carved and the meat left on the bone,
or the meat can be pulled from the bone. Either way, remove and discard
the skin.

SAUTÉ
12 mins.

15–20 mins.

Vegetables
In a saucepan sauté celery, endive, lettuce, and onion in butter until the
vegetables are limp, about 12 minutes. Pour in the water and bring to a
boil, then simmer until the vegetables are just tender, 15 to 20 minutes.
Set aside.

BOIL
6 mins.

5 mins.

Pasta
Heat the chicken stock in a medium (3½-quart) saucepan. Add macaroni and saffron, return to a boil, and cook 6 minutes. Add vermicelli
and continue boiling 5 more minutes. Pasta should be just tender—
al dente—not overcooked. Add salt to taste and the pepper.

ASSEMBLE

If you are serving the soup from a tureen or casserole, arrange the pieces of chicken on the bottom of the vessel. Cover the chicken with vegetables and their broth. Finally, add the soup and two pastas.

FINAL STEP   Stir the soup to blend just before serving. Serve with saltines or homemade French bread.

Chicken Soup with Stuffed Lettuce Pillows (Italian)
Serves 6 to 8

The proper name for this dish made with quite ordinary ingredients but put together in a unique way is Chicken Soup with Stuffed Lettuce Pillows, but at our house it goes as "Pillows."

Pillows came to my kitchen by the circuitous route of many good recipes. It is an adaptation of a recipe by Julia Huxley that in turn was inspired by a recipe by Marcella Hazan, the author of several fine volumes on Italian cooking. Huxley wrote for The Washington Post.

The little forcemeat pillows in the soup are reminiscent of the most delicate wontons without the envelope of dough. The original recipe called for veal to be mixed with the chicken. I used ham—a piece left over from a holiday Smithfield. A piece of pork (or veal) will do as well.

While the layers of pillows simmer on the bottom of the pot—held down by the weight of a plate or pot lid—they impart to the broth a special flavor that the broth alone does not have; hence it is possible to use canned broth and still get the good, made-at-home taste.

INGREDIENTS   *Forcemeat*
½ pound ham or other cut of lean pork
1 whole chicken breast, boned and skinned
4 tablespoons butter
Salt to taste
Pinch of freshly ground black pepper
¼ cup minced onion
¼ cup minced celery
2 tablespoons minced carrot
2 tablespoons ricotta cheese or sour cream
¼ cup freshly grated Parmesan cheese
1 teaspoon fresh marjoram or ¼ teaspoon dried
1 tablespoon minced parsley
2 egg yolks

Pillows
2 heads lettuce, iceberg preferred
2 quarts chicken stock, fresh or canned

(continued)

SPECIAL EQUIPMENT	Food processor or blender
PREPARATION	*Note:* The ham or pork and chicken will be cooked separately but later put through the food processor together.
SAUTÉ *4 mins.*	Cut the meats in 1-inch pieces but keep separate. Melt the butter in a skillet and brown the ham or pork on all sides, about 4 minutes. Salt and pepper as desired. Lift pieces out of the skillet with a slotted spoon and reserve in a bowl.
4 mins.	Brown the chicken with a little salt and pepper. Add the pieces to the pork in the bowl.
8 mins.	Drop the onions into the skillet and cook until they are slightly browned and tender, about 8 minutes. Add the celery and carrots and
10 mins.	cook for an additional 10 minutes. Scrape the vegetable mixture into a medium bowl and set aside.
PROCESS *1 min.*	Chop the meats in a food processor or blender until very fine. If using a blender take care not to overprocess. Add the meats to the vegetables.
BLEND	Blend in the ricotta or sour cream, Parmesan, marjoram, parsley, and egg yolks. Mix well—the mixture should be moist but not wet.
TEST	Fry a spoonful of the mixture in a small skillet, then taste (do *not* taste it raw). Correct seasoning if necessary, and set aside until the lettuce leaves are ready.
BOIL *2 mins.*	Bring to a boil sufficient water to cover a whole head of lettuce. While the water is heating, discard colored or torn outer leaves, and core each head. Ease a head into the water and when water comes back to a boil— about 2 minutes—lift out with a slotted spoon. Drain in a colander. Repeat with the second head.
	When the lettuce has cooled, carefully peel back the leaves. Cut each leaf vertically along the heavy rib in the lower part of the leaf, making two pieces. Discard the rib. Flatten the halves and lay aside. (The deep inner leaves are often too small and crumpled to use.)
STUFFING	Place about 1 teaspoon of the stuffing on each leaf half and roll the leaf to completely envelop the stuffing, turning in the ends and folding under as it is rolled. Each pillow should be bite-size, about 1½ inches long and ½ inch thick. Set the tightly wrapped pillows aside, seam side

down, and continue with the stuffing until it is all used. The pillows may be covered with plastic wrap and refrigerated for a day or two.

ASSEMBLE

When assembling, place the rolled pillows on the bottom of a large saucepan that has a cover, packing them tightly together with no space between them. Put down as many layers as necessary, although one will usually do it.

Place a plate or lid small enough to fit *inside* the pot on top of the pillows holding them in place as they cook.

SIMMER
30 mins.

Heat the chicken stock and, taking care to keep the plate or lid in place, pour it over the pillows to a level about 2 inches above them.

Cover the pot and bring the broth to a simmer; anything more robust may break the pillows apart. Cook for 30 minutes from the time the simmer begins.

In a separate saucepan, heat the remaining stock. (Pouring all the stock into the pot initially would make it difficult to lift out the pillows later.)

Remove the cover and the inside plate or lid. With a slotted spoon, carefully lift out the pillows and divide them among the soup plates, seam side down.

FINAL STEP

Ladle the hot stock over the pillows and serve.

Delicious Chicken Noodle Soup

Serves 8 to 10

Mrs. Regina Hollander calls this her "delicious chicken noodle soup"—a lovely dish she has made once each week in a long lifetime spent in a Jewish kitchen that has produced some exceptional dishes. (Her retes—Hungarian apple strudel—is in my earlier cookbook on pastries.) Regina, born in the nineteenth century, was given this recipe by her mother when she was a young girl in Hungary. The store-bought noodles were not a convenient staple available to either mother or daughter in the beginning, but Regina approves of the high quality of noodles that can be purchased today.

There are dividends that come with this golden noodle-strewn soup—beef left over for hash or sandwiches and chicken for salad or an entrée. Mrs. Hollander, a purist, does not garnish her soup with bits of meat, but I do, on occasion.

A 3-pound pullet, a piece of beef which Regina describes as "bony meat" (a soup bone with some flesh), and noodles, homemade or store-bought, are the triad that go together to make this a delicious and nourishing dish.

Finally, true to her origin, Regina adds a small sprinkle of pungent Hungarian paprika.

INGREDIENTS	3-pound chicken, whole or quartered, rinsed
	1½ pounds fleshy beef soup bone, rinsed
	1 teaspoon salt
	3 quarts cold water
	1 medium onion, peeled
	1 bay leaf
	2 carrots, cut into 1-inch pieces
	2 stalks celery, plus leaves, cut into 1-inch pieces
	4 sprigs parsley, roughly chopped
	1 clove garlic, quartered, bruised
	2 tablespoons tomato juice
	1½ cups (2 ounces) fine noodles, packaged or homemade, cooked separately
	2 cups boiling water
	1 teaspoon salt, if desired
	Pepper, to taste
	⅛ teaspoon Hungarian paprika
	Chopped parsley, for garnish

SPECIAL EQUIPMENT	One large (5- to 6-quart) pot and one medium (1½-quart) pot
PREPARATION BOIL/SIMMER *15 mins.* *60 mins.*	Place chicken, beef bone, and salt in large pot with cold water, which will allow it to come to a boil slowly. Skim surface. Simmer 1 hour, uncovered. Add water if needed to maintain level in pot.
BOIL/SIMMER *5 mins.* *60 mins.*	Add onion, bay leaf, carrots, celery, parsley, garlic, and tomato juice. Bring to a boil and simmer 1 hour.
STRAIN	Strain and reserve soup. Meat will fall easily from the bones. Cut 1 cup of chicken into bite-size pieces and add to soup, if desired. Reserve the rest of both meats for other uses.

Note: The chicken portion of the soup may be prepared ahead of time, then chilled, and the fat lifted off. When the soup is hot the fat can be skimmed off, but it is more difficult to trap all of the fat globules.

Note: The noodles are cooked separately during the final 20 minutes of preparation and added to the soup after it has been strained and the meat and vegetables have been removed.

BOIL/SIMMER
5–10 mins.

Drop the noodles into boiling salted water. Cook packaged noodles according to label instructions, taking care not to overcook. Drain, rinse with cold water, drain again, and add to the soup.

SEASON

Salt and pepper to taste. Add paprika.

FINAL STEP

Heat soup bowls and have ready to serve. Return soup to a simmer and serve. Garnish with a sprinkle of finely chopped parsley.

Smoky Chicken Soup

Serves 8

A faint smokiness permeates this delicious soup of chicken, beans, and pasta. It is made with a home-smoked chicken, which provides both the white meat to be shredded for the soup and the stock from the stripped-down carcass. Dark meat is reserved for other uses.

Smoke gives this hearty soup a touch of elegance.

If smoking your own chicken is not feasible, smoked chicken, whole or parts, can be purchased at many meat counters or ordered from food catalogs. Smoked turkey parts do equally well. If you buy the meat and have no carcass, a rich but unsmoked stock will do reasonably well.

Allow two days to smoke the chicken, beginning with rubbing the bird with coarse salt and allowing it to season for 48 hours before steaming. Smoking instructions follow.

This inspired recipe came from Mrs. London's Bakeshop and Restaurant in Saratoga Springs, New York, where she created the recipe to utilize what remained of the smoked bird after it made its contribution to chicken sandwiches.

INGREDIENTS

To smoke
4-pound chicken
½ cup coarse salt, kosher or sea type
Handful of hickory chips, soaked for several hours in water;
    or ¼ cup raw rice, ¼ cup black tea leaves, and 1 tablespoon sugar

Soup
Chicken carcass from above
1 large onion, coarsely chopped
1 large carrot, coarsely chopped
1 clove garlic, crushed

(continued)

1 bay leaf
1 sprig parsley
8 ounces dried Great Northern beans, rinsed and picked over
4 ounces noodles or macaroni or other pasta
2 tablespoons olive oil
1 large onion, finely chopped
8 ounces (1 cup) Italian plum tomatoes, canned or fresh
Smoked breast of chicken, from above, skin removed, shredded
1 teaspoon fresh basil, chopped, or ¼ teaspoon dried
Pinch of fresh oregano
2 tablespoons chopped fresh parsley if fresh basil and oregano are not
     available
Salt to taste, if desired (usually about 1½ teaspoons)
½ teaspoon freshly ground black pepper

SPECIAL EQUIPMENT

A steamer or pot with cover large enough to hold chicken in a deep dish (a large Pyrex bread pan is good). Meat smoker or a wok with cover, both upper and lower pieces lined with heavy aluminum foil.

Chicken (a 3-step operation)

PREPARATION SEASON
2 days

Wash chicken, dry well, and rub thoroughly with salt. Place in bowl, cover with plastic wrap, and refrigerate for 2 days, turning once. When ready to steam, rinse chicken and dry with paper towels.

STEAM
45 mins.

Place the chicken in a deep, ovenproof dish. If using an ordinary saucepan or pot, pour 1½ inches of water into the bottom and place a rack under the dish to hold it above the water. Cover the vessel tightly and steam over medium-low heat for 45 minutes. For a steamer, follow directions.

COOL

Take chicken out of the saucepan or steamer and allow it to cool completely, at least 2 to 3 hours.

SMOKE
15–20 mins.

If a wok is used, drop handful of hickory chips on the foil-covered bottom. Place chicken on oiled rack above the chips and place wok over high heat. Cover tightly with foil-lined lid. Chicken will be golden brown and well smoked in 15 to 20 minutes, depending on size of chips used. Smoke 15 minutes if using the rice, tea, and sugar mixture, then turn off heat and allow the chicken to remain covered for an additional 15 minutes.

Cool or refrigerate the smoked chicken. Remove the breast meat.

Cut in 3 pieces across the grain and shred with a fork. Cover and reserve. The legs, thighs, and wings are disjointed and held for other uses—they are not used in this soup. The carcass is now ready to make into the smoky stock.

Soup

BOIL/SIMMER
2 hours

Press the carcass flat and place it with onions, carrots, garlic, bay leaf, and parsley in a medium (3-quart) saucepan. Barely cover with water, about 4 or 5 cups. Bring to a boil, lower heat, and simmer for 2 hours. Strain the stock through a fine-mesh sieve, pressing down on the vegetables and bones to extract all juices.

BOIL
2 mins.
1 hour 15 mins.

While the stock simmers, cover beans with cold water in a small saucepan and bring to a rapid boil for 2 minutes. Turn off heat and let stand for 1 hour; return to a simmer and cook until the beans are barely done—still with some crunch. Drain but save the liquid to thin out the soup later if necessary.

COOK
4–5 mins.

Cook pasta in a medium (3-quart) saucepan in boiling water until al dente; drain and reserve the pasta, tossing with a little olive oil to keep the strands from sticking together.

SAUTÉ
8 mins.
SIMMER
20 mins.

In a large soup pot or saucepan (4-quart) sauté the onion in olive oil for 8 minutes or until translucent. Add chopped tomatoes, smoky broth, and herbs. Simmer for 20 minutes. Add the reserved beans, pasta, and shredded chicken pieces.

SEASON

Return to a simmer for a moment or two while tasting for seasoning—add salt and pepper if necessary.

FINAL STEP

Ladle into a heated tureen and serve in heated soup plates. Serve with saltines or a peasant bread and lots of butter.

Avgolemono Soup (Greek)
Kotosoupa Avgolemono

Serves 6

The most popular of all Hellenic soups, avgolemono has a creamy texture and a refreshing tang that come from an uncomplicated blend of stock, eggs, lemon juice, and rice.

Avgolemono can be made with chicken, lamb, beef, or fish stock. All are equally good. Any kind of pasta can be used instead of rice, with the small ricelike orzo preferred.

This recipe came from Frank Martinez, an outstanding chef and a fellow student at Hyde Park's famous culinary institute. He adds a dash of Worcestershire sauce, which I have not included among the ingredients because it is little known in Greece.

INGREDIENTS	6 cups chicken, lamb, beef, or fish stock
	3 tablespoons long-grain rice or pasta
	4 eggs, separated, at room temperature
	½ teaspoon salt, if desired
	4 tablespoons lemon juice
	¼ cup white wine, optional
	1 tablespoon freshly ground black pepper, to garnish,
	or 3 tablespoons finely chopped fresh dill, to garnish

SPECIAL
EQUIPMENT   Whisk or electric mixer

PREPARATION   *Note:* The sauce of lemon and egg is blended into the soup just before it is served.

BOIL/COOK
15 mins.   In a medium (3-quart) saucepan, bring stock to a boil, add rice, cover, and cook over medium heat until the rice is tender but not soft, about 15 minutes.

    Remove the pot from the heat. Dip out 1 cup of stock and set aside to use in making the sauce.

BEAT
5 mins.   Separate eggs. Pour egg whites into mixing bowl (for hand or electric beater) and beat whites with salt until stiff. Add yolks, still beating, then add lemon juice very slowly. Slowly pour the reserved cup of stock, and optional wine, into the mixture and continue to beat rapidly until well blended. Pour the sauce into the soup and return pot to low heat. Stir for

2 mins.   about 2 minutes until steaming hot. Remove from heat.

FINAL STEP   Pour the avgolemono into heated bowls and serve with freshly ground black pepper or sprinkles of dill.

Chicken Lemon Soup (Greek)

Serves 4

Three ingredients—chicken stock, eggs, and lemon juice—are all that is needed to make this delicious light, yet creamy, Greek soup that is put together in minutes. Its lemony tang is enjoyable as the first dinner course, or as an appealing luncheon dish.

Thin slices of lemon are floated on the surface just before serving.

INGREDIENTS	4 cups chicken stock
	4 eggs
	4 tablespoons fresh lemon juice
	½ cup heavy cream, optional
	Thin slices of whole lemon, seeded, to garnish
SPECIAL EQUIPMENT	Whisk
PREPARATION 5 mins.	Heat chicken stock to boiling. Beat eggs with a whisk until they are light. Beat in the lemon juice.
SIMMER 3 mins.	Slowly pour 2 cups of the hot stock into the egg/lemon mixture, stirring constantly.
4 mins.	Pour the egg mixture into the remaining stock in the saucepan, stirring with a whisk as the soup thickens, about 4 minutes over low heat.
FINAL STEP	For a richer, creamier version add ½ cup heavy cream. Float a lemon slice on each serving.
VARIATION	Instead of lemon slice, float 3 cooked asparagus tips to radiate from the center of each serving.

Clear Chicken Soup (Japanese)
Tori No Suimono

Serves 4

The Japanese word for the large family of soups to which this delicious one belongs is suimono, *meaning "something to drink." It is more than that, of course; it is a sparkling, elegant soup to be served as a prelude to a Western meal or following the appetizer as the first course of the Japanese meal.*

"Clear" Chicken Soup is not quite clear, because a teaspoon of light soy sauce gives it a touch of color.

Traditionally this and other Japanese soups are served in covered lacquer bowls. Because of the wood base, the bowl is insulated and not uncomfortable when it is held in the hand and the soup is sipped—sipped gently, not slurped.

When I was in Japan as a war correspondent at the end of World War II, there was so little food in the cities that soup was almost the only dish available. I had nothing so delicious as this Clear Chicken Soup. I have not been back since then, but I have adapted a fine recipe by Shizuo Tsuji from his book Japanese Cooking, a Simple Art.

Although edible chrysanthemum leaves are grown year-round in Japan, they are available in the United States only in Japanese and specialty food stores, principally on the Pacific Coast.

INGREDIENTS	5 cups Chicken Stock (page 20)
	8 fresh spinach leaves, preferably young and tender,
	    or 10 sprigs edible chrysanthemum leaves, coarsely chopped,
	    if available
	1 small carrot, peeled and cut into very thin rounds
	4 to 6 okra pods, washed and caps removed
	Salt
	4 fresh shiitake mushrooms or 4 small button mushrooms
	1 teaspoon light soy sauce
	½ cup cooked white meat of chicken, cut into bite-size pieces
	4 very thin lemon slices
	¼ cup very thinly sliced scallions

SPECIAL EQUIPMENT	None
PREPARATION	*Beforehand:* Make 5 cups chicken stock, or use frozen stock if available. Prepare the vegetables that will be arranged in an artistic pattern on the bottom of each serving bowl.
PARBOIL 1 min.	Cut and discard the thick center rib from the spinach leaves; parboil in lightly salted water for about 1 minute or until limp. Lift out of the water with a slotted spoon or chopsticks and rinse under cold running water. Set aside for the moment. Or, if using chrysanthemum leaves, wash and coarsely chop. Do not parboil.
5 mins.	Cook the thin carrot slices in boiling salted water until tender, about 5 minutes.
1–2 mins.	Rub the okra pods with salt to remove the fuzz, then parboil about

1 to 2 minutes. Drain but do not rinse. Cut the pods into ¼-inch rounds to reveal their symmetrical pattern of green and white.

If shiitake mushrooms are used, cut a cross design on the cap of each. Do the same with button mushrooms, or remove stems and cut the caps into attractive thin slices.

8 mins. Complete the broth, if you are making it from scratch; strain, clarify, and add soy sauce.

Remove the skin from the chicken and dice ½ cup meat into ⅜-inch pieces no larger than the carrot rounds.

HEAT To serve, bring stock to a simmer.

ASSEMBLE Place a small portion of the chicken in each individual soup bowl. Alongside the chicken, artistically arrange spinach or chrysanthemum leaves, slices of carrot and okra, and a mushroom. Use chopsticks or a slotted spoon to lift the vegetables from the saucepan to the bowls.

FINAL STEP Carefully ladle the hot broth over the arranged ingredients and garnish with a thin slice of lemon and the sliced scallions.

Serve immediately.

Mulligatawny

Serves 8

India is not a travel destination for many Americans, but the taste of it can be enjoyed with mulligatawny. The British brought mulligatawny home with them from India, where originally it was milakutanni, "pepper-water." It is the kind of soup you will long remember, and later wish for a bowl of.

The recipe below can be made with curry powder from the spice shelf or one can be put together with a selection of exotic but easily obtainable spices. While some curries are made with as many as 16 spices, this one has only 6. This homemade seasoning is far better than store-bought curry powder, especially if the latter is not fresh.

This is a robust, spicy (but not too spicy) dish, rich with pieces of chicken and a sprinkling of coconut flakes floating on top. Rice is usually served as a side dish.

INGREDIENTS *Homemade Curry Seasoning*
1 teaspoon coriander seeds
½ teaspoon whole cumin seeds
8 cardamom pods
3 cloves

(continued)

¼ teaspoon black peppercorns
½ teaspoon dried hot red chili flakes

Note: If pressed for time, or if ingredients are not available, you may substitute 1 tablespoon curry powder. Be certain it is fresh.

4 teaspoons finely chopped onion
1 clove garlic, minced
1 teaspoon turmeric

Soup
2 medium onions, sliced
½ cup *each* finely sliced carrots and celery
4 tablespoons butter
4-pound stewing chicken, cut into pieces, or 4 pounds drumsticks, thighs, giblets, and backs
1 cup yogurt
Curry seasoning from above
2 quarts water
Salt, if desired (usually about 2 teaspoons)
½ cup coconut, toasted, to garnish (unsweetened preferable)
4 cups boiled rice, optional

SPECIAL
EQUIPMENT

Blender or mortar and pestle

PREPARATION
OVEN
200°
30 mins.

Homemade Curry Seasoning
Preheat oven to 200°. Spread all the dry seeds, pods, and flakes in one layer in a shallow pan. Roast for 30 minutes but do not brown. Stir and turn the mixture several times. Remove the pan from the oven and, when cool, break the cardamom pods. Take out the tiny seeds and combine with all the other spices.

GRIND
2–3 mins.

Grind the spices in an electric blender until pulverized into a powder.
    This small amount may also be pulverized using a mortar and pestle. I sometimes use a marvelous piece of Japanese kitchen equipment, a *suribachi*. A wooden pestle grinds the spices against ridges baked into a stoneware bowl.
    Note: This spice mixture (*garam masala* in India) may be mixed in larger quantities and stored at room temperature for up to 5 or 6 months.

MIX *3 mins.*	Mix the powder with the onion, garlic, and turmeric and blend into a paste. Set aside.
SWEAT *15 mins.* *20 mins.* *20 mins.*	*Soup* In a large (5- to 6-quart) soup kettle, sweat the onions, carrots, and celery in the butter for about 15 minutes. Add the chicken pieces and cook for about 20 minutes, turning the pieces over once or twice. Stir in the yogurt, curry seasoning, and salt, if desired, and stew until the juices become a brownish crust on the bottom of the pan. This will take an additional 20 minutes. Watch carefully and do not let the mixture burn.
SIMMER *1 hour* *20 mins.*	Pour in the 2 quarts of water; cover and simmer for an hour over medium-low heat, or longer if the chicken is an older and tougher bird. When the meat is tender and pulls easily from the bones, take the pot off the heat. When the soup has cooled a bit, pick the meat off the bones and cut into bite-size pieces. Discard the bones, skin, and cartilage. Return the meat to the soup pot.
FINAL STEP	Taste for seasoning. Reheat soup until it is simmering. Pour into a heated tureen. Sprinkle coconut over each serving. Serve a separate bowl of boiled rice, if desired. Each guest may drop a spoonful of rice into his or her individual soup serving. Pass the coconut again, as well as the rice.

Egg Drop Soup (Japanese)
Tamago Toji

Serves 4

This delightfully light soup—with a golden swirl of egg through it—can be made with either dashi, the basic sea-flavored stock, or chicken stock clarified with egg or eggshells. Don't think of dashi as fishy; it is not. It has a lovely smoky flavor all its own. This soup is appropriate to be served with almost any meal.

*   The spice used by the Japanese in this soup is* sansho, *the leaves of the prickly ash plucked in early springtime and powdered. Sansho is available in shops specializing in Asian foods.*

*   To mix the egg in a colorful pattern, the soup is first stirred clockwise, and then the egg swirled in and immediately stirred counterclockwise.*

INGREDIENTS   **3 cups Dashi (page 24) or Chicken Stock (page 20)**
¼ teaspoon salt

(continued)

½ teaspoon soy sauce

2 or 3 small fresh button mushrooms, trimmed, thinly sliced, optional—
   but good

1 egg, lightly beaten

2 or 3 stalks coriander, chopped, or ½ teaspoon chopped chives

Pinch of *sansho,* if available, or pinch of paprika (hardly authentic but
   effective)

SPECIAL
EQUIPMENT

None

PREPARATION

Heat the basic stock, dashi or chicken, in a medium (2½-quart) saucepan and season *lightly* with salt and soy sauce.

BOIL/SIMMER
3–4 mins.

Bring the stock to a gentle boil over medium-low heat. Add mushroom slices if using them. Reduce heat and simmer for 3 to 4 minutes.

Gently move the soup clockwise with a slotted spoon or chopsticks. Pour in the beaten egg. Remove the soup from heat and stir counterclockwise. Sprinkle in the finely chopped coriander or chives. Cover the

1 min.

soup for 1 minute, then uncover and season with a light sprinkling of *sansho* or paprika.

FINAL STEP

Serve the soup immediately in heated cups or, as the Japanese do, in lacquered bowls with covers.

Chili

MENTION CHILI and watch the gleam in the eyes of those around you when they think of their own version of a steaming bowl of this special kind of spicy stew. It is the subject of much contest and controversy.

What is there about chili that brings such a happy glint to all eyes but means something different to each person? Only two things are consistent—it is hot and its color is red. Beyond that, anything seems to go. To some, the wilder the selection of ingredients the better.

Chili had its humble origin in the southwestern section of the United States, probably at campfires along the early cattle trails, where tough unaged beef was disguised by a fiery seasoning of the region's chili peppers.

Then in 1967 the chili contest was born, and with it, a new proliferation of recipes. It is enough to mention but a few—Gross National Product, Rebel Roulette, Red Chili Nightmare, Hot Pants, Buzzard's Breath, Survival, and False Alarm (no chilies). Desperate to make their chilies different, contestants reached for anything in the kitchen including applesauce, marinated artichoke hearts, cinnamon, goat cheese, booze, and beer. Chocolate found its way into chili because it is a staple in Tex-Mex cooking. One contestant attributed her winning ways to the fact that she tied the chilies in the toe of her discarded panty hose.

This book does not contain the ultimate chili recipe, because, as any chili-head knows, his own is the best. Nor does this chapter espouse way-out chilies. None will force you to run for a fire extinguisher. Nevertheless, each has the potential for doing so if you simply increase the amount of peppers or chili powder.

While chili simmers, taste and test its heat *(picante)*. If some like it hot and some like it mild, divide the pot and season portions accordingly.

For the true believers—those who hold to meat and seasonings only—the list of *verboten* things is impressive: celery, carrots, parsley, Worcestershire sauce, sugar, sherry, and rice, to name but a few.

Chili is essentially a meat dish, highly seasoned, though vegetarian chili has slipped in along the way. In the Southwest, markets sell "chili ground" meat, a coarse grind that leaves the meat fibers in evidence. Some like all of the meat ground while others demand small chunks or cubes. I have discovered that a blend of 40 percent cubed and 60 percent ground meat is good. Something to chew on, but not a challenge. A home grinder with ½-inch holes or a food processor zapped on and off briefly is excellent for this kind of grind. Or ask the meat man to use the same blades as for Italian sausage. Cubes can range from ¼ inch to ½ inch. Meat chilled in the refrigerator is easier to cut.

One of the great controversies within chili circles is whether or not to include beans in the mixture or exile them to a side dish. Here simple economics may come into play. A kettle of pure chili will serve eight persons. But a dozen can be served if beans are added. It is a simple way to extend the chili.

The heart and hot soul of chili are peppers.

Chili peppers are hot. Chili peppers are mild. Chilies are long, short, and fat. Chilies are yellow, green, brown, and red. There are roughly 200 different types of chili peppers in the world, over 100 of which are to be found in Mexico and the U.S. Southwest.

To complicate the study of peppers further, the names given to various chilies vary from one locale to another. Chili poblano, for example, is known as chili *para rellenar* near the Texas border, and as ancho or *pasilla* in Baja California. In addition, a chili will be known by one name fresh (chili poblano) and, by another when dried (chili ancho). Chili peppers are now in almost every store across the country.

A convenient way to add peppers to chili is to first make a puree (see Hernandez Chili, page 76) that can be meted out by degree, rather than to dump in all the peppers at once.

If not chilies themselves, then use chili powder, which is a blend of more ingredients than just peppers—cumin, oregano, garlic, and salt are also included. However, a chili made with a selection of peppers has greater substance, greater depth of flavor, and a more delightful afterburn than a chili made with only chili powder.

Rather than adding the chili powder as it comes from the jar or can, a Mexican friend suggests blending 1 tablespoon of powder, 1 teaspoon of flour, and 1 tablespoon of cold water. The paste is brought to bubbling over medium heat. The quantity replaces one whole pepper and seasons evenly and well.

Here is a guide to peppers for the serious chili cook:

VARIETY	PHYSICAL CHARACTERISTICS	HOTNESS
Ancho* (dried Poblano)	3"–5" long; brownish red to chocolate brown; turns red after scalding; wrinkled skin	Mild, flavorful
Cascabel*	About 1" diameter; small, round, brownish red; smooth skin; seeds rattle when shaken	Medium-hot, nutty flavor when toasted
Jalapeño	About 2" long, 1" diameter; dark green, firm, waxy skin, blunt tip	Very hot, fresh are hotter than pickled
Muleto*	Brown-black, same shape as ancho; tough skin, slightly less wrinkled than ancho	Sweeter than ancho
Pasilla*	About 6" long; brownish-black; wrinkled skin, slender	Very piquant, rich, slightly hotter than ancho
Pequin	Pea-size oval	Very hot
Poblano	About 5" long; dark green, almost black; triangular; shape, size, color vary by where, when grown	Mild to hot; flavor similar to bell pepper
Serrano	About 1½" long; light green, ripening to bright red; thin, narrow tip	Hot to very, hotter than jalapeño; seeds and ribs very hot

* Dried; all others fresh

Courtesy The Cook's Magazine

Six chili recipes follow. Four come from the Southwest, where, happily, the region is returning to the traditional Texas chili, which essentially consists of meat and chilies. Beans are rarely included. The fifth recipe, by Minnie Roach, is the least potent of the bunch and would not get far among the chili-heads, but I have included it because it is delicious and easy to make on the spur of the moment from ingredients at hand or available at a nearby supermarket. For this one you need not develop an expertise in chili craft or maintain an inventory of chili peppers. The sixth recipe is a regional favorite along the Ohio River—Cincinnati Chili.

Hernandez Chili con Carne

Serves 4 without beans, 6 with

The purist should not be put off by the inclusion of beans in this otherwise authentic recipe that started in San Antonio, was polished in Mexico, and finally came to rest in my kitchen.

Milton Hernandez was born in Texas, moved to Mexico City, and then returned to the United States, where he was discovered by Craig Claiborne, the noted food writer for The New York Times.

His is a chili that can be made fiery or not so fiery. The beans are cooked separately and added to the stew later, or served as a side dish. While specific chilies are listed among the ingredients, substitutions can be made freely—but do taste and test as you go. Each chili or combination of chilies will give a different flavor, so feel free to go in any direction the palate suggests.

The preparation of a puree is an unusual way to introduce the chilies. When the chilies are blended and cooked, the puree can be used to season the meat as the cooking progresses. Instead of dumping all the chilies into the brew at once—a step from which there is no return—a portion at a time can be added to allow you to judge the intensity of the chili as you go. The puree can be made days or weeks in advance and kept refrigerated until the chili assemblage begins. The unused portion can be frozen for later use. I sometimes whip up a triple batch to have on hand to use myself or as a small gift to a chili-head.

The beauty of the puree is that it allows one to be moderate at the start and build slowly to a climax.

INGREDIENTS

Meat

2 pounds round steak, in one piece

1 cup finely chopped onions

2 finely minced cloves garlic

2 tablespoons cooking oil

3 cups water, or enough to cover

1 cup tomato sauce or 2 cups tomato puree

2 teaspoons cumin seeds, roasted in a small skillet and ground

1 tablespoon oregano

2 teaspoons paprika

Salt, if desired

Chili Puree
6 to 8 dried ancho peppers
2 *guajillo* peppers
2 New Mexico peppers
2 to 10 chilies *de arbol,* depending on hotness desired
1 whole clove garlic
½ cup water
2 tablespoons cooking oil

Beans
2 cups red kidney or pinto beans
Salt to taste
2 bay leaves
1 small ham hock or 1 pork rind
6 to 10 cups water

SPECIAL
EQUIPMENT

Mortar and pestle to grind roasted cumin. Food processor to puree chilies and to cut meat coarsely. Otherwise, use a blender to puree chilies and a meat grinder with coarse blade to chop meat.

PREPARATION

Meat
Beforehand: Trim fat off the meat. Cut half of the meat into 1-inch chunks and feed through the meat grinder or food processor. The meat should be coarsely shredded. Cut the balance of the meat into ½-inch, or smaller, cubes. Set the meat aside.

SAUTÉ
10–12 mins.

COOK
6–8 mins.

Sauté the onions and garlic slowly in oil in a large kettle, preferably a black iron one. When the onions and garlic have cooked over medium heat for 10 to 12 minutes, add the meat. Cook the meat, stirring frequently, until it has lost its redness, about 6 to 8 minutes. Add enough water to barely cover the meat, about 3 cups. Add tomato sauce (or puree), cumin, oregano, paprika, and salt, if desired.

COOK
1 hour

Bring the chili to a boil, reduce heat, and cook over low heat while it slowly bubbles for 1 hour.

Chili Puree
While the meat is cooking, puree the chilies and garlic.

Break the stems of dried chilies, pop open the pods, and shake out and discard the seeds. Break the pods into small pieces and drop into the processor bowl or blender.

PUREE
5 mins.
5 mins.

Pour in ½ cup water and blend briefly, about 1 minute with off-and-on bursts. Scrape down the sides of the container. Let the mixture stand for about 5 minutes. Blend once more and allow to rest again for 5 minutes. Process again until the puree is smooth and uniform.

COOK
10 mins.

Heat oil in a small saucepan and add the puree. Cook over low heat so that it bubbles (but does not burn) for about 10 minutes.

CAUTION

Add a portion of the puree to the meat mixture, blend well, and judge for potency! Add more (or all of it if you wish); but remember, some guests may wish for moderation. Additional puree can be added anytime, now or days later.

COOK
10 mins.–
2 hours

Cook the completed chili over a medium-low flame until it boils down to the consistency pleasing to you—anywhere from 10 minutes to 2 hours.

If you want thicker chili, add ⅓ cup masa harina, the Mexican corn flour, and cook for an additional 10 to 15 minutes.

The chili is ready to be served unless you wish to add the beans now. Or they may be served as a side dish.

BOIL/SIMMER
1–2 hours

Beans
Put the beans in a saucepan and add salt, bay leaves, ham hock or pork rind, and 6 cups of water. Bring to a boil, reduce heat, and simmer until beans are tender but not mushy, about 1½ to 2 hours. Add more water if it cooks away.

Drain the beans and add the liquid to the chili for more flavor. Cut off what meat there is on the ham hock, chop it into small bits, and add to the chili. Discard bay leaves and pork rind.

COOK
10–15 mins.

Set beans aside if they are to be a side dish, or add some or all to the chili pot, stirring and cooking together for another 10 to 15 minutes.

FINAL STEP

Serve the chili hot in a heated tureen and heated bowls. Saltines, oyster crackers, or chunks of a country loaf are ideal companions. So is cold beer, preferably a Texas brew such as Lone Star or Pearl.

Pedernales River Chili

Serves 10 to 12

One of the most famous chili recipes is the creation of Lyndon Baines Johnson. Named for his beloved ranch along the Pedernales River in Texas, it was much publicized and eaten during his years as president in the White House. It still is.

It is a straightforward presentation that has the basic ingredients—cumin, oregano, and chili powder. The beef broth gives it a special lift.

LBJ did not thicken his chili, so I have amended his recipe slightly by adding a bit of masa harina, the Mexican corn flour used in making tortillas and tamales. It not only gives the chili more body but adds a subtle flavor as well.

INGREDIENTS	3 cups chopped onions
	2 cloves garlic, finely minced
	2 tablespoons oil or bacon drippings
	4 pounds beef, chopped or coarsely ground
	1 teaspoon oregano
	2 teaspoons cumin seeds, roasted in a small skillet and ground
	2 tablespoons chili powder, or more to taste
	4 cups tomatoes, fresh, frozen, or canned; crushed
	Salt, if desired
	2 cups hot beef stock or boiling water
	⅓ cup masa harina
SPECIAL EQUIPMENT	None
PREPARATION SAUTÉ *10 mins.*	In a large saucepan sauté onions and garlic in oil (bacon drippings are good) until tender and translucent, about 10 minutes.
10 mins.	Add the meat, breaking up clumps with a heavy wooden spoon. Sauté, stirring often, until lightly cooked—no red showing, about 10 minutes. Sprinkle in the oregano, ground cumin, and chili powder. (The chili powder can be mixed into a paste with an equal amount of water and one third the volume of flour.) Stir to blend.
BOIL/SIMMER *1 hour*	Add the tomatoes, salt, if desired, and hot beef stock or water. Stir in masa harina. Bring to a boil, cover, and let simmer, stirring frequently, about 1 hour. Check the meat for tenderness. Taste for a final adjust-

ment of the seasonings. If a hotter chili is wanted, add more chili powder and cumin, a powerfully pungent spice much overlooked in the home kitchen.

FINAL STEP   Ladle hot soup into tureen and bowls.

Pinto or kidney beans, cooked with a bit of ham, make a fine accompaniment. Overall, a marvelous bowl of red.

"Mom" Unser's Chili

Serves 4 to 6

Mary "Mom" Unser was a legend at every racetrack in the country where her famous sons drove, but at none more so than the Indianapolis Motor Speedway where the two boys were each three-time winners of the 500-mile race. Her own fame rested on her chili, and it grew as she made chili for more and more race drivers and crew members. Her chili bash at Indianapolis was as much an annual event as the race itself. It grew from a one-pot affair to an event that had to be catered. The chili grew in intensity as she added more jalapeños and tequila as the years went on. Mom, who grew up with her family in New Mexico, created a chili that was known to have made race drivers cry.

This is a middle-of-the-road version of her famous chili, but it can be speeded up with additional peppers. Vroom! On a scale of 10 this is a 5.

The Unser chili is different from other chilies in the book in that it is made with pork. Mom used pork shoulder, but on occasion I have cut up thinly sliced pork chops. Delicious!

INGREDIENTS   2 tablespoons oil or bacon drippings

4 cups finely chopped onions

2 cloves garlic, minced

1 to 1½ pounds lean pork shoulder, trimmed and cut into ¼-inch cubes

2 tablespoons masa harina or all-purpose flour

1 15-ounce can tomatoes, coarsely chopped

5 jalapeño peppers, split, seeded, stems and seeds discarded

½ cup water

1 tablespoon paprika

1 teaspoon oregano

2 teaspoons salt, if desired

1½ cups water, or more to control consistency

1 15-ounce can pinto or red kidney beans

1 cup tequila, optional

SPECIAL EQUIPMENT	Processor or blender to puree peppers

| PREPARATION SAUTÉ *8 mins.* COOK *10 mins.* | Pour oil into a medium (4-quart) saucepan or kettle and sauté onions and garlic until soft and transparent, about 8 minutes. Drop pork in with the onions and cook until all redness in the meat is gone. Sprinkle on the masa harina or flour and blend. Stir frequently to prevent the meat from sticking, about 10 minutes.

Chop tomatoes and add them to the kettle. |

| PUREE | Meanwhile, cut open the jalapeños and discard seeds. Cut pods into pieces and place in the work bowl of a food processor or blender. Add ½ cup water and puree.

Pour a portion of the pepper puree into the cooking mixture and taste for *picante* (heat). Decide whether to use the balance of the puree or hold it in reserve. Five jalapeños create a dish that is hot but not unbearably so. But taste and make your own determination.

Add paprika, oregano, salt, if desired, and additional water. As the chili cooks down it may need more water or it could become too thick. |

| COOK *1 hour or longer* *30 mins.* | Cover the pot and cook, slowly bubbling, over low heat for at least 1 hour.

During the last ½ hour of cooking add the beans, including the water in which they were packed.

Stir the pot frequently to prevent the chili from sticking.

Taste for seasoning midway through the cooking process and decide if more of the jalapeño puree should be added. Also check for saltiness. |

| FINAL STEP | If desired, pour in 1 cup tequila before serving. Present the cooking pot at the table and ladle directly into hot bowls.

Saltine crackers and the Unser chili go together. |

Minnie's Mild Chili

Serves 6

For those who like chili, but in its mildest form, I have included the dish brought to perfection by Minnie Roach, my mother-in-law. It is not far from the truth that I married into the family not only to get her daughter but also to get this chili recipe, plus her grandmother's recipe for canned smoked sausage.

It is a fine basic recipe that is easy to make and one that can be made hotter with more chili powder and/or chili peppers.

While Minnie's recipe calls for beef ground for hamburger, the texture will be more exciting if half the meat is cubed and half coarsely ground.

INGREDIENTS	2 slices bacon, chopped into ½-inch pieces
	1 pound ground round beef
	1 tablespoon flour
	1 cup finely chopped onions (about 2 medium)
	1 small green pepper, minced
	2 tablespoons brown sugar
	4 cups tomato juice
	1 15-ounce can red kidney beans
	1 cup water
	1 4-ounce can mushroom pieces
	2 teaspoons chili powder
	¼ teaspoon cayenne (red pepper)
	1 teaspoon flour
	¼ cup water
	Salt, as desired
	½ teaspoon freshly ground black pepper
SPECIAL EQUIPMENT	None
PREPARATION TRY OUT	Try out the bacon in a medium saucepan (3 quarts).
COOK 5 mins. 12 mins.	Stir in the meat and brown lightly. Sprinkle on the flour. Cook for 5 minutes before adding the onions and green pepper. Cook until the onions and peppers are somewhat soft, about 12 minutes over medium heat.
	Add the brown sugar. Pour in the tomato juice. Add the beans, water, and mushrooms.
PASTE	In a small bowl mix the chili powder, cayenne, flour, and water. Stir well to blend. It is now possible to *gradually* introduce the chili powder mixture—teaspoon by teaspoon—without overdoing it. Taste. If you want it hotter, add more of the mixture.
COOK 2 hours	Add the chili paste, stir well, and cook, bubbling slowly, for 2 hours. Cover loosely. If the chili is thin, uncover pot and allow it to cook down.

Taste and determine if either salt or pepper is needed. The hot pepper may carry the flavor without salt or pepper.

FINAL STEP

Serve hot in large bowls. Pass saltines or oyster crackers.

Cincinnati Chili

Serves 4 (or 8 over spaghetti)

Unlike its namesake, the vibrant Queen City on the Ohio River, Cincinnati Chili did not come from the South and West on steamboats up the great rivers; it is the fairly recent creation of a native who now has some ninety parlors serving his dish.

This chili is unusual in several ways. Chocolate and vinegar are among its ingredients; some like the beef and onion to be put through a food processor or blender before they are added to the soup pot; it is creamy-smooth and is served in Cincinnati on a bed of spaghetti and under layers of grated cheese, finely chopped onions, and oyster crackers.

While to some it may sound more like spaghetti sauce with Mexican overtones, it is a good and filling dish. I like it unadorned.

INGREDIENTS

2 medium onions, finely chopped
4 cloves garlic, optional, finely minced
1 tablespoon olive oil
2 pounds lean ground beef
4 cups beef broth
1 15-ounce can tomato sauce
1 teaspoon ground allspice
3 tablespoons chili powder
½ teaspoon cayenne, or more if you want it hotter
1 teaspoon cumin seeds, freshly roasted in a small skillet and ground
1 teaspoon flour
2 tablespoons water
1 bay leaf
¼ teaspoon ground cloves
2 tablespoons white or cider vinegar
½ ounce unsweetened chocolate
Salt, if desired
Spaghetti, chopped onions, cheese, and oyster crackers—selection
    as desired

| SPECIAL EQUIPMENT | None |

| PREPARATION SWEAT 8 mins. | In a covered medium (4-quart) saucepan, sweat onions and garlic in oil over a medium flame until soft and translucent, about 8 minutes. With a slotted spoon lift out the onions and garlic and set aside. |

| COOK 6 mins. | Drop meat into the saucepan and cook over medium-high heat until all the redness is gone and the meat is a light brown, about 6 minutes. Break up the clumps of meat with a wooden spoon to ensure that it is thoroughly cooked. Add the cooked onions and garlic to the meat and stir well to mix. Add the beef broth, tomato sauce, and allspice. Cook over low heat, barely simmering, for about ½ hour. |
| 30 mins. | |

| PASTE | Make a thin paste with the chili powder, cayenne, freshly ground cumin, 1 teaspoon flour, and about 2 tablespoons water. The chili puree or paste in this form makes it easier to control the amount of hot stuff to be added. |

Begin with 2 tablespoons of the chili paste mixed into the saucepan, and stir to blend it well. Taste. Add more by the single tablespoon until the desired seasoning is reached.

Add the bay leaf, ground cloves, vinegar, and chocolate, and salt to taste.

| COOK 1 or more hours | Cover and cook over low heat for at least 1 hour. Some Cincinnati cooks let the pot simmer for up to 3 hours. But don't let the chili turn into a solid before adding more beef stock or water. |

| FINAL STEP | Taste and test one more time and correct seasoning to suit the tongue and the occasion. |

Serve chili in heated bowls—and pass saltines.

Or, as in Cincinnati, layer spaghetti, chili, onions, cheese, and oyster crackers.

Green Chili Stew

Serves 8 or more

There are two doors in Charlie Elias's restaurant in Albuquerque: Front Door and Back Door. One leads into a dining room more formal than the room in back, but in both rooms you can get his famous Green Chili Stew. Charlie loves food in the tradition of the Southwest—hot from a variety of chilies!

Green Chili Stew is delicious and filling, a meal in itself, great for the meeting of robust appetites such as is found at tailgate parties or après-toboggan on the big hill out in back, or when the kids are home from college.

Green chilies are also known as New Mexico chilies and, if dried, as chile colorado. *You may substitute fresh poblano or dried ancho or guajillo.*

INGREDIENTS	½ cup lard or shortening of choice
	2 pounds lean pork, cut into 1½-inch cubes
	¼ cup all-purpose flour
	2 pounds potatoes, peeled and diced
	6 cups crushed or finely chopped tomatoes
	1½ cups chopped green chilies, fresh or frozen
	(This is for "medium" hot—add more for "hot" hot.)
	3 cloves garlic, finely minced
	1 tablespoon *chile pequin* or Tabasco sauce
	1 teaspoon salt
	4 quarts water

SPECIAL EQUIPMENT

6-quart heavy saucepan or kettle

PREPARATION
15 mins.

Heat the lard or other shortening over medium heat in the saucepan. Dredge the pork cubes in the flour and drop into the saucepan to brown, about 15 minutes. Watch carefully that the flour does not burn.
  When the pork is well browned, add remaining ingredients.

SIMMER/BOIL
1½ hours

Simmer, covered, over low heat for 35 minutes. Bring to a boil for 20 minutes, then return to a simmer for 30 minutes to finish. Taste and adjust the seasoning. Perhaps more Tabasco?

FINAL STEP

Serve hot with warm tortillas. And perhaps a cold Mexican beer.

Chowders

THE WORD *CHOWDER* is derived from the French *chaudière,* a three-legged heavy iron pot sitting above glowing coals and bubbling with a thick seafood soup. The dish may have found its way via French Canada to New England, where the seafood became almost exclusively clams.

Hungry colonists watched wild pigs rooting in the shore sands for clams, and they soon realized the value of those meaty clams for making their first clam chowder. A rivalry now exists between New England purists, who want their chowder made with milk but no tomatoes, and those farther south, who want their chowder made with tomatoes and water, hence a thinner brew. The latter became Manhattan or Long Island chowder, in which there is another distinction—a pronounced flavor of thyme. The bits of thyme are left floating on the surface and do not detract from the soup's eye appeal. New Englanders place their thyme in a muslin bag, which is discarded before serving.

Clam stock should never be weak or lifeless in flavor. This means using enough clams to produce a strong clam broth or else reducing the broth to concentrate its flavor. Canned or bottled clam broth or juice is a weak substitute for broth made with fresh clams, but it can be strengthened by boiling down.

Potatoes are always used, and the preference is for diced salt pork rather than bacon.

Hard-shell clams called quahogs are the ones used in chowder. Soft-shell clams or steamers are eaten in other ways.

Clams may be opened with a clam/oyster knife, but for the tyro it may be less trying to use the following method: Arrange them on a rack or an inverted pie tin resting on the bottom of a pot with a tight-fitting lid. Add a cup or so of water. Cover. Boil over medium heat until the clams open. Shake the pot once or twice during the steaming. Live clams will open when steamed, so discard those that don't. Remove clams from pot with slotted spoon or tongs and let them cool slightly before pushing out the meat with the thumb.

In preparing all clam chowders, clams should be scrubbed and well rinsed to remove grit and other particles. Nevertheless the clam juice still may be sandy, so strain through a double or triple thickness of muslin or cheesecloth. Discard sediment left in the bottom of the pot after the liquor has drained off.

Clams, even in their raw state, are somewhat chewy. Overcooked, they become almost inedible, so take care when preparing clams not to overcook.

The strict discipline over what went into chowder was finally broken when cooks turned back to an earlier version—a fisherman's stew of the catch of the day.

Then came chowders from inland—corn, cheese, tomato, and on and on. Chowder today encompasses anything made with three common ingredients: salt pork pieces fried to crisp bits, onions cooked in the fat, and potato cubes. These are the foundation for almost all chowders, seafood or vegetable.

A collection of both sea- and land-based chowders follows.

Fish Chowder

Serves 6 to 8

The New England way with chowder is to allow the dish to rest at least 1 or 2 hours before serving. The good flavors blend. This recipe takes a bit longer than some, so plan to give it 24 hours to prepare and allow it to mature. It can be done in less time, but scheduling it in large blocks of time may be more convenient.

There are two beforehand steps: (1) Cube the fish, rub with the salt mixture, and put aside; and (2) prepare stock with fish frames or skeletons. Other fish stock may be used, of course, but this stock is so good-tasting and easy to make that taking 20 minutes to prepare it seems well worth the effort.

INGREDIENTS

Fish
1 teaspoon coarse salt (kosher is good)
2 cloves garlic, minced
½ teaspoon dried thyme
2 pounds lean fish fillets—haddock, cod, hake—in 2-inch cubes

(continued)

Stock, if needed (I keep a supply frozen)
Heads and bones of filleted fish
6 cups water
I cup dry white wine

Chowder
4 cups thinly sliced onions
I clove garlic, minced
¼ cup olive oil
¼ cup flour
5 to 6 cups stock (from above or prepared otherwise)
    or bottled clam juice

Sachet d'épice
2 teaspoons dried basil
½ teaspoon dried summer savory
2 bay leaves, crumbled into small bits

½ teaspoon saffron threads
2 teaspoons salt, if desired
2 pounds (about 5 cups) new potatoes, peeled and cut into ¼-inch slices
½ cup light or heavy cream (you may wish to use more)
Minced fresh basil or thyme, optional, to garnish

SPECIAL
EQUIPMENT

Mortar and pestle. Cheesecloth.

PREPARATION

Fish
In a mortar crush the coarse salt, minced garlic, and thyme and mash to a paste, or chop with a heavy knife.

Cut the fish into 1½- to 2-inch cubes and drop into a bowl. When the fish is cut, sprinkle salt mixture over the pieces and, with hands or a wooden spoon, spread thoroughly over the fish.

SEASON
*overnight or
2–3 hours*

Cover the bowl tightly with plastic wrap and let rest at room temperature for 2 to 3 hours, or overnight in the refrigerator.

Stock
With kitchen shears or knife cut out and discard fish gills, which are bitter.

SIMMER *5 mins.*	Chop the frames or skeletons into large pieces and combine with water in a large kettle. Simmer, partly covered, for about 5 minutes or until meat can easily be pulled off the bones. Reserve and refrigerate meat.
20 mins.	Return bones to the kettle, add wine, and continue to simmer gently for 20 minutes. Strain through a sieve, then through double thickness of dampened cheesecloth. Discard bones.

Chowder

SWEAT *12 mins.* *2 mins.*	Sweat onions and garlic in olive oil in a large (4-quart) covered saucepan until soft, about 12 minutes over medium-low heat. When cooked, sprinkle in the flour and stir while it cooks for 2 minutes.
BOIL/SIMMER *5 mins.*	Pour in the fish stock and add the sachet. Steep saffron in ¼ cup hot water; add to the pot. Also taste for salt and add if desired. Bring to a boil, stirring occasionally so ingredients don't stick to the bottom of the pan.
SIMMER *15 mins.* *2 mins.*	Add potatoes and simmer gently for 15 minutes or until potatoes are cooked. When potatoes are done, stir in both the cooked and raw fish pieces. Gently cook for about 2 minutes or until the outsides of the fish pieces turn white. Do not overcook fish.
COOL	Cool pot of chowder as rapidly as possible. In winter I sometimes set it in a snowbank. Other times I set the pot in the sink and run cold water around it. Refrigerate, covered, overnight or for 1 or 2 days, during which time it will develop a fine flavor.
FINAL STEP	Warm the soup over low heat, stirring gently so as not to break up the fish. Add cream to give chowder desired color and richness. Sprinkle with fresh herbs, if available, and serve in hot bowls. Pass oyster crackers or saltines.

Bahamian Fish Chowder

Serves 6

The layers build up in a Bahamian fish chowder to a delicious climax: first, a layer of fish, followed by layers of potatoes, green peppers, crackers, and, to top it off, a spicy tomato mixture of no fewer than nine ingredients. Two hours of cooking blend together all these good things. A meal in itself, this is a thick chowder that can be thinned to taste with fish stock, clam juice, or water.

Guests in the famous old Buena Vista guest house and restaurant on the hill above Nassau Harbour were served this unusual but delicious chowder. It was placed on the menu when the 200-year-old mansion became a hotel after World War II.

INGREDIENTS

½ pound salt pork, in ¼-inch cubes

3 medium onions, thinly sliced

1 16-ounce can tomatoes or 5 fresh tomatoes, peeled and chopped

2 tablespoons tomato paste

½ cup *each* ketchup and chili sauce

2 teaspoons Worcestershire sauce

½ teaspoon Tabasco sauce

1 teaspoon thyme

2 bay leaves

Juice of 1 lime

Salt, to taste, if desired

½ teaspoon freshly ground black pepper

1½ pounds potatoes, peeled and thinly sliced

3 green or red sweet peppers, in ¼-inch dice

2 pounds fillet of grouper, sea bass, drum, or red snapper, cut into 1-inch pieces

½ pound unsalted crackers (or saltines will do)

4 or 5 cups fish stock or clam juice, approximately

1 cup dry sherry or white wine

SPECIAL
EQUIPMENT

None

PREPARATION

Note: All of the first dozen ingredients, down to the potatoes, will be cooked into a thick sauce to ladle on top of all the layers.

TRY OUT
8 mins.

In a medium (3-quart) saucepan or casserole, try out salt pork cubes to release all fat and until brown and crisp, about 8 minutes. Take care they do not burn. Lift out the pork with a slotted spoon. Pour off and discard all but 2 tablespoons of fat.

SAUTÉ
10 mins.

Sauté the onions in the pot over medium heat until they are well cooked and translucent, about 10 minutes. Do not brown or burn.

COOK
10–12 mins.

Add the chopped tomatoes, tomato paste, ketchup, chili sauce, Worcestershire sauce, Tabasco, thyme, bay leaves, and lime juice, and stir well to blend. Cook over medium heat for 10 to 12 minutes. Taste for saltiness and add salt if desired. Grind on pepper.

SLICE	While the sauce is cooking, peel potatoes and slice thinly. Also slice the peppers.
LAYER	In a medium (4-quart) kettle, put down, in order, layers of fish, raw potatoes, sweet peppers, a dozen or so dry crackers, and, finally, the tomato mixture.
STOCK	Add stock or clam juice to 1 inch above the top layer.
SIMMER *2 hours* *10 mins.*	Simmer over low heat for 2 hours. Keep the level of liquid constant with the addition of stock or clam juice during the simmering, if necessary. When the chowder is nearly done—10 minutes to go—add sherry or white wine.
FINAL STEP	Bring the kettle to the table and ladle into large heated bowls. It is a spectacle that the guests should not be denied. Serve with a green salad and fruit for a satisfying meal.

Catfish Chowder

Serves 6

Some would have you believe that fish chowder can be found at its best only along coastal waters, but they overlook one of freshwater's best-tasting inhabitants—the catfish. Along the river deltas in the South the catfish is as much a mainstay in the soup kettle as it is in the frying pan.

This is an adaptation of a recipe from a fine Southern cook and author, Lillian Marshall, a good friend as well.

If you have fish stock on hand, perhaps frozen, you may wish to skip the stock making from the fish bones or use bottled clam juice. Cream gives this chowder color and richness.

INGREDIENTS	*Stock* Heads and bones from filleted fish (below) 5 cups water 2 teaspoons salt *Chowder* 5 cups fish stock or bottled clam juice 2 cups minced onions 4 cups diced potatoes (about 3 potatoes) 1 16-ounce can tomatoes plus their liquid

(continued)

2 tablespoons tomato paste
¼ teaspoon freshly ground black pepper
I teaspoon salt, if desired
2 pounds catfish fillets, in I½-inch cubes
I cup light cream
I tablespoon lemon juice
2 tablespoons chopped parsley, to garnish

SPECIAL
EQUIPMENT

None

PREPARATION
BOIL/SIMMER
10 mins.

Stock

Combine fish bones, water, and salt in a large pot such as a Dutch oven or saucepan. Bring to a boil and reduce heat to simmer for 10 minutes over medium-low heat.

Lift out the bones and pick off whatever pieces of meat are on the bones and reserve.

BOIL/SIMMER
20 mins.

Add to the stock the onions, potatoes, tomatoes, tomato paste, freshly ground black pepper, and salt. Bring to a boil, reduce heat, and cook over low heat until the potatoes are al dente, barely fork-tender, about 20 minutes.

The addition of the fish, presumably taken from the refrigerator, will cool the stock, so allow several minutes for it to return to a simmer. When the stock and fish are hot—but not boiling—cook for no longer than 5 minutes.

5 mins.

Pour in the cream, stir, and allow chowder to reheat for a moment or so.

Remove from heat and add lemon juice.

FINAL STEP

Serve in heated bowls. Garnish with parsley.

A tasty companion for this chowder is a crisp hush puppy.

Note: To make a delicious hush puppy, combine 2 cups self-rising corn-meal and 1 small onion, finely chopped. Add ¾ cup milk and 1 egg, slightly beaten. Mix well. Drop batter by tablespoonfuls into deep hot oil (370°); cook only a few hush puppies at a time, turning once. Fry 3 to 5 minutes until golden brown. Drain. This recipe will make about 24 hush puppies.

Southern Shrimp Chowder

Serves 6

A raft of shrimp bobbing about in a pinkish broth, seasoned with a dash or two of Tabasco, is a fine chowder presentation. This one found its way from Memphis via St. Louis to my kitchen, where I gave it a northern home.

INGREDIENTS

¼ pound salt pork, in ¼-inch dice
1 medium onion (1 cup), finely chopped
½ cup green pepper, in ¼-inch dice
3 cups boiling water
2 cups potatoes, peeled and cut into ½-inch cubes
1 16-ounce can tomatoes, chopped, juice reserved
1 bay leaf
½ teaspoon salt, if desired
¼ teaspoon freshly ground black pepper
1 or 2 dashes of Tabasco sauce, to taste
1½ pounds shrimp, cooked, shelled, and cleaned*
3 tablespoons chopped parsley

* If you clean the shrimp yourself, freeze the shells for the day when you have enough for Shrimp Bisque (page 179).

SPECIAL
EQUIPMENT

None

PREPARATION
TRY OUT
8 mins.
SAUTÉ
10 mins.

In a medium (3-quart) saucepan, try out the salt pork to release its fat and until crisp, about 8 minutes over medium heat. Add the onion and green pepper and sauté until tender, about 10 minutes.

BOIL/SIMMER
15 mins.

Pour in the hot water. Add potatoes, tomatoes, bay leaf, salt, if desired, pepper, and Tabasco. Bring slowly to a boil and then turn heat to low to simmer for about 15 minutes or until potatoes are tender but not mushy.

3–4 mins.

Add shrimp and parsley and continue cooking 3 to 4 minutes. Remove bay leaf and discard.

FINAL STEP

Serve in heated bowls with saltines on the side.

New England Clam Chowder

Serves 6 to 8

There are those who hold that the only true clam chowder is the New England type. When well made, they say it can hold its head proudly among its peers, even including bouillabaisse from Marseille and environs.

Ideally the clam should be a quahog, the hard-shelled Venus mercenaria, a remarkable bivalve that keeps well and maintains both flavor and texture under refrigeration because it has the powerful adductor muscles that enable it to close its shell tightly for protection. There are also other hard-shell types on the East Coast. From the Pacific Coast come the pismo clam, the butter clam, the razor clam, and the flesh of the big geoduck.

True believers also hold that the ration of the three basic ingredients—clams, potatoes, and onions—should be 5-5-3, as it is in the recipe that follows.

The outside meat of clams in this recipe is chopped into small bits, while the soft center part (the stomach) is cut in half to be added to the chowder during the final 3 minutes of simmering.

A final note of caution: Don't be misled into believing, as I once was, that store-bought clam juice has a potency equal to the liquor collected from freshly opened clams or from the bottom of the steamer, where the juice mixes with whatever water is left after steaming. Similarly, canned clams can also be used in chowders, but don't expect them to carry the flavor load alone.

INGREDIENTS

5 dozen hard-shell clams or 3 cups shucked clams
1 cup water
3 cups potatoes, peeled and cut into ½-inch dice
2 ounces salt pork or slab bacon, in ¼-inch dice
2 cups onions, chopped into ¼-inch pieces
1 clove garlic, minced
¼ teaspoon thyme
2 quarts milk (or 2½ quarts if cream is omitted)
1 pint heavy or light cream if extra richness is desired
1 teaspoon salt, if desired
Pinch of cayenne pepper
Freshly ground black pepper
Paprika to dust over servings

SPECIAL
EQUIPMENT

Steamer or large covered kettle with shallow pan to hold clams above water while steaming. Food processor or meat grinder, if desired. Cheesecloth, to strain.

PREPARATION **STEAM** *10 mins.*	Scrub clams under running water, place them in a steamer or large covered kettle with 1 cup water to cover the bottom, and cook gently over medium heat for about 10 minutes or until the shells open. Stir the clams once or twice while steaming.
COOK	Remove clams from vessel and set aside to cool before removing meat. Continue cooking the broth until it is reduced in volume to about 1½ cups. Set aside.
BOIL *12 mins.*	In a small saucepan, cover potatoes with lightly salted water and cook until tender but not mushy, about 12 minutes, over medium heat. Drain and set aside.
TRY OUT *8 mins.*	In a skillet, try out the diced salt pork or bacon bits over medium-low heat, about 8 minutes, or until the pieces are browned. Turn the heat down when almost cooked so pieces do not burn.
SWEAT *10 mins.* **COOK** *3 mins.*	Lift the fried bits out of the skillet with a slotted spoon and reserve. Drain all but 1 tablespoon of fat from the skillet. Add the diced onions, garlic, and thyme; cover the skillet and sweat over medium-low heat until they are soft and translucent, about 10 minutes. Remove the lid and cook over medium heat until they are lightly browned, about 3 minutes.
CHOP	Remove the clams from the shells and, with a sharp knife, cut away the tough meat surrounding the soft centers. Chop or process this meat but reserve the soft gray centers.
SCALD *180°–198°* *5–6 mins.* *3 mins.*	Over moderate heat and without stirring, heat the milk to scalding hot. A skin will form on the surface and the temperature will be between 180° and 190°. Add the chopped portions of the clams, potatoes, and onions. Add cream if desired. Bring the temperature back to scalding. Strain the reserved 1½ cups of clam broth through a double thickness of cheesecloth and add to the pot. Allow the chowder to cook at this temperature for 5 to 6 minutes. Add the reserved soft clam pieces, salt, and cayenne pepper 3 minutes before the chowder is taken off the heat. Taste for seasoning.
FINAL STEP	Serve hot in deep bowls with a light sprinkling of black pepper and a dusting of paprika on the surface of each.

Southern New England Clam Chowder

Serves 6 to 8

The only ingredients in this dish are quahogs, salt pork, potatoes, and onion (or not) to taste. Nothing else other than salt and pepper.

This recipe was a family treasure handed down to Robert Greenleaf, a friend who grew up on that part of the Atlantic Coast. He defines "solid territory" for this chowder to be from Groton, Connecticut, to Point Judith, Rhode Island. When he was young, it was an area boasting of more chowder restaurants than any other kind; traditionally, chowder was always served as the main course.

The quahog is a hard-shell clam that lives in sand (never mud) covered with brackish water. Its inner shell is white with purple lips, the raw material of wampum. Commercially it comes in three sizes—littleneck, cherrystone, and the big chowder clams. The number or size of the clams is relatively unimportant; it is the volume of the meat and liquor that is the prime consideration.

The chowder has the clear, strong, delicious flavor of clams, though it is not clear in the sense that consommé is clear, nor is it creamy or thickened with flour, arrowroot, or mashed potato.

The essence of the chowder flavor is the quahog liquor; save or buy all you can. Commercial clam juice is not as good—it comes from the quite different steamer clam.

INGREDIENTS	1 pint quahog meat and liquor (usually about 18 to 24 clams)
	¼ pound salt pork, diced
	2 quarts water
	6 medium potatoes (Maine preferred), in ¼-inch cubes
	2 medium onions, diced
	Salt, if desired, to taste
	Sprinkling of freshly ground black pepper when served
SPECIAL EQUIPMENT	If quahogs are to be steamed to open, a steamer or large covered kettle with rack or inverted pie pan on bottom
PREPARATION STEAM 10 mins.	Scrub clams and either open with knife over bowl or pan to catch liquor or steam over 2 cups of water in the steamer for about 10 minutes or until shells open. As soon as shells open, remove from heat immediately or meat will get tough. Let cool. Remove meat; discard shells. Reserve the clam broth collected in the steamer and strain through double thickness of cheesecloth to remove sand and grit.

With a heavy knife chop clam meat into pieces. Don't grind, process, or blend—it will make the clams too mushy for this particular recipe. The meat should be chopped into pieces no larger than bite-size that will fit comfortably into a soupspoon when eaten.

TRY OUT
6–8 mins.

Wash salt pork and cut into ¼-inch dice. Try out in a heavy skillet until all of the fat is rendered, turning down the heat at the end, as the fat "husks" burn easily after the fat is drawn off. Lift the pork husks out of the skillet with a slotted spoon. Set aside.

BOIL
8–10 mins.

Bring the 2 quarts of water to boil in a medium (4-quart) saucepan and add potatoes and pork husks. Cook the potatoes over medium heat for 8 to 10 minutes. They should be al dente, not soft or mushy.

COOK
10 mins.

Cook the onions in the rendered fat over medium-low heat until soft and glistening, about 10 minutes.

When the potatoes are cooked, remove pan from the heat and add clams plus the strained broth. Add the onions and rendered fat, scraping every bit of the latter into the mixture. Clam liquor tends to be naturally salty, so taste before seasoning with salt. The pepper will be sprinkled on at serving time.

LOW BOIL
3–4 mins.

Return the chowder to a low boil for 3 to 4 minutes. Then turn off heat and let the chowder rest for an hour or more. If the chowder is too thin and watery it can be simmered down. In any event, kept warm at the back of the stove it will continue to gain flavor.

Note: If there isn't time to let the chowder rest the initial hour, increase quahogs and liquor from 1 to 1½ pints.

FINAL STEP

Ladle into heated tureen and large bowls. Sprinkle light dusting of black pepper across the surface of the chowder.

Confirmed New England chowder buffs want nothing more served with this dish than thin pilot crackers and a green salad.

Manhattan Clam Chowder

Serves 6

Manhattan Clam Chowder is also known as Long Island Clam Chowder and Philadelphia Clam Chowder. Whatever its name, some describe it simply as vegetable soup with clam overtones. It is far more than that, of course. Thanks to tomatoes, red is its distinguishing color.

This recipe offers a different ending. Caraway seeds are added just before the chowder is taken from the heat. Tabasco sauce gives it a spicy kick. Both are optional.

INGREDIENTS

12 large fresh hard-shell clams, shucked, and clam liquor reserved,
    or approximately 1 cup water, to steam clams
½ pound salt pork or slab bacon, in ¼-inch dice
2 medium onions, chopped into ¼-inch pieces (about 1½ cups)
4 medium carrots, diced (about 1½ cups)
2 stalks celery, diced (about 1½ cups)
½ cup diced green pepper
3 tablespoons finely chopped parsley
1 16-ounce can tomatoes or 4 ripe tomatoes, skinned and chopped into
    ½-inch pieces
Water to be added to tomato and clam juice to make 2 quarts

Sachet d'épice
6 peppercorns
1 bay leaf
½ teaspoon thyme

2 medium potatoes, peeled and cut into ½-inch cubes (about 2 cups)
½ teaspoon caraway seeds, if desired
Tabasco sauce, optional
Water crackers or hot biscuits

SPECIAL
EQUIPMENT

Steamer for clams or covered saucepan. An old pan with holes punched in the bottom to allow the steam to escape easily can be set into a larger pot.

PREPARATION

STEAM
10 mins.

Scrub clams with stiff brush under running water. Shuck the clams or place them in the steamer over water to barely cover the bottom. Steam over medium heat until all the shells are open, about 10 minutes, shaking steamer once or twice to shift clams about. Remove from heat and set aside to cool.

TRY OUT
8 mins.

In a medium (4-quart) saucepan, try out salt pork or bacon until brown and fat has been rendered, about 8 minutes.

SWEAT
10 mins.
10 mins.

Sweat onions in fat until they are tender and translucent, about 10 minutes. Add the carrots, celery, green pepper, and parsley. Cook an additional 10 minutes.

    Tomatoes will be less messy to chop if the juice is first poured off and reserved. Strain the clam juice to remove the sand and combine it with tomato juice. To bring the volume to 2 quarts, add water if necessary. Pour the liquid and the chopped tomatoes into the pot.

SIMMER
30 mins.

Add sachet d'épice and diced potatoes. Simmer for 30 minutes over medium-low heat. Vegetables should be fork-tender but not mushy.

PROCESS

Chop the tough white flesh of the clams or put it in a food processor— 1 or 2 quick zaps—or through a meat grinder. The pieces should be the size of small peas, no larger. The soft dark center (stomach) can be left whole or cut into two pieces, depending on size. Combine with the clam bits.

COOK
6–7 mins.

Add clams to the chowder. Cook over low heat 6 to 7 minutes. If caraway seeds are to be added, do so with the clams. Do not boil, or the clam meat will toughen.

FINAL STEP

Serve in heated bowls. Guests may enjoy a few drops of Tabasco in each serving. Serve with water crackers or hot biscuits.

Nora Bennett's Clam Chowder

Serves 8 to 10

Nora Bennett's clam chowder was among the first things we heard about when we arrived on the eastern tip of Long Island to celebrate the publication of Craig Claiborne's new book and his birthday. We were among the chefs and authors invited to participate in a food extravaganza to which some 300 guests were invited. Each participant stayed with a neighbor who welcomed us as guests and turned over the kitchen so we could prepare for "A Feast Made for Laughter," also the title of Claiborne's book.

The Claytons stayed with Kay and Berton Roueché, and it was while baking in her kitchen that I heard from Kay the highest praise for the Bennett chowder. The inference was clear— you will not have savored East Hampton clam chowder until you have eaten hers. She was so right.

Nora does two things that make her chowder different from other Manhattan-type chowders. The vegetables and clams are ground or fed into a food processor before cooking, and milk and cream, rather than water, are included. Tomatoes, which distinguish Manhattan chowders from all others, also are included, of course.

Nora Bennett, born in County Galway, and the cook for many years in one of the big houses in the Hamptons, had created a very special dish of chowder.

INGREDIENTS

1½ quarts chowder-clam meat, fresh or canned
3 cups clam juice, fresh, or canned to supplement
3 cups water
4 to 5 stalks celery
3 to 4 carrots
4 to 5 medium onions
6 medium potatoes, peeled
1 16-ounce can tomatoes or 5 or 6 ripe fresh tomatoes
Pinch of baking soda
6 tablespoons butter
1 teaspoon salt, if desired
⅛ teaspoon freshly ground black pepper
1½ cups milk
½ cup light or heavy cream
Paprika, to garnish

SPECIAL
EQUIPMENT

Grinder or food processor. Don't use a blender, as the result will be too mushy.

PREPARATION
GRIND

Rinse clams, grind, and set aside. (Half will be used shortly; the balance will be refrigerated and used later.)

SIMMER

Pour strained clam juice and water into a large (4-quart) kettle and bring to a simmer.

GRIND

Meanwhile, grind the celery, carrots, onions, and potatoes, or process coarsely—only a zap or two. Do not puree. Stir to mix and add to the kettle. Add half the ground clams; refrigerate the balance.

Add tomatoes, baking soda, butter, and salt and pepper to taste.

BOIL/SIMMER
5–6 hours

Bring the chowder to a boil, lower heat, and cook gently, partially covered, barely above a simmer—an occasional bubble—for 5 to 6 hours.

Note: This is an ideal chowder to do in a slow cooker.

AFTER 3 HOURS

Add the milk to the chowder after 3 hours.

Do not let the chowder boil above an occasional bubble or two. Stir occasionally. If at any time the chowder appears too thick, thin with milk.

REFRIGERATE

Refrigerate overnight or for 2 or 3 days, if desired. Before reheating add the reserved clams and the cream.

HEAT
15 mins.

Heat for about 15 minutes but do not boil. Correct seasonings.

FINAL STEP

Serve in heated bowls with a sprinkling of paprika over each to garnish. Excellent with saltines.

Shrimp and Corn Chowder

Serves 6

I have made this chowder with both fresh and frozen corn—and can hardly tell which is which. I have also used frozen shrimp with excellent results.

My notes remind me that in my first endeavor I used a blender; the food processor was yet to come to this country. Since then I have used the processor a great deal. The chowder is not as creamy made with the processor, but it produces a textured soup that is appealing.

The thin white sauce that gives the chowder its special creaminess is made separately and brought together with the other ingredients later in the preparation.

INGREDIENTS

White Sauce
1 tablespoon butter
1 tablespoon flour
2 cups scalded milk
½ teaspoon salt, if desired
Pinch of freshly ground white pepper

Chowder
1½ cups frozen whole kernel or freshly grated corn
1½ cups scalded milk
2 slices onion
2 egg yolks
½ cup light cream or milk
1 cup chopped shrimp, uncooked, fresh or frozen
2 tablespoons butter
Salt, if desired
Pinch of freshly ground white pepper
Nutmeg, freshly grated, to garnish

SPECIAL
EQUIPMENT

Food processor or blender

| PREPARATION | *White Sauce* |
| | First, prepare white sauce and set aside until needed. |

| COOK 90 secs. | In a medium (3-quart) saucepan, melt 1 tablespoon butter and sprinkle on it the tablespoon of flour. Cook the roux over low heat, stirring constantly, until it bubbles and foams, about 90 seconds. |

| 5 mins. | Gradually add the scalded milk, stirring vigorously with a wire whisk until the sauce is smooth. At this stage it will appear not to have body, but it does. |

| SIMMER 5 mins. | Add salt, if desired, and pepper, and simmer over low heat for about 5 minutes or until the flour has cooked thoroughly.
    Set aside at the back of the stove to keep warm. |

| | *Chowder* |
| COOK 20 mins. | In the top of a double boiler, combine the corn, scalded milk, and onion slices. Cook the mixture, stirring occasionally, for 20 minutes. |

| PROCESS 2 mins. | When the mixture is cooked, you may wish to remove the onion rings (I like them left in) before putting it through the food processor. There is a nice texture to the processed corn, but it can be made creamier in a blender. |

| SIMMER 10 mins. | Pour the puree into the reserved white sauce and bring the mixture to a simmer. Beat the egg yolks with the light cream or milk and stir into the soup. |

| SAUTÉ 2–3 mins. | Chop the shrimp into ¼-inch pieces and sauté in butter in a skillet over medium heat for a few moments. Stir the shrimp into the chowder.
    Season with salt, if desired, and pepper. |

| FINAL STEP | Bring the soup to a simmer and serve. Grate nutmeg over each bowl and pass saltines. |

Nantucket Scallop Chowder

Serves 6

Tenderness, sweetness, and depth of good flavor give this scallop chowder an A plus in my kitchen notebook. The sweetness is not saccharine but a sweetness that reminds one of a warm spring breeze coming off the shore.

While there are many ways to serve scallops, chowder is often the last to be considered. A pity. In my view there is no tastier way to present this delicate shellfish.

We once spent a weekend following World War II on Nantucket and ate all the good things there except the island's scallop chowder. That is something I have regretted to this day, and with this recipe I seek to make amends.

The secret of this chowder is low heat. Let nothing come to a boil (except the potatoes). Simmering is the key.

INGREDIENTS	¼ pound butter
	2 medium onions, cut into slices
	4 cups milk or 2 cups milk and 2 cups light or heavy cream, depending on richness desired
	1 medium potato, cut into ½-inch cubes
	Water to cover potato
	1 tablespoon salt
	1 pound sea scallops
	Pat of butter to float on each serving
	Sprinkle of paprika, to garnish

SPECIAL EQUIPMENT
There will be 3 vessels used in preparation—a heavy 3-quart saucepan, a small saucepan, and a heavy 10-inch skillet.

PREPARATION
Note: The chowder progresses in 3 separate stages, which are brought together moments before the chowder is presented at the table.

COOK
10 mins.
In the large saucepan, melt 4 tablespoons of butter over moderate heat. When the foam subsides, add the onions, stirring frequently. Cook for about 10 minutes until soft and translucent. Take great care not to brown or burn the onions, as the dark specks would be unattractive later in the creamy white chowder.

15 mins.
Pour in the milk or milk-and-cream combination and bring the mixture to a gentle simmer over moderate to low heat. Do not boil! Partially cover and simmer for 15 minutes. At this time the onions will impart their flavor. Take pan off the heat and set aside for a moment.

COOK
4–5 mins.
In the small saucepan, drop the diced potato into salted boiling water to cover by 1 inch. Cook over moderate to high heat until al dente—just tender but still firm. Drain. Set aside.

DICE
To dice scallops, cut into ½-inch slices across the grain and then into ½-inch cubes. If frozen, be certain the scallops are completely thawed.

SAUTÉ *2–3 mins.*	In a large skillet, melt 2 tablespoons of butter and drop in the scallops. Sauté over high heat for 2 or 3 minutes, turning them constantly with a spatula, until they are opaque. Set the scallops aside with the potatoes.
STRAIN	Strain the onion/milk mixture through a fine sieve into a bowl. Discard the onions and return the onion-flavored liquid to the saucepan. Add the scallops and potato.
SIMMER *2–3 mins.*	Bring to a simmer over low heat for 2 to 3 minutes until the chowder is heated. Stir frequently.
FINAL STEP	Taste for seasoning. Ladle the chowder into individual bowls and place a pat of butter on the surface of each. Sprinkle with a pinch of paprika. Serve at once.

Lobster Chowder

Serves 6 (6 cups)

This is a superior dish for the lobster lover. All the essence of this prized shellfish is here. It gets its rich lobster flavor not only from the meat but from the shells, legs, tomalley, and other bits and pieces from hard-to-reach places in the lobster. The chowder is a velvety combination of these.

The chowder makes it possible to extend lobster for two diners to lobster for six with no loss of enjoyment.

Milk and cream are crucial to the chowder, so be certain each is fresh. Bring each to a boil beforehand. If the milk or cream "breaks" into small particles or flakes it is not fresh and should not be used in this dish.

Pouring milk and cream over a collection of broken shells may seem an odd way to arrive at such a good dish, but New Englanders have been doing it for generations.

Don't make this chowder unless you use a whole lobster (or lobsters)—not tails only—because the essence is chiefly forward of the tail—head, claws, legs, tomalley, etc. The lobster meat will not be introduced into the chowder until just before serving.

The lobsters, of course, can often be steamed in the market where they are purchased.

INGREDIENTS	2 cups water 1 tablespoon coarse sea salt 1 handful seaweed, if available 2 live lobsters, 1½ to 2 pounds each, or one 3- to 3½-pound lobster 4 cups light cream 2 cups milk

2 medium onions, peeled and thinly sliced

1 clove garlic, crushed

2 sprigs parsley

1 bay leaf

2 cloves

4 whole black peppercorns

2 tablespoons softened butter

2 tablespoons fine cracker crumbs

2 beaten egg yolks

2 tablespoons dry sherry, optional

1 teaspoon salt, if desired

¼ teaspoon freshly ground black pepper

1 tablespoon finely chopped parsley

SPECIAL EQUIPMENT

8½-quart (or larger) pot (with basket insert, if available) in which to steam lobsters. Chinois or fine sieve and cheesecloth, to strain.

PREPARATION

Note: The lobster or lobsters may be prepared 1 to 2 days in advance and refrigerated until needed.

STEAM
18–20 mins.
35–45 mins.

Into a very large saucepan or pot with tight-fitting lid, pour water, salt, and seaweed. Bring to a boil. Drop in the lobster(s), cover, and cook briskly—18 to 20 minutes for small lobsters and 35 to 45 minutes if large.

Take a lobster from the pot to test for doneness. Jerk sharply on one of the small legs. If it pulls away from the body, the shellfish is done. If not, steam for a few minutes longer.

While steaming lobster(s), maintain a medium heat sufficient to create an abundance of steam but not so high as to bring the water boiling over the edge of the pot.

COOL

Transfer the lobster(s) to a platter and allow to cool before twisting off the large claws. Crack each claw in several places with a hammer, nutcracker, or pliers. Split the lobster(s) lengthwise and lift out the tail meat. Discard the stomach but retain the greenish-brown tomalley (liver), as well as red coral (roe) if there is any. Remove all the meat from the claws, legs, and body. Cut the meat into bite-size pieces (½ inch or so) and set aside. Reserve the shell(s).

(The meat may be refrigerated at this point to be added to the chowder later.)

SIMMER
45 mins.

Crush shells, chop them into 2-inch pieces, and place in a heavy 5-quart saucepan. Cover with the cream and milk and add onion, garlic, parsley sprigs, bay leaf, cloves, and peppercorns. Bring to a simmer over medium heat. When tiny bubbles begin to form around the edge of the liquid, reduce heat and continue to simmer, partially covered, for 45 minutes. Stir the contents occasionally. Watch carefully so that a slow simmer doesn't become a violent boil, which can happen in an instant if the pot is left unattended.

STRAIN
15 mins.

Remove from heat. Strain the contents through a chinois or fine sieve set over a large bowl to catch the liquid. Press and crush the shells with a heavy spoon or pestle to extract all of the flavorful liquid. Discard the shell material. Rinse chinois or sieve, line with double thickness of dampened cheesecloth, and pour the liquid through it into the saucepan, which has been rinsed. This double-sieving produces a smooth, velvety chowder.

In a small bowl blend softened butter and cracker crumbs into a paste, which will become the thickening agent for the chowder. Push the tomalley and coral (if any) through a fine sieve with the back of a spoon. Add to the cracker paste and blend.

5 mins.

Pour ½ cup of the liquid into the cracker mixture. Stir to blend. Pour back into the saucepan and stir well until blended thoroughly into the rest of the liquid. (The liquid can be refrigerated at this point for a day or two.)

When almost ready to serve, add the lobster meat and, over low heat, bring to a simmer—but barely.

3 mins.

Blend together in a small bowl the egg yolks, sherry, if using, salt, and ground pepper with a fork or whisk. Add ½ cup of the hot liquid. Pour the contents of the small bowl into the larger pot.

SIMMER

Simmer for a few minutes until all elements of the chowder—meat and stock—are heated. Be very careful that the chowder does not come to a boil, or it will curdle!

FINAL STEP

Taste for seasoning. Serve at once from a heated tureen into heated bowls. Garnish each serving with a sprinkle of parsley.

The completed chowder may be refrigerated for one or two days and reheated. Freezing after milk and cream have been added is not recommended.

Abalone Chowder

Serves 4

Abalone chowder is delicious—well worth the strenuous chore of whacking the abalone with a mallet or rolling pin to break down its muscular fibers. (I use a heavy Hawaiian stone poi pounder against a thick maple block.)

The good flavor and interesting texture of abalone have resulted in an overharvesting of the pink-and-red mollusk in waters off the Pacific Coast. Happily for the cook, there are other sources. Some come from Mexico, and I have used an abalone-type shellfish, concholepas-concholepas, caught in Chilean waters. Abalone can be bought in markets both canned and frozen.

Abalone pieces, even after beating, have an al dente quality, so there is no mistaking cubes of abalone for dice of potato even though they may look alike.

INGREDIENTS	1 pound abalone, tenderized and cut into ¼-inch dice (frozen, fresh, or canned) ¼ pound salt pork, in ¼-inch dice 1 large onion, chopped 2 cups boiling water 2 medium potatoes, peeled, in ⅜-inch dice 1 bay leaf 2 cups milk or light cream, heated 1 tablespoon butter Salt, if desired (the pork will make its salt contribution) Pinch of freshly ground black pepper 3 tablespoons chopped parsley Snippets of chives, to garnish
SPECIAL EQUIPMENT	Mallet or rolling pin with which to tenderize abalone against a sturdy surface. (I once started pounding on the counter beneath my spice rack and all tumbled down!)
PREPARATION	Tenderize the abalone. It will take 20 to 30 minutes to beat 1 pound of meat. Invite friends to help. Dice meat uniformly.
TRY OUT *8 mins.*	Try out pork in a medium (3-quart) saucepan over medium heat to release all fat and until the pieces are crisp.
SAUTÉ *10 mins.*	Add onions and abalone and sauté until onions are glistening and tender, about 10 minutes.

COOK *15 mins.*	Pour the boiling water over the onions and abalone. Add potatoes and bay leaf. Cover and cook slowly until abalone and potatoes are tender, about 15 minutes. Add heated milk or cream, butter, salt, if desired, pepper, and parsley.
BLEND *1–2 mins.*	Leave over heat for 1 or 2 minutes to blend the flavors.
FINAL STEP	Serve in heated bowls. Garnish with snippets of chives.

Curried Chicken Chowder

Serves 8

Cubes of chicken combined with a vegetable puree, barley, and mushrooms, mildly seasoned with curry, were first served in my kitchen during the finals of a basketball tournament. The game is not remembered by my guests, but the chowder is. It has since become traditional.

INGREDIENTS	3-pound chicken, cut up 1 cup finely chopped carrots 1 cup thinly sliced celery, with leaves 1 medium onion, quartered 4 whole cloves 1 tablespoon salt, if desired 1 bay leaf 10 cups water, approximately ½ cup uncooked barley 2 cups thinly sliced carrots 3 tablespoons butter 8 ounces fresh mushrooms, thinly sliced 1 tablespoon finely chopped shallots 3 tablespoons flour ½ teaspoon salt ½ teaspoon or more curry powder, as desired ¼ cup dry sherry 1 cup light cream Avocado slices, to garnish
SPECIAL EQUIPMENT	Food processor or blender. Chinois or colander.

PREPARATION	In a large (4-quart) saucepan or Dutch oven, place the chicken pieces, 1 cup of carrots, celery, onion quarters studded with cloves, salt, and the bay leaf. Add water to cover, about 10 cups.
BOIL/SIMMER *1 hour*	Bring to boiling; reduce heat, cover, and simmer over low heat until chicken is tender, about 1 hour. Remove chicken and put aside to cool. Pull meat from the bones; discard skin. Cut into ½-inch cubes. Set aside.
STRAIN	Strain chicken stock through chinois or colander. Reserve stock and vegetables. Allow the stock to cool, and spoon fat from the surface. Discard cloves and bay leaf.
PUREE	Pour vegetables and 1 cup of stock into food processor or blender. Blend until pureed.
BOIL/SIMMER *12 mins. or* *30 mins.* *30 mins.*	Heat remaining stock in a large saucepan to boiling. Stir in the barley. If quick-cooking barley is used, cook 10 to 12 minutes. If regular barley, cook for 30 minutes. Simmer uncovered. Stir in vegetable puree and the last 2 cups of sliced carrots. Heat to boiling, reduce heat, and simmer uncovered for 30 minutes.
SAUTÉ *3 mins.* *3 mins.*	In a small skillet heat butter until it foams. Stir mushrooms and shallots into butter and cook for 3 minutes. Stir in flour, ½ teaspoon salt, and curry. Cook over low heat for another 3 minutes.
SIMMER *15 mins.*	Stir mushroom mixture into the chicken stock. Simmer uncovered for 15 minutes.
HEAT	Stir in chicken pieces, sherry, and cream. Heat until hot and steaming— about 3 minutes over medium heat.
FINAL STEP	Pour into heated bowls. Garnish with avocado slices. Delicious!

Chicken and Corn Chowder

Serves 6

Chicken and corn have always gone well together, but never more deliciously than as companions in this chowder.

The corn can be fresh or frozen, and processed or blendered into a creamy puree rather than by the old-fashioned way of cutting down the row of kernels with a sharp knife to release the milk. The breast is considered by some to be the best part of the chicken for this dish, but I sometimes use thigh or leg meat. A bit more chewy, perhaps, but a good texture.

INGREDIENTS	1 pound chicken breast(s), skinned and boned
	Salt and freshly ground black pepper
	3 tablespoons butter
	3 cups corn kernels, fresh or frozen (about 8 ears if to be cut off cob)
	3 ounces lean salt pork or bacon, in ¼-inch dice
	¾ cup finely chopped onion
	½ cup finely chopped celery
	2 cups potatoes, in ½-inch dice (about 2 medium potatoes)
	4 cups chicken stock
	1 cup heavy cream
	1 tablespoon finely chopped parsley

SPECIAL
EQUIPMENT

Food processor or blender

PREPARATION

Dry the chicken breast(s) with a paper towel and season with salt and a few grindings of pepper. Melt butter in a heavy skillet over medium heat. When hot add the chicken and turn several times with tongs. Do not let it brown. When it has taken on a milky cast and all the rawness is gone, reduce heat to low, cover the skillet, and cook until the chicken is firm to the touch, about 6 minutes. Set aside until cool, then cut into ½-inch cubes and reserve.

PUREE
2 mins.

Process or blend 2 cups of the corn until a smooth puree. Scrape down the sides of the container once or twice during the operation.

TRY OUT
10 mins.

Try out the pork or bacon dice in a medium (4-quart) saucepan over medium heat until the bits have given up their fat and are crisp and brown. Lift out the bits with a slotted spoon and add to the chowder later.

SWEAT
8–10 mins.

Pour off all but 2 tablespoons of fat. Add the onion and celery, lower heat, and cook until the vegetables are soft and a light brown, about 8 to 10 minutes.

BOIL/SIMMER
15–18 mins.

Stir in the chicken cubes, pureed corn, whole corn kernels, potatoes, and chicken stock. Bring to a boil over high heat, reduce to low, and simmer, partially covered, for about 15 to 18 minutes until the potatoes are tender.

3 mins.

Stir in the cream and parsley and continue to simmer for another 3 minutes.

FINAL STEP

Serve immediately in a heated tureen or in heated individual soup plates. Garnish with parsley.

Corn Chowder

Serves 6

In earlier days summertime was the time for this corn chowder prepared the old-fashioned way. The corn was picked and rushed to the kitchen, where the kernels were cut and scraped from the cob. The cobs were then boiled for a cupful of corn essence, which was blended with chicken broth.

But times have changed. Ear corn is now in the market for most of the year as well as corn frozen at its peak of goodness both on and off the cob.

If the choice is corn without the cob, the cup of broth from the boiled cobs will be missed only slightly. It lends a country touch I like, but the taste without it will not be dramatically diminished.

INGREDIENTS

5 ears corn or 3 cups corn kernels
Water to cover cobs above (if using ears)
2 cups stock (corn broth and/or chicken stock)
¼ pound salt pork or bacon, in ¼-inch dice
1 cup finely sliced celery (about 2 stalks)
2 cups thinly sliced onions (2 medium)
1 clove garlic, minced
3 medium potatoes, peeled and cut into ½-inch dice
1 16-ounce can tomatoes, chopped
¼ teaspoon baking soda
2 cups milk or light cream
1 teaspoon Worcestershire sauce
Salt to taste
Freshly ground black pepper
Chopped parsley, to garnish

SPECIAL EQUIPMENT

Food processor or blender. A food mill can be used.

PREPARATION

Note: In chowders, ingredients such as potato, celery, and onions should be cut the same size to make a harmonious blend. In this chowder, the principal ingredient is the corn kernel, so everything should be cut approximately to its size.

PUREE *2 mins.*	Cut and scrape the corn from the cobs. Puree 2 of the 3 cups of corn in the food processor or blender, and set aside for later use. Break the cobs in half, place in a saucepan, and add water to cover.
BOIL *20 mins.*	Boil the cobs for about 20 minutes. Discard the cobs. There should be about 1 cup of broth in the pan. Supplement this with chicken stock to make 2 full cups of liquid, and set aside.
TRY OUT *10 mins.*	In a medium (3-quart) saucepan, try out the salt pork or bacon until all the fat is rendered and the pieces are brown and crisp—about 10 minutes over medium heat. Remove bits with slotted spoon and set aside. (Some cooks discard the pork or bacon bits, but I like them as part of the chowder.) There should be about 2 tablespoons of grease. Pour off the excess.
COOK *12 mins.*	Add celery, onions, and garlic to the saucepan and cook over medium heat until the vegetables are somewhat tender and translucent, about 12 minutes.
BOIL/SIMMER *12 mins.*	Pour the stock (corn broth and/or chicken stock) into the saucepan and add diced potatoes, tomatoes, and baking soda (soda to counter the acid of tomatoes when mixed with milk). Cook until the potatoes are almost tender—al dente, about 12 minutes.
10 mins.	Add both the pureed and the whole corn kernels to the pot and continue cooking for another 10 minutes. Stir frequently. Potatoes and corn should be tender. The chowder may be prepared in advance to this point and set aside. To serve, add milk or cream and Worcestershire sauce, season with salt and pepper, and reheat gently. Do not boil. When steam begins to rise from the surface, the chowder is heated.
FINAL STEP	Pour into hot bowls and garnish with a sprinkling of parsley. Pass oyster crackers or saltines.

Parsnip Chowder

Serves 6

The parsnip is a pale, slim root vegetable, a member of the carrot family, and when it is diced, as in this recipe, it looks like potato. It soon proves its identity with the sweet taste for which it is known.

I have also been struck by how easy it is to hold a parsnip to peel.

INGREDIENTS	4 cups diced parsnips
	5 slices bacon (to be used later for garnish)
	1 cup finely sliced onion
	3 cups new potatoes, peeled and cubed (about 1½ pounds)
	2 cups boiling water
	4 cups milk
	3 tablespoons butter
	Salt, to taste, if desired
	¼ teaspoon freshly ground black pepper
	1 cup light cream or half-and-half
	2 tablespoons chopped parsley, to garnish

SPECIAL EQUIPMENT

None

PREPARATION

Cut parsnips into ½-inch dice, discarding any part of the core that is hard and woody, especially in larger (older) parsnips. Set dice aside.

TRY OUT
7 mins.

Try out the bacon in a large skillet over low heat until it is crisp. Remove the bacon and set aside on a paper towel to drain (bacon will be used later for garnish).

SAUTÉ
10 mins.

Place the onions in the skillet and cook gently over medium-low heat until tender and lightly browned, about 10 minutes.

COOK
30 mins.

Spoon the onions into a large (4-quart) saucepan, reserving the fat. Add the parsnips and potatoes to the saucepan and pour in the boiling water. Cover and cook over medium-low heat for about 30 minutes or until the vegetables are tender.

HEAT
5 mins.

When the vegetables are cooked, add milk and return just to the boiling point—but not beyond! Stir in the butter and leftover fat. Season to taste. Stir in the cream.

FINAL STEP

When the chowder is steaming hot, pour into a heated tureen. Crumble the bacon into bits to garnish the chowder. Sprinkle with parsley. Serve.

Cheese

IN MY SMALL INDIANA TOWN in the 1920s when I was growing up, my mother knew of only two kinds of cheese—Kraft's pimiento and that cut by the grocer from a large wheel resting on the back counter and called, simply, rat cheese. Fortunately, I was to discover the glory of cheese in all its many forms when I moved to the city. But it was another decade or so and in another part of the world that cheese in soup first delighted me.

Stilton/Cheddar Cheese Soup

Serves 8

Scotland and Texas came together in my kitchen in this velvety soup, rich with the taste of two of the best of cheeses—Stilton and Cheddar.

Two friends came across this soup in different parts of the world. Craig Claiborne found his at Ardsheal House, Kentallen, Scotland, while a Texas friend, Lucetta Teagarden, sent this recipe found in the 1886 Tea Room of the Driskill Hotel in Austin. There were minor differences in the recipes but the results were surprisingly alike and equally delicious.

The Scottish recipe called for equal amounts of Stilton and Cheddar while the Texas recipe suggested only that it be made with an English cheese of good quality. The Scottish version was made with only onions and garlic, while the Texas restaurant's called for carrots and celery as well.

If Stilton is difficult to find, make the soup with Cheddar alone. Better to have a slight difference in taste than to do without.

INGREDIENTS	2 tablespoons butter
	½ cup *each* finely chopped onion, carrot, and celery
	1 teaspoon finely minced garlic
	⅓ cup flour
	2 teaspoons cornstarch
	3 cups chicken stock
	½ pound *each* Stilton and Cheddar, crumbled or cut into bits
	⅛ teaspoon baking soda
	1 cup heavy or light cream, as desired
	⅓ cup dry white wine, optional
	Salt, if desired
	Dash of cayenne
	¼ teaspoon freshly ground black pepper
	1 bay leaf
	¼ cup chopped fresh parsley or dusting of paprika, to garnish

SPECIAL
EQUIPMENT

None

PREPARATION
SWEAT
8 mins.

Melt the butter in a large (4-quart) saucepan; add the onions, carrot, celery, and garlic, and cover. Sweat until wilted and tender, about 8 minutes.

COOK
2 mins.

Stir in the flour and cornstarch; cook until bubbly, about 2 minutes. Pour in the stock. Add the two cheeses, baking soda, cream, and wine, if using. Blend with a large wooden spoon until smooth and thickened. Add optional salt, cayenne, black pepper, and bay leaf.

SIMMER
8–10 mins.

Bring to a lazy boil and let simmer over very low heat for 8 to 10 minutes.

Remove the bay leaf. The soup may be thinned with a little milk, if desired.

FINAL STEP

Serve in heated bowls, garnished with either a sprinkling of finely chopped fresh parsley or a dusting of paprika.

Be forewarned: This deliciously rich soup may go right to the top of the list of family favorites.

Brie Soup

Serves 8

Brie, a cheese not usually associated with the soup pot, is the foundation of this dish to be served hot or cold. Brie may raise eyebrows among the guests, but only because of its unexpected appearance, not because of its unexpectedly good flavor.

Some may comment that this is not the proper use of such a celebrated cheese, but that is before they taste this velvety-smooth creation.

The taste of a fine Brie has been described as a mixture of part mushrooms, part cream, part Cognac, part earth—and all become part of the taste of this soup.

However, the fine flavor can be easily overpowered by other ingredients usually found in this kind of soup—hence the reliance here on the equally delicate flavors of leeks and celery rather than onion.

This soup need not be confined to Brie alone but can be made with other soft cheeses such as Camembert, Crema Danica, Danish Crème Royale, Pont-l'Evêque, or, if you are daring, a Liederkranz. Many other cheeses make fine soups, but they are of different families and call for different preparations.

Brie soup may start the meal, or it may be served as the dessert/cheese course to end it.

The recipe was the inspiration of my mentor at the Culinary Institute of America, Chef Elliott Sharron.

INGREDIENTS

3 ounces butter or margarine
6 ounces leek, chopped into ½-inch pieces, no green
6 ounces celery, chopped into ½-inch pieces
4 cups milk
4 cups chicken stock, heated
12 ounces Brie (not too ripe), cut into chunks
⅔ cup white roux (see page 337)

Sachet d'épice
1 clove
1 bay leaf
4 peppercorns
Pinch of thyme

Salt and freshly ground black pepper to taste
24 julienne strips leek, to garnish hot soup
Snippets of parsley or chives, to garnish cold soup

SPECIAL EQUIPMENT	Blender or food processor
PREPARATION SWEAT *20 mins.*	Place butter or margarine in medium (3-quart) pot and add chopped leeks and celery. Cover. Turn heat to medium-low and sweat until softened and translucent, about 20 minutes.
MILK TEST *10 mins.*	Bring milk to a boil in a separate saucepan to be certain it is fresh (if not, it will "break" into particles).
BOIL/SIMMER *45 mins.*	When vegetables are cooked, pour in chicken stock and milk and add chunks of cheese. Bring to a boil and reduce to a simmer. Stir in the roux to thicken soup. Drop sachet into pot 30 minutes after the soup begins to simmer. The soup will be velvety and the consistency of light cream, but if it is too thick, thin with stock or milk. Remove and discard pieces of rind from cheese as they float to the surface. Add salt and pepper to taste.
BLENDER *20 mins.* *5 mins.*	Remove pot from heat and allow soup to cool 15 or 20 minutes so that it can be worked. Remove sachet. Use blender or food processor to achieve a velvety texture. If to be served hot, return to heat and bring to a simmer again. If to be served cold, chill rapidly in a running water bath and refrigerate.
FINAL STEP	Ladle the hot soup into individual bowls and garnish with the julienne leek. If the soup is to be served cold, sprinkle snippets of parsley and chives over the surface.

Note: The heated soup will have more flavor of the Brie than the chilled soup.

Cold Roquefort Soup
Potage Glacée au Roquefort

Serves 6 (6 cups)

A hint of Roquefort (the real thing—no blue cheese) sets this apart from vichyssoise, which is also basically a potato-leek soup. The taste is undeniable, yet not so pronounced as to turn aside someone who might not fancy this blue-veined cheese made in the small town of Roquefort in the province of Rouergue in southern France. The cheese, expensive, is made exclusively with ewe's milk, whereas the more available (and less costly) U.S. domestic blue-veined cheeses are made with cow's milk.

Any one of the many blue-veined cheeses available in the United States may be substituted, but the soup will lack Roquefort's characteristic suggestion of slight mustiness that it would have otherwise.

(If there is Roquefort left, consider a loaf of Roquefort bread. Add 1½ cups of crumbled cheese to a recipe that makes 2 loaves of a basic white bread. Toast a slice for a memorable breakfast experience.)

INGREDIENTS	3 leeks, washed, trimmed, and chopped
	4 tablespoons (½ stick) butter
	3 baking potatoes, diced (about 5 cups)
	6 cups chicken stock
	1 cup half-and-half or light cream
	1½ ounces Roquefort, broken into pieces or mashed
	Salt and white pepper to taste
	1 teaspoon minced chives, to garnish
SPECIAL EQUIPMENT	Blender or food processor
PREPARATION **5 mins.**	Cut heavy green leaves off leeks and discard. Carefully wash leeks under running water to remove sand and dirt; chop. Melt butter in a medium soup pot and add leeks.
SWEAT **10–12 mins.**	Cover and sweat slowly over medium to low heat until tender and translucent. Add potatoes and stock.
SIMMER **30–35 mins.**	Simmer for about 30 to 35 minutes or until the vegetables are tender.
PUREE	Choose between a blender (for a velvety texture) and the food processor (for coarse creaminess). Place the vegetables in the work bowl and puree. Add the cream and cheese. Continue processing. Strain the soup through a sieve.
SEASON	Salt and pepper to taste after the cheese has been blended in.
CHILL **6 hours to overnight**	Refrigerate soup for at least 6 hours or overnight, which may be more convenient. Also chill soup cups or bowls.
FINAL STEP	Serve in chilled cups or bowls. Sprinkle with chives to garnish.

Cream of Gouda/Edam Soup (Dutch)

Serves 6

While neither Gouda nor Edam is much recommended for cooking, this recipe captures their light, clean, buttery taste. Edam, the one with the red rind, is made with reduced-fat milk. Gouda, the one encased in yellow, is prepared with whole milk.

This is a good soup to serve with a special array of condiments: chopped green pepper, thin pimiento strips, toasted slivered almonds, crumbled crisp bacon, and buttered popcorn. Fun and tasty.

INGREDIENTS	3 ounces (about 4 strips) bacon, chopped
	¼ cup butter or margarine
	1 medium onion, peeled and minced
	⅓ cup tomato puree or 2 tablespoons tomato paste
	1 teaspoon sharp prepared mustard
	1 teaspoon Worcestershire sauce
	½ teaspoon paprika
	2 teaspoons salt, if desired
	¼ teaspoon freshly ground black pepper
	4 cups chicken stock
	½ pound (2 cups) shredded Gouda or Edam
	2 cups light cream, heated
	Condiments (see above)

SPECIAL
EQUIPMENT

None

PREPARATION

SAUTÉ
5 mins.

In a large saucepan, fry bacon until almost crisp. Pour off fat and drop in the butter or margarine. Let it melt before adding the onion. Sauté onion until soft and glistening, about 5 minutes. Mix in the tomato puree or tomato paste, mustard, Worcestershire sauce, paprika, salt if desired, and pepper. Stir to mix well.

COOK
1–2 mins.
30 mins.

20 mins.

Cook for 1 or 2 minutes to blend flavors. Add chicken stock and bring to a boil over medium heat. Simmer slowly for 30 minutes over reduced heat.

Add cheese and stir well to break apart the shreds. Simmer for about 20 minutes. Not all of the cheese will be absorbed, but the stringy pieces give an interesting texture to the soup.

3 mins.   Add the heated cream (chilled cream would shock the soup and take more time to bring to serving temperature).

FINAL STEP   Remove from the stove and pour at once into heated bowls. Each guest is to add his or her own condiments to this smooth cheese soup.

Double Gloucester Cheese Soup (English)

Serves 6

Double Gloucester cheese and this namesake soup come from Gloucestershire in the heart of England, where the milk from the big black-and-white Gloucester cattle is processed not once but twice. There is a "single" Gloucester cheese, but it does not travel well and is kept close to home.

This soup reflects the qualities of the cheese, which is considered the one hard English cheese that can be compared to the great blue cheeses. "Put a crumb no bigger than a pin-head on your tongue and it will fill your whole mouth with its savor," said one admirer.

It was a cool, clear evening when we arrived at the old manor house on the Usk River, a famous trout stream in Wales, not far from Gloucestershire. The soup served that night in Gliffaes Country House Hotel was a Gloucester cheese soup.

Not all of the cheese is used in the preparation of the soup. Some is put aside to sprinkle over the hot soup just before it is served—with croutons and chopped parsley to garnish.

The original recipe calls for the soup to be strained through a fine sieve and the vegetables discarded. However, on occasion I have pureed the vegetables to produce a thicker soup.

INGREDIENTS   3 tablespoons butter
½ cup *each* leeks, carrots, turnips, celery, onions, potato—cleaned or peeled and chopped
2 tablespoons cornstarch
2 tablespoons water
5 cups chicken stock

Sachet d'épice
12 black peppercorns
2 cloves
½ teaspoon thyme
2 cloves garlic, crushed

6 or 8 sprigs parsley, tied in a bundle
1½ cups (8 ounces) shredded Double Gloucester

1 teaspoon salt, if desired
Pinch of freshly ground black pepper
½ cup light cream, warmed
1 cup freshly toasted croutons
¼ cup finely chopped parsley

SPECIAL
EQUIPMENT

Fine chinois or strainer. A blender or food processor, if vegetables are to be pureed.

PREPARATION
SWEAT
20 mins.
10 mins.

Melt butter in a medium (3-quart) saucepan and drop in the prepared vegetables. Stir and cover. Cook gently over medium-low heat until the vegetables are tender but not colored, about 20 minutes.

Stir together the cornstarch and water and add the mixture to the vegetables. Continue cooking over low heat for an additional 10 minutes.

BOIL/SIMMER
1 hour

Pour in the stock, stirring continuously. Add the sachet and parsley sprigs and bring to a boil. Add two thirds of the cheese, reserving the balance until the soup is served. Reduce the heat, cover, and simmer over low heat for 1 hour.

Taste for seasoning and add salt, if desired, and black pepper.

STRAIN

Discard sachet and parsley bundle. Pass the soup through a fine strainer, or blend or process the vegetables and add to the soup if a thicker soup is desired.

REHEAT

Reheat the soup, remove from heat, and stir in the warmed cream.

FINAL STEP

Pour the soup into heated bowls. Top each serving with croutons and sprinkles of the cheese. Garnish with chopped parsley.

Serve immediately.

Fruit

A SPOONFUL OF FRUIT soup is a long step beyond a sip of fruit juice, yet they are sometimes mistakenly equated. Fruit soup may be drunk from a frosted glass or cup as one might a fruit drink, but there the similarity ends. Fruit soups quickly establish themselves as dishes with substance and subtle flavors. Curried Pippin Soup (page 123), for instance, is not a simple fruit juice but a soup with many ingredients, including onion, curry powder, light cream, and lemon juice. Decidedly apple, nonetheless.

Apple Soup Polonais

Serves 4 to 6

Apples are for eating out of hand, bobbing for at Halloween, and adapting into a delicious cold soup from Poland. It is a lovely off-white color and a bit frothy when poured and looks richer and creamier than it really is. This is ideal for someone seeking a cold soup not laden with calories. It is made with the addition of buttermilk (90 calories) or low-fat cottage cheese (160 calories) whipped in a blender or food processor. But it can also be made with sour cream or whipping cream (480 calories) for those who wish it to be as rich in content as in appearance.

In early July I begin watching my apple trees for the first half dozen or so ripe Lodis so I can make this soup. Lodi apples are tart, and apples bought later in the summer should be chosen from among the tart ones. Avoid the mild Delicious.

This is a versatile soup that can be served either to begin the meal or to end it as the dessert course. For the latter, serve with Calvados or a fine brandy.

INGREDIENTS	**6 large, tart apples**
	4 cups water
	1 cinnamon stick
	1 teaspoon grated lemon rind
	½ cup sugar
	½ cup dry white wine
	1 cup buttermilk or other choices (see above)
	Fresh mint leaves, to garnish

SPECIAL
EQUIPMENT

Food mill, processor, or blender

PREPARATION
15 mins.
BOIL/SIMMER
8–10 mins.

Peel, core, and quarter apples and drop them into water in a large saucepan. Add cinnamon stick and lemon rind. Bring to a boil. Reduce heat and cook slowly, covered, until the fruit is soft, about 8 to 10 minutes. Remove from the heat and allow to cool somewhat before processing. Remove cinnamon stick. Puree apples.

Combine with sugar, wine, and buttermilk in a large bowl. Sieve through fine mesh if you want soup of a velvety texture.

CHILL
2 hours
or longer

Place in the refrigerator to chill for 2 or more hours, or hold, chilled in the refrigerator, for up to 48 hours. Also chill cups or bowls in which the soup is to be served.

FINAL STEP

Serve in cups. Drop a fresh mint leaf to float on each serving.

Curried Pippin Soup

Serves 8 to 10

Curried Pippin Soup came at the end of an uncommon day in August that began with a flight out of Indiana, a touchdown in New York, a momentary pause to disembark at London's Heathrow Airport, and a brief respite in Bath alongside a pool in which Romans swam and otherwise disported themselves in the first century.

(I thought little of the wonder of flying across continents and oceans but marveled at the still intact, original lead piping connecting the many Roman baths, saunas, and pools.)

It had been a hot day and the discovery of a delicious cold curried apple soup at Bath's Beaufort Hotel was made in a quiet moment just before jet lag moved in!

Few pippin apples are now grown commercially in the United States, but here and there in old orchards and backyards one can find them. This apple is known also as an Albemarle pippin, Newtown pippin, and yellow or green Newtown. Granny Smith, a bright green, tart apple found seasonally in most supermarkets, is an acceptable substitute if a pippin cannot be found.

INGREDIENTS	2 pounds pippin or other tart cooking apples
	Lightly salted water to cover
	2 tablespoons butter
	1 medium onion, peeled and sliced
	3 teaspoons curry powder, or to taste
	5 cups chicken stock
	1 tablespoon cornstarch
	1 tablespoon water
	1 tablespoon lemon juice
	1½ cups light cream, warmed
	2 egg yolks
	Salt, to taste, if desired
	Pinch of freshly ground white pepper
	1 tablespoon finely chopped parsley, to garnish

SPECIAL EQUIPMENT

Food processor, blender, and chinois or sieve

PREPARATION

Peel, core, and slice the apples. Cover with lightly salted water and set aside.

SWEAT
15 mins.

In a large (4-quart) saucepan, melt butter; add onion and sweat, covered, until soft and translucent, about 15 minutes. Do not let the onion slices brown.

Stir in the curry powder and follow with the stock. Mix the cornstarch and water together and stir into the stock.

SIMMER
15–20 mins.

Rinse apples, sprinkle with lemon juice, and add to the saucepan. Bring to a gentle boil, reduce to a simmer over low heat, and cook until the apple slices are soft, about 15 to 20 minutes.

PUREE
5 mins.

When the apples have cooled for a few moments, put the mixture through a food processor or a blender, depending on the degree of smoothness desired. (I like the blender, which produces a very smooth soup.) The soup may also be sieved, if an even finer texture is desired.

Heat the cream gently to remove the chill, then beat in the egg yolks until fully incorporated. Combine with soup.

CHILL
2 hours or more

Season to taste with salt and pepper. Refrigerate 2 or more hours to chill.

FINAL STEP

Ladle soup into chilled cups and garnish lightly with the chopped parsley.

Bluenose (Blueberry) Soup

Serves 5 (4 cups)

The blueberries are suspended in an almost clear soup in this unusual dish from The Blueberry Connection, *a small cookbook put together from "memories, libraries, and kitchens" in and around Granville Centre in Nova Scotia, which is one of the largest producers in the world of low-bush (wild) blueberries.*

We once bicycled from stem to stem in Nova Scotia (Yarmouth to Dingwall and back), regretting all the way that we had not chosen the blueberry season for an otherwise delightful excursion.

Bluenose was the name of a privateer in the war of 1812 that had a cannon in the bow painted a bright blue. Later, in 1921, the name was given to a newly launched deep-sea schooner of the Nova Scotian fishing fleet that challenged and beat the finest of the Gloucester fleet, the Gertrude L. Thibaud.

A fine fillip for Bluenose is a dollop of salted whipped cream.

INGREDIENTS

4 cups water
¾ cup sugar
2 lemon slices
2 cinnamon sticks
2 teaspoons vinegar
1 tablespoon white rum, optional
¼ cup quick-cooking tapioca
2 cups (1 pint) blueberries, fresh or frozen
½ cup heavy cream, whipped, to garnish
¼ teaspoon salt

SPECIAL
EQUIPMENT

None

PREPARATION 10 mins.	In a heavy saucepan, combine all of the ingredients *up to* the blueberries. Let the pan set for 5 minutes while the tapioca softens.
BOIL/SIMMER 20 mins.	Bring to a boil over medium heat. Immediately turn down to simmer for about 20 minutes. Remove from the heat and lift out the lemon and cinnamon sticks. Discard. When the mixture is cool, stir in the blueberries.
HEAT	If the soup is to be served hot, reheat but don't boil.
CHILL 3 hours or longer	If the soup is to be served cold, chill in the refrigerator for at least 3 hours.
WHIP 5 mins.	Meanwhile, whip the cream with the salt.
FINAL STEP	Serve hot or cold, with a dollop of salted whipped cream. Chill bowls first if serving cold.

Chilled Cherry Soup

Serves 6 (6 cups)

Cherry soup is eaten in triumph at our house because it means a victory over the robins, jays, and blackbirds that wait for days for the cherries to ripen on our one tree. Then all of us—birds and humans—make a dash for the tree. We get some. They get most of them. Some years we have only soup. In those years when we are quicker we also have a cherry pie or two. But not often.

If I must, I buy frozen or canned cherries, which are equally good in this soup, but it means a defeat for man.

This is not only a good soup to eat but a soup to admire—cherry red!

INGREDIENTS	4 cups tart red cherries, fresh, frozen, or canned
	3½ cups water
	1 3-inch cinnamon stick
	2 whole cloves
	¼ cup sugar
	1 tablespoon cornstarch
	2 tablespoons water
	2 tablespoons lemon juice
	¼ cup dry red wine or Cherry Heering
	Whipped sour cream and/or whole cherries, or mint leaves, to garnish

SPECIAL EQUIPMENT	Food processor or blender

PREPARATION	*Note:* If canned or frozen cherries are used, substitute the juice for the water or a portion of it.

BOIL/SIMMER *30 mins. or 10 mins.*	Combine cherries, water, cinnamon stick, cloves, and sugar in saucepan and bring to a boil. Reduce heat and simmer fresh or frozen cherries for 30 minutes; canned, 10 minutes. When cooked, mix corn-starch and water; stir into cherries and simmer until liquid is clear and slightly thickened.

PUREE *5 mins.*	*Note:* You may wish to reserve 1 or 2 cups of the whole cherries and return them to the soup after it has been pureed. It gives the soup a different character—one I like.
	Remove cinnamon stick and cloves; puree. Add lemon juice and pour into a large bowl.

CHILL *2 hours or longer*	Chill soup 2 hours or longer. Also chill the soup bowls. Before serving, stir in wine or Cherry Heering.

FINAL STEP	Garnish with whipped sour cream and/or whole cherries, or mint leaves.

Chocolate Soup

Serves 6

Where but at the Hotel Hershey in Hershey, Pennsylvania, would you expect to find chocolate soup presented daily—hot or cold? Its base is chocolate pudding, thinned considerably, and flavored with crème de cacao to boost its chocolateness and amaretto for a distinctive almond flavor. Combined with light cream, this produces a marvelous dessert soup or a soup for brunch.

Sprinkle with toasted almond slivers or coconut shreds before serving.

INGREDIENTS	4 cups light cream
	1 5½-ounce package chocolate pudding, such as Jell-O
	⅓ cup crème de cacao
	2 tablespoons amaretto
	½ cup toasted almond slivers or coconut shreds, to garnish

SPECIAL EQUIPMENT	None

PREPARATION	In a medium (3-quart) saucepan, combine 3 cups of the light cream and
BOIL	the package of chocolate pudding powder. Cook and stir over medium
4–5 mins.	heat until mixture has come to a full boil.

Remove from heat. Add the additional cream, crème de cacao, and amaretto. The liqueurs will lose their alcoholic content—but not their good flavor—when heated in the hot chocolate.

CHILL	If to be served cold, chill in the refrigerator overnight or for at least
4 hours to overnight	4 hours.

FINAL STEP	Pour the cold soup into chilled bowls. Sprinkle toasted almonds or co-
	conut over the surface and serve.

To serve hot, present in heated bowls with either of the garnishes.

Chilled Melon Soup

Serves 8 (6 cups)

Fragrant and rich in flavor, chilled melon soup—served in glasses rimmed with sugar—is made with the meat of the fruit cooked in apricot nectar and sweetened with a light touch of honey. Ginger sprinkled on the melon is among several subtle seasonings.

The cantaloupe or muskmelon and the crenshaw have golden peach tones and good taste that are just right for this recipe. The fruit, when chosen, should be fairly bursting with ripeness and good color.

This recipe may also be used to make a delicious apple soup. Substitute peeled tart apples for the melon, cook with cider, and garnish with toasted almonds or toasted coconut. A touch of apple brandy will give the apple soup a delicious fillip just as apricot or peach brandy will for the melon soup.

In my kitchen the season for this soup begins when the regional melons come on the local market—cantaloupe, May through September; crenshaw, August into October; honeydew, July through October; and casaba, July through November. Melons imported from faraway places can be bought almost any time of year, but they are high in price and low in quality. I prefer to freeze the cooked puree in midsummer to make a surprise soup for the off-season.

INGREDIENTS	2 medium cantaloupes
	2 cups apricot nectar
	1 cup water
	2 tablespoons honey

1 tablespoon lemon juice
Pinch of salt

Sweet sachet
1 cinnamon stick
3 whole allspice
1 clove
Gingerroot (small ½-inch chunk)

1 cup light cream, chilled
1 tablespoon apricot or peach brandy, optional
Choice of garnishes—tiny melon balls, mint leaves, whipped cream, sour cream, or yogurt

SPECIAL EQUIPMENT	Food processor or blender
PREPARATION	Cut the rind from the fruit; seed fruit and slice it into 1-inch chunks; place in saucepan with apricot nectar, water, honey, lemon juice, and pinch of salt. Stir together well. Add sweet sachet.
BOIL/SIMMER *15 mins.*	Bring the mixture to a boil; reduce heat so it simmers gently for about 15 minutes or until fruit is soft. Remove from heat and allow to cool somewhat before processing. Remove sweet sachet.
PUREE *5 mins.*	Puree mixture in food processor or blender. It will become a light golden color.
CHILL *2 hours or longer*	Refrigerate puree. Cream will be added later.
FINAL STEP	This soup takes on a special excitement when it is served in wineglasses or sherbet glasses with the rims dipped into lightly beaten egg white and then into sugar. Chill glasses. Stir chilled cream into the soup just when ready to serve and add the optional brandy, if desired. Garnish. Serve immediately. (This soup separates quickly.)

Champagne Melon Soup

Serves 6 to 8

Cantaloupe joins with honeydew to give a delicious base to this unusual combination—a blend of melon, orange juice, and champagne. Both melons should be summer-ripe for the best flavor. The light green of the honeydew mingles with the peach tones of the cantaloupe to make a light golden presentation.

INGREDIENTS	3 cups *each* (a total of 6) cantaloupe and honeydew (about ½ melon, or a little less, is needed for each cup), peeled, seeded, and chopped coarsely 1 cup fresh orange juice or ⅓ cup frozen orange juice concentrate 2 tablespoons fresh lime juice 1½ tablespoons honey 2 cups brut champagne 12 fresh mint leaves, to garnish
SPECIAL EQUIPMENT	Blender or food processor
PREPARATION *10 mins.*	Peel each of the 2 melons, or scoop out the flesh with a spoon.
BLEND *5 mins.*	Process the melon pieces. Add orange juice (or concentrate), lime juice, and honey and continue processing until smooth.
CHILL *3 hours or overnight*	Refrigerate the soup and chill the bottle of champagne to be opened later.
FINAL STEP	Within ½ hour of serving, pour the champagne into the soup. Stir to blend well. Serve in chilled wineglasses or glass cups rimmed with sugar (see page 129). Garnish with mint leaves.

True Melon Soup

Serves 6

When cantaloupe are ripe from the center through to the skin, and farmers seem to be at every rural intersection hawking their fruit from truck beds, it is time for a pure melon soup. This is melon only, with a bit of cream, a touch of lime or lemon, and a pinch of salt.

The melons must be ripe and smell of a harvest field hot under a summer sun, because it is the melon alone that must carry this soup. No half-ripe fruit will do.
The salt and lime are concessions to those who like one or the other on their melon.
The soup was named by my wife, who exclaimed, "Now that's a true melon flavor!"

INGREDIENTS	5 cups (1 melon about 6 inches in diameter) cantaloupe, seeded, peeled, and cut into chunks
	1 cup light cream
	1/8 teaspoon salt, or to taste
	Juice of 1 lime
	12 mint leaves, to garnish

SPECIAL EQUIPMENT

Blender (for a velvety texture) or food processor (for a somewhat rougher texture)

PREPARATION
20 mins.

Note: I prepare melons either by cutting off the peel with a very sharp knife or by scooping out the ripe flesh with a large spoon.

Place the melon chunks in food processor or blender and process until smooth. Add cream, salt, and lime juice. Blend. Check for additional salt, if needed.

CHILL
6 hours or overnight

Refrigerate the soup until it is well chilled, about 6 hours. Overnight may be more convenient.

FINAL STEP

Pour soup into chilled cups or bowls and serve garnished with mint leaves.

This soup may be held in the refrigerator for a week while retaining its good flavor. If it is to be frozen, do so before adding the cream.

Chilled Black Olive Soup

Serves 6

Bits of black olives bobbing in a golden soup make a striking presentation, hot or cold. Olives may be thinly sliced or put through a food processor in one or two short bursts.
The ingredient that gives the soup an unexpected boost is steak sauce.

INGREDIENTS	1 cup pitted ripe olives
	3 cups chicken broth
	1 1/2 cups minced onions
	1 clove garlic, minced

(continued)

1 egg
1 cup light cream
1 teaspoon thick bottled steak sauce
    (Crosse & Blackwell, for example)
¼ cup dry sherry

SPECIAL   Food processor, optional
EQUIPMENT

PREPARATION   *Note:* Some may prefer olives sliced wafer-thin while others will want
                olives chopped into bits in a food processor. Try slices and, if still too
                large, drain and process the balance.

BOIL/SIMMER   Place chicken stock in a medium saucepan and bring to a boil. Add
10 mins.   onions and garlic. Simmer 10 minutes.
                    Remove pan from heat, strain out onion and garlic bits, and discard.
                Return soup to the pan and add olives. Beat egg in a bowl and slowly
                add a cup of hot soup while continuing to beat, taking care not to curdle
                the egg. Pour soup/egg mixture into the soup. Add light cream, steak
                sauce, and sherry.

CHILL   Refrigerate for several hours or overnight.

FINAL STEP   Serve chilled in chilled soup bowls.

Chilled Teahouse Orange Soup

Serves 4

Chilled Teahouse Orange Soup is an intriguing name for an intriguing but easy-to-make cooked soup—served cold. It has not only orange but pineapple and lemon juices accented with clove and mint. It may be made with either fresh or frozen juices.

INGREDIENTS   3 cups orange juice
                1 cup pineapple juice
                5 cloves
                ⅓ cup sugar
                2 tablespoons cornstarch
                ⅔ cup lemon juice
                Fresh mint leaves, to garnish

SPECIAL EQUIPMENT	None
PREPARATION	In a medium (3-quart) saucepan, combine orange and pineapple juices and cloves. Remove ½ cup of the liquid to blend with the cornstarch.
BOIL *4 mins.*	Bring the juices to a gentle boil. In a small bowl stir together the sugar and cornstarch. Stir in the ½ cup of reserved juices and mix well. If lumps persist, put the mixture through a sieve before slowly adding to the simmering juices. Stir constantly until the soup thickens, about 4 minutes.
COOL	Remove from heat and leave at room temperature to cool. When cool stir in the lemon juice.
REFRIGERATE *Overnight*	Pour the soup into a plastic or glass container and refrigerate overnight.
FINAL STEP	Stir the soup before ladling into chilled bouillon cups. Decorate with mint leaves.

Peach Buttermilk Soup

Serves 8 (6 cups)

Peaches are scarce in my part of the country after a hard winter, so when the luscious ripe fruit is on the market I make one of my favorite cold soups—peach laced with buttermilk (another favorite). It is not cooked.

INGREDIENTS	2 pounds ripe peaches, peeled, seeded, and cut into chunks ⅓ cup frozen orange juice concentrate I cup buttermilk I cup light cream ⅛ teaspoon cinnamon ⅛ teaspoon ground cloves ⅛ teaspoon allspice Slivered or shaved almonds or toasted coconut, to garnish
SPECIAL EQUIPMENT	Blender or food processor
PREPARATION	Drop peaches into boiling water for no longer than a count of 10. Peel under cold running water and remove pits. Puree in a blender or food

processor. Pour into a medium bowl and add the next 6 ingredients. Stir to blend well.

CHILL
6 hours or
overnight

Place soup in refrigerator for 6 hours or overnight.

FINAL STEP

While soup is being chilled, also chill the soup cups or bowls. Serve garnished with slivered or shaved almonds. Toasted coconut is also good.

Brandied Peach and Plum Soup

Serves 4 or 5

Peaches and plums make their annual debut at about the same time in regional orchards and together they make a delightful soup to be served cold or hot. Plus a bit of wine and brandy. Light plum-colored, naturally.

The most memorable peach and plum soup in our kitchen was made with fruit bought at a roadside stand in the rich Canadian orchard district near Niagara-on-the-Lake.

INGREDIENTS

2 cups *each* ripe peaches and plums, peeled, pitted, and cut into chunks
1½ cups water
1½ cups dry white wine
⅔ cup sugar
1 slice lemon
1 cinnamon stick
2 tablespoons brandy
Mint leaves, to garnish

SPECIAL
EQUIPMENT

Chinois or sieve

PREPARATION

Drop peaches into boiling water for 5 seconds to loosen the skins. Slip off the skins, pit, and cut into chunks. Wash plums, pit, and cut into chunks.

BOIL/SIMMER
10 mins.

Place the peaches, plums, water, wine, sugar, lemon, and cinnamon in a medium (3-quart) saucepan. Bring to a boil, lower heat, and simmer gently for about 10 minutes or until fruit is fork-tender.

SIEVE

Allow mixture to cool somewhat so it can be comfortably worked through the chinois or sieve. Discard coarse pulp.

Set soup aside to cool. Add brandy and adjust to taste—add sugar and/or brandy as needed.

CHILL   Chill for 3 hours or longer.

FINAL STEP   Serve in chilled cups and garnish with finely chopped mint leaves.

The soup may also be served hot. Try it first hot, then again after it has been chilled, before deciding on your preference.

Red Raspberry Soup

Serves 6

The taste of raspberry soup is clear and pronounced—nothing artificial about it (as with many things boasting of a raspberry flavor).

The fruit is cooked, but slightly. When the soup is served, a few berries are dropped into each bowl.

Fresh strawberries, washed and hulled, may be substituted for raspberries to make another excellent soup. Black raspberries may also be used, but they are so scarce in my part of the country that I eat them only au naturel, covered with thick cream.

INGREDIENTS   **2 quarts ripe raspberries**
3 cups water
Juice of 2 lemons

Sweet sachet
⅛ teaspoon mace
Pinch *each* of cayenne and marjoram
4 cloves
I bay leaf, crumbled

¼ cup sugar
1½ tablespoons cornstarch
Whipped cream or 6 orange sections, peeled and seeded

SPECIAL   Sieve or chinois
EQUIPMENT

PREPARATION   Put aside 24 ripe berries to be added to the soup later. Don't cook these. Stem all the berries.

Place the raspberries to be cooked in a medium (3-quart) saucepan and add water, lemon juice, and sweet sachet.

SIMMER
10 mins.

Bring the mixture to the boiling point, reduce heat, and simmer for about 10 minutes, or until the fruit is soft and breaking apart.

Pour the mixture through a sieve or chinois, first removing the sachet. Discard pulp. Blend sugar and cornstarch in a small amount of cold water before adding them to the raspberry liquid.

COOK
10–12 mins.

Cook soup over low heat, stirring constantly (4 to 6 minutes), until mixture begins to thicken. Cook for an additional 6 minutes, stirring constantly.

Remove from heat. Chill.

FINAL STEP

Serve the soup in chilled cups. Drop 4 of the reserved berries into each cup. Garnish with whipped cream or an orange section.

Iced Fruit Soup (French)
Potage de Fruits Glacés

Serves 4 to 6

There is a tang about rhubarb that underscores the bland but distinctive taste of banana in this delicious chilled French soup. Tanginess of a different kind comes from orange, lemon, and lime. While rhubarb is a vegetable, it marries well with fruit. The final touch is blending in yet another fruit, diced apple.

Rhubarb (sometimes known as pieplant in my part of the country) is chiefly a springtime treat, which can be frozen at home or bought in the supermarket and frozen to be used in this dish at any time of year. In or out of season, this is a refreshing soup to be served in bowls nestled in ice. Try it as a first course or as dessert. It is especially good at a brunch or luncheon.

This recipe came to my kitchen in one of Dione Lucas's fine books on French cooking.

This soup has everything going for it except its color—a subdued gold that does not match its upbeat flavor. A few drops of red food coloring will give it life.

INGREDIENTS

½ pound rhubarb (about 6 stalks), cut into 1-inch pieces
⅓ cup sugar
¼ cup water
2 teaspoons lemon juice
Juice of 1 lime
4 ripe bananas, sliced
2 cups fresh or frozen orange juice
⅓ cup light rum, optional
Drops of red food coloring (about 10 or so, optional)

1 eating apple, peeled, cored, and cut into ¼-inch dice
Crushed ice, to surround serving cups
2 or 3 thin slices lime, cut in half, to garnish

SPECIAL EQUIPMENT	Blender
PREPARATION	Preheat oven to 325°.
	Clean the rhubarb and cut it into 1-inch lengths. Place the pieces in a heavy saucepan. In a separate saucepan, heat the sugar and water and
COOK 5 mins.	stir to dissolve the sugar. Cook to a light syrup without stirring, about 5 minutes.
BAKE 15 mins.	Pour the syrup over the rhubarb; add the lemon and lime juices. Place the pan on a top burner and heat until the mixture just begins to bubble. Cover with a piece of wax paper cut to fit down over the rhubarb, and bake for 15 minutes. Remove from the heat and allow to cool.
BLEND	Place the rhubarb and sliced bananas in the blender work bowl. Puree the mixture until smooth. Mix in the orange juice and the rum, if using it.
	If the soup needs color, blend in 8 to 10 drops of red food coloring. Stir in the apple.
FINAL STEP	Serve in chilled bowls, preferably glass, surrounded with crushed ice. Float half of a very thin slice of lime on the top of each bowl.

Strawberry Wine Soup

Serves 6

Strawberries are combined with dry white wine to achieve a lovely cold soup that may be served at brunch or dinner as a first course, or as the dessert course.

The combination of cooked and uncooked fruit gives the soup a complete strawberry flavor that one without the other would miss.

INGREDIENTS	3 cups ripe strawberries, washed, stemmed, and cut into pieces
	⅓ cup sugar
	1¼ cups water
	1 tablespoon cornstarch or arrowroot
	2 tablespoons cold water

(continued)

              1 cup dry white wine
2 tablespoons lemon juice
2 teaspoons grated lemon peel
Lemon peel slices or ¼ cup sour cream, to garnish

SPECIAL EQUIPMENT	Blender, food processor, or food mill
PREPARATION	*Note:* Two of the 3 cups of strawberry puree will be cooked. The remaining cup will be added uncooked to the soup.
PUREE 5 mins.	Puree 2 cups of the strawberries. Place the puree in a saucepan over medium heat. Reserve third cup. Add sugar and the 1¼ cups water; simmer for 5 minutes.
5 mins.	Mix cornstarch with the 2 tablespoons water; stir into the puree. Cook until thickened, about 5 minutes. Remove from heat. Add reserved uncooked berries, wine, lemon juice, and grated peel.
CHILL 1 hour or longer	Refrigerate and, when cold, season to taste with additional wine or lemon juice, if desired.
FINAL STEP	Garnish soup with slivers of lemon rind or sour cream. Yogurt also may be used as garnish.

Chilled Strawberry Soup

Serves 6

There can be no better use for a red-ripe strawberry than to become part of this creamy chilled soup created by Chef Frank Martinez, my colleague at the Culinary Institute of America.

It takes the gardener longer to pick the strawberries than it does to blend them into this lovely, velvety soup. The hidden flavors are Calvados, the French apple brandy, and a hint of cinnamon. Applejack may be substituted for the Calvados, in which case reduce the amount by half. The domestic version does not have the smoothness of its French cousin.

INGREDIENTS	1 quart ripe strawberries, washed and hulled
	2 cups (1 pint) heavy cream, chilled
	¼ cup Calvados, optional
	1 bay leaf
	½ teaspoon cinnamon

2 tablespoons sugar
½ cup sour cream or yogurt, to garnish

SPECIAL
EQUIPMENT

Blender or food processor

PREPARATION
20 mins.

Note: Reserve 5 or 6 berries to be sliced and dropped later on the top of each bowl or cup of soup.

You'll probably have to blend or process the berries and other ingredients in two batches.

Place fruit, cream, optional Calvados, bay leaf, cinnamon, and sugar in receptacle. Blend in short bursts. Don't overblend, or the soup may become frothy, a stage beyond velvety.

CHILL
I hour or longer

Pour into a container and chill until time to serve.

FINAL STEP

Glass bowls and cups are ideal for service because they show off the beauty of the cold soup.

Drop a dollop of sour cream or yogurt—topped with a strawberry half—on the soup when it is served.

Grains

S URELY CERES, the Roman goddess of agriculture, would have given high marks to soups made with grains from her domain, even though it is unlikely the Romans of that day would have prepared them in this manner. While one of the grains, wild rice, is not a true rice but the seed of a different aquatic grass, we can be certain Ceres would have embraced it along with the others.

Barley Prosciutto Soup

Serves 6

Be it thin slivers of prosciutto or another dry-cured ham, in this recipe the meat has a happy affinity for the grain. This soup is easy to make, and equally delicious without the cream. For richness, cream, yes, but the taste rests with the ham and barley.

I reduced the amount of peas in the original recipe by half because they seemed to overpower the other good flavors.

INGREDIENTS	4 tablespoons (¼ cup) butter or margarine
	¼ cup finely chopped shallots
	1 cup pearl barley
	5 cups chicken stock

¼ pound prosciutto or other dry-cured ham, cut into julienne strips
¼ teaspoon freshly ground black pepper
1 cup heavy cream, optional
5 ounces (½ package) frozen *petits pois*, thawed
1 cup (4 ounces) grated or shredded Parmesan cheese and whole
    nutmeg, to be grated as garnish

SPECIAL EQUIPMENT	None
PREPARATION *14 mins.*	Stir butter and shallots in a 4- to 5-quart saucepan. Cover and cook over medium heat until the shallots are translucent and soft, about 6 minutes. Add barley and stir constantly until it turns a light golden color, about 8 minutes. Stir in the chicken stock, the thin-sliced prosciutto or other ham, and the pepper.
BOIL/SIMMER *30 mins.*	Cover and bring to a boil. Reduce heat and simmer over low heat until the barley is tender but *not* mushy, about 30 minutes. Add cream and peas. Heat through before serving. Don't bring to a boil.
FINAL STEP	Serve in hot tureen and bowls. Pass the cheese and the grated nutmeg.

Beer Soup (Finnish, Swedish)

Serves 4 (very rich)

It is kaljakeitto *in Finland and* biersuppe *in Sweden. The chief ingredient—light or dark beer or ale—never varies; nevertheless, it has many variations. (It may be clear or creamy, hot or cold, and perhaps flavored with eggs, cream, lemon juice, sugar, sour cream, and on and on. An English spiced ale soup includes vegetables, while the Danes take particular delight in one made with lumpy curds of whey.*

The Finnish recipe here differs from a favorite Swedish beer soup in that it does not have 3 egg yolks added. (But add these if you wish.)

The original Finnish recipe called for double the amount of sugar and corn syrup, but for many it is far too sweet. I have reduced the sugar content considerably.

The cheese dice at the bottom of the bowls melt to give a pleasant contrasting texture and flavor.

This is a tasty first-course dish.

INGREDIENTS	2 cups milk
	2 tablespoons flour
	Pinch of salt, if desired
	1 cup beer
	½ tablespoon corn syrup
	½ teaspoon chopped fresh or ground ginger
	1 cinnamon stick
	1 clove
	Pinch of freshly ground white pepper
	1 cup diced Swiss-type cheese
	⅓ cup finely chopped parsley

SPECIAL EQUIPMENT	None

PREPARATION BOIL *1 min.*	Mix the milk, flour, and salt in a medium saucepan. Heat to boiling while stirring constantly to avoid suddenly boiling over. Boil and stir 1 minute. Remove from heat; cover.
BOIL/SIMMER *5 mins.*	Put beer, corn syrup, ginger, cinnamon stick, and clove into a saucepan. Heat to boiling, stirring constantly, then reduce heat and simmer for 3 or 4 minutes. Stir the mixture into the thickened milk. Return to heat and bring to a boil—but watch it carefully so it doesn't boil over.
STRAIN	Add white pepper and perhaps more salt (which accentuates the sweetness). Discard cinnamon stick and clove. Strain out lumps.
FINAL STEP	Serve immediately in heated bowls in which you have placed the cheese, and garnish with sprinkles of parsley.

Oatmeal Soup (Scottish)

Serves 4

Oats and oatmeal have not led the glamorous life that other grains have, yet oats have been eaten by man (and his horse) for several thousand years. Oats, which flourish in a cool, rainy climate, have for years been at the center of the Scottish cuisine. Oats appear most often as the familiar hot porridge, but they are enjoyed in a variety of other ways, served in scones, gingerbread, biscuits, puddings, desserts, and soups.

Oats have a unique, pleasant taste as well as a high nutritional rating. They are a better source of protein than wheat, and contain less than 8 percent fat. They also add a healthy ration of fiber to the diet.

This recipe elevates oatmeal into an onion-flavored soup that is rich and tasty.

INGREDIENTS	**2 tablespoons butter** **2 medium onions (about 2 cups), thinly sliced** **¼ cup quick-cooking or rolled oats** **2 cups rich chicken stock** **½ teaspoon salt, if desired** **¼ teaspoon freshly ground white pepper** **1½ cups light cream** **Fresh minced parsley, to garnish**
SPECIAL EQUIPMENT	Food processor or blender and fine-mesh sieve
PREPARATION COOK *8 mins.*	In a large saucepan, melt butter over medium heat. Add onions, cover, and cook until soft and glistening, about 8 minutes. Stir occasionally.
TOAST *2–3 mins.*	Meanwhile, toast oats over medium flame in a dry skillet until they are lightly browned and smell pleasantly like freshly harvested hay.
PROCESS *1 min.*	Process toasted oats in a blender, preferably, or a food processor until whirled to a fine powdery texture.
COOK *5 mins.*	Stir the powdered oats into the onions. Cook, stirring frequently, over medium heat for about 5 minutes. Gradually stir stock into the pot with the onions and oats. Season to taste with salt and pepper.
SIMMER *30 mins.*	Simmer mixture, covered, for 30 minutes. Remove from heat and allow to cool somewhat before pureeing.
PUREE *3 mins.*	Puree soup in blender or food processor. If you want a truly velvety soup, press through a fine-mesh sieve or chinois with a wooden spoon or pestle after processing. Combine puree and cream in the saucepan.
HEAT *barely*	Heat but don't boil before bringing to the table for serving.
FINAL STEP	Serve in heated tureen and bowls, garnished with minced parsley.

Sizzling Rice Soup

Serves 6

A lovely, light, creamy soup, this unusual dish gains a new personality when hot deep-fried rice is dropped into the bowls just before serving. It sizzles. The soup is of Chinese origin by way of Honolulu. The rice is cooked in the Asian way (the grains stick together) and then dried before being fried to a crispy golden brown.

The preparation needs planning to ensure that the soup and the rice are brought to the table at the same moment.

INGREDIENTS	1 cup long-grain rice (not converted)
	1 cup water
	1 whole chicken breast, skinned, boned, and cut into julienne strips
	3 tablespoons cornstarch
	3 tablespoons water
	1 tablespoon soy sauce
	6 cups chicken stock
	2 cups shredded fresh watercress, lettuce, or spinach
	½ cup finely chopped green onions
	1 teaspoon Chinese sesame oil, if desired (it is very potent)
	Salad oil for deep frying
SPECIAL EQUIPMENT	Deep-fat fryer or heavy deep saucepan
PREPARATION	*Rice* This first step is done the night before, or 1 hour before if the rice is to be dried in a microwave oven.
BOIL *10 mins.* *30 mins.*	In a large heavy saucepan or Dutch oven, combine rice and water over high heat. Bring to a boil, cover, reduce heat to medium, and cook 10 minutes. Drop heat to low and cook for an additional 30 minutes *without* removing lid. The crusty rice around the sides and bottom will stick to the pan. This will be used in the soup. Take off the top layer of softer rice and reserve for another use.
OVERNIGHT	Lift out the crusty rice and place on a cookie sheet to dry at room temperature, or place in a glass baking dish in a microwave oven for 10 minutes on low.

Soup

Toss the strips of chicken breast with 1 tablespoon of the cornstarch. Set aside. In a small container combine remaining 2 tablespoons of cornstarch with water and soy sauce. Heat stock just to boiling. Stir in soy mixture and chicken. Simmer 5 minutes. Add the shredded greens, onions, and sesame oil, if desired.

BOIL/SIMMER
5 mins.

Keep the soup hot (but not boiling) while frying rice. Heat oil to 375° in a deep-fryer or heavy saucepan. Fry rice 3 to 5 minutes until puffed and lightly browned. Be watchful because it can burn quickly. Lift rice out of the fat with a slotted spoon.

FRY
3–5 mins.

Drain the rice on paper towels and place in heated tureen or bowls. Pour in the soup. Serve at once. Additional fried rice may be passed during this course.

FINAL STEP

Any crispy rice left over is delicious used in salads or eaten out of hand as a snack.

Wild Rice Soup *en Croûte*

Serves 5

Wild rice soup—served under a covering of flaky pastry—is an outstanding presentation of this unusual foodstuff. Wild rice is not true rice, of course, but the seed of a grass growing wild in wet places, mainly in the northern states and Canada.

I discovered this soup (without its pastry canopy) on the menu of the Marquette Hotel while dining on the balcony overlooking the attractive IDS Center of Minneapolis. It was rich and delicious, and later, when I prepared it in my kitchen, I decided to cap this special dish with pastry, which rises into a golden brown dome as it bakes. (The soup may be prepared without its pastry top, of course, but the effect and taste of the pastry are worth the effort.)

Minnesota seemed the logical place to find this soup. It was there for many years that Indians in canoes were the chief harvesters of wild rice. The bulk of wild rice is now produced in commercial paddies, most of them farther north, in Manitoba.

The pastry covering can be made with packaged crescent dinner roll dough or homemade puff pastry.

Wild rice soup is an ingenious and tasty way to stretch an expensive ingredient.

INGREDIENTS

Stock, optional (The Marquette makes this stock especially for this soup. Chicken stock may be substituted, of course, but this richer stock, with its hint of smokiness from the ham hock, stands up nicely to the hearty, nutty flavor of the wild rice.)
2 chicken or duck carcasses (or equivalent quantity wings and backs)
2 ham hocks
1 medium onion, sliced
1 bay leaf
3 teaspoons protein seasoning (such as Maggi)
¼ cup chopped celery
1 cup chopped carrots
5 cups water
Salt, if desired, and freshly ground black pepper to taste

Soup
4 tablespoons butter
⅓ cup raw wild rice, rinsed (or 2 cups cooked wild rice)
2 tablespoons sliced almonds
½ cup finely chopped onion
½ cup finely diced carrots
¼ cup finely chopped celery
4 cups rich stock (see above)
2 teaspoons arrowroot, or as needed
2 cups heavy cream

Pastry covering, store-bought or homemade, if desired
1 egg beaten with 1 tablespoon light cream, to brush pastry

SPECIAL
EQUIPMENT

Select ovenproof soup bowls no larger than 4 to 5 inches in diameter. French earthenware soup pots with little handles are best.

PREPARATION

1½ *hours*

Marquette Stock, optional; see above
Combine all the stock ingredients and bring to a boil. Simmer approximately 90 minutes. Strain and reserve stock. Discard bones and vegetables. Meat from ham hocks may be used for other dishes.

SAUTÉ
8 mins.

Soup
Melt butter in a medium saucepan and lightly sauté rice, almonds, onions, carrots, and celery until the onions are translucent and soft, about 8 minutes.

BOIL/SIMMER *1½ hours*	Add the stock to the mixture, bring to a boil, and lower heat to simmer for about 90 minutes, covered.

The soup should have body and not be too watery, so, if necessary, thicken with arrowroot dissolved in a small amount of cream.

Stir in the cream. If the soup is to be served *without* pastry top, reheat gently before bringing to the table.

BAKING *375°* *15–18 mins.*	If the pastry is to be used, preheat oven to 375°. If using packaged crescent dough, gently roll pieces to flatten and enlarge. The size of packaged crescent dinner rolls varies, but as a rule 2 to 3 pieces rolled out and joined by pressing the edges together will be enough.

Homemade puff pastry is usually rolled out in large sheets so it is easy to cut each circle of dough to size, and in one piece. Allow the dough to relax for 4 to 5 minutes *after* rolling it out so that it will not shrink and pull back when it is cut to fit the tops. Allow for a generous overhang of ½ inch when cutting the dough or fitting the crescent pieces.

Fill the bowls with hot soup, and fit the dough over the tops of the bowls. Press the dough gently against the rims and down against the sides. Take care not to tear the dough when pressing it down. Brush with the egg mixture. The dough on the rim and against the sides will be delicious broken and eaten with the soup.

FINAL STEP	When the pastry is baked to a golden brown, remove from oven and serve. Break through the crusts with spoons.

Rice Soup with Egg (Greek)
Soupa Rizi Avgolemono

Serves 4

Eggs give this Greek soup its creaminess, while lemon gives it tang. It is simple and easy to make—no more than 30 minutes from start to table.

INGREDIENTS	1½ quarts (6 cups) chicken or beef stock
	⅓ cup raw, unprocessed rice
	Salt, if desired, to taste
	2 eggs
	2 to 3 tablespoons fresh lemon juice
SPECIAL EQUIPMENT	None

PREPARATION BOIL/SIMMER *15 mins.*	Bring the stock to a boil in a medium (3-quart) stockpot. Add the rice, cover, and cook gently until the rice is tender, about 15 minutes. Taste, and add salt if needed.
TEMPER *3 mins.*	Beat the eggs and lemon juice together in a small bowl. Temper the egg/lemon mixture with 2 or 3 tablespoons of the hot stock, stirring constantly. Pour all the mixture into the pot and stir to blend.
HEAT *2 mins.*	Heat the soup over low heat, stirring constantly. Don't allow to boil.
FINAL STEP	Serve at once in heated bowls. Pass saltines or a waferlike bread.

Barley Soup with Mushrooms and Chicken

Serves 6

There is a surprising clarity of flavor in this barley soup. Delicious. This is a great cold-weather dish.

Making the rich stock is the first easy step. Inexpensive chicken backs and/or wings and a pound of beef bones provide the sturdy underpinning. The recipe will make about 2 quarts (8 cups) of fine stock that can be used in many soups, in addition to this one.

To parch the barley, lard is used because it imparts a country taste that I like. Use butter or a combination of butter and lard, if you wish.

INGREDIENTS

Stock
1½ pounds chicken wings and/or backs
1 pound beef or veal bones
1 carrot, sliced
2 stalks celery, sliced
3 quarts water
1 tablespoon salt, if desired
½ teaspoon freshly ground black pepper

Soup
1 cup pearl barley
2 tablespoons lard or butter or a combination of both
1 large onion, chopped
1 clove garlic, minced or mashed
2 cups thinly sliced fresh mushrooms
2 tablespoons chopped parsley

Salt, if desired (there will already be some in the stock)
2 tablespoons light (Chinese) soy sauce, optional but tasty
Paprika, to garnish

SPECIAL EQUIPMENT	None

PREPARATION
BOIL/SIMMER
2–3 hours

Stock

Place the wings, backs, bones, carrot, and celery in a large stockpot and cover with 3 quarts of water. Bring to a boil, reduce heat, and simmer until the chicken and beef are tender and fall off the bones, about 2 to 3 hours. Add the salt and pepper. Skim occasionally.

When the stock is cooled, pick all choice meat from the bones and strain stock through a sieve. Discard bones, gristle, and vegetables. Cut the meat into ½-inch pieces (bite-size).

COOK
30 mins.

Soup

Return stock to heat and add ½ cup of the barley. Cook at a simmer for about 30 minutes. Add salt, if desired.

SAUTÉ
20 mins.

Place 1 tablespoon of lard or ½ tablespoon each of butter and lard in a skillet. Pour the remaining ½ cup of barley into skillet. Sauté until the barley begins to brown and crackle slightly, about 6 to 8 minutes. Add the onions and garlic, stirring, until the vegetables are soft and translucent.

30 mins.

Add to the stock and cook for 30 minutes.

In the meantime sauté the mushrooms and parsley in the balance of fat for about 8 minutes. Set aside.

When the soup has cooked for 1 hour, add the sautéed mushrooms and parsley as well as the chicken, beef pieces, salt, if using, and soy sauce. Simmer for 10 additional minutes.

REST
30 mins. or more

Remove from heat, cover, and let stand for at least 30 minutes to blend flavors before reheating and serving.

FINAL STEP

Serve in heated bowls. Give the tops a sprinkling of paprika. Serve this hearty dish with chunks of French bread.

Lamb

L AMB IS A MEAT enjoyed by most of the world, yet there is a puzzling avoidance of it in some places, especially in my part of the Midwest. When I was a boy we had lamb only when my Grandfather Condon came to visit. We liked it, and even my father vowed we should have it more often, but we never did. These lamb soup and stew recipes will surely win converts.

Lamb Shank and Lima Bean Soup

Serves 4 to 6

The shank of the lamb is an underrated piece of meat. I prefer it to almost any other part of the animal, including leg of lamb. I like it served in two ways—one, roasted slowly in the oven for several hours, rubbed with a garlic clove, and presented at the table with mint sauce; and the other in this lima bean potage garnished with fresh mint.

The soup is unpretentious and hearty—a perfect choice for supper on a chilly evening.

The lima bean is an excellent companion. It is rich and starchy, with a distinctive flavor. The bean originated in South America, where it remains a popular legume. It has been cultivated in this country since the eighteenth century.

INGREDIENTS   I pound dried lima beans

1½ pounds lamb shank(s)

1 tablespoon butter (if little fat on meat)
4 cups chicken stock
4 cups water
1 clove garlic, crushed
1 cup finely chopped onions
1 cup finely diced carrots
½ cup finely chopped celery
Salt, if desired (about 2 teaspoons for me)
½ teaspoon freshly ground black pepper
2 tablespoons butter, to swirl in when served
⅓ cup finely chopped fresh mint, to garnish

SPECIAL EQUIPMENT	None
PREPARATION	*Note:* Soak the beans overnight in cold water to cover by about 2 inches. A quicker method is to boil the beans in water to cover, as above, for 2 minutes, and set aside to soak for 1 hour. Cooking follows either method.
SAUTÉ 10–12 mins.	In a large (4-quart) saucepan, brown the shank(s) over medium-high heat. If the meat has little fat and sticks to the bottom of the pan, drop in a tablespoon of butter. Turn the meat several times so all sides get browned in 10 to 12 minutes.
BOIL/SIMMER 1 hour	Pour off any fat that has accumulated in the pan. Drain the beans and add them to the pot, along with the chicken stock, water, and crushed garlic clove. Cover partially, bring to a boil, and reduce heat so the soup simmers gently for about 1 hour.
30 mins.	In the meantime, prepare the onions, carrots, and celery and add to the pot at the end of the hour. Season to taste with salt and pepper. Continue cooking for an additional 30 minutes.
DEBONE	At the end of the cooking period, lift out the shank(s). Place on a cutting board and allow to cool for a few minutes. Pulling the meat from the bones with a fork will hasten the cooling process. Cut the meat into bite-size pieces, discarding cartilage and bones.
REHEAT	Return the meat pieces to the saucepan and reheat to serve.
FINAL STEP	Just before ladling the soup into a heated tureen or individual soup bowls, swirl in the 2 tablespoons of butter. Sprinkle with the mint to garnish.

Irish Stew

Serves 6 to 8

Irish stew is laid down in five layers—potato, onion, lamb pieces, onion, and, to top it off, another layer of potato. It is an economical dish that can be put together in about 2 hours, or simmered all day in a slow cooker. It is a marvelous stew for a cold blustery day when active kids (and guests) come to the table famished.

My Irish stew is cooked in a heavy black iron Dutch oven that has been in the family for years. At the table the stew is ladled directly from the Dutch oven into the individual bowls. The layers blend as the ladle dips down to the bottom and comes up brimful and steaming with good things. In Ireland I have watched the cook suspend a big iron pot over the turf fire in the fireplace while glowing red embers were put on the top of the lid to give extra heat from above.

The original Irish stew was made not from mutton or lamb, but from kid. Sheep were too valuable to be put into the pot for a poor man's family dinner. The young male kids had little value except for their skins, which were sold for a few pence. The flesh went into the stew pot.

INGREDIENTS	6 medium potatoes (about 2 pounds), peeled and sliced ½ inch thick
	4 large onions (1½ pounds), peeled and sliced ¼ inch thick
	3 pounds lean, boneless lamb, neck or shoulder, trimmed and cut into 1-inch cubes
	3 teaspoons salt, or as desired
	3 grindings of black pepper
	¼ teaspoon thyme
	Cold water to cover, about 5 cups
SPECIAL EQUIPMENT	Large (4-quart) casserole, Dutch oven, or kettle, with cover and suitable to bring to the table
PREPARATION LAYER	In the appropriate stew pot, arrange half the potatoes in a layer over the bottom. Add half the onions in a layer and then all of the lamb pieces. Season with salt, pepper, and thyme. Cover the lamb with the remaining onions and, finally, the balance of the potatoes.
	Pour in cold water to barely cover the last layer of potatoes, usually about 5 cups.
BOIL/SIMMER *1½ hours*	Bring the stew to a boil, cover, and simmer over low heat for about 1½ hours or until the vegetables and meat are tender. Check the stew occasionally and if the liquid seems to be cooking away, add water a tablespoon at a time.

OVEN
350°

Rather than cooking on top of the stove, the stew can be done in a 350° oven after having been brought to a boil as above. Look at the stew after the first half hour and reduce heat if it has come to an active boil rather than a gentle simmer.

FINAL STEP

Serve in heated bowls. A crusty peasant loaf is excellent to serve with Irish stew. If it's a family affair, dipping the bread into the stew may be allowed.

Scotch Broth

Serves 8

Scotch broth is not a broth but a stew of lamb and vegetables thickened with barley. In Scotland and all of the British Isles it is made more often with mutton, while in this country lamb is used for its more delicate taste and texture. I discovered this recipe in Pitlochry, a small town in the Highlands, where I found an equally delicious buttermilk bread. They are delicious together.

Adding the mushrooms to Scotch broth was the inspired touch of the noted food writer Craig Claiborne.

INGREDIENTS

2½ pounds stewing lamb, with bones (neck or breast)
1 beef marrowbone (about ½ pound)
2 quarts water
1 teaspoon salt (add more later if desired)
1 cup carrots (2 medium), peeled and thinly sliced
¾ cup white turnip (1 small), peeled and thinly sliced
½ cup celery (2 stalks), thinly sliced
1 cup onions (2 medium), peeled and thinly sliced
½ cup leek (1 small), washed well and thinly sliced
1 clove garlic, finely minced
1 bay leaf
½ cup quick-cooking pearl barley
¼ teaspoon freshly ground black pepper
¼ pound mushrooms
1½ teaspoons butter

SPECIAL
EQUIPMENT

None

PREPARATION	It is important that all the fat be cut away from the meat and discarded. Place the meat and bones in a large (4-quart) soup pot or saucepan and cover with cold water.
FIRST BOIL	Bring to a boil slowly and then immediately pour off the water. Rinse the meat under the cold water tap and return to the washed pot.
SECOND BOIL	Pour 2 quarts of water over the meat and bring to a second boil. Add all the vegetables, except the mushrooms. Add the bay leaf.
SIMMER *1 hour 30 mins.*	Turn the heat to low and simmer, partially covered, for 1 hour. Skim from time to time. After 1 hour, stir in the pearl barley and continue cooking for an additional 30 minutes. Remove the pot from the heat. Lift out the bones and meat and place on a cutting board. Pick the meat from the bones, cut into 1-inch chunks, and return to the soup pot. Discard the bones. The fat can be skimmed off while the broth is hot, or, if time allows, let the fat congeal at room temperature or in the refrigerator. Lift the congealed fat off with a slotted spoon and discard.
REHEAT	Reheat the broth and continue with the cooking. Add the pepper.
SAUTÉ	Brush or wipe the mushrooms clean if necessary. Heat the butter to foaming in a medium skillet. Thinly slice and sauté 2 mushrooms, which will be used to garnish the soup when served. Set them aside. Cut the remaining mushrooms into quarters and sauté.
SIMMER *15 mins.*	When the mushrooms are cooked to the point that they have lost their springiness, transfer them to the soup pot. Continue simmering the broth for 15 more minutes.
FINAL STEP	Ladle the hot broth into heated bowls and garnish with the slices of sautéed mushrooms. Serve.

Lamb Soup with Egg and Lemon (Greek)
Arni Soupa Avgolemono

Serves 6

Egg and lemon combine in a sauce that gives this hearty lamb soup a special Hellenic fillip. It is a pleasing dish to set before a guest—brown bits of lamb bubbling about in a creamy white soup.

Another Greek touch is manestra *or* kritharaki, *perhaps better known by its Italian name,* orzo—*a pasta that looks like cantaloupe seeds and is widely used in soups and main dishes. If orzo is not readily available, substitute other small pasta or rice.*

INGREDIENTS

¼ cup olive oil

3 pounds lean shoulder of lamb, cut into 1-inch chunks

2 pounds lamb bones, cut into 2-inch pieces

2 stalks celery, chopped

1 large onion, sliced

1 carrot, chopped

10 cups cold water

Sachet d'épice

2 teaspoons dried rosemary

1 teaspoon dried thyme

1 bay leaf

8 peppercorns

6 sprigs parsley

½ teaspoon salt

½ cup orzo (see above) or rice

5 eggs

½ cup lemon juice

½ cup heavy cream

¼ cup snipped fresh dill

6 sprigs mint, to garnish

SPECIAL
EQUIPMENT

Chinois or other strainer

PREPARATION
COOK
5 mins. each

Pour olive oil into a large saucepan or kettle and lightly brown the lamb pieces and bones over medium to high heat for about 5 minutes. It may be necessary to brown them in more than one batch.

SWEAT
8 mins.

Remove the browned meat and bones from the pot with a slotted spoon and set aside. Place the prepared celery, onion, and carrot in the pot, cover, and sweat for about 8 minutes over medium heat.

BOIL/SIMMER
*1½ hours
approximately*

Return the lamb and bones to the kettle; add cold water and sachet of spices. Cover. Slowly bring the soup to a boil, reduce heat, and simmer for about 1½ hours or until the meat is tender. The time will depend on the quality of meat. Skim off froth as it rises to the surface.

STRAIN	When the meat is cooked, pour the contents of the kettle through a chinois or other strainer. Pick out the meat pieces and reserve. Press the juice out of the vegetables.
CHILL	Chill the stock. Lift off and discard the fat. If there isn't time to chill, carefully skim the fat off the surface.
BOIL/SIMMER 15 mins.	Bring the stock to a boil in a saucepan; add lamb pieces and pasta or rice. Simmer, covered, for about 15 minutes or until the pasta or rice is tender.
8 mins.	Beat eggs in a bowl until thick and light. Add lemon juice and 1 cup of hot stock in a slow stream, beating constantly. Combine with cream and slowly pour the mixture into the saucepan, stirring constantly. Simmer for about 8 minutes. Do not boil, or the eggs will curdle, making a less than attractive soup.
FINAL STEP	Stir in the dill and taste for additional salt and pepper. Pour the hot soup into a heated tureen and ladle into hot bowls. Garnish each bowl with a sprig of mint.

Lamb-Barley Soup

Serves 5

Small pieces of lamb from the shank, cooked in a barley broth, make a flavorful soup for serving on a cold, blustery day in ski country or in a snowbound townhouse in Manhattan.
Make no mistake—this has a strong lamb flavor that will please a lover of lamb. It is a near cousin to Scotch broth but not as thick.

INGREDIENTS	5 cups water
	2 lamb shanks (about 1½ pounds)
	¼ cup pearl barley
	1 bay leaf
	2 whole cloves
	1 medium onion, coarsely chopped
	1 garlic clove, mashed
	1 medium carrot, peeled and grated
	1 large stalk celery, thinly sliced
	½ teaspoon salt, if desired
	¼ teaspoon freshly ground black pepper
	½ cup chopped parsley, to garnish

SPECIAL EQUIPMENT	None
PREPARATION BOIL/SIMMER 1½ hours	Pour water into a medium (3-quart) saucepan; bring to a boil and add lamb, barley, bay leaf, and cloves. Simmer, covered, until meat is tender and can easily be taken from the bones, about 1½ hours.
BOIL 15 mins.	Remove lamb from bones, discard bones and tough pieces of gristle, and reserve the meat. Remove bay leaf and cloves and discard. Add onion, garlic, carrot, and celery to the soup. Boil gently until vegetables are tender, about 15 minutes.
SIMMER 10 mins.	Meanwhile cut the lamb into bite-size pieces. Return to the soup and allow to simmer together with the other ingredients for about 10 minutes. Season to taste.
FINAL STEP	Serve soup in hot bowls and garnish with parsley. Serve with big chunks of French bread or other peasant bread (see "Two Breads," page 360).

Greek Lamb Stew

Serves 6

Greek lamb stew is worth one of the best cuts of lamb—the leg. No need to buy the entire leg, since most markets now sell pieces or the butcher will cut a leg in half if you ask. The chunks from the leg are sweet and tender.

The stew is ladled on top of a mound of rice when served. Delicious.

Why not lamb stock for lamb stew? I find beef stock with lamb to be milder and more appetizing.

INGREDIENTS	2 pounds boneless lamb, cubed
	⅓ cup flour
	1 teaspoon salt, if desired
	½ teaspoon freshly ground black pepper
	¼ cup olive oil
	8 small white onions, fresh and peeled, or canned
	2½ cups beef stock
	1 8-ounce can tomato sauce
	½ teaspoon (or more) cinnamon
	1 teaspoon oregano
	2 cups cubed eggplant

(continued)

½ pound green beans, ends trimmed, and beans cut into 1-inch pieces
Rice, cooked to accompany

SPECIAL EQUIPMENT	None
PREPARATION	*Beforehand:* Trim fat from lamb and cut meat into ¾-inch cubes or ask the butcher to do so.
DREDGE 3 mins.	Mix flour, salt, and pepper on a piece of wax paper or in a pie pan. Dredge the lamb cubes in the flour, shaking off the excess.
COOK 8 mins. 5 mins.	Heat oil in a medium saucepan, casserole, or Dutch oven with lid. Drop the lamb pieces into the oil and cook uncovered, stirring frequently, until the meat is a crusty brown. Remove the meat with a slotted spoon and set aside. Drop the onions into the vessel and partially cook for about 5 minutes. Stir them around as they cook.

Return the meat to the vessel and add ¾ cup of stock, tomato sauce, ½ teaspoon of cinnamon, and the oregano. |
| SIMMER 1¼ hours 30 mins. | Cover vessel and over low heat simmer for about 1¼ hours or until the meat is fork-tender. Bubbles should come slowly up through the stew.

Stir in the eggplant, beans, and remaining 1¾ cups of stock. Stir frequently to prevent the stew from sticking to the bottom of the pan. Cook until the vegetables are tender, about 30 minutes over low heat.

More cinnamon may be added, but taste before doing so. Check other seasonings as well. |
| RICE | While the stew is cooking, prepare the rice. |
| FINAL STEP | Bring the lamb stew to the table in its cooking vessel. Ladle the stew over the rice in large shallow bowls or deep-sided plates. |

Seafood

FOR THE KITCHEN there are two kinds of fish—finfish and shellfish. Finfish include all edible saltwater and freshwater fish possessing fins. Shellfish are the crustacea (lobster, crayfish, shrimp, crab) and the mollusks (clams, oysters, scallops). All these fish are rich in nutritive value and are an excellent source of protein, vitamins, and minerals. In soups and stews they are a perpetual source of pleasure to the cook and the diner alike.

Fish and Mussel Soup *Normandie*

Serves 6 to 8

The shellfish in this soup are the base for the broth in which the fish is cooked. The French serve this thrifty and delicious soup with a spicy and garlicky rouille (page 366), stirred into it at the table. This recipe has the rouille built into the soup as part of the dish itself.

A touch of hot red pepper adds spiciness while tomatoes give the soup a warm pink color to show off the white fish pieces. This is an excellent soup that can be prepared in less than an hour. Serve it with garlic croutons; southern-style corn sticks, though not French, are surprisingly complementary.

INGREDIENTS *Note:* If mussels are in short supply, substitute bottled clam juice, fish stock, or light chicken broth.

1½ pounds mussels, scrubbed and bearded
1 cup water
1 teaspoon saffron threads, optional
¼ cup olive oil
1½ cups finely chopped onions
1 cup *each* finely sliced celery and peeled carrots
4 cups water
1 cup red wine
4 cups fresh or canned tomatoes, peeled, seeded,
   and finely chopped
1 teaspoon dried thyme
2 bay leaves
1 hot red pepper, ground or crushed
Salt to taste, if desired
½ teaspoon freshly ground black pepper
1 tablespoon finely chopped garlic
2½ to 3 pounds of at least 2 kinds of fish, cut into 1½-inch pieces

Note: The fish may be chosen from among cod, haddock, red snapper, sea
bass, sole, dab, flounder, mullet, catfish, and others that are not oily.

½ cup finely chopped parsley, to garnish

SPECIAL EQUIPMENT	Steamer for mussels, optional. Cheesecloth, to strain.
PREPARATION	*Broth*

Scrub the mussels with a stiff brush or a steel-mesh scouring pad. With a knife scrape or pull the black tufts off the shells and discard them. Discard the mussels that are open and, after steaming, those that are still closed.

Pour 1 cup of water into a medium (4-quart) saucepan or kettle. Cover and bring to a boil. Add the mussels.

STEAM
3–4 mins.

Replace cover and steam for 3 to 4 minutes until the shells have fully opened. Remove the pot from the heat and allow to cool before slipping each mussel out of its shell. Place the meat in a bowl and keep warm. Discard the shells.

STRAIN

Strain the mussel juice into another bowl through a double thickness of moistened cheesecloth. Reserve for the moment.

Pour ½ cup of the hot broth over the saffron threads in a bowl. Allow them to soak for a few minutes.

Rinse the saucepan for the next step.

Soup

SMOTHER   Pour the olive oil into the saucepan and heat over a medium flame. Add the onions, celery, and carrots; cover and cook for 10 minutes or until the vegetables are soft and translucent.

BOIL/SIMMER   Pour in the reserved stock, water, and wine and bring to a boil. Add
10 mins.   tomatoes, thyme, bay leaves, red pepper, salt, black pepper, and garlic. Return to a boil, turn the heat down to low, cover, and simmer for
25 mins.   25 minutes. Discard the bay leaves.

Cut the fish into 1½-inch pieces while the soup is simmering.

5 mins.   Add the fish, and when the soup has returned to the simmer, cook for 5 minutes. Add the steeped saffron threads and their broth. If the soup is quite thick at this stage, thin with additional wine or water.

Remove the saucepan from the heat and drop in the reserved mussels. They will quickly warm in the hot soup.

FINAL STEP   Serve the soup in large bowls with garlic croutons either in it or on the side, or with corn sticks. Garnish with parsley.

Cioppino, a Seafood Stew

Serves 6 to 8

Cioppino is to the Italian fishing colony in San Francisco what bouillabaisse is to the French fishermen in Marseille. Both are seafood stews. Created by Italian fishermen who settled in California, many from Genoa, cioppino takes its name from the word for fish stew in Genoese dialect. Cioppino is a combined treasure of fish and shellfish.

Seldom are cioppino ingredients the same because much depends on what is available from the sea that day. If clams are not to be had, increase the number of mussels. If crab is scarce, substitute lobster tails. Nothing is sacred. The end result, whatever its makeup, will be delicious.

It is a minor exercise in logistics to bring everything to fruition at the moment of presentation at the table, but with a little planning it can be done with great success.

With all seafood, there is a precise moment when it is exquisitely cooked; from that point on it is all downhill (or downstream). Better to undercook the fish and mollusks than to over-

cook. Don't give in to the temptation to let seafood steam or cook another moment because you fear it might not be done. Be firm with yourself. Remember, the seafood will continue to cook in the hot broth even after it is removed from the heat.

The preparation is in three parts: first, the making of the fish stock from the fish frames, i.e., the heads and skeletons of the filleted fish to be used in the cioppino; second, making the sauce or broth in which the seafood is to be cooked; and third, cooking the seafood. The third and final step presents an option: The mollusks may be (1) steamed and the upper shell discarded beforehand, or (2) added to the soup pot as part of the final preparation.

INGREDIENTS

Seafood

3 pounds fillets from firm white-fleshed fish such as red snapper, sea bass, halibut, etc., *plus* frames of these fish to make the stock (page 22)

1 pound jumbo shrimp, shelled and deveined

1 large cooked Dungeness crab or cooked lobster

2 dozen or so mussels in their shells

2 dozen or so small hard-shell clams in their shells

(Keep within the broad framework for cioppino, but don't hesitate to substitute, add, or delete.)

Sauce (in which seafood will be cooked)

⅓ cup olive oil

2 cups finely chopped onions

3 cloves garlic, finely chopped

1 cup finely chopped green peppers

2 pounds ripe tomatoes, peeled, seeded, and chopped, or 1 1-pound-12-ounce can tomatoes

1 15-ounce can tomato puree

2 cups red wine

4 tablespoons chopped parsley

4 cups fish stock (homemade) or clam juice

Salt, if desired, and freshly ground black pepper

Several dashes of Tabasco, to taste

½ cup minced parsley, to garnish

SPECIAL EQUIPMENT

Large pots

PREPARATION

Stock

Use fish frames (heads, tails, bones) to make fish stock. Set aside. This can be done a day or so in advance and refrigerated.

Note: The balance of the seafood does not go into the cioppino in the order of the ingredients as listed. They are grouped to facilitate shopping.

SAUTÉ
15 mins.

Sauce

Pour olive oil into a large 4-quart saucepan and over medium heat sauté onions, garlic, and green peppers until they are tender, about 15 minutes.

BOIL/SIMMER
30 mins.

Add the chopped tomatoes, tomato puree, wine, and parsley and 4 cups of the reserved fish stock (or clam juice). Bring to a boil, lower heat, and simmer for 30 minutes. Remove from heat and set aside.

Seafood

Note: The mussels and clams may be steamed earlier, and the top shell removed and discarded. The other half of the shell, with the meat and the broth, is set aside. This cuts down on the bulk of shells in the final assembly and at the table. (Traditionally, the uncooked clams and mussels are added at the last moment, their juices blending with the sauce.)

Prepare the clams and mussels by scrubbing with a stiff brush under cold running water and remove the black ropelike tufts—the beards— from the mussel shells.

STEAM
4–5 mins.

To prepare the mussels and clams in advance, place an inverted pie pan on the bottom of a large kettle and pour in a cup or so of water—just to the edge of the pan. Arrange the mollusks on the pan, cover tightly, and bring to a boil. Stir or vigorously shake the kettle so they will steam and open uniformly. Steam briefly—only until the shells open—about 4 to 5 minutes.

Allow to cool. Break off the top shell and discard. Reserve the shell with the meat and the liquor—which must be strained to remove sand and possible broken pieces of shell. Discard any mollusks that remain closed.

15 mins.

To prepare the shrimp, cut up the back of the shell with scissors. Peel, leaving only the end of the tail, which makes a good handle for holding later. Devein.

10 mins.

To prepare the cooked crab, lift off the large top shell and discard. Under cold running water wash away spongy gray material and the intestines in the center. Turn the crab over and pry off the pointed flap or apron. Holding the crab in both hands, break into two pieces. Break off

3 mins.
each leg. Crack each joint with a nutcracker or pliers. (This can be done a day in advance and the crab refrigerated.)

Cut the fish into 3-inch pieces and set aside.

To Assemble
This demands a large kettle or casserole with cover, 8 to 10 quarts.

COOK
Arrange the crab on the bottom of the kettle. Lay the mussels and clams on top and pour in the tomato sauce.

BOIL/SIMMER
12–15 mins.
8–10 mins.
Bring to a boil over high heat, reduce the heat to low, cover tightly, and cook for 12 to 15 minutes. Add the fish and shrimp and continue to cook for 8 to 10 minutes longer.

The cioppino is done when the fish flakes easily when prodded gently with a fork.

REST
5 mins.
Allow the cioppino to rest for 5 minutes. Taste for seasoning. Add salt, pepper, and Tabasco, if needed.

FINAL STEP
The fish and shellfish may be arranged on a large platter and served, with the broth ladled separately. Sprinkle liberally with minced parsley.

Furnish guests with bibs as well as large napkins because fingers are expected to augment forks.

Pass nutcrackers and picks to get meat out of stubborn crab shells.

Serve with hot crusty peasant bread in big chunks, plenty of butter, and a hearty red wine.

And you will have a taste of San Francisco!

Clam Soup

Serves 4

In many kitchens clams are served only on the half shell or as the principal ingredient of a great chowder. Seldom are they considered as a base for a lovely cream soup, a velouté, fine for brunch, luncheon, or the first course of a dinner.

This is an adaptation of a recipe by my friend Chef Pierre Franey, who was also a food columnist for The New York Times *and a cookbook author. Together we stood overlooking the waters of Long Island Sound where, among other things, we talked about clams, which he harvests very near his East Hampton home.*

The size of the clam determines which of two ways to make Pierre's soup. If the clams are small—littlenecks or cherrystones—the shelled meat may be served intact as a garnish. That was Pierre's way. If the clams are larger (and most are, in my local seafood market), turn to the food processor, which will quickly reduce the largest and most formidable-looking clam to a delicate puree.

INGREDIENTS	36 to 48 clams, the smaller the better
	2 tablespoons butter
	2 tablespoons finely chopped shallots
	¼ cup finely chopped onion
	1 clove garlic, finely minced
	½ teaspoon finely chopped fresh thyme, or ¼ teaspoon dried
	½ teaspoon hot red pepper or whole pod
	1 tablespoon cornstarch
	2 cups dry white wine
	1 egg yolk
	1 cup heavy cream
	Salt and freshly ground black pepper, if desired
	¼ cup chopped fresh basil

SPECIAL EQUIPMENT

Food processor or blender—the latter makes the soup very creamy.

PREPARATION

Scrub the clams, rinse well, and drain.

SWEAT
6–8 mins.

In a large (4-quart) saucepan, heat the butter until it foams and add the shallots, onion, and garlic. Stir to blend. Cover and sweat over medium heat until the vegetables are tender, about 6 to 8 minutes. Stir occasionally so vegetables do not brown or burn.

Uncover and add thyme and hot red pepper and sprinkle with the cornstarch. Stir. Add the wine and stir to blend. Bring to a boil.

BOIL
6–8 mins.

Drop the clams into the pot, cover tightly, and return to a boil over medium heat. Let cook 6 to 8 minutes, stirring occasionally, until the clams are open.

With a slotted spoon remove clams to a bowl or pan to cool a bit before taking out the meat. Discard clams that do not open.

Also discard red pepper if it was used whole rather than crushed.

In the meantime, blend the egg yolk and cream. Add this mixture to the soup, stirring.

PUREE

If the clams are small you may wish to serve them in the soup as a garnish. If not, put the meat in the work bowl of a food processor or blender and puree.

REHEAT

Add the clam puree to the soup and bring just to a bubble. Remove from the heat immediately; it should not boil.

Caution: Don't add salt to the soup until the puree has been blended in. The soup always *seems* saltier afterward. Also taste for pepper. It is not likely to need much, because of the other seasonings.

FINAL STEP

Spoon immediately into hot bowls, sprinkle with basil, and serve with crusty French bread.

Crab Soup

Serves 6 to 8

There is an elegance about crab soup. It looks elegant. The smell of it is elegant. It tastes elegant. It is proper for an elegant brunch, lunch, or first course of any other elegant meal.

The soup is expensive, as are all crab dishes—lump crabmeat at a good fish store is pricey, but for the proper, elegant affair, it's worth the money.

Crabmeat comes from several types of edible crabs. The big solid chunks are usually reserved for cocktails and salads, where texture and appearance are important. Meat for this soup is the small pieces known as back fin. The third grade is flake meat—flakes and shreds are also suitable for soup. But as the pieces get smaller it becomes more difficult to extract all of the bits and pieces of shell.

She-crab soup, a special delight in southern coastal states, is simply the addition of roe carried by the female. In some coastal areas, however, the egg-carrying females must be returned to the water to keep the breed ongoing. Lacking roe, a tablespoon of mashed hard-cooked egg yolk may be substituted.

INGREDIENTS

1 pound crabmeat (and roe, if available)
4 tablespoons butter
1 tablespoon flour
2 cups milk
2 cups light cream
1 teaspoon Worcestershire sauce
2 teaspoons grated lemon rind
⅛ teaspoon ground mace
1 teaspoon salt, if desired
¼ teaspoon freshly ground white pepper
5 soda crackers (saltines)
3 to 4 tablespoons sherry
3 to 4 hard-cooked egg yolks—if roe not available

½ cup whipping cream, whipped, to garnish
Paprika, to garnish

SPECIAL
EQUIPMENT

Double boiler (improvise one, if necessary)

PREPARATION

Crab: Almost all crabmeat picked from the shell, whether this is done by the expert or the novice, has its share of bits and pieces of shell and cartilage—some more, some less. Pick over the crab carefully, feeling for the little hard pieces. Some are certain to slip by, it seems.

Note: The secret of this soup, like so many other cream- and milk-based soups, is not to bring it to a boil; that is the reason for the double boiler. (It can be made directly over the heat, however, but this requires great care. Stand over it.) This soup is almost too much for my 1½-quart glass double boiler, so I improvise with a small pot resting on a metal trivet in a larger pot, and I add an inch or so of water. *Voilà!*

COOK
20 mins.

In the top of the double boiler, melt the butter and blend in the flour. Add milk and cream, stirring constantly. Add the Worcestershire sauce, lemon rind, mace, and crabmeat (plus roe, if you have it). Stirring frequently, cook over a gentle boil (which occurs in the lower part of pot) for about 20 minutes.

SEASON

Season with salt and pepper.

THICKENER

Place the crackers between sheets of wax paper and crush with a rolling pin. Add to the soup and blend well.

KEEP HOT
10–15 mins.

Lift the double boiler off the heat and move to the back of the stove. Allow to stand over the hot water for an additional 10 to 15 minutes before serving.

FINAL STEP

Serve in heated soup bowls. Add ½ tablespoon of sherry to each bowl. If no roe has been added, stir in ½ tablespoon of egg yolk, pressed through a sieve. Top with a dollop of cream. Sprinkle with paprika. Elegant!

Creole Crabmeat Soup

Serves 4 to 6

Creole Crabmeat Soup is a close cousin to a recipe from a New Orleans cookbook, The Picayune Cookbook, *first published in 1901 and, more than a hundred years later, given new life by food writer Julia Reed.*

Today's soup is made infinitely easier by the availability of fresh lump crabmeat already out of the shell.

The soup itself, without the crabmeat, is so good that the crab seems to come along for the ride (or swim).

I have also made it with shrimp. Whichever, it is delicious.

INGREDIENTS	2 large lemons
	3 tablespoons butter
	1 medium onion, chopped
	2 cloves garlic, minced
	4 cups fresh or canned Italian tomatoes, seeded and chopped, with their juice
	4 cups fish stock or clam juice
	1 bay leaf
	1 large sprig parsley
	1 sprig marjoram
	1 tablespoon chopped tarragon
	2 tablespoons chopped mint
	1 pound lump crabmeat
	Salt to taste
	Pinch of cayenne pepper or more to taste

PREPARATION
20 mins.

Using a vegetable peeler, remove the zest from 1 lemon in one long strip, if possible; this makes it easier to retrieve later. Set aside. Juice the peeled lemon; set aside. Thinly cut the remaining lemon into 4 to 6 slices; set aside for garnish.

SWEAT
6 mins.

Melt the butter in a medium (4½-quart) saucepan over medium heat and sweat the onions and garlic until translucent and somewhat tender.

BOIL/SIMMER
1 hour

Add the tomatoes, with their juice, and stock. Bring to a boil over medium-high heat. Reduce the heat to low and simmer. Add the bay leaf, parsley, marjoram, tarragon, and 1 tablespoon of the mint. Add the lemon zest and lemon juice.

10 mins.

Add the crabmeat and simmer gently for 10 minutes. Don't allow to boil. Add salt and cayenne. Discard the bay leaf and parsley.

FINAL STEP

Stir in the remaining tablespoon of mint. Top off each serving with a thin slice of lemon.

Billi-bi

Serves 4 or 5

Billi-bi is a rich, elegant bisque made with the least of the shellfish—the mussel, which hardly has the stature of an oyster or a clam. This soup is named for a customer of Ciro's, a famous Parisian restaurant. In 1925 he asked the chef to create a dish with the essence and good flavor of mussels, but without the mussels. This creamy and velvety bisque, served hot or cold, was the happy result.

This recipe for an especially creamy billi-bi (pronounced to rhyme with sea*) came from the kitchen of the LaGrange restaurant in the Homestead Inn in Greenwich, Connecticut. It was given to me by Jacques Thiebeult, who ruled the kitchen of one of the most beautiful inn-restaurants in the country.*

INGREDIENTS	**4 pounds mussels, washed and scrubbed**
	1½ cups white wine
	2 tablespoons chopped onion
	½ cup chopped shallots
	2 sprigs fresh parsley
	½ bay leaf
	Salt, to taste, if desired
	White pepper to taste
	2 cups heavy cream
	2 cups light cream or half-and-half
	1 egg yolk, lightly beaten
	Sprigs of fresh parsley or snippets of chives, to garnish
SPECIAL EQUIPMENT	Chinois or colander and cheesecloth
PREPARATION	Scrub mussels under running water to remove sand and beards.
BOIL *4 mins.*	Into a large kettle, pour wine and put in onions, shallots, parsley, and bay leaf. Boil over high heat to reduce liquid by half, about 4 minutes.
6 mins.	Add mussels, cover, and cook over medium heat until the shells open, about 6 minutes. Remove from heat and pour through a chinois or colander to remove mussels and other solids. Put the mussels aside for the moment.
	Strain the broth again, this time through a double thickness of moistened cheesecloth.
	Note: For the authentic billi-bi remove mussels for another use. Or a

few mussels may be taken from their shells and used as a garnish for the soup. A variation is billi-bi chowder, in which the mussels in their shells are served in the soup.

BOIL
5 mins.
approximately,
but watch
closely

Bring the strained liquid to a boil in a medium (3½-quart) saucepan over medium heat. Taste for salt and add white pepper. Add the cream and return just to the boil. Immediately remove from the heat. In a small bowl add a cup of the bisque to the beaten egg. Blend well and pour back into the saucepan of bisque. Return to the heat long enough for the soup to thicken slightly. Do not boil.

FINAL STEP

Pour into heated bowls and drop a tiny sprig of parsley or a few chive snippets onto each serving. Or chill, if to be served cold.

Mussel and Shrimp Soup (French)
Potage Dieppoise

Serves 4

A mussel is a blue-black jewel among shellfish, yet it is not appreciated as such in this country. Lobster, crab, shrimp, and scallops outrank it by far. But the popularity of this sleek and tender mollusk is growing as Americans realize what the Europeans have known for centuries—the mussel is delicious. It is also inexpensive.

Potage dieppoise is a combination of mussels and shrimp or fish in a rich golden soup touched delicately with garlic. It can be savored in restaurants and cafés along the coast of Normandy.

The shapely elongated shells hold a bite-size creamy morsel. The mollusk is characterized by its "beard," which is a mass of slender but tough threads spun in a special gland and cast out to grab a foothold in the ocean. Most cooks pull off and discard the beard but some leave it on to flavor the cooking stock.

Mussels for centuries have been held in high esteem in Europe, where they are cultivated on ropes dangling from acres of rafts anchored in the sea. But only recently have such off-bottom growing techniques been introduced on the East Coast of the United States to produce cleaner, healthier mussels.

INGREDIENTS

36 mussels (about 2 pounds)
3 cups Fish Stock (page 22) or high-quality clam broth
2 tablespoons finely chopped fresh parsley
2 tablespoons Cognac or good brandy
1 tablespoon arrowroot or cornstarch

2 tablespoons water

1 teaspoon finely minced garlic

3 tablespoons butter

Salt, if desired (I use about 1 teaspoon)

¼ teaspoon freshly ground black pepper

¾ cup light cream

1 pound shrimp, cooked and shelled, or 1 pound *each* of two kinds of
    fish—fillets of sole, flounder, halibut, or haddock

2 raw egg yolks

2 tablespoons water

1 cup freshly toasted or sautéed croutons, to garnish

SPECIAL EQUIPMENT	Cheesecloth, to strain
PREPARATION	Scrub mussels in cold running water and remove stringy beards. Discard any mussels that are broken, open, or empty.
STEAM 4–5 mins.	Into a large (8-quart) stockpot, pour the fish stock and bring to a boil. Add the mussels, cover tightly, and steam over medium heat for 4 to 5 minutes or until shells have opened. Stir once or twice during the steaming. Remove mussels from the broth. Discard any that have failed to open. The mussels are to be served on the half shell, so discard the empty half of each mussel. Put the full halves together in a bowl. Sprinkle with parsley and Cognac. Cover with foil to keep warm while the rest of the soup is prepared.
STRAIN	Strain the mussel broth through a double thickness of moistened cheesecloth and return the liquor to the pot.
SIMMER	Dissolve the arrowroot or cornstarch in 2 tablespoons of water and stir into the stock. Bring to a simmer, stirring the broth until it thickens slightly.
SAUTÉ 4 mins.	In a small skillet, sauté the garlic in the butter over medium heat for about 4 minutes. Scrape the mixture into the soup pot and stir together.\n Taste for seasoning.\n Slowly stir in the cream.\n If shrimp are to be used, add them and the reserved mussels to the broth at the same time. No further cooking is required except to reheat.
POACH 5 mins.	If fish, rather than shrimp, are to be added, cut the fillets into 2-inch pieces. Drop them into the pot. Allow about 10 minutes for fillet pieces

10 mins.	1 inch thick to poach. Thinner pieces will be poached in 5 minutes or less. When the fish is poached, return mussels to the soup to reheat for about 2 to 3 minutes. Simmer only. Do not let the soup boil.
REHEAT	Beat the egg yolks together with water. Remove the pot from the heat and slowly stir in the egg-water mixture. Reheat but do not boil.
FINAL STEP	Taste again for seasoning. Serve with buttered croutons. Absolutely delicious.

Fish Ball and Watercress Soup (Chinese)

Serves 4 or 5

A delicate and delicious offering at any meal, Chinese or other, is this Fish Ball and Watercress Soup. The recipe came from Ken Hom, one of the country's best Chinese chef-authors. He and I shared the food adventure at Craig Claiborne's birthday-and-autograph affair on Long Island.

A food processor is a tremendous time-saver, whirling the fish into a smooth paste in a fraction of the time it would take to first chop the fish with a cleaver or knife, and then put it through a food mill to remove any filaments.

The paste is used for many of the classic Chinese dishes besides fish balls.

When the fish balls are formed, they are moist and somewhat sticky, but after 1 or 2 minutes in simmering water they are cooked and firm.

INGREDIENTS	*Fish Balls* (makes 20 to 24)
	¾ pound fish fillets (rock cod, sea bass, or any white-fleshed fish)
	2 tablespoons dry sherry (or *shao hsing* wine)
	2 tablespoons minced scallions
	1 teaspoon sesame oil
	3 tablespoons finely chopped ham fat or chicken fat
	(a blender may be used for this)
	Salt to taste, if desired (1½ teaspoons is the usual amount)
	1 egg white
	2 tablespoons cornstarch
	1 tablespoon cold chicken stock
	Soup
	4 cups chicken broth
	Salt to taste, if desired

¼ teaspoon freshly ground black pepper
1 cup loosely packed watercress or spinach leaves, chopped coarsely
Fish balls, above

SPECIAL EQUIPMENT	Food processor, blender, or food mill (if chopped by hand). One bowl of ice water to cool and moisten hands while forming balls.
PREPARATION PROCESS *5 mins.*	*Fish Paste/Balls* Process the fish into a smooth paste. (Don't process or blend the other ingredients into a puree, or the paste will be too smooth and bland. However, if the fat is firm, it may need to be processed.) Add the remaining ingredients and stir the mixture together with a large spoon or, even better, by hand, forcing it between the fingers to mix it well.
CHILL *15–20 mins.*	Place the paste in the refrigerator for 15 or 20 minutes to stiffen. In the meantime bring to a simmer enough water to completely cover the fish balls when they first sink to the bottom. Fill a bowl with ice and water in which to dip the hands before working with the paste. This will make it much easier to manage.
FORM	Place about 3 tablespoons of the fish paste in one hand and squeeze out a small amount into a spoon held in the other hand. Pat and mold into a 1-inch ball. Set aside.
SIMMER *1–2 mins.*	Shape 10 or 12 balls before carefully dropping them into the simmering water. When they rise to the surface (in a surprisingly short time), lift them out with a slotted spoon. Set the balls aside in a bowl with some of the stock to keep them warm. Continue with the remainder of the mixture.
SIMMER BLANCH	*Soup* Heat the chicken broth to simmering over low heat in a medium (3-quart) saucepan. Add salt, if desired. In a small saucepan, pour boiling water over the watercress or spinach leaves to blanch. Drain off the hot water and plunge into cold water. Drain and reserve.
SIMMER	Drop the fish balls carefully into the hot broth and simmer for 1 to 2 minutes to reheat.
FINAL STEP	To serve, place a few of the blanched leaves in each serving bowl and ladle in the hot broth and fish balls. Serve immediately. This soup will be just as delicious if held 1 or 2 days.

French Oyster Soup

Serves 6

For those who especially love seafood, this oyster stew made with fish stock is a double reward.
The fine cookery author Jane Grigson found this soup in L'AberWrach, on the French Chan-nel coast north of Brest. Later my wife and I bicycled there in search of recipes.
Mussels may be substituted for oysters. Steam open over high heat in a pan with a cover and add their liquor to the soup.

INGREDIENTS	½ pound leeks, white part only, chopped
	4 tablespoons butter
	I medium potato, diced
	4 cups Fish Stock (see page 22)
	I quart oysters, shucked, or mussels (steamed open) and their liquor
	I cup heavy cream
	2 tablespoons chopped parsley, to garnish

SPECIAL EQUIPMENT	Food processor, blender, or food mill

PREPARATION 10 mins. COOK 15–20 mins.	Cook the leeks in butter in a skillet over low heat until translucent, about 10 minutes. Put leeks and diced potato into the fish stock in a large (4-quart) stockpot. Cook stock and vegetables over medium heat for 15 to 20 minutes or until vegetables are soft. Remove from heat.

PUREE 5 mins.	When the leeks and potato have cooled somewhat, put them through a food processor, blender, or food mill. Set aside the puree.

COOK 2 mins.	Pour the oysters or mussels and their liquor into a shallow frying pan and cook gently, stirring frequently, until edges curl, about 2 minutes. Drain the liquor into the pureed vegetables. Pour the cream into the oysters in the skillet. Bring to just below a boil. Remove from heat; add to the pureed mixture gradually.

FINAL STEP	Pour the soup into a large, heated tureen and sprinkle with parsley. Serve in warm bowls. Rye bread is a good accompaniment.

Stone Crabber Oyster Stew

Serves 4

Bake a pan of corn bread to begin this uncommon stew. The choice will probably be yellow cornmeal in the North, and white in the South. The oysters will follow in due course.

The stew, coarse-looking but fine-tasting, was created years ago in Apalachee Bay in the Gulf of Mexico, south of Tallahassee. At low tide women waded out on the sandbars to harvest oysters. At noontime they came ashore, built a fire to warm themselves, and cooked their meal. Oysters were shucked, then dropped into a tin can or bucket along with a piece of fatback and chopped onions. Corn bread, brought from home, was added to the pot.

The original recipe has been changed only with the addition of milk rather than water.

INGREDIENTS	½ stick butter or 4 bacon slices, cut into small pieces
	2½ cups oysters and their liquor
	2 cups crumbled corn bread
	1 cup milk, approximately
	Salt, if desired, and freshly ground black pepper to taste
	Dash of Tabasco or other hot sauce
	1 medium onion, chopped
	Choice of garnishes: slivers of pimiento, chopped parsley, chopped chives, or light dusting of paprika
SPECIAL EQUIPMENT	None
PREPARATION	*Note:* Bake the pan of corn bread beforehand using yellow or white cornmeal.
SAUTÉ 10 mins.	If using butter, sauté the chopped onions; if bacon, fry it and the onions together.
	While the onions are cooking, separate the oysters from their liquor. If oysters are large, cut in half. There will be about a cup of liquor to set aside.
COOK 3 mins.	Pour the oysters into the onion-butter (or onion-bacon) mixture and cook until the edges curl, about 3 minutes—no longer, or they will get tough. Add oyster liquor and crumbled corn bread. Pour in the milk. Blend the ingredients and heat until steaming. Remove immediately from the heat. Season with salt if desired, black pepper, and Tabasco.
	If the stew seems thick, add more milk. If thin, add corn bread crumbs.

FINAL STEP   Ladle into heated soup bowls and top with one of the garnishes. Serve additional corn bread with the stew.

Oyster Stew

Serves 4

This is a straightforward presentation of oysters, with no intrusion by other flavors—an oyster-lover's stew.

At the turn of the twentieth century express trains from the Atlantic coast rushed seafood to cities, towns, and hamlets in Middle America. My mother's kitchen was one terminus, particularly for oysters, in this vast distribution network.

At our table the family's favorite garnish was a big dab of butter swirled over the surface of the stew at the moment it was ladled. A large bowl of crisp oyster crackers stood by. There was nothing better, as I remember.

This is my mother's recipe, simple but very good.

INGREDIENTS
1 pint oysters, with their liquor
3 cups light cream
1 cup scalded milk
Pinch of cayenne pepper
½ teaspoon salt, if desired
4 tablespoons unsalted butter, at room temperature
Sprinkles of paprika

SPECIAL
EQUIPMENT   None

PREPARATION   Pour the liquor off the oysters; reserve.

COOK
5 mins.   Combine in a bowl the cream, milk, cayenne pepper, and salt. In a medium (3-quart) saucepan, melt 2 tablespoons of butter over medium heat and add the oysters. Cook gently, stirring occasionally, until they plump, about 5 minutes.

3–4 mins.   Pour the reserved oyster liquor and the cream/milk mixture into the saucepan. Heat the stew, stirring, and simmer gently for 3 or 4 minutes until the edges of the oysters curl. Don't overcook, or they will become tough.

FINAL STEP   Ladle the stew into heated soup plates and swirl a dab of butter into each. Sprinkle with paprika. Serve at once with traditional oyster crackers.

Oyster Soup Hollandaise

Serves 6

The smooth blend of oysters and spinach—speckled green against creamy white—is topped at the last moment with a dollop of whipped cream mixed with hollandaise and placed under the broiler to brown.

The shellfish flavor is subtle. This soup could be served as the first course for any dinner, even a state dinner.

INGREDIENTS	1 8- or 10-ounce container of oysters, with their liquor
	1 10-ounce package frozen chopped spinach, thawed
	3 tablespoons chopped onion
	2 cups light cream
	1 teaspoon Worcestershire sauce
	Dash of Tabasco
	2 tablespoons lemon juice
	Salt to taste, if desired
	¼ cup whipping cream
	¼ cup hollandaise sauce, freshly made or bottled
SPECIAL EQUIPMENT	Food processor or blender
PREPARATION	*Note:* You may wish to include whole oysters in the soup. If so, reserve a few and add them to the soup 2 minutes before it is finished cooking.
PUREE 2 mins.	Puree raw oysters, spinach, and onion in a food processor or blender until smooth. For an even finer texture force through a sieve.
COOK 8 mins.	In a medium (3-quart) saucepan, combine the puree with the light cream, Worcestershire, Tabasco, lemon juice, and salt to season. Heat soup to simmering and cook gently over low heat for about 5 minutes. (Add whole oysters if desired.) Pour the hot soup into ovenproof bowls.
WHIP 3 mins.	Whip the cream and fold in hollandaise sauce—the result will be golden in color. Float a portion on the surface of each bowl.
BROIL 1–2 mins.	Place soup about 6 inches below heat and broil to a light brown, about 1 to 2 minutes.
FINAL STEP	This is a handsome dish to present at the table. Serve with rye crisps.

Saimin (Hawaiian)
Asian Noodles with Pork in Broth
Serves 6

Saimin is peculiarly of the Hawaiian Islands—a hybrid creation of many cultures. There was a time before and during World War II when there was a saimin stand in every block in Honolulu. Or so it seemed. The front was usually open to the weather, the roof and sides were of corrugated iron, and inside were two or three worn tables.

This soup is inexpensive to make. It is nourishing and its recuperative powers are considered providential by late homeward-bound partygoers. It is said that saimin will cure a hangover even before one begins.

Most of the old saimin stands have been crushed under the bulldozer in Hawaii's frantic building boom, but happily a few remain to keep the tradition and recipe alive.

I fell in love with saimin—for all the prescribed reasons—when I was a war correspondent stationed in the Islands, and the affair has continued to this day.

Note: The authentic saimin calls for several ingredients that are found only in Asian food stores, so check availability before beginning. Ramen noodles can be purchased in most large supermarkets, and the packets of instant broth can be added to the stock. However, don't hesitate to make saimin even lacking an ingredient or two.

INGREDIENTS

Soup
3 pounds pork bones
3 quarts water
1 small onion, quartered
¼ cup dried shrimp
4-inch square kombu (dried kelp)
2 tablespoons sake
2 teaspoons shoyu (soy sauce)
Salt, if desired, to taste

Bowl Items
1 pound ramen or other thin, flat Asian noodles
½ pound roast pork, thinly sliced, or ½ pound thick pork chop, roasted and thinly sliced
½ pound *kamaboko* (fish paste), thinly sliced
8 scallions, cut 2 inches long and sliced lengthwise in julienne strips

SPECIAL
EQUIPMENT

Sieve or chinois and cheesecloth

PREPARATION	*Note:* There are two steps in the preparation of saimin. The first is the broth itself; then the 4 additional ingredients are placed in the bottom of each bowl and the soup is ladled on.
BOIL SIMMER *1½ hours*	In a large saucepan, cover the pork bones with water, bring to a boil, and drain off the water. Rinse the bones under running water and return them to the pot. Add the 3 quarts of water, onion, and dried shrimp. Bring to a boil, reduce heat, and simmer for 1½ hours.
STRAIN	Line a sieve or chinois with a double thickness of moistened cheesecloth and strain the soup, discarding the solids. (The meat can be picked off the bones and used for other purposes.)
SIMMER *20 mins.*	Pour the broth back into the saucepan, add the kombu, and cook at a bare simmer for 20 minutes. Be careful—boiling the kombu will make the soup bitter. Lift out the kombu with a slotted spoon and discard. Add sake (or another dry white wine) and shoyu, and salt to taste, if desired.
COOK *3 mins.*	Cook the ramen noodles according to instruction on the packet (about 3 minutes). Cut the pork slices and the *kamaboko.* Slice the scallions.
FINAL STEP	Divide the 4 items among the heated bowls and ladle the hot soup into each. Chopsticks may be used for the solid ingredients and the soup drunk from the bowl. Aloha!

Shrimp Bisque

Serves 4 to 6

The essence of the flavor of shrimp is in the shell, its skeleton, rather than in the meat. To make this full-flavored bisque, the shells are seared over high heat, cooked with mirepoix, chopped, pounded, and put through a sieve and/or cheesecloth to extract all of the goodness. This is the traditional method for soups that are defined as "bisques."

Shrimp are too expensive to buy just for their shells, and too little of the meat is used as a garnish to justify the cost. This dish should go hand in hand with an occasion calling for shrimp itself as a cocktail, a dip, a casserole, or whatever. Or freeze the meat for another day, or better yet, make the bisque with shells that were previously frozen. It is prudent to think of two uses.

This crustacean acquired its name because of its relatively small size. The Middle English word for a small person is "shrimpe," and the Swedish word for shrimp is skrympa.

There is no better way to capture the rich yet light and sweet taste of shrimp than in this recipe. It makes an elegant first course or main course for brunch, served with bread and cheese.

INGREDIENTS

Note: The bisque is made with the ½ pound of shells from 2 pounds of shrimp. Adjust the ingredients according to the weight of the shells.
2 tablespoons high-quality olive oil
½ pound uncooked shrimp shells
¼ cup chopped shallots
1 cup chopped onion
1 cup chopped celery, with leaves
¾ cup chopped carrots
⅓ cup flour
3 tablespoons brandy
¼ cup dry white wine
2 quarts fish stock or fumet

Sachet d'épice
½ teaspoon thyme
1 clove garlic, minced
⅓ teaspoon black peppercorns
3 sprigs parsley, chopped

3 ounces tomato puree
Salt, if desired
2 tablespoons butter
½ pound raw shrimp meat (from above)
1 cup light cream (or heavy cream for a richer bisque)
Snippets of chives or green onions, to garnish

SPECIAL
EQUIPMENT

Food processor, chinois or strainer, cheesecloth

PREPARATION

Note: The shells must be seared over high heat to set the color and draw out the flavor. Do not burn.

SEAR
5 mins.

In a large skillet, heat the olive oil to smoking and drop in the shells. Stir frequently until shells are a bright pink, about 5 minutes. Do not cover during searing.

SWEAT *8 mins.*	Add the shallots, onions, celery, and carrots; cover and sweat over medium heat until vegetables are translucent and somewhat tender, about 8 minutes.
COOK *2–3 mins.*	Sprinkle flour over the mixture and stir to blend well. Cook uncovered for 2 or 3 minutes.
FLAMBÉ **REDUCE** *3 mins.*	Splash 2 tablespoons of brandy over the mixture and flambé. When the flames have died, add white wine and reduce. This will take about 3 additional minutes.
BOIL/SIMMER *1 hour*	Pour the stock into a medium (3-quart) saucepan and add the contents of the skillet. Scrape the skillet clean. Add the sachet and the tomato puree, which is for color. Increase the amount if you wish the soup to be pinker. Bring to a gentle boil, partially cover, reduce heat, and simmer for 1 hour. During the cooking, taste for seasoning, especially salt. When the bisque has cooked, the extraction begins. Remove the sachet and discard.
STRAIN	Pour all the contents of the saucepan through a chinois or sieve into a clean saucepan. Push as much of the mass through as possible with a wooden spoon.
PUREE	Ladle shells and vegetables into the work bowl of a food processor and puree. If you do not have a food processor, the mixture may be put through a food mill.
EXTRACT	Moisten a generous length of cheesecloth, spread it on the counter, and empty the contents of the work bowl onto its center. Fold the cloth over the puree, leaving enough length to grip on either end. Twist the cloth to extract every bit of liquid from shells, over the saucepan. It helps a lot to do this step with another person. When you can twist out no more of the essence, discard the cloth and dry shell residue. While it isn't absolutely necessary, I often pour the bisque through the chinois or a sieve with a smaller mesh a second time to produce a perfectly smooth texture. Set the saucepan of bisque aside.
SAUTÉ *3 mins.*	Heat the butter in a skillet and sauté the raw shrimp over medium heat until they turn pink, about 3 minutes. Flambé with the remaining tablespoon of brandy. Remove from heat and chop into ¼-inch pieces. Add the meat to the bisque.

REHEAT	Pour in the cream and, over low heat, bring back to steaming hot, but not quite to a simmer (about 175°).
FINAL STEP	Ladle the bisque into a heated tureen and bring to the table. Serve in heated soup bowls garnished with snippets of chives.
VARIATIONS	This recipe can be used to make delicious bisques with crayfish, crab, or lobster shells—crustaceans all.

Turtle Soup au Sherry

Serves 6 to 8

Turtle, delicious as it is, is an uncommon meat. When I want turtle, I can't find it. Once, when I was not looking for it, my grandson and his friend brought home an angry 18-pound snapping turtle, which they turned loose in my bird pond. I drove 100 miles to Louisville to get the turtle to make the soup below; I sent my grandson's turtle back to the farm pond.

The turtle meat came to Kentucky from Florida but it was not from the green sea turtle, which is on the endangered list. It was snapper. Beef tongue can be substituted for turtle meat because it has much the same texture and taste. Turtle meat, like chicken, is both light and dark. It is quite tender and there is a wild sweetness about it.

August is a time for the traditional turtle soup festivals in the rolling hills of southern Indiana, near the Ohio River. They are popular among parishes in German Catholic farm communities. It takes 300 pounds of snapping turtle from nearby creeks and rivers to provide enough meat for the 400 gallons of soup, which also includes 2 dozen chickens, 250 pounds of beef, okra, celery, a variety of chilies, and tomato and other sauces.

I enjoyed a big bowl of the soup at St. Boniface Catholic Church in Fulda and brought home 2 gallons to freeze for another and cooler day (it was 101° around the 50-gallon gas-fired kettles).

INGREDIENTS	1½ to 2 pounds turtle meat
	Water to cover, boil, and discard
	2 quarts water for soup
	2 stalks celery, finely chopped
	1 carrot, finely sliced
	1 clove garlic, minced
	1 medium onion, finely chopped
	2 teaspoons salt

Sachet d'épice
2 bay leaves
½ teaspoon thyme
12 black peppercorns

2 tablespoons mixed olive oil and other cooking oil
3 tablespoons flour
1½ cups finely sliced leek
1 cup chopped tomatoes
½ cup sherry
2 hard-cooked eggs, sliced, to garnish

SPECIAL EQUIPMENT	None
PREPARATION BOIL RINSE	Place the turtle meat in a large (4- to 5-quart) soup pot and cover with cold water. Bring to a boil, remove from heat, and pour off water through a colander. Rinse the meat under running water and return to the clean pot. *Note:* The meat will be picked from the bones after cooking.
BOIL/SIMMER *30 mins.*	Cover the meat with 8 cups of water and add celery, carrot, garlic, onion, and salt. Bring to a boil, add sachet, partially cover, lower heat, and simmer over medium-low heat for 30 minutes.
SAUTÉ *10 mins.* *5 mins.*	While the meat is simmering, pour the oils into a medium skillet, sprinkle in the flour, and brown, stirring. Add the leeks and sauté until soft and slightly browned, about 10 minutes. Stir in the tomatoes and cook for an additional 5 minutes. Stir frequently. Set aside for the moment. Lift the turtle meat from the stock and allow it to cool for a few minutes before taking the meat off the bones. Cut the meat into small ½-inch pieces; discard the bones. Return the meat to the stock in the saucepan. Scrape in the flour/leek/tomato mixture and stir together.
20 mins.	Simmer the soup for 20 minutes.
FINAL STEP	Pour the soup into a heated tureen and swirl in the sherry. Ladle into individual soup bowls and garnish with egg slices.

Bouillabaisse Provençale

Serves 8

> *"This bouillabaisse a noble dish is—*
> *a sort of soup, or broth or brew."*
> THE BALLAD OF BOUILLABAISSE
> *THACKERAY*

Bouillabaisse is legendary among the fish stews, having a reputation enhanced by the aura of waterfront excitement and seafaring adventure of its home port, Marseille.

All along the Mediterranean coast, from Cape Cerbère near the Spanish frontier to Menton near the Italian border, a great variety of bouillabaisse is prepared. But it is in Marseille where, according to the purists, one finds the authentic bouillabaisse.

True bouillabaisse—bouillabaisse provençale—is a saffron-flavored soup prepared with olive oil and tomatoes, among many other things. The true bouillabaisse does not contain mussels, clams, or oysters, and never potato or spinach! The bread over which the bouillabaisse broth is ladled is never toasted or fried. Fish stews that do include these ingredients may be equally delicious but that's not the way bouillabaisse came to be in Marseille. In Paris, for example, it is the wont of many restaurants to add mollusks, an affront to the true believer.

In the beginning, bouillabaisse was put together by fishermen from whatever they caught that day and could not sell. Seldom was the mix of fish in the bouillabaisse the same from day to day. This remains true today, with the cook assembling the bouillabaisse from among what's available in the market.

The American bouillabaisse, obviously, cannot be made with some of the fish found only in the Mediterranean, such as the rascasse and the Saint-Pierre, but there is an equally impressive choice available in this country. Witness this list:

Flounder	Trout
Pollack	Haddock
Halibut	Cod
Mackerel	Sea Bass
Turbot	Red Snapper
Tuna	Sole
Perch	Eel
Pike	Whitefish
Grayling	Whiting (Hake)

As well as lobster, shrimp, and crab.

Four or more of these fish, together with the crustaceans, can be the foundation of a delicious and authentic bouillabaisse. Several are seasonal or available only frozen (which is acceptable for bouillabaisse).

The richer, heavier fish—haddock, cod, bass, and eel—go into the kettle first, followed a few minutes later by the more delicate fish.

The hot peppery rouille, a sauce that accompanies the bouillabaisse, is the crowning touch to the fish supper. A little of the rouille is thinned with a few tablespoons of soup and poured into the broth. The balance of the sauce is passed separately so that each guest can have his or her bouillabaisse as spicy as desired.

INGREDIENTS

Bouillabaisse
½ cup olive oil
4 cloves garlic, chopped
1 large onion, chopped
2 leeks, white part only, washed and chopped
1 stalk celery, chopped
4 large tomatoes (or 1 large can), skinned, seeded, and chopped
4 cups fish stock or clam juice
¼ teaspoon crushed saffron threads
4 or 5 sprigs parsley, tied in a bundle
1 bay leaf, crumbled
¼ teaspoon thyme
2 teaspoons salt, if desired
3 turns of freshly ground black pepper
3 small lobsters (1 to 1½ pounds); see note, page 187
1 pound *each* 5 kinds of fish (see list above), cut bite-size
1 pound eel, filleted or cut into 2-inch pieces, optional
1 pound raw medium-size shrimp in shells
1 to 2 cups dry white wine

Rouille
For ingredients and preparation see page 366. The sauce may be made a
    day or so in advance.

SPECIAL
EQUIPMENT

Chinois or sieve—if the vegetables are to be strained and discarded after they have given up their flavor, rather than served in the bouillabaisse

PREPARATION

Note: If a stock is to be made from fish heads, bones, and trimmings, it can be done beforehand and set aside (see Fish Stock, page 22). On the other hand, an equally delicious stock can be made in a few minutes with fish base (page 15).

SWEAT
15 mins.

In a large (8-quart or larger) saucepan or kettle, heat the olive oil and drop in the garlic, onion, leeks, and celery. Cover and sweat over medium-low heat for 15 minutes or until translucent.

BOIL/SIMMER
30 mins.

Add the tomatoes and the fish stock or clam juice. Bring to a boil. Add the saffron, parsley, bay leaf, and thyme and continue cooking over medium-low heat for a total of 30 minutes or until the vegetables are quite soft.

Season with salt and pepper. (If a commercial fish base is used, be certain to taste for saltiness before adding additional salt.)

Note: Either the contents of the pot can be strained through a chinois or sieve, and the vegetables pressed dry with a large spoon (and discarded); or the vegetables can be left in the broth to be served with the fish. In either case, discard the parsley bundle.

BOIL

Bring the stock to a boil over medium heat. Check again for seasonings.

COOK
5 mins.

Drop the uncooked lobster pieces into the boiling stock. Cover and cook for 5 minutes—no longer. (If the lobster was cooked previously, eliminate this step.)

4 mins.

Add the heavier fish pieces (see above), cover, and cook for 4 minutes.

4 mins.

Add the shrimp, the wine, and the remainder of the fish. Cook for an additional 4 minutes or a total of 13 minutes—no longer, or the fish will fall apart.

REST
15 mins.

Remove from the heat to allow the bouillabaisse to rest for 15 minutes before serving.

FINAL STEP

Everything is to be served at the same time. Arrange the fish pieces and crustaceans on a large platter and pour the broth into a heated tureen. Bring both to the table.

Place a ½-inch-thick slice of peasant bread (see page 360) in each soup bowl. Lightly spread the slices with the rouille before placing pieces of seafood on the bread. Ladle the broth over the fish.

Pass the rouille to guests who may want more of the spicy sauce. French bread and a green salad complete this outstanding fish stew dinner.

Bouillabaisse can be frozen and kept at 0° for at least 6 to 8 months.

Note: To Prepare Lobster

Lobsters, expensive and delicious, deserve a special note. Cooked lobsters may be used in bouillabaisse, but it adds more flavor to both the lobster and the soup to cook the lobster and fish together.

If the fish dealer cannot be induced to cut up the lobsters, begin by washing them in cold water. Lay one lobster at a time on a cutting board. With a large, heavy sharp knife or cleaver, slice off the tail section to cut the spinal cord to kill the lobster. Cutting is easier if you put the knife across the underside of the tail and hit it with a wooden mallet or rolling pin. Slice the tail into several crosswise pieces and, with scissors, cut lengthwise through the thin undershell to make it easy to pick out the meat later.

Cut the claws from the lobster and separate the joints from the claws. Crack the sides of the claws with a hammer. Remove and discard the feelers, then cut the body in half lengthwise. Scoop out and save the tomalley and coral, if any. Discard the gelatinous sac near the head.

Refrigerate the pieces if they are not to be used immediately.

Vegetables

T REAT ALL VEGETABLES as if they were precious luxuries, even though their cost be minimal when compared with that of other items of the daily menu," wrote Alex D. Hawkes, author of *A World of Vegetable Cookery*. "Afford each vegetable the attention its character so richly deserves and you, your family, and your guests will be more than amply pleased and rewarded."

No higher tribute to vegetables can be found than in their use in these hundred or so recipes. They range through the garden from artichokes and asparagus to watercress and zucchini.

Cream of Artichoke Soup

Serves 6

There are 87 fully formed leaves in a single artichoke. This recipe calls for four artichokes, or a total of 348 leaves, to be scraped to reap the harvest of soft pulp that is the essence of this fine cream soup.

Plan to make this soup in the spring when artichokes appear in quantity in our markets. The velvety soup should be accompanied by plain, unseasoned toast bits or crackers. Once I spoiled the taste experience by serving light rye crisps, which overpowered the soup's delicate flavor.

INGREDIENTS	4 medium to large fresh artichokes
	Water to depth of 1 inch around artichokes
	1 tablespoon salt
	1 tablespoon olive oil
	2 tablespoons lemon juice
	1 cup heavy cream
	2 cups chicken stock
	½ teaspoon salt
	Freshly ground black pepper to taste
	¼ teaspoon basil
	2 tablespoons minced fresh parsley

| SPECIAL EQUIPMENT | Food mill, blender, or food processor |

PREPARATION
15 mins.

Artichokes
Wash artichokes and cut off the stems flush with the bases of the leafy bracts. Fit artichokes snugly, upright, side by side in the kettle. Add water 1 inch deep. Add 1 tablespoon salt and pour the oil into the crowns of the artichokes.

BOIL/SIMMER
40–45 mins.

Cover and bring to a quick boil. Reduce heat and simmer about 40 to 45 minutes or until an outside leaf can easily be pulled off.

COOL
30 mins.
or longer

Remove the kettle from heat and pour off water. Allow the artichokes to cool, about 30 minutes or longer. They may be refrigerated for 1 or 2 days if it is more convenient to scrape leaves later.

SCRAPE
20 mins.

Remove all of the leaves from one artichoke down to the cluster of thin undeveloped center leaves. Remove this prickly part, the choke, with a knife or sharp-edged spoon (a grapefruit spoon with a serrated edge is good for this). Set the cleaned bottom aside. Hold each leaf by its sharp tip, flesh side up, against the work surface and with a large spoon held in the other hand scrape out the soft inner pulp. Place the pulp from all leaves, and the cleaned bottom, in a bowl.

Repeat with others.

PUREE
5 mins.

When all the leaves have been scraped, discard them. Puree the leaf pulp and bottoms in a food mill, blender, or food processor, depending on the degree of smoothness desired. If in a blender or food processor, add ½ cup of the chicken stock to moisten puree to make it easier to process.

BLEND

In a large bowl mix puree with lemon juice, cream, chicken stock, salt, pepper, and basil. Mix well and chill.

FINAL STEP

Serve cold. Garnish with minced fresh parsley. This soup freezes well and can be kept, frozen, for 2 or 3 months.

Asparagus and Crab Soup (Vietnamese)
Súp Mang Tây Nâú Cua

Serves 6

Crab is an expensive seafood and thus deserves the best. One of the best soups is Vietnamese—Súp Mang Tây Nâú Cua, asparagus and crab.

Tender white asparagus are mixed with crabmeat flakes in a smooth chicken broth spiced with just a trace of Asian fish sauce.

This recipe was given to me by a lovely Vietnamese woman, Thoa Fink, who, with impeccable taste in both food and decor, ruled over an outstanding Denver restaurant, Chez Thoa.

INGREDIENTS

1 tablespoon vegetable oil
1 clove garlic, finely minced
2 tablespoons minced shallots or whites of scallions
½ to ¾ pound flaked crabmeat
2 quarts chicken stock
3 tablespoons fish sauce, optional (available at Asian markets)
3 tablespoons cornstarch
3 tablespoons water
1 10-ounce can white asparagus, drained and cut into ½-inch lengths
Salt to taste, if desired
¼ teaspoon freshly ground black pepper
Toasted croutons, to garnish

SPECIAL EQUIPMENT	None
PREPARATION SAUTÉ 6 mins. 4 mins.	Heat the oil in a large (10-inch) skillet and sauté the garlic and shallots or scallions over medium heat until tender, about 6 minutes. Stir the crabmeat into the garlic/shallot mixture. Raise the heat to medium hot and continue cooking for an additional 4 minutes, stirring constantly. Take the skillet off the heat and set aside.
BOIL/SIMMER 5 mins. 5 mins.	In a medium (4-quart) saucepan, heat the chicken stock to a gentle boil and stir in the fish sauce if you are using it. (Fish sauces vary in strength and composition. Taste the broth after the addition of the sauce. There should be just a hint of flavor. Do not overpower.) Scrape the contents of the skillet into the saucepan and return to a simmer. Blend together the cornstarch and water and stir into the soup. Simmer until thickened, about 5 minutes. Add the asparagus and bring the soup back to a simmer. Taste for salt and pepper.
FINAL STEP	Ladle into heated bowls and garnish with a sprinkling of croutons.

AVOCADO

One of the most pleasing, velvety tastes on the tongue is avocado, and it is especially so in two *sopas*—one hot, one cold—both from Mexico, where the fruit has been cultivated since pre-Columbian days.

While it is often treated as a vegetable on our tables, it is really a fruit, a member of the laurel family, and is also known as "alligator pear."

The body of a ripe avocado will yield slightly to gentle pressure. Unripened avocados should be placed in a brown paper bag to mature. They darken when they are cut, but if the seed is left in place in the unused portion, the discoloration will be slight for a day or two. Cover the avocado with plastic wrap or foil and hold in the refrigerator.

The third soup is the creation of an excellent cook, Betty Smith, who lives in the heart of avocado country in Southern California. Her husband, an executive in a produce firm, buys tons of avocados for shipment to the Midwest and the East. Needless to say, Betty is accustomed to the very best fruit.

Avocado Soup Acapulco
Sopa de Aguacate Acapulco

Serves 6

The meat of the avocado is broken up with a fork and mashed into a coarse pulp rather than pureed in a blender or processor. It is presented in shades of green—the darker green of the mashed avocado against the lighter green of the liquid. The cold soup is not without its touch of heat—chili powder, cayenne, onion, and dill weed.

INGREDIENTS	2 ripe avocados 3 cups consommé madrilène, fresh or canned, or chicken stock ½ cup sour cream 1 teaspoon grated onion ⅛ teaspoon cayenne pepper ⅛ to ¼ teaspoon chili powder, to taste 1 teaspoon finely minced fresh dill weed
SPECIAL EQUIPMENT	None
PREPARATION *20 mins.*	Split, seed, and peel avocados. Cut into several pieces and drop into a mixing bowl. Mash with fork into a coarse pulp. Don't stir the meat into a puree! Combine with consommé madrilène or chicken stock, sour cream, onion, cayenne, and chili powder. Gently blend all together with a whisk.
CHILL	Place a piece of plastic wrap on the surface of the soup to exclude air that might discolor it, cover the bowl, and chill in the refrigerator for 1 hour or more. Do not keep longer than 6 hours or the flavor of the avocado will grow bitter.
FINAL STEP	Serve in chilled bowls (over ice, perhaps), garnished with a sprinkling of minced fresh dill weed.

Avocado Cream Soup (Mexican)
Sopa de Aguacate

Serves 6

One of the traditional ingredients in this Mexican hot soup is thick cream, but I have found that it is even more delicious (and less caloric) made with yogurt. Despite my best efforts, the mixture of avocado puree and yogurt will sometimes curdle a little when I introduce the hot chicken stock. I add one extra step—press mixture through a sieve and return it to the pot for a final heating.

This soup may also be chilled and served cold.

Small pieces of crisply fried tortillas may be floated on the surface of the hot soup as an alternative to thin slices of avocado.

INGREDIENTS	2 large ripe avocados
	¾ cup plain yogurt
	4 cups chicken stock
	1 tablespoon pale dry sherry, optional
	Salt to taste
	¼ teaspoon freshly ground white or black pepper
	Avocado slices or 2 crisply fried tortillas, to garnish, if desired
SPECIAL EQUIPMENT	Optional: blender or food processor. Sieve with fine mesh.
PREPARATION *20 mins.*	*Note:* Half an avocado may be reserved and thinly sliced to be floated on top of the soup (hot or cold) when served.

Peel, halve, and pit the 2 avocados. Reserve ½ avocado for garnish. Dice the remaining 1½ avocados into the work bowl of a blender or food processor. Add the yogurt; then blend and process until the mixture is smooth, about 30 seconds at high speed. To make the puree by hand, force the meat through a sieve set over a bowl, using the back of a large spoon.

In a medium (4-quart) saucepan, bring the stock to a boil over high heat, then reduce heat to low. When the stock is simmering, stir several tablespoons into the avocado puree and blend. Then stir the avocado into the stock. If the mixture should separate, force through a fine-mesh sieve. Return to the saucepan and reheat. Add sherry, salt (if needed), and pepper. Taste for seasoning.

FINAL STEP

To serve soup hot, pour into a heated tureen or bowls and float avocado slices or pieces of fried tortillas over the surface of the soup.

The soup may also be refrigerated and served cold, in which case use only avocado slices for garnish.

Cold Avocado Soup

Serves 6 to 8

A tot of light rum distinguishes this cool, smooth avocado soup from the others. My friend Betty Smith, whose creation this is, garnishes each bowl with a spoonful of whipped cream and a slice of lemon. An alternative is to pass crisp corn chips for each diner to sprinkle over the light green soup.

INGREDIENTS	3 ripe avocados (about ½ pound each), peeled and cut into chunks to blend
	2 cups chicken stock
	2 cups light cream
	¼ teaspoon onion salt
	I teaspoon salt, if desired
	Pinch of white pepper
	¼ cup light rum
	I cup whipped cream or sour cream
	I teaspoon lemon juice
	6 to 8 thin lemon slices or I cup crisp corn chips, crushed, to garnish
SPECIAL EQUIPMENT	Blender or food processor. A food mill can also be used.
PREPARATION PUREE	Place all the ingredients *except* the lemon juice and garnishes in the blender work bowl. If the volume is too great for your blender, do it in 2 batches. Blend to a creamy puree stage. A food processor or food mill can also be used but the soup will not be quite as smooth. The soup should be the consistency of heavy cream. If it is too thick, stir in additional stock or light cream.
CHILL *6 hours*	Pour the puree into a container. Drop a piece of wax paper or plastic wrap down on the surface of the soup to prevent discoloration. Chill for 6 hours. Use immediately after removing from the refrigerator. Avocado does not keep well and will discolor and lose flavor if stored for a long period.
BLEND	Add the lemon juice and stir to blend.
FINAL STEP	Serve immediately with a spoonful of whipped cream and a slice of lemon on each serving.
	The soup may also be garnished with corn chips, freshly toasted to crisp them, and crushed into small pieces.

BEANS

The bean is one of the most important staples in the human diet and the basic ingredient for many of the world's most delicious soups. Members of this far-flung family include not only the adzuki, black, bonavist, broad, and green bean but the jack, kidney, cannellini, lima, navy, pinto, scarlet runner, and yam bean and others.

While many recipes are made with the fresh bean, both in and out of the pod, most soups call for the dried legume because it is so available and convenient.

A wonderful source of protein, the bean, alas, is also the source of occasional gas discomfort. However, when beans are soaked, they become far less disturbing after the water in which they have soaked is poured off and discarded. The beans are then cooked in new water or stock.

Tufts University explains that soaking beans extracts complex sugars, which can otherwise cause digestive problems.

There are two ways to soak dried beans before cooking. The least complicated—if you plan ahead and have the time—is to soak them overnight in water to cover 2 to 3 inches above beans, to allow for absorption. Drain the beans, discard the water, and cook.

If time is a factor, the beans may be quick-soaked by covering them with water and bringing to a boil for 2 minutes. Set aside and allow to soak for 1 hour. Drain and discard the water. Blanching beans for 2 minutes and soaking for 1 hour is the equivalent of 6 to 8 hours of soaking.

Lentils do not have to be soaked before cooking, nor do those beans with package directions that say soaking is not required.

Always wash and pick over beans before putting them to soak. Discard any beans that are discolored as well as any pebbles or floating particles.

Stuffed Bean Curd Soup (Chinese)

Serves 6

Stuffed bean curd soup is an intriguing Cantonese presentation—a chopped shrimp/ham mixture spooned into a recess cut into a small cube of bean curd, resting in a rich chicken broth. The green of spinach leaves floating in the golden soup is the backdrop for the filled white cubes. But this pretty soup is as good to eat as it is to behold.

My Chinese recipe called for a combination of dried and fresh shrimp, but the dried ones are too high in both taste and odor for me. I did not use them, but increased the number of fresh shrimp instead. The stuffing can also be made with only ham or pork loin, leaving the shrimp out entirely—equally delicious.

INGREDIENTS

Stuffing

3 ounces raw shrimp, shelled and deveined

3 ounces ham, ground

1 teaspoon dry white wine

¼ teaspoon salt, if desired

¼ teaspoon MSG, if desired

¼ teaspoon freshly ground black pepper

2 teaspoons plus 1 teaspoon cornstarch

1½ tablespoons water

1 pound fresh bean curd (in a block 4 x 3 x 2 inches; see note below)

Soup

6 cups chicken stock

1¼ teaspoons salt, if desired

½ teaspoon MSG

½ pound spinach leaves, washed, trimmed of coarse stems, and chopped

½ cup finely chopped coriander or parsley

SPECIAL
EQUIPMENT

Food processor or blender. Steamer (see note below).

PREPARATION
PROCESS

Stuffing

Process the shrimp only until finely chopped—not pureed. Process or grind the ham and place it and the shrimp in a medium bowl. Mix in the wine, salt, MSG, and pepper. In a small cup mix together the 2 teaspoons of cornstarch with 1½ tablespoons water. When smooth, pour into the meat mixture. Blend well. Set aside.

BLEND

Note: There are several sizes of bean curd cakes (tofu) manufactured across the country. Chinese bean curd is a little firmer than the Japanese because the excess moisture has been pressed out of it; hence the cakes tend to be smaller. The Japanese tofu (my preference) is whiter and more delicately flavored than the Chinese type and is the one generally stocked in American stores. Either can be used in this recipe.

In either case, cut and divide the cake into cubes, if possible, or blocks no smaller than 1 inch on the narrow side. Most 1-pound cakes cut easily into 16 pieces. If cut into 12 larger pieces, these may be too large to be attractively presented in a soup bowl.

Sacrifice the first two or three cubes if necessary while developing your technique for cutting out the center recess. A knife will cut through bean curd almost with its own weight, so use a delicate touch. While the bean curd is soft, it is remarkably resilient and will bend before it breaks except in areas flawed by air bubbles. Lift out the center with the knife or a very small spoon. Discard the scraps or reserve for another use. It makes little difference if the recess of the cube is rough and irregular—the stuffing covers it.

Sprinkle the center of each piece lightly with the remaining 1 teaspoon cornstarch and stuff each with the meat mixture. Smooth the surface with a spoon moistened with water to prevent sticking.

Soup
Note: The soup can be assembled *with* the filled pieces or the pieces can be steamed separately and placed in the bowls, and the hot soup ladled over them.

BOIL

Heat the stock to boiling in a medium (3½-quart) saucepan. Add salt and MSG. Add the stuffed pieces and bring the liquid to a boil.

SIMMER
6 mins.
BOIL

Turn heat to low and simmer for about 6 minutes. Add the chopped spinach and coriander or parsley. Heat to bring it back to a boil—and remove from heat.

Or make soup and add steamed, stuffed tofu pieces just before serving.

FINAL STEP

Arrange the stuffed pieces in each dish and cover with hot soup. Arrange the green spinach leaves attractively around the cubes.

Bean Sprout Soup (Korean)

Serves 6

During the years we lived in Hawaii I ate many Korean dishes, but none better than bean sprout soup. It has flavor and a crisp texture, thanks to the bean sprouts.

(I must confess that despite admiration for Korean cooking I never succumbed to the national dish, kimchi, made with fermented cabbage and a lot of garlic. I prefer this soup.)

INGREDIENTS

¾ pound lean stew beef, in ¼-inch dice or processed briefly

3 tablespoons peanut or soy oil

½ cup coarsely chopped onion

2 cloves garlic, finely minced

2 teaspoons salt, if desired

¼ teaspoon freshly ground black pepper

2 quarts beef stock

(continued)

3 tablespoons soy sauce
2 cups bean sprouts, fresh or canned, drained
3 scallions, with green tops, coarsely chopped
Tabasco sauce, to taste

SPECIAL
EQUIPMENT

Food processor, optional

PREPARATION

Chop the beef into small ¼-inch dice by hand or coarsely in a food processor. Heat the oil in a medium (4-quart) saucepan and add the meat, together with onions, garlic, salt, and pepper.

COOK
5 mins.
15 mins.

Over high heat, cook for 5 minutes, stirring constantly.
    Add the beef stock and soy sauce, cover the saucepan, reduce heat, and simmer until the meat is tender, about 15 minutes.

SIMMER
4–5 mins.

Add the bean sprouts to the soup as well as the scallions and Tabasco sauce to taste (usually a dash is sufficient), cover again, and simmer 4 to 5 minutes. The sprouts should still be crisp.

FINAL STEP

Serve piping hot.

Austrian Green Bean Soup

Serves 4 to 6

From Vienna, this delicious soup for all seasons blends mushrooms, barley, and green beans. If young tender green beans are not available, use frozen ones.

INGREDIENTS

¾ pound young green beans or
    1 10-ounce package frozen cut beans, thawed
6 tablespoons butter
1 medium onion, finely chopped
1 clove garlic, minced
½ cup finely chopped celery
2 quarts chicken stock
⅓ cup pearl barley
½ teaspoon dried tarragon or 1 tablespoon fresh
6 to 8 sliced fresh mushrooms or 1 4-ounce can, drained
2 tablespoons butter
2 tablespoons flour

½ cup sour cream
¼ cup chopped parsley, to garnish

SPECIAL EQUIPMENT	None
PREPARATION	If using fresh beans, trim the ends and line up on a cutting board a handful at a time. Chop with a heavy knife until the beans are the size of peas. If frozen, thaw and chop as above.
SMOTHER 8 mins. 10 mins.	In a medium (4-quart) saucepan, heat 6 tablespoons butter until it foams, and add onion, garlic, and celery. Cover and cook for 8 minutes. Add the chopped beans and continue to cook, covered, for an additional 10 minutes over medium-low heat.
BOIL/SIMMER 30 mins.	Pour the stock into the saucepan with the vegetables. Add the barley and tarragon. Bring to a gentle boil, reduce heat to a simmer, and cook for 30 minutes.
SAUTÉ 10 mins. 15 mins. 2 mins.	Meanwhile, sauté the mushrooms in 2 tablespoons of butter in a medium skillet over medium heat for about 10 minutes. Set aside. When the soup has cooked for 30 minutes, transfer the mushrooms to the saucepan with a slotted spoon. Simmer for 15 more minutes and then remove from heat. Whisk together the flour and sour cream. Beat 1 cup of hot soup gradually into the sour cream. While stirring, slowly pour the sour cream mixture back into the saucepan.
FINAL STEP	Serve hot with a sprinkling of parsley.

White Bean Soup (French)
Potage Haricot Blanc

Serves 8

This delicious soup is creamed with its own ingredients—no outside thickeners such as flour or cornstarch. No egg yolk. No cream. Just beans and vegetables. The optional cabbage and turnips add their flavor, yet let the taste of beans comes through.

INGREDIENTS	3 cups dry white beans (navy, marrow, or Great Northern) Water to soak 2 quarts chicken stock

(continued)

1 tablespoon olive oil
1 onion, finely minced
1 carrot, finely chopped
2 leeks, finely chopped, including some green
¼ pound lean salt pork or 1 ham bone

Sachet d'épice
1 cup peeled turnip, cubed (½ inch), optional
1 cup shredded green cabbage, optional
4 sprigs parsley
2 leafy celery tops
2 bay leaves

Salt to taste, if desired
¼ teaspoon freshly ground white pepper
2 tablespoons soft butter
2 tablespoons chopped parsley or chives, to garnish

SPECIAL EQUIPMENT	Food processor or food mill. Colander or sieve.
PREPARATION	*Note:* To prepare dried beans for cooking, see page 195. Regardless of how the beans have been soaked, they are to be put into a large (5- to 6-quart) soup pot or kettle and covered with the 8 cups of chicken stock before proceeding. If the beans have been quick-soaked in stock, add enough to bring the amount to 8 cups.
SMOTHER *8 mins.*	Pour the olive oil into a medium skillet and add the onion, carrot, and leeks. Cover and cook over medium heat until the vegetables are soft and translucent, about 8 minutes. Stir frequently. Set aside in the skillet.
BLANCH *10 mins.*	Meanwhile, blanch the salt pork or ham bone in 2 cups of water in a small saucepan over medium heat. Simmer uncovered for 10 minutes. Drain and set the pork aside.
BOIL/SIMMER *2 hours*	Add the vegetables and blanched salt pork or ham bone and the sachet d'épice to the pot. Bring to a boil, lower heat, partially cover, and simmer for 2 hours. By then, the beans and vegetables should also be tender. Discard the salt pork or ham bone and the sachet d'épice.
PUREE	Drain the beans and vegetables through a colander or sieve and reserve the stock. Puree the bean mixture in a food processor (with 1 or 2 table-

spoons of stock) or through a food mill or sieve. Return the pureed beans to the pot and add enough of the stock to make the soup the consistency of heavy cream.

Taste and season with salt and pepper.

REHEAT   Return the pot to the stove and bring to a simmer over moderate heat. Cook until it is hot and steaming.

Remove the pot of soup from the heat and swirl in the 2 tablespoons of butter.

FINAL STEP   Ladle the soup into a large tureen or into individual soup bowls and garnish with parsley or chives.

Seven-Bean Soup

Serves 14

This is a wonderful soup for the neighborhood party to which each neighbor brings one kind of bean, or when cleaning out the pantry and finding a number of kinds of beans tucked away in jars and bags. Substitute freely. One variety more or less will make little difference in the blended taste.

Visually this soup is fun. Guests throughout the meal will ask—"Tell me again, which bean is this one?"

This is a large recipe that will feed a Boy Scout patrol, a young football team, or a crew freshly returned from a sail.

INGREDIENTS

½ cup *each*, dried
- navy beans
- pinto beans
- cranberry beans
- kidney beans
- black-eyed peas
- garbanzos (chickpeas)
- lima beans

Water to cover
2 smoked ham hocks
1 pound soup bones, preferably veal
Water to cover (about 10 cups)
2 tablespoons butter
2 medium onions, finely chopped

(continued)

2 medium carrots, finely chopped
4 stalks celery, finely chopped
I clove garlic, minced
I pound garlic sausage: Portuguese, Italian, kielbasa, or other
I 28-ounce can tomatoes, including liquid
Salt, if desired or necessary
Freshly ground black pepper to taste

SPECIAL
EQUIPMENT

None

PREPARATION

Note: To prepare dried beans for cooking, see page 195.

BOIL/SIMMER
2½ hours

In a medium (4-quart) saucepan, cover ham hocks and soup bone with water to 2 inches above the meat, about 10 cups. Bring the water to a boil, partially cover with lid, reduce heat, and simmer over low heat for 2½ hours. Skim off brown film as it collects on the surface.

I hour

Drain the beans. While the meat is cooking, place the beans in another saucepan; add water to cover plus 2 or 3 inches, about 4 quarts all together. Bring to a boil, reduce heat, and simmer for about 1 hour or until the beans are al dente—not mushy.

Drain the beans through a colander into a bowl. Reserve the liquid in the event it is needed to thin the soup.

SMOTHER
8 mins.

In a large skillet, heat the butter to foaming. Add the onions, carrots, celery, and garlic. Cover the skillet and cook—but do not brown—until translucent, about 8 minutes. Put aside for the moment.

TRY OUT
10 mins.

At the same time cut the sausage into diagonal ¼-inch slices and try out in the skillet. Cook until the fat is released and the meat is browned, about 10 minutes. Lift out the pieces with a slotted spoon. Discard the fat.

When the ham hocks are cooked, take the saucepan off the heat. Lift out the ham and cut off the thin strip of meat beneath the layer of fat. Cut into bite-size pieces and return to the saucepan. Discard fat and bones, including the veal bones.

ASSEMBLE

When the beans are cooked, drain and pour them into the ham/veal stock. Reserve the water in which they have been cooked in the event it is needed later.

Add the vegetables, including the tomatoes. Add the sausage slices.

SIMMER	Simmer the completed soup over medium-low heat for 30 to 45 min-
30–45 mins.	utes. Taste for seasoning. Salt cautiously, if at all, because the ham will
	have made its contribution. Add black pepper to taste.
FINAL STEP	This is a great dish to bring to the table in the pot in which it is cooked. Ladle into heated bowls. Serve a green salad and plenty of country bread. And lots of butter.

U.S. Senate Bean Soup

Serves 6 to 8

The U.S. Senate has come to stand for many things in this republic. One is its bean soup. There is also a bean soup served in the House of Representatives, but it lacks both the pres- tige and the taste of that of the upper house. Between the two, however, cooks ladle out gal- lons of 8-ounce servings each day in the eleven dining rooms on the Hill.

I had my first bowl of Senate bean soup in 1940 as the guest of Senator Charles M. McNary of Oregon. I was a brand-new Life *magazine correspondent in the capital and he was then the running mate of Republican presidential hopeful Wendell Willkie. I don't recall what we talked about, but I have never forgotten the soup.*

Senate bean soup can be served on any occasion that warrants a hot, steamy, filling, thick soup such as an election eve party or a modest precinct gathering.

INGREDIENTS	1 pound dried white beans, Great Northern, or navy
	Water, to soak
	1 meaty ham bone or 2 smoked ham hocks
	3 quarts water, to cook
	3 medium onions, finely chopped
	3 cloves garlic, minced
	3 stalks celery, finely chopped
	¼ cup finely chopped parsley
	1 cup cooked mashed potatoes
	or ⅓ cup instant potato flakes
	Salt to taste, if desired
	¼ teaspoon freshly ground black pepper
	Snippets of parsley or chives, to garnish
SPECIAL EQUIPMENT	None
PREPARATION	*Note:* To prepare dried beans for cooking, see page 195.

| BOIL/SIMMER | Drain the beans and place them with the ham in a large (5-quart) soup |
| *I hour* | kettle. Add 3 quarts of cold water. Bring the water to a boil, reduce heat, |

BOIL/SIMMER
I hour

Drain the beans and place them with the ham in a large (5-quart) soup kettle. Add 3 quarts of cold water. Bring the water to a boil, reduce heat, and simmer over low heat for 1 hour. Skim if necessary.

In the meantime, chop the onions, garlic, celery, and parsley. When the beans and meat have cooked 1 hour, add the chopped vegetables and the potatoes to the pot.

I hour

Simmer for 1 hour longer or until the beans are tender.

Season with salt and pepper

Remove the bones and meat from the soup. Dice the meat into ½-inch pieces and return to the pot. Discard the bones. Reheat to serve.

FINAL STEP

This is a hearty, robust dish and so it should have a hearty, robust service—from the pot at the table, ladled into heated soup bowls. Garnish with snippets of parsley or chives.

ALTERNATIVE

The House version: Only beans, ham hock, and seasoning. The beans are bruised with a spoon or ladle to barely cloud the soup before serving.

Shaker Bean Chowder

Serves 6 to 8

The celibate Shakers left no children but they did leave an enduring legacy of simple and beautifully crafted furniture and simple, delicious food. They left much more, of course, but it is their food that is remembered in kitchens across the country.

This chowder, from a hundred-year-old recipe, is a delicate light pink. It is almost wholly beans and tomato—and one glug* of molasses—with thickening coming from a puree of the cooked beans. Simple. Delicious. Inexpensive.

INGREDIENTS

2 cups dried white beans

Water, to soak

½ pound salt pork, diced

2 onions, finely chopped

6 cups water, to cook

4 cups chopped tomatoes, fresh or canned

2 teaspoons salt, if desired

¼ teaspoon freshly ground black pepper

2 tablespoons dark molasses or brown sugar

* In early kitchens, the measurement, by sound, of molasses as it is poured from a jug.

1 cup toasted croutons, to garnish
2 tablespoons snipped parsley, to garnish

SPECIAL
EQUIPMENT

Food processor, blender, or sieve

PREPARATION

Note: To prepare dried beans for cooking, see page 195.

TRY OUT
15 mins.

In a medium skillet, try out the salt pork dice until they begin to lose their fat. Add the onions and cook over low heat until pork bits are brown and onions are soft and translucent, about 15 minutes.

BOIL/SIMMER
30 mins.

In the meantime, pour the water off the beans and discard. Add 6 cups of cold water to the pot and bring to a boil. Lift the pork and onions out of the skillet with a slotted spoon and add to the pot. Discard the grease. Reduce heat to a simmer and cook for about 30 minutes or until the beans are just getting tender, al dente. Remember, they have another 30 minutes to cook.

30 mins.

Add tomatoes, salt, if desired, pepper, and molasses or brown sugar. Stir into the soup and continue simmering for an additional 30 minutes.

PUREE

Take the soup off the heat and when it has cooled a bit dip out about half the beans and puree in a food processor or blender. They can also be pushed through a sieve. Return the puree to the soup to thicken it.

FINAL STEP

Ladle into a heated tureen and serve in warmed soup bowls. Garnish with croutons and snipped parsley.

Bean and Pasta Soup (Italian)
Pasta e Fagioli

Serves 6 to 8

Traditionally pasta e fagioli *is from Naples. This version, from northern Lombardy, is quite different—it has more vegetables, and the usual roast pork is replaced with pancetta (when obtainable), the peppered bacon doted upon by the Alpine Italians. The soup also contains lots of rosemary, one of the classic herbs of the region's cuisine.*

Susan Crosby Marshall, an exceptional cook whose kitchen overlooks the Italian section of San Francisco's North Beach, found this recipe and worked out alternative ingredients for those difficult to find in some parts of the country.

The Italians love the pink-and-white-marbled cranberry bean in this soup. The bean has a distinct and wonderful flavor. If the cranberry (or Roman) bean is not available substitute either cannellini (white kidney beans) or pinto beans.

INGREDIENTS	½ pound pancetta or pork chops or Canadian bacon
	2 tablespoons olive oil, or less, depending on the fat in the meat above
	2 tablespoons butter
	2 medium onions, finely chopped
	2 carrots, cut into thin (⅛-inch) rounds
	2 stalks celery, thinly chopped
	½ cup finely chopped fresh parsley
	1 28-ounce can Italian plum tomatoes, chopped, with juice
	2 bay leaves
	2 teaspoons dried rosemary, crushed
	1 teaspoon dried basil
	3 cups chicken stock or water
	1 cup white wine
	1 pound dried beans (see above for choice)
	or 2 15-ounce cans beans of choice, above
	Salt to taste, if desired
	Freshly ground black pepper—4 or 5 twists of the mill
	6 ounces small pasta shells or homemade pasta
	1½ cups grated Parmesan cheese, to garnish

SPECIAL EQUIPMENT

Mortar and pestle to powder rosemary. Food mill or food processor.

PREPARATION
SAUTÉ
5 mins.
8 mins.
10–12 mins.

Cut the meat into ¼-inch dice. Sauté in oil and butter over medium heat in a large (6-quart) saucepan or casserole until meat is browned on all sides, about 5 minutes. Add the onions and cook until translucent and soft, about 8 minutes. Add the carrots, celery, and parsley. Cover pot and cook until carrots begin to get tender, about 10 to 12 minutes.

BOIL
3 mins.

Pour in the chopped tomatoes and their juice. Bring the liquid to a boil for about 3 minutes. Add bay leaves, rosemary, basil, stock or water, and wine.

If rehydrated dried beans are used, drain and add them to the saucepan. (If canned, beans will be added later.)

25–30 mins.

Return to a gentle boil and cook for 25 to 30 minutes or until firm-tender.

5 mins.

If the beans are canned, put 2 cups aside and add the balance to the pan. Boil gently for an additional 5 minutes.

PUREE | If rehydrated dried beans are used, lift out approximately 2 cups with a slotted spoon and put them through a food mill or mash them into a puree with a heavy fork or spoon. A food processor can be used, but a blender makes the beans too creamy. Do the same for the 2 cups of reserved canned beans. Add pureed beans to the soup.

Check the soup for saltiness (the meat will have contributed some salt, and the broth as well, if canned). Add freshly ground black pepper.

BOIL
1 min. or
5–8 mins.

Bring the soup to a steady boil over medium heat. Add the pasta. Cook fresh pasta in the soup for just 1 minute and remove from the heat. If dry pasta is used, cook 5 to 8 minutes—taste for doneness, and when it is firm to the bite, remove the pot from the heat.

REST
10 mins.

The soup should rest about 10 minutes before it is served. The pasta will continue cooking in the hot liquid and will be tender, but not mushy.

FINAL STEP

Swirl a tablespoonful of cheese into each serving. Pass thick slabs of peasant bread and plenty of butter.

Italians like to sprinkle a small spoonful of extra-virgin olive oil over the top. This is a rich, fruity green oil from the first pressing.

Black Bean Soup

Serves 8 hungry guests (12 cups)

The black bean is a standout among beans, and this is a standout among soups. The black bean, also called a turtle bean, has an especially hearty, distinctive flavor. It is widely used in the tropics of this hemisphere.

This is an ambitious undertaking with an utterly delicious result. The finished soup is not black, as you might expect, but a rich brown. In addition to the beans, there are two dozen other ingredients, several of which are only fractional teaspoons of spices, as well as three different meats. Obviously the absence of one or two of the spices will not affect the soup in a substantial way, so don't hesitate to go ahead without them.

Do not process or sieve the soup too fine. It is a robust soup and it should have a degree of roughness. I do not like mine pureed—only 2 or 3 short bursts of the processor will give the right texture.

The garnishes are important to the success of this soup. One among them is sliced banana (via Mexico).

INGREDIENTS	2 cups (about 1 pound) dried black beans
	¼ pound salt pork
	Ham bone with some meat (2 or 3 ham hocks may be substituted)
	¼ pound lean smoked slab bacon (or thickly sliced bacon),
	in ½-inch cubes
	3 cups water
	3 cups beef stock
	2 tablespoons butter
	1 medium onion, peeled and chopped
	1 carrot, peeled and chopped
	¼ cup chopped celery tops
	2 small leeks, chopped (about 1 cup)
	1 tomato, peeled, seeded, and chopped,
	or ½ cup tomato puree
	2 cloves garlic, finely chopped
	¼ teaspoon dried thyme
	¼ teaspoon turmeric
	½ teaspoon cumin seeds
	1 bay leaf
	½ teaspoon freshly ground black pepper
	2 or 3 dashes of Tabasco
	Salt, if desired, after tasting for the saltiness of the smoked meats

To Garnish
2 hard-cooked eggs, minced
1 tablespoon minced parsley
1 banana, thinly sliced
8 lemon slices
1 medium onion, finely chopped

SPECIAL EQUIPMENT	Large (6-quart) soup pot; food processor; mortar and pestle
PREPARATION	*Note:* To prepare dried beans for cooking, see page 195.
15 mins.	Place salt pork in a small saucepan with water to cover and bring to a boil for 1 minute. Drain and rinse under cold water. Add to the beans. Drop in the ham bone or hocks and the bacon cubes. Add 3 cups water
BOIL	and 3 cups beef stock and bring to a boil.
SIMMER	Lower heat, cover, and simmer 3 hours.

3 hours

While the meats and beans are simmering, prepare the vegetables and measure the spices onto a length of wax paper for convenience in adding them to the soup later. Roast the cumin (see "Spices, Herbs, and Seasonings," page 372) and crush to powder in mortar.

SMOTHER
10 mins.

In a large skillet, melt the butter over medium heat and add the onions, carrot, celery tops, and leeks. Cover and cook until the onions are translucent and the other vegetables are soft—about 10 minutes.

Stir the vegetables into the soup. Add the tomato and garlic as well as the thyme, turmeric, cumin, bay leaf, and pepper. Add 2 or 3 dashes of Tabasco.

SIMMER
2½ hours

Cover the pot and continue simmering until the beans are soft, about 2½ additional hours. Stir frequently.

COOL

Remove the pot from heat and allow soup to cool somewhat before removing salt pork and ham bone. Pick off the ham meat, if any, and discard the bone.

Note: If time permits, allow the soup to cool at room temperature or in the refrigerator in order to congeal the fat and make it easier to lift off and discard. If not, skim the fat off the hot soup with a ladle.

PROCESS

While the beans and vegetables can be mashed against the sides of the pot with a wooden spoon or pushed through a coarse sieve or food mill, I think the most satisfactory method is with the food processor. Check the soup after a burst or two to make certain the texture is as you want it. I don't blender this soup because that makes it too creamy and leaves it with little character.

REHEAT

Reheat the soup before serving—adjust the consistency (and add more beef broth if it seems too thick) and seasoning. Add salt if desired and needed.

FINAL STEP

Stir together the minced eggs and parsley. Sprinkle a bit of this mixture over the soup as it is served. Place a lemon slice on the top of each serving. The banana is a surprise garnish, to be passed at table, along with additional mixed egg and parsley, and the chopped onion.

Brazilian Black Bean Soup
Feijoada

Serves 8 (8 cups)

Brazil's feijoada completa, *the country's national dish, is considered by some to be a meat dish rather than a stew because the traditional recipe includes a smoked beef tongue, corned spareribs, beef jerky, smoked spiced sausage, pork sausage, bacon, beef chuck, Canadian bacon, and, finally, a pig's foot. This version of* feijoada *is not a* completa *but it is delicious and will make you wish to try the* completa *the next time you are south of the border.*

The cookery author Geoffrey Tomb adapted this recipe, which has only four meats. And, as with completa, *orange slices are simmered in the stew the final 5 minutes of cooking. The Latin American volume of the Time-Life* Foods of the World *series has the nine-meat* completa *recipe.*

INGREDIENTS	1 pound (2½ cups) black beans
	½ pound spicy Italian sausage
	½ pound spareribs, trimmed of fat
	1 cup beef stock
	6 cups water
	1 smoked ham hock or ¼ pound ham, chopped
	¼ pound pepperoni, thinly sliced
	1 onion, sliced
	2 green peppers, seeds and membrane removed, sliced
	2 cloves garlic, mashed
	1 teaspoon oregano
	1 teaspoon crushed dried chili peppers
	½ teaspoon ground cumin
	Salt, if desired, and freshly ground black pepper
	3 ripe tomatoes, skins and seeds removed,
	or 1 cup canned tomatoes, drained
	¾ cup red wine
	2 oranges, peeled and sectioned, membrane removed
	Orange rind, slivered, to garnish
SPECIAL EQUIPMENT	Food mill or food processor, optional
PREPARATION	*Note:* To prepare dried beans for cooking, see page 195.
FRY *20 mins.*	While the beans are soaking, brown the sausage and spareribs in a large skillet over medium heat. Reserve fat, if any.

Drain the beans and place in a large (5-quart) saucepan or kettle. Add the stock, 6 cups of water, and all the meats.

SAUTÉ

Pour the reserved fat (add more oil if needed) into the skillet and sauté the onions, peppers, garlic, herbs, and spices. Cover and cook over medium-low heat until onions are translucent. Add this to the bean pot and stir together.

BOIL/SIMMER
1–1½ hours

Partially cover pot, bring to a boil, reduce heat, and simmer until the beans are soft, about 1 to 1½ hours. Stir frequently so beans don't stick to the pot.

As the meats may be salty, check seasoning before adding any salt. Add black pepper.

30 mins.

Add tomatoes and wine and continue cooking for another 30 minutes.

Stir in the orange sections a few minutes before the soup is done.

If a different and thicker texture is desired, mash some of the beans against the sides of the pan with a large wooden spoon or put 1 or 2 cups through a food mill or food processor.

FINAL STEP

Serve in heated bowls; garnish with slivers of orange rind.

Cold Green Bean Soup (Hungarian)
Habart Bableves

Serves 6

Soup and strudel are not often the specialties of the same cook, but they were in the case of Iréne Jánosné, one of Budapest's finest cooks. I had traveled across Europe to her big kitchen in the Grand Hotel Margitsziget to learn the secret of her rétes, the famous Hungarian multilayered strudel, for the book on pastries I was then writing. The visit paid an unexpected dividend, for I discovered that she was also noted for her soups. Her dominion was not only over bake ovens but over soup kettles as well.

Soups and stews are the mainstays of Hungarian cuisine, and cold soup, such as this one done by Jánosné, is especially esteemed. Vinegar and sour cream are among its ingredients.

INGREDIENTS

1 pound fresh or frozen green beans, cut into ½-inch lengths
5 cups water
3 tablespoons white vinegar
2 tablespoons chopped onion

(continued)

2 tablespoons sugar
I teaspoon salt, if desired
I clove garlic, crushed
I cup sour cream
2 tablespoons flour
I tablespoon tarragon vinegar
Paprika, to sprinkle over soup
I cup toasted croutons, to garnish

SPECIAL
EQUIPMENT

Food processor, if desired

PREPARATION

Note: The availability of young tender green beans may determine whether you wish to leave the cooked beans in small pieces or chop them into small fragments in the food processor. Give them only 1 or 2 short bursts—don't puree finely.

Place the cut beans in a medium (3-quart) saucepan, with lid. Add the water, white vinegar, onion, sugar, salt, and garlic.

BOIL/SIMMER
30–60 mins.

Bring the soup to a boil, reduce heat, cover, and simmer for 30 minutes or until the beans are tender but not mushy. Cooking may require more time if the beans are tough and fibrous.

BLEND

SIMMER
5 mins.

In a small bowl, combine the sour cream and flour. When the beans have cooked, ladle out ½ cup of the bean liquid and stir it into the sour cream/flour mixture. Return the blended sour cream to the soup and simmer, stirring, for 5 minutes. Add tarragon vinegar. Remove the saucepan from the heat.

Taste the soup. Bite into a bean to check the texture and tenderness. If desired, put the soup in the food processor and cut the beans into smaller bits. I find the latter method most attractive.

CHILL
*3 hours
or overnight*

Allow the soup to cool at room temperature before chilling in the refrigerator 3 hours or longer.

FINAL STEP

Serve the soup in chilled bowls. Sprinkle with paprika. Pass the toasted croutons.

Sunday Soup (Cream of Bean)

Serves 6

The Amish are a plainspoken and plain-living people, and nothing bespeaks this better than a favorite recipe called "Sunday Soup" by Sister Nancy Underhill found in a worn copy of the 1901 edition of the Old Order cookbook cherished by my wife's grandmother, a member of the Brethren Church.

Here is the recipe as she wrote it more than a hundred years ago, including the times and occasions when it is to be prepared. It needed seasoning other than salt. I also process 1 cup of the cooked beans in a blender to give the soup more body because the cream available in the market today can in no way compare to the thick cream separated at home by Sister Underhill.

Her recipe:

At night wash a pint of dried beans, place them on the back of the stove in a porcelain vessel, with 2 quarts of cold water and a pinch of soda. In the morning, when they have simmered half an hour or until breakfast, pour off the water through a colander; return beans to cooking vessel; add 2 quarts of hot water; let boil until nearly done, then place the vessel where it will keep warm, but not boil. After church, a visit or washing (according to the day), add to your beans a teacupful of sweet cream; salt to taste, and serve. They should simmer before serving.

Although Sister Underhill did not suggest corn bread to accompany the soup, the two are good companions deserving of each other.

INGREDIENTS

2 cups (1 pint) dried navy beans
2 quarts water, to soak beans
Pinch of baking soda
2 quarts hot water

Sachet d'épice
½ teaspoon thyme
10 black peppercorns
1 bay leaf, crumbled
1 clove garlic, mashed

2 teaspoons salt, or to taste
1 cup light cream
2 tablespoons finely chopped parsley, to garnish

SPECIAL EQUIPMENT	Blender, food processor, or food mill. Beans may also be crushed against the sides of the saucepan with a fork or heavy spoon.
PREPARATION	Wash and pick over beans. Place the beans in a medium (4-quart) saucepan, cover with water, and add the pinch of soda. Soak the beans overnight.
SIMMER *30 mins.* BOIL/SIMMER *1½ hours*	The following morning place the saucepan over low heat and bring to a simmer. Cook for 30 minutes. Drain. Replenish with hot water; bring to a boil, reduce heat, and allow beans to cook slowly until tender, about 1½ hours, over medium-low heat. Assemble the ingredients for the sachet and place in a metal ball-type tea infuser or tie in a cheesecloth bag. Add the sachet to the soup for the final 30 minutes of cooking.
BLENDER	When the beans are cooked, remove the saucepan from the heat. Discard sachet. When the soup has cooled somewhat, remove 1 cup of beans and puree. Return the pureed beans to the pot and blend with the soup. Add salt, if wanted. Add cream. Carefully reheat before serving, not allowing soup to come to a boil.
FINAL STEP	Sprinkle each serving with parsley. Delicious every day, but especially on Sunday.

Vinegar Bean Soup (German)
Schnippel

Serves 8 (10 cups)

Fresh-picked green beans, cooked slowly with a ham bone for 2 or more hours over a low fire, create a broth that I fell in love with as a child, and the romance continues to this day.

Now that flavor has been carried a delicious step further by a German soup, Schnippel, so named for the word that describes the diagonal cut the beans are given before they are dropped into the pot.

The soup is made with two kinds of beans—green and navy—plus a splash of red wine vinegar to give it an unexpected piquancy. At one time green beans were "laid down" in brine in a crock for wintertime use, much like cabbage for sauerkraut. It is that acidulous taste that the vinegar here provides.

This is a large recipe (10 cups) made to fully utilize a ham bone and a bountiful harvest of bush or pole green beans. It can be made with either 1 or 2 pounds of schnippeled *green beans, depending on how thick you like your soup.*

The recipe came to me from my friend Ken Moeller, whose great-great-grandmother brought it from Germany. On a trip to Germany I was delighted to find the same recipe myself. It is a meal in itself when accompanied with a green salad and chunks of country bread.

INGREDIENTS

Shopping note: To make the soup, buy a 4- or 5- pound smoked pork shoulder or a meaty ham bone generously overlaid with meat.

1 cup navy beans
1 pork shoulder or ham bone (see above)
4 quarts water, to cover
1 onion
6 cloves
1 clove garlic, mashed
1 to 2 pounds green beans
1 cup chopped green onions
(No salt until tasted)
½ teaspoon, or to taste, freshly ground black pepper
¼ cup good-quality red or white wine vinegar

SPECIAL
EQUIPMENT

None

PREPARATION

Note: Two things are to be done overnight. The navy beans must be soaked and the pork shoulder or ham bone cooked so the stock can be chilled and the congealed fat lifted off and discarded before proceeding.

OVERNIGHT

In a medium bowl, soak navy beans overnight with water to cover. Place meaty ham bone in large (6-quart) pot and add 4 quarts of water, the onion stuck with cloves, and the crushed garlic clove. Bring to a boil slowly. Skim.

SIMMER
2 hours
30 mins.

Reduce heat and simmer covered for 2 hours. Cool overnight. Fat will rise to the surface to be skimmed off later and discarded.

Carefully skim off fat. Remove bone and meat. Strain stock to re-move onion and garlic and return stock to pot. Pick meat from the bone and cut into bite-size pieces—it should yield about 2 cups. Return the meat to the stock.

Pour water off the navy beans and add them to the stock.

SIMMER

Bring the stock to a boil, reduce heat, and simmer navy beans for 1 hour.

I hour	In the meantime, wash, clean, and *schnippel* the green beans into diagonal pieces about 2 inches long. Add these and the chopped green
I hour	onions to the pot and continue to simmer for an additional hour, or until the green beans are tender but not falling apart.
15 mins.	Remove soup from the heat. Taste for saltiness and add a small amount of salt if needed, but use caution, as the ham may be quite salty.

Pepper is important to the flavor of this soup but don't overdo it. Start with no more than ½ teaspoon and then add more if desired.

Finally, pour in the vinegar and stir to blend well. Taste. If more piquancy is desired, add 1 additional tablespoonful.

FINAL STEP   Serve hot with a coarse bread, perhaps slices of a French country loaf.

Borscht (Russian)

Serves 6 to 8

The classic borscht is always thick with vegetables, but if you prefer a less robust soup, strain it when finished cooking and serve as a clear liquid, hot or cold.

The Russian peasant created out of simple ingredients an attractive style of cooking that is epitomized in this one dish, borscht. If there was to be a single nourishing dish served in the peasant home it probably was a steaming bowl of borscht accompanied with sour, dark Russian bread in thick slabs. Only shchi, *a cabbage soup, was more common. The basic ingredients were about the same. If cabbage predominated, it was* shchi; *if it was red with beets it was borscht.*

There are more versions of borscht than can be tasted or counted. There are meatless ones made with mushrooms, borshchok *made with almost no vegetable other than beets,* borshch *made with young beets and their green tops, and a clear soup with fat and vegetables removed. Ukrainian* borshch *has tomatoes, pork as well as beef, and a greater variety of vegetables, including garlic.*

The name comes not from the beet but from an old Russian word signifying either a parsnip or a wild plant known as cow parsnip. And it can be spelled borscht, borsch, bortch, borschschock, borshch, bortsch, and so on, ad infinitum.

This borscht has a variety of vegetables and small pieces of beef, flavored with garlic and vinegar. At serving, a spoonful of blended sour cream and heavy cream is swirled over the top.

INGREDIENTS   2 tablespoons butter
I pound lean stew beef, cut into ⅜-inch cubes, or processed briefly

3 stalks celery, trimmed and cut lengthwise into julienne strips
    1 ½ inches long
½ cup coarsely shredded carrots
1 turnip, diced
1 large onion, peeled and finely chopped
1 pound beets, fresh or canned, cut into strips (julienne), about 5 cups
1 clove garlic, minced
5 cups beef stock
⅓ cup tomato paste
1 tablespoon white vinegar
Salt, if desired
¼ teaspoon freshly ground black pepper
½ cup sour cream
½ cup heavy cream

SPECIAL EQUIPMENT	Food processor, optional
PREPARATION	*Note:* While canned beets may be used, the borscht has a fresher taste made with beets from the garden plus their leaves and stems. Wash the beets and leaves well. Break off the leaves and separate them from the ribs. Cut the leaves into fine shreds and chop the stalks and ribs finely. Peel the beets and cut into julienne strips. *Note:* The meat may be cubed by hand or chopped coarsely in 1 or 2 short bursts of the food processor.
SAUTÉ *20 mins.*	Drop the butter into a medium (4-quart) saucepan and heat to bubbling. Add the meat and cook over medium heat for 20 minutes until all the redness is gone and the meat is somewhat tender.
SMOTHER *15 mins.*	Add the celery, carrots, turnips, onions, beets, and garlic. Cover and cook over medium heat for 15 minutes. Stir frequently.
BOIL/SIMMER *30–40 mins.*	Pour in the beef stock and add the tomato paste, vinegar, and beet leaves and stalks, if to be used. Bring to a boil, reduce heat, and simmer until the vegetables, especially the beets, are fork-tender—about 30 minutes over medium-low heat. If canned beets are used add them only during the last 10 minutes of cooking. Stir occasionally. Add salt, if needed, and black pepper. In a small bowl combine the sour and heavy creams.

FINAL STEP   Serve very hot in heated bowls. Swirl a teaspoonful or more of the cream blend in each serving. Also pass additional cream. Serve with a coarse peasant bread and plenty of butter.

Cream of Broccoli Soup

Serves 4 or 5

For a long time broccoli was not high on my list of preferred vegetables. That was before I discovered it in this delicious soup, which is speckled with finely chopped broccoli florets and green onions. The original recipe called for a potato to be added, but it makes the soup quite thick.

Broccoli probably is the parent of cauliflower, and in England it is often called winter cauliflower. It was valued by the Romans some 2,000 years ago; however, not until the 1920s was it cultivated in the United States.

The broccoli pieces in this soup are not to be overcooked. They should be al dente, somewhat crisp to the bite.

INGREDIENTS   1 pound broccoli (about 3 stalks)
2 tablespoons butter
1 medium onion, peeled and chopped
1 quart chicken stock

Sachet d'épice
2 teaspoons thyme
2 bay leaves, crumbled
½ teaspoon black peppercorns
1 clove garlic, mashed

4 sprigs parsley, tied together
2 tablespoons cornstarch
2 tablespoons water
¾ cup light or heavy cream, depending on thickness desired
2 tablespoons finely sliced green onions
1 to 2 tablespoons lemon juice, to taste
Salt, if desired
White pepper to taste
1 tablespoon butter, to swirl into finished soup
4 to 5 thinly cut lemon slices, to garnish
Paprika, to dust

SPECIAL EQUIPMENT	Food processor, blender, or food mill
PREPARATION	Cut broccoli florets off stalks and reserve. Peel thick stems and stalks to their centers. Set aside.
SMOTHER 8 mins.	In a medium (3-quart) saucepan, melt butter and add onion. Cover and cook until soft and translucent, about 8 minutes.
BOIL/SIMMER 5 mins.	Pour in the chicken stock, add the sachet and parsley sprigs, and bring to a boil over medium heat. Boil gently for 5 minutes. Mix the cornstarch and water together in a small bowl. Pour the mixture slowly into the stock, stirring constantly, until it thickens to the consistency of heavy cream.
5 mins.	Add broccoli stalks and stems; simmer uncovered for 5 minutes.
3 mins.	Set ½ cup of florets aside and add the rest to the simmering stock. Simmer for 3 minutes, or until both large pieces and small ones are somewhat tender—not thoroughly cooked. Remove from the heat.
PUREE	Puree soup in processor or blender, or put through a food mill. Return the puree to the clean saucepan. Add cream, green onions, lemon juice, salt if desired, and white pepper.
BLANCH 1 min.	Blanch the reserved ½ cup of florets in water to cover in a small saucepan. Boil for 1 minute and immediately plunge into cold water. Drain, dry, and roughly chop the florets. Add to the soup.
REHEAT	Reheat soup to hot but not boiling.
FINAL STEP	Whisk the tablespoon of butter into the soup and ladle into heated individual soup plates. Garnish with lemon slices and dust with paprika.

Cabbage Soup

Serves 6 to 8

One of the most popular vegetables in the American cuisine almost from the beginning has been cabbage. It is recorded in Thomas Jefferson's garden book and the Dutch prepared it in New Amsterdam as kool sla, cabbage salad.

Properly cooked, cabbage has a gently sweet flavor and little or no odor.

This is a fine soup for a one-dish meal. It can be reheated time and again, and reheating seems only to enhance its flavor.

INGREDIENTS	I cup chopped onion
	I cup diced celery
	5 tablespoons butter
	I-pound solid head white cabbage
	I tablespoon minced parsley
	6 tablespoons flour
	2 quarts chicken stock
	6 to 8 thinly sliced mushrooms, including stems
	½ pound high-quality frankfurters, cut diagonally into ⅜-inch slices

Note: I despair at times of finding a good frankfurter or wiener and turn instead to garlic- or spice-seasoned Portuguese sausage or kielbasa.

8 ounces frozen peas, cooked
Salt, if desired
Pinch of freshly ground black pepper

SPECIAL EQUIPMENT	None

PREPARATION SMOTHER 10 mins. 10 mins.	Cook onions and celery in 4 tablespoons of butter over medium heat in a large (4-quart) covered saucepan until tender and translucent, about 10 minutes.
	Cut the cabbage lengthwise into quarters. Cut away the tough core and slice into ⅜-inch shreds. Add the cabbage and parsley to the saucepan and continue to cook, covered, for 10 additional minutes. The cabbage will shortly wilt and collapse among the other vegetables.
2–3 mins.	Stir in the flour and cook for 2 or 3 minutes.
SIMMER 30 mins.	Pour in the stock, bring to a simmer, and cook for 30 minutes. Stir well to blend the flour with the stock.
SAUTÉ	Sauté the mushrooms in the remaining 1 tablespoon of butter and set aside.
BOIL/SIMMER 10 mins.	Ten minutes before the soup is done add the frankfurters or sausages, cooked peas, and mushrooms. Bring to a boil, reduce heat, and simmer for about 10 minutes. Season with salt, if desired, and pepper.
FINAL STEP	The soup may be prepared several hours or a day or so in advance. Reheating only seems to make it better. Serve hot in a heated tureen and ladle into heated individual soup plates.

Cabbage Soup (Russian)
Shchi

Serves 6 to 8 bountifully

Shchi (also shchee) is one of the most famous of the Russian soups. While it is essentially cab-bage, it also includes potato, tomato, and celery root (celeriac), among other vegetables.

Shchi is a hearty affair, the principal item on the menu served on a wintry evening, with thick slabs of Russian pumpernickel or black bread and sweet butter on the side.

The soup, thick enough to be a stew, is made with a firm head of white cabbage (the kind available in most markets). The cabbage should have crisp, unblemished greenish outermost leaves. A very white color indicates an overripe head that is apt to be tough.

There are some five hundred varieties of cabbage offered by commercial seed suppliers in this country. Cabbages can be green, white, or red; conical, round, or flattish; and with the leaves smooth to elegantly puckered and crinkled. The French call it chou, *the Germans* Kraut, *the Portuguese* repolho, *and the Italians* verza.

This shchi recipe is adapted from one passed along by Alex D. Hawkes in his fine book on vegetable cookery.

INGREDIENTS	2 1-pound solid heads young cabbage
	2 quarts beef stock
	2 tablespoons butter
	1½ cups coarsely chopped onions
	1 cup finely chopped carrots
	2 cups (8 ounces) celery root (celeriac), scraped and cut into fine strips
	1 teaspoon salt, if desired
	1 bay leaf
	1 teaspoon dill weed
	1 pound garlic sausage or kielbasa, cut diagonally into ¼-inch slices
	2 tablespoons minced parsley
	2 cups tomatoes, peeled, seeded, and chopped
	2 cups diced potatoes
	Freshly ground black pepper, to taste
	Sour cream, to garnish
SPECIAL EQUIPMENT	None
PREPARATION	Slice the cabbages into quarter wedges, cutting away the core and any hard ribs. Coarsely chop the cabbage and put it aside.

HEAT	Pour the stock into a large (6-quart) pot or kettle and bring to a simmer while preparing the vegetables.
SMOTHER
10 mins.	In a large skillet, melt the butter until bubbling and add the onions, carrots, and celery root. Cover and cook for about 10 minutes over medium-low heat until the vegetables are translucent and somewhat tender.
SIMMER
20 mins.	Turn the contents of the skillet into the stockpot and add salt to taste (pepper will come later). Also add the bay leaf and dill weed. Bring to a simmer.
TRY OUT
10 mins.	In the same skillet, try out the sausage pieces until slightly browned and the fat has been released. Lift the meat out of the skillet with a slotted spoon. Discard the fat.
SIMMER
20 mins.	Add the sausage, parsley, tomatoes, and potatoes to the soup. Continue to simmer for an additional 20 minutes, or a total of 40 minutes.
BOIL/SIMMER
4–5 mins.	Add reserved cabbage, bring to a boil, reduce heat, and simmer over low heat for 4 to 5 minutes. Do not overcook.
FINAL STEP	Serve while very hot, with freshly ground pepper to be added by each diner. Pass sour cream to be stirred into the soup at the table.

Old Country Cabbage and Pork Soup

Serves 8 to 10

The humble but flavorsome cabbage is a fine kettle companion for pork pieces and sausage bits in this delicious soup, which has its roots in the peasant kitchens of middle Europe.

It is a tasty soup to serve at a tailgate party or at home after the football game—whether college, pro, or high school. Great for the ski hut, too. Serve it with big chunks of French peasant bread and plenty of butter. Calories don't count at these moments!

| INGREDIENTS | 3 medium-size (1½ pounds) pork shoulder or blade chops
¼ pound salt pork or bacon
1 large onion, chopped
3 quarts beef stock
4 cloves garlic, minced
2 turnips, cubed
3 carrots, chopped
3 medium potatoes, peeled and cubed
1 pound garlic sausage or kielbasa |
| --- | --- |

1 medium (1½ pounds) cabbage, shredded
Freshly ground black pepper to taste
Salt, if desired

SPECIAL EQUIPMENT	Food processor
PREPARATION *20 mins.*	Cut meat from chops, discard excessive fat, and cut meat into bite-size pieces. Place meat and bones in a medium (4-quart) saucepan. Cut salt pork or bacon into chunks and add to pot. Cook over medium-high heat, stirring, until meat browns.
10 mins.	Add onion and cook until translucent. Stir in stock. Add garlic, turnips, carrots, and potatoes.
BOIL/SIMMER *1 hour* *8 mins.*	Cover and bring to a boil; reduce heat and simmer for about 1 hour or until vegetables are tender. While pot is simmering, remove casings from sausage and cut the meat into small pieces. Fry briefly in hot skillet to render out fat, and discard this. Set meat aside.
10 mins. *5 mins.*	Coarsely shred cabbage (slicing disk of food processor). Set aside. After simmering 1 hour, discard pork bones and add sausage pieces and cabbage. Return to a boil but immediately reduce heat to a simmer.
SIMMER *20 mins.*	While soup simmers, taste for seasoning and add pepper and salt, if desired. Cover and simmer until cabbage is tender, about 20 minutes.
DEGREASE	Spoon off shiny fat globules from hot soup or, ideally, chill soup and allow hard disk of cooled fat to form on top; then lift off fat and discard. Reheat soup to serve.
FINAL STEP	Heat soup bowls and tureen before ladling soup into them. This soup freezes well.

Puree of Carrot Soup (French)
Potage Crécy

Serves 6

A crisp bite of carrot is at the other end of the spectrum from a spoonful of this rich and creamy potage purée. With the exception of a small amount of onion, this is pure carrot, with rice as the liaison. The soup is a lovely pink, and its taste makes it a perfect first-course dish or a potage for a lunch or brunch. Equally good hot or cold, but if served chilled, be certain all the butter from sautéing has been taken off.

INGREDIENTS

3 cups thinly sliced carrots (about ¾ pound)
2 tablespoons chopped onion
6 tablespoons butter
Pinch *each* of salt and sugar
4 cups consommé
⅓ cup uncooked rice
1 tablespoon chopped fresh chives, to garnish
2 teaspoons chopped fresh parsley, to garnish
1½ cups small croutons fried in butter

SPECIAL
EQUIPMENT

Blender, food processor, food mill, or sieve

PREPARATION

Note: If the carrots are old and tough, parboil them for about 15 minutes.

SMOTHER
15 mins.

Place the carrots and onions in 3 tablespoons of butter in a medium (3-quart) saucepan, cover, and cook over medium-low heat until soft, about 15 minutes. Stir frequently and don't allow to brown or burn. Season with salt and sugar.

SIMMER
20 mins.

Pour the consommé into the saucepan and bring to a simmer. Add the rice and cook gently with the lid on for 20 minutes or until rice is soft.

PUREE

Take the soup off the heat and set aside to cool. Puree in blender, food processor, or food mill, or rub through a sieve.

REHEAT

Reheat the soup. If it is too thick, dilute with consommé or water.

FINAL STEP

When the soup is hot, swirl in the remaining 3 tablespoons of butter and take the pan from the heat. Ladle into a heated tureen or warm bowls and sprinkle with chives and parsley. Pass a separate bowl of croutons.

If the soup is to be served cold, omit the butter and skim off butter left from sautéing.

Cream of Carrot with Ginger (French)
Crème de Carottes à Gingembre

Serves 6

On the two-hundredth anniversary of the first manned balloon flight, which occurred in France, I climbed out of the wicker basket hanging beneath a giant pear-shaped balloon—in the same country—to celebrate with the traditional bottle of champagne both that historical event and my own return to earth.

These festivities were closely followed by the discovery of Crème de Carottes à Gingembre on the table spread for two dozen fellow balloon passengers, the pilots, and the ground "chase" crews. It all happened in a château near Beaune, in Burgundy, the headquarters for the remarkable food-and-flying adventure put together by the Buddy Bombard Society.

While the pilots handle things aloft, on the ground the adventure is in the skilled hands of an experienced young chef, Robert Jackson Chambers, who has among his impressive credentials the Grand Diplomate from the École de Cuisine La Varenne, Paris. He arrived in France by the way of hotels and restaurants in Oregon and in North Dakota, where he was born.

Because of the vagaries of free-flight hot-air balloons, Chef Chambers each evening fashions an elegant cold buffet beginning with a superb hot soup. This gives him and his small staff maximum flexibility in feeding balloonists whenever they return to the château, from wherever their balloons land.

This soup is equally delicious with minced fresh dill weed instead of the ginger.

INGREDIENTS	2 tablespoons butter
	2 medium onions, peeled and coarsely chopped
	1½ pounds young carrots, peeled and sliced
	3 tablespoons shredded fresh gingerroot
	6 cups chicken stock
	1 cup milk
	1½ cups light cream
	1 teaspoon salt or to taste, if desired
	Large pinch of freshly ground white pepper
	Optional: ¼ cup, or to taste, minced fresh dill weed instead of ginger
SPECIAL EQUIPMENT	Food processor or blender
PREPARATION COOK *15 mins.* *20 mins.*	Melt the butter in a medium (3-quart) saucepan. Cook the onions uncovered over low heat until translucent, about 15 minutes.

Add the carrots and shredded ginger, cover, and cook over medium-low heat for 20 minutes. Bring the chicken stock to a simmer in a sepa- |

rate saucepan while the carrots are cooking. Add the stock to the carrot mixture and boil gently over medium heat for about 20 minutes or until the carrots are fork-tender.

PUREE

Remove from the heat and add the milk. Allow to cool for a few minutes before putting the soup into a food processor or blender. (The food processor will produce a pleasant graininess.)

Stir in the cream, and add salt and pepper to taste.

OPTION

Minced dill weed, in place of ginger, may be added.

FINAL STEP

Reheat the soup gently; don't let it come to a boil. Ladle soup into heated bowls.

Cream of Cauliflower Soup

Serves 6

Cream of cauliflower soup, served hot or chilled with a few snippets of fresh chives over a dollop of sour cream, is elegant, yet not often encountered.

The soup can be enjoyed year-round, since fresh cauliflower is available in markets most of the time. If not, there is always the frozen vegetable. One word of caution—overcooking can be disastrous for this lovely edible, so take care that the pieces remain firm.

Beyond the arcaded court of the two-hundred-year-old Science Hill Inn in Shelbyville, Kentucky, is the Georgian Room, one of the best dining rooms in the state. This cauliflower soup is a favorite from its menu. It is a cream soup, pleasingly light.

INGREDIENTS

1 medium head cauliflower
6 tablespoons clarified butter, divided
1 cup finely chopped celery (about 4 stalks)
½ cup finely chopped carrot (1 medium)
½ cup finely chopped onion
2 tablespoons finely chopped parsley, divided
4 cups beef or chicken stock

Sachet d'épice
½ teaspoon black peppercorns
1 bay leaf, crumbled
1 teaspoon dried tarragon

2 tablespoons cornstarch
2 cups milk

1 cup light cream
Salt to taste, if desired
1 cup sour cream
2 tablespoons finely chopped chives, to garnish

SPECIAL EQUIPMENT	None
PREPARATION	Cut away the heavy cauliflower stems. Break the head into small florets and set aside—there should be about 4 cups.
SMOTHER 5 mins. 5 mins. 10 mins.	In a large (4-quart) saucepan, melt 2 tablespoons butter and add the celery and carrot. Cover and cook over medium heat for 5 minutes. Add the onion and cook for an additional 5 minutes. Stir frequently. Add the cauliflower and 1 tablespoon of the parsley. Keep covered and cook for 10 more minutes.
BOIL/SIMMER 10 mins. 15 mins.	Pour the stock into the saucepan and add the sachet. Bring to a boil, reduce heat, and simmer over medium-low heat for 10 minutes.

While the stock is simmering, melt the remaining 4 tablespoons of butter in a small saucepan. In a small bowl blend together the cornstarch and milk. Stirring constantly, add the cornstarch mixture to the butter. It will thicken immediately into a white sauce of medium consistency. Remove from heat and dilute with the light cream. Pour this mixture into the soup. Stir gently and let simmer for another 15 minutes. |
| FINAL STEP | Place sour cream in a heated tureen. Mix with it the remaining tablespoon of parsley. Remove sachet from soup. Ladle 2 cups of hot soup into the tureen and stir it into the sour cream. Pour the remaining soup into the tureen. Add salt to taste. Serve immediately. Garnish with chives. |
| VARIATION | The soup is equally good chilled, but in that case it should be pureed first. When it is cold, the fat, if any, will rise to the surface and can be lifted off and discarded. Garnish with chives. |

Cream of Celery Soup

Serves 4 to 6

Celery has a wonderful clear, clean taste. It doesn't intrude or overpower. Most of the time it is just one of the several vegetables in soup; and it is always in mirepoix, that bundle of onions, carrots, and celery that blends to give a classic seasoning to stocks and soups.

Worth only 9 calories to the cupful, celery can be used from the very bottom of the stalk up to and including its vivid green foliage.

This soup is put together in two stages and brought together just 10 minutes before it is served. To prepare it longer in advance would allow the potato to thicken the soup too much.

INGREDIENTS

Puree
8 stalks celery (½ pound), chopped into 1-inch lengths
2 medium potatoes (5 ounces), sliced ¼ inch thick
4 cups water
1 teaspoon salt

Soup
2 tablespoons butter
1 cup finely chopped onion
¼ teaspoon salt, if desired
1 cup finely minced celery
½ teaspoon celery seed
1 cup milk
½ cup sour cream or heavy cream
White pepper, to taste
2 tablespoons thinly sliced pitted black olives, to garnish
2 tablespoons finely chopped pimiento, to garnish

SPECIAL
EQUIPMENT

Food processor, blender, or food mill. Double boiler, optional.

PREPARATION

In a medium (3-quart) saucepan, with lid, place the celery and potatoes and add 4 cups of water. Sprinkle with salt.

GENTLE BOIL
15 mins.

Bring the contents to a boil and cook, covered, until the celery and potatoes are fork-tender, about 15 minutes. Remove from heat.

PUREE

When the potato/celery mixture has cooled for a few minutes, pour it, including the liquor, into the work bowl of a processor or blender. It may be necessary to do this in two batches if the bowl is small. The mixture may also be put through a food mill. Pour the mixture into the saucepan and set aside.

SMOTHER
6 mins.

8 mins.

In a medium skillet, melt the butter and add the finely chopped onions. Cover and cook over medium-low heat until translucent, about 6 minutes. Add minced celery and celery seed, keep covered, and cook for an additional 8 minutes or until celery is tender.

Scrape the contents of the skillet into the saucepan with the celery/potato puree.

Ten minutes before serving, add the milk and sour or heavy cream. Season with white pepper. Heat the soup carefully in a double boiler or by placing the saucepan on a heat-absorbent plate. Don't boil or overcook.

FINAL STEP   Ladle the soup into heated individual bowls. In a moment or so, when the soup has formed a supporting film over the surface, garnish with sliced olives and chopped pimiento.

Celery and Herb Soup

Serves 4

Celery is one of the important mainstays of the kitchen, called on time and again to strengthen and underscore a developing flavor with its clear, fresh taste. Yet it seldom has the opportunity to stand alone. And only 9 calories to a cupful!

In this recipe celery is front and center with a supporting cast of herbs. The soup is a panade—soup ladled over toasted sturdy peasant bread, not the squeezing-fresh kind which would disintegrate into mush.

This recipe is from New Harmony, the small southern Indiana settlement where Robert Dale Owen welcomed his "Boatload of Knowledge." Earlier, in 1814, Father George Rapp had established a communal society there. The Harmony Herb Shop, which specializes in herbs used by the Harmonists, is where I found it.

INGREDIENTS
2 tablespoons butter
2 cups finely chopped celery
1 tablespoon snipped fresh chives or 1 teaspoon dried
1½ teaspoons minced fresh tarragon or ½ teaspoon dried
1 teaspoon minced fresh chervil or ¼ teaspoon dried
4 cups chicken stock
Pinch of sugar
Salt to taste, if desired
Freshly ground black pepper to taste
4 thin slices French peasant bread (page 360)
Pinches of freshly grated nutmeg, to garnish

SPECIAL
EQUIPMENT
Food processor, optional

PREPARATION	*Note:* The celery may be hand-chopped or done in a food processor, but if using the latter, don't make a pulp. Chop only into small particles to give the soup texture.
SMOTHER *5–6 mins.*	Melt the butter in a medium (3-quart) saucepan and when foaming, add the celery, chives, tarragon, and chervil. Cover and cook for 5 to 6 minutes or until the celery has softened somewhat.
SIMMER *20 mins.*	Pour in the chicken stock, add a pinch of sugar, and add salt and pepper to taste. Simmer over low heat for 20 minutes.
TOAST	Meanwhile, toast the bread in the oven or toaster.
FINAL STEP	Place a piece of bread in each warmed soup bowl. Ladle the soup over the bread and garnish each portion with a pinch of freshly grated nutmeg.

Cream of Cucumber (Spanish)
Crema de Pepinos

Serves 6 to 8

Crema de Pepinos *is the creation of one of Barcelona's most respected restaurateurs, Ramon Cabau, whose Agut d'Avignon is noted for its outstanding Catalan cuisine and its ambiente típico. A dapper and grandly mustached gentleman, Señor Cabau earned three doctoral degrees (in law, medicine, and music) before he turned with equal dedication to food.*

The Agut d'Avignon is dimly marked at the end of a narrow passageway in the old Barri Gòtic district. That's the way he wanted it. (Put your faith in a taxi driver. Address: Trinitat 3.)

When I asked Señor Cabau for his finest summertime soup he unhesitatingly chose Crema de Pepinos. *It is a cold soup that conveys a very real sense of iciness. The nutty flavor and texture of the almonds blend with the cucumber and yogurt to make a delicious soup.*

The skin of garden-fresh cucumbers need not be removed, but cucumbers found in supermarkets have usually been waxed—for color and preservation—and should be peeled.

INGREDIENTS	5 pounds (4 or 5 large) cucumbers, peeled (if not freshly picked), seeded, and coarsely sliced
	4 ounces (¾ cup) blanched almonds
	1 clove garlic
	1 teaspoon lemon juice
	2 cups plain yogurt
	2 cups light cream

1 teaspoon salt, if desired
¼ teaspoon freshly ground white pepper
½ cup finely chopped fresh parsley or chives, to garnish

SPECIAL EQUIPMENT	Food processor or blender, depending on degree of smoothness desired
PREPARATION PUREE *5 mins.*	Puree the cucumber pieces in 2 or 3 batches, according to the capacity of the work bowl, and pour into a mixing bowl. In the last batch add the almonds, garlic, and lemon juice.
BLEND *2 mins.*	Add the yogurt and cream to the mixture and stir to blend. Season with salt and pepper.
CHILL *2 hours or more*	Refrigerate the soup for at least 2 hours or until it is thoroughly chilled. Also chill the cups or bowls in which it is to be served.
FINAL STEP	Ladle the soup into bowls and garnish with either parsley or chives.

Indian Hominy Stew

Serves 4 or 5

Indian Hominy Stew is a good choice for the days following Thanksgiving when there are bits of leftover bird—be it turkey, chicken, goose, or duck—to combine with the hominy. A creation to warm the heart of the coldest Pilgrim.

The Indians had little to do with developing this particular dish. I am fond of hominy and this is my tribute to it and to the people who first harvested corn. Hominy is made by treating the kernels of corn with lye, which dissolves their skin. Afterward the hominy is washed and then boiled.

INGREDIENTS	2 cups (1 pint) milk
	2 cups tomatoes, fresh or canned, drained
	1 16-ounce can hominy, drained
	1 tablespoon finely chopped onion
	1 teaspoon butter
	1 teaspoon salt
	1 teaspoon sugar
	⅛ teaspoon paprika
	1 to 2 cups bite-size pieces of meat of choice, above, at room temperature

(continued)

1 tablespoon cornstarch or arrowroot, to thicken
¼ cup water
½ cup finely chopped parsley or celery leaves, to garnish
1 cup popcorn, to garnish

SPECIAL EQUIPMENT	None
PREPARATION *8 mins.*	Bring milk to boil in a medium (3-quart) saucepan, add tomatoes and hominy, and return to a boil. Turn down heat and simmer while sautéing the chopped onion in butter in a small skillet, about 8 minutes.
SIMMER *20 mins.*	Add the onion to the milk mixture—also the salt, sugar, paprika, and meat. Blend thickening agent with water in a small bowl and pour into the stew.
20 mins.	Continue to simmer until all ingredients are heated, about 20 minutes. Stir frequently.
FINAL STEP	Serve in large soup bowls with crackers on the side. Garnish with parsley, celery leaves, and/or popcorn.
VARIATION	With the addition of 3 or 4 pork chops, chopped hot green chilies, cumin seed, oregano, and chicken or beef stock rather than milk, this becomes posole, the Mexican pork and hominy stew. It is also delicious with a stock made from pork bones, pig knuckle, fresh pork hock, and boneless lean fresh pork.

Dandelion Soup (Italian)
Zuppa di Cicoria

Serves 8

When dandelions blossom yellow in the spring, think of them as the important ingredient of a delicious soup, not as weeds unwanted and unloved. The pleasant bitterness the greens impart to this soup brings a rush of childhood remembrances of my mother's special treat for me—a mess of dandelion greens simmered with bacon or ham bits, served with slices of hard-cooked egg and awash in vinegar (the latter was my idea).

This recipe was given to me by Harry Lordino, who was with Footers Restaurant in Denver. It was brought to this country from Northern Italy by his grandmother, Giuseppa Tramutola Lordino.

The young leaves picked in springtime are the best, for they are the most tender. Later in the summer, as the plants grow older, the leaves develop a fibrous character. Long cooking, un-fortunately, seems only to make them tougher. Bunches of fresh dandelion greens can be found in the spring in many markets in the larger cities. Alas, you miss the fun of uprooting the plant.

If in the winter you have a hunger for zuppa di cicoria *and simply can't wait for spring, try curly endive—a highly satisfactory substitute.*

INGREDIENTS	
	½ pound dandelion greens or endive, well washed
	2 quarts water
	½ pound bulk Italian or other mildly hot garlic sausage
	1 pound ground beef
	1 onion, finely chopped
	3 cloves garlic, peeled and minced
	3 eggs
	1 cup shredded mozzarella cheese (grated Parmesan or Romano can substitute)
	2 tablespoons cider vinegar
	Salt to taste, if desired (about 2 teaspoons usually)
	¼ teaspoon freshly ground black pepper
	8 slices hard-cooked egg, to garnish
	1 cup shredded cheese, to garnish, if desired

SPECIAL EQUIPMENT

A heavy knife to cut through the root of the dandelion when picking

PREPARATION

Note: It will take one soaking and several rinsings to thoroughly clean the greens. After washing, pick through the greens, discarding discolored leaves and odd bits and pieces of grass. With scissors, cut the plant just above the root so the leaves will fall free. Rinse as often as necessary to get rid of all the dirt. The greens may be picked and cleaned 1 or 2 days ahead of time, bagged, and refrigerated.

Pile the greens on a cutting block and with a large knife chop leaves into pieces no more than 1 inch in length.

BOIL/SIMMER
6–8 mins.

Into a medium (3-quart) pot, pour the water and add the greens. The leaves will protrude far above the waterline but will quickly cook down. Cover the pot and bring the water to a boil. Reduce heat to a simmer and cook the greens for 6 to 8 minutes or until tender but not mushy. Do not overcook. A little crunch in the bite is good. Bite into a leaf or two to test.

SAUTÉ *6–8 mins.* *10 mins.* *6 mins.*	While the greens are cooking, prepare the meats. In a large skillet place the sausage and cook over medium heat until brown, about 6 to 8 minutes. Add the ground beef, break apart with a wooden spoon, and cook with the sausage until well browned, about 10 minutes over medium heat. Add the onion and garlic, cover, and continue to cook until the onion is soft, about 6 minutes.
DRAIN	Take the skillet off the heat. Tilt it to allow the grease to drain to one side. Lift the grease out with a large spoon and discard.
SIMMER *10 mins.*	Scrape the meat mixture into the soup pot and let the meat and greens simmer together for 10 minutes. Beat the eggs in a small bowl and pour into the soup, stirring constantly. Next add the cheese in small portions at a time, again stirring constantly—it will become delightfully stringy in the process. Stir in the 2 tablespoons of vinegar—more if you like the sour touch it gives the soup.
FINAL STEP	Bring the soup back to a simmer so that it is steaming hot before ladling into hot soup bowls. Decorate with the egg slices. Pass shredded cheese so that the guests may add more to the soup if they desire. A crusty bread is a great companion for the *zuppa*.

Chickpea Soup (Spanish)
Caldo Gallego

Serves 10 to 12

Caldo Gallego is a thick, delicious wintertime soup—nearly a stew—from the Spanish province of Galicia. Some believe it should be so thick that a spoon will stand upright in it.

Tomato can be included and ham or pork substituted for the beef. Fishing folk along the Spanish coast use whichever is in the larder at the moment. Sausage is a constant, however, and the best for this soup is chorizo, found in Hispanic markets.

The chief ingredient, the chickpea or garbanzo bean, is used in similar soups in Mexico and many other parts of Spanish-speaking America. In many lands it is probably the most important source of protein.

INGREDIENTS	1 pound dried chickpeas (garbanzos) or 3 15-ounce cans 1 tablespoon salt Water to cover

1 pound boneless beef chuck, cut into ½-inch pieces
1 pound veal bones, sawed into 2-inch pieces
10 to 12 cups water

Sachet d'épice
1 tablespoon chopped parsley
1 bay leaf, crumbled
1 clove garlic, crushed
½ teaspoon black peppercorns

Salt, to taste
4 slices bacon
1½ cups chopped onions
1 pound chorizo, sliced ⅜ inch on the diagonal, or other spicy,
    hot sausage links
2 medium potatoes, peeled and cut into ½-inch cubes
1 pound fresh young spinach leaves
½ cup minced parsley, to garnish

SPECIAL EQUIPMENT	Food processor or food mill
PREPARATION SOAK *Overnight*	Soak the chickpeas overnight in salted cold water to cover, or boil for 3 minutes and set aside in the water for 1 hour. Canned chickpeas are equally good in this recipe. Drain, if using the canned.
BOIL/SIMMER *2 hours*	In a large (4-quart) saucepan or kettle, place the beef, veal bones, and chickpeas. Add water to cover (about 10 cups), bring to a boil, reduce heat, and simmer for about 2 hours. Salt to taste. A half hour before chickpeas are cooked, add the sachet.
TRY OUT *7 mins.*	Try out the bacon strips in a skillet over medium heat. When the bacon pieces are crisp, lift out and place on paper towels to drain. Set aside.
SAUTÉ *8 mins.*	Leave the fat in the skillet and add the onions. Sauté onions uncovered for about 8 minutes or until soft and translucent. With a slotted spoon lift out onions and reserve.
TRY OUT *8 mins.*	Drop the sausage slices into the skillet and try out over medium heat until the fat has been released and pieces are glossy and lightly browned. Lift out with a slotted spoon and reserve.

If the liquid in the pot boils down, replenish with 1 or 2 cups of water.

When the meat and beans are cooked, remove the pot from the heat. Cut off any meat on the veal bones and add to the pot. Discard the bones.

PUREE

About half the chickpeas will be pureed or mashed, depending on the texture desired in the soup. Place in a food processor, with some of the liquid, for a fine chop, or put through a food mill for a coarser one. (Cooks simply mash some of the chickpeas against the sides of the pot with a large wooden spoon.) Return the chickpeas to the pot.

BOIL/SIMMER
15 mins.

Add crumbled bacon, onions, sausage, and cubed potatoes. Bring to a boil, reduce heat, partially cover, and simmer for about 15 minutes or until the potatoes are fork-tender.

Meanwhile tear the spinach leaves from the heavy stems; wash all sand from the leaves and chop coarsely.

5 mins.

Drop the leaves on top of the soup, cover, and allow the leaves to steam for 5 minutes. Remove from heat and stir the leaves into the soup.

If the soup is too thick, add water. Taste for seasoning. Remove and discard sachet.

FINAL STEP

This is a hearty, robust, family-style dish that should be ladled into large heated soup plates. Garnish with parsley. Serve with a new red wine, a green salad, and thick slices of peasant bread.

Spicy Garlic Soup (Spanish)
Sopa da Ajo

Serves 5

Sopa de ajo is a national dish with as many variations as there are regions of Spain. In some areas the garlic cloves are sautéed in olive oil to a golden color, while in others they are gently cooked with no browning. In coastal provinces, fish or shellfish are included, but in Madrid sopa de ajo is made with only garlic, bread slices, paprika, olive oil, and eggs.

This adaptation has a beef stock rather than water for a richer flavor. The eggs are slipped into the simmering soup and poached. Beaten egg may also be swirled into the hot soup (in the Chinese manner) or poured over the top of the soup and placed under the broiler for a moment until barely set.

INGREDIENTS

3 tablespoons olive oil

10 cloves garlic

5 slices peasant-type bread, cut ¼ inch thick

4 teaspoons paprika

6 cups rich beef stock or water

½ teaspoon cumin seeds, roasted and crushed
(see "Spices, Herbs, and Seasonings," page 372)

1 teaspoon salt, if desired

5 eggs (1 per serving)

1 tablespoon chopped parsley

SPECIAL
EQUIPMENT

Individual ovenproof bowls or oven- and flameproof casserole or saucepan in which to make the soup and poach the eggs

PREPARATION

Note: If individual bowls are to be used, make the soup in a separate saucepan and ladle the soup into each ovenproof bowl. Bowls are placed in the oven until the soup comes to a simmer. An egg is then added to each bowl to set. If using a casserole, however, use the same vessel for all steps.

SAUTÉ
4 mins.

4 mins.

Spoon the olive oil into a medium (3-quart) saucepan or casserole. Heat over medium-high heat. Drop the garlic cloves into the oil. Sauté, stirring frequently, until golden brown, but do not allow to burn. They will be soft and puffy. Remove the cloves with a slotted spoon and set aside.

Drop the bread slices into the pot and brown on both sides. Lift out the slices and put aside. Remove the pan from the heat to allow to cool somewhat, about 3 minutes. Stir in the paprika, which will absorb the balance of the oil.

When the paprika has been well blended, pour in the beef stock or water. Add the cumin. Crush the garlic cloves with a fork and return to the soup. Stir well and check for taste, especially salt.

PREHEAT
400°

Preheat the oven to 400°.

COOK
8 mins.

Cook the soup over medium heat for 8 minutes.

SIMMER

Ladle the soup into ovenproof bowls and place in the oven until the soup returns to a simmer. Break an egg into a saucer and slip it into one of the bowls. Repeat for the others. Place a piece of the toasted bread on top of the egg and soup.

If using a casserole, slip the eggs into the simmering soup one at a time, and cover with the toasted bread.

BAKE
4 mins.

Place the soup in the oven and bake until the eggs are set, about 4 minutes. Don't overcook. The eggs should be soft so the yolks will mix with the soup when they are broken.

FINAL STEP

Garnish with parsley and serve.

VARIATION

Instead of whole eggs, it is also common to cover the top of the soup with beaten eggs (use only 2) and place the casserole briefly under the broiler.

"Boiled Water" Soup (French)
L'Aido Boulido

Serves 4

"Boiled water"—essentially a garlic/cheese soup—has a sharp, clear flavor. In the south of France, in Provence, it is believed to have great restorative powers, for ailments ranging from gout to a toothache.

It is, in addition, one of the least expensive of soups, consisting of nothing more than water, garlic, cheese, and stale bread.

L'Aido Boulido has a tanginess that is delightful.

INGREDIENTS

4 cups water
1 teaspoon salt, if desired
1 dozen cloves garlic, peeled and lightly mashed
2 bay leaves
1 sprig fresh sage or ¼ teaspoon dried
¼ cup olive oil
4 slices day-old dry French peasant bread
1½ cups freshly grated Parmesan or Gruyère cheese

SPECIAL
EQUIPMENT

None

PREPARATION
COOK
10 mins.
5 mins.

Pour water into a medium (3-quart) saucepan; add salt and garlic. Place over medium heat and bring to a gentle boil. Cook for 10 minutes.

Add the bay leaves, sage, and a tablespoon of the olive oil, and cook for an additional 5 minutes.

REST *10 mins.*	Remove from the heat, cover, and let stand for 10 minutes. Strain. Discard garlic buds and herbs.
	Place a slice of stale bread in each heated bowl, cover with a large helping of cheese, and sprinkle with the remaining olive oil.
	Pour the strained broth over the bread and cheese
FINAL STEP	Serve and watch the pleasantly surprised faces of your guests. This is an excellent first course for a heavy meal to follow.

Gazpacho Verde

Serves 4

In Spain this refreshing chilled soup is called gazpacho blanco, *but in Hawaii, where I was given the recipe by a well-known Island cook, Esther Wetzel, it had become* gazpacho verde.

White became green when Wetzel and friends decided that the soup needed something more, and, in a moment of inspiration, added watercress. This gave the soup a slight pungency that it had lacked. Delicious.

Urge your diners to use the condiments liberally. The soup might be described as condiments with soup rather than soup with condiments.

INGREDIENTS	**Soup** ⅓ cup sour cream ⅓ cup mayonnaise 2 tablespoons white wine vinegar 2 cups chicken stock 1 medium onion, sliced 1½ cups coarsely chopped watercress leaves 2 tablespoons chopped dill leaves 1 teaspoon sugar ½ teaspoon salt ¼ teaspoon white pepper 1 cup soft bread crumbs **Condiments** 1 tomato, peeled and seeded ½ green pepper ½ cucumber

(continued)

½ Maui onion*

2 hard-cooked eggs

¾ cup chopped celery hearts

* The mild Maui onion is an Island product and is seldom found in mainland markets. However, Bermuda white, Georgia Vidalias, or any other mild onion may be substituted. (Vidalias—as in Vidalia, Georgia—are the rage of the onion world. Can be eaten out of hand. Ask your greengrocer.)

SPECIAL EQUIPMENT	Use a food processor for a speckled shade of green (my preference) or a blender for overall light green coloring.
PREPARATION *20 mins.*	*Note:* The bread crumbs dissolve and thicken the soup into a kind of *panade.* Use a high-quality white bread, one with substance.
	In a bowl combine the sour cream, mayonnaise, and vinegar. Set aside. Put chicken stock, onion, watercress, dill, sugar, salt, and pepper into a food processor or blender. (Don't overload the machine—process half at a time if necessary.) Blend well. Stir this into the sour cream mixture. Stir in fresh bread crumbs.
CHILL *6 hours or overnight*	Cover and place in the refrigerator for at least 6 hours or overnight, if more convenient.
PREPARE CONDIMENTS	While the soup is chilling, prepare the condiments, all diced—tomato, green pepper, cucumber, onion, eggs, and celery.
FINAL STEP	Place condiments in small dishes to serve with the cold soup. The more condiments in the soup, the better.

Herb Soup

Serves 6

Herb soup is a delight for the gardener or for friends who have access to these herbs. Most of them can be purchased fresh in summer and autumn months in supermarkets, herb shops, and farm markets, but it may take a concerted effort to collect all of them. Doing without one or two of the herbs will not greatly affect the good flavor of the soup, but try to get them all.

Chef Kusuma Cooray created this soup at Willows in Honolulu, where she does wonderful things with food, and that is where I found it.

INGREDIENTS	2 tablespoons clarified butter
	½ teaspoon *each* fennel, cumin, and dill seed

2 tablespoons chopped onion

½ cup *each* coarsely chopped leafy tops of parsley, coriander, and fennel

¼ cup *each* coarsely chopped sweet basil and mint

2 medium tomatoes, finely diced

6 cups chicken stock

¼ teaspoon freshly ground black pepper

Salt, if desired, to taste

2 tablespoons lemon juice or to taste

1 cup yogurt, to garnish

SPECIAL EQUIPMENT	Food processor or blender, optional

PREPARATION	In a medium (3-quart) saucepan, heat the clarified butter over low heat.
COOK	Add fennel, cumin, and dill seed; cook and stir for 1 minute.
1 min.	
8 mins.	Add the chopped onion and cook, stirring occasionally, until the onions are soft and light gold in color. Add the herbs—parsley, coriander, fennel, basil, and mint—then the diced tomatoes. Cook over high
1 min.	heat for 1 minute.
SIMMER	Add the chicken stock. Season with pepper, salt, and lemon juice to
5 mins.	taste. Simmer for 5 minutes.
	There is a choice of texture: Serve as is, or put through a food processor or blender for a creamier soup.
FINAL STEP	Serve hot, with a dollop of yogurt in each bowl.

Leek and Potato Soup (English)

Serves 4

The leek, one of the most honorable of vegetables, was the badge of a high-spirited and fiery nation, the ancient Britons. Today, in Britain and elsewhere, the leek is looked upon as an essential flavoring agent for all sorts of culinary masterpieces.

This delicious leek and potato soup was being made in the kitchen of Drovers, a great house in West Sussex, south and west of London, years before Louis Diat, chef de cuisine of the Ritz-Carlton, created his leek and potato masterpiece, vichyssoise.

Drovers, now a hotel about 40 miles down the road from Heathrow airport, is an ideal place to stay for a day or two to accommodate jet lag, with the bonus of a top-notch cuisine, including this soup.

INGREDIENTS

I pound (about 6 cups) leeks, white part only, washed and finely chopped
¾ pound boiling potatoes, peeled and thinly sliced
¼ cup (½ stick) butter
4 cups chicken stock

Sachet d'épice
I bay leaf
2 or 3 parsley stems
8 peppercorns
¼ teaspoon dried thyme

2 egg yolks
I cup heavy cream, or, if preferred, light cream
Salt to taste, if desired
Snippets of chives or parsley, to garnish

SPECIAL
EQUIPMENT

Food processor or blender

PREPARATION
SMOTHER
8 mins.

In a medium (3½-quart) saucepan, place the leeks and potatoes; cover and cook in butter for about 8 minutes.

BOIL/SIMMER
30 mins.

Add the stock and the sachet, bring to a boil, cover, reduce heat, and simmer for 30 minutes. The potatoes should be fork-tender.

PUREE

Allow the soup to cool for a few minutes before pouring it into a food processor or blender. You may need to process the soup in batches.

SIMMER
3 mins.

Pour the pureed soup back into the rinsed saucepan and return to a simmer. When the soup is hot but not boiling, whisk together 1 cup of the soup, the egg yolks, and the cream in a small bowl. Return the mixture slowly back into the soup. Add salt, if desired.

3 mins.

   Simmer the soup over low heat for about 3 minutes. Do not let it boil.

FINAL STEP

Ladle the soup into preheated bowls and garnish with snippets of chives, if available, or parsley. A rich touch is a tablespoon of heavy cream spooned into each bowl just before serving.

Cock-a-Leekie (Scottish)
Chicken-and-Leek Soup

Serves 6 to 8

Come, my lords and lieges, let us all to dinner,
for the cocky-leeky is a-cooling!
SIR WALTER SCOTT

The name honors the chicken (cock) and the leek (leekie). The traditional cock-a-leekie soup came from Scotland, but long ago variations sprang up across the British Isles, especially in Wales and the West Country.

The addition of prunes is controversial among the soup's admirers. The prunes add sweetness to the soup, which some like and some don't. A Scot is quoted: "The man was an atheist that first polluted it with prunes!" Try one prune in each bowl or serve them as a side dish. Or not at all.

Some cock-a-leekie recipes include ½ cup of quick-cooking pearl barley added when the stock is poured over the leeks. A thicker soup is the result.

INGREDIENTS

4- to 5-pound stewing chicken
4 quarts water
I onion, unpeeled, washed and quartered
2 carrots, unpeeled, washed and coarsely chopped

Sachet d'épice
I clove
I blade fresh mace or ¼ teaspoon dried
2 sprigs parsley
6 peppercorns
I bay leaf

2 tablespoons butter
2 pounds leeks, including 2 inches of green part, washed thoroughly and
    cut diagonally into ½-inch slices (about 8 cups)
Salt, to taste, if desired
¼ teaspoon or 2 grinds of black pepper
12 to 16 dried prunes, optional
2 tablespoons finely chopped parsley

SPECIAL
EQUIPMENT

None

PREPARATION

Wash the fowl inside and out with cold running water. Remove chunks of fat from the cavity and discard. (Or render the fat for another use.)

BOIL/SIMMER
1½–2 hours

Place the chicken in a large (6- to 8-quart) soup pot. Pour in the 4 quarts of water and bring to a boil over high heat. Add onion, carrots, and the sachet (tied in a cheesecloth or placed in a metal tea ball). Reduce heat and cook gently for 1½ to 2 hours, depending on the age of the bird, or until the meat comes easily off the bones.

Remove the chicken from the pot and put it aside until it is cool enough to handle. Strain the stock into a large bowl and discard the solids, including the sachet. The stock may be refrigerated to bring the fat to the surface to be discarded, or the fat can be blotted from the hot stock with paper towels.

Note: There are several ways to include the chicken. The wing meat only can be cut into thin strips and put in the soup while the larger and more choice pieces can be served separately with vegetables. Or all the meat can be cut into bite-size pieces and added to the soup. Your choice. The soup with all the chicken added becomes a full meal in itself.

SMOTHER
10–12 mins.

Meanwhile, heat the butter in a medium (4-quart) saucepan, with lid, and add the leeks. Cover and cook over medium heat 10 to 12 minutes or until they are soft and translucent.

BOIL/SIMMER
15 mins.
12 mins.

Pour in the stock, bring to a boil, and season with salt and pepper to taste. Simmer over medium-low heat for about 15 minutes.

Add the chicken strips or pieces in whatever quantity desired and simmer for a further 12 minutes.

Note: If the traditional prunes are to be served, drop them in the simmering stock about 15 minutes before the soup is done.

FINAL STEP

Swirl in the chopped parsley just before serving. Put 1 prune in each individual bowl and ladle in the soup.

LENTILS

Lentils are inexpensive, versatile, nutritious, and very good to eat. They do not require soaking; but if they are soaked overnight, the short cooking time—15 minutes to 1 hour—can be made shorter by half.

There are two main varieties. The Chilean is the one found most often at the grocer's. It is brown, yellow, or gray. The other is the Persian, widely used in Middle Eastern cuisines and is reddish or orange-red. It is most readily available from health food, Middle Eastern, and East Indian markets but is rapidly moving onto supermarket shelves along with the others.

Lentils are *not* dried beans, although they belong to the same plant family. They are the seeds of a small scrubby plant (*Lens culinaris*) cultivated since prehistoric times in Mediterranean regions and in India. The seeds are used in a tremendous array of dishes, while the leafy stalks are fed to livestock. The optical lens, upon its invention, was named for the lentil because of the marked similarity in shape.

High in vegetable protein, lentils are rich in iron and other minerals and in vitamins B and A, and low in sodium. One pound of raw lentils equals 2⅓ cups, and about three times that volume when cooked.

Lentils should be picked over and washed before cooking. Spread them on a cookie sheet and discard any foreign matter or broken seeds. Place them in a colander and wash under cold running water.

Here are three lentil soup recipes. One is from Sri Lanka, by way of Honolulu, and spiced with cayenne and curry powder. The second—which actually appears first below—was created by Chef Elliott Sharron at the Culinary Institute of America. It is a more traditional soup, made with a combination of beef and chicken stocks and with sausage or ham hocks cooked in it. The third was sent to me by a reader.

Lentil Soup

Serves 8 to 10

Lentil soup is among almost everyone's favorite dishes and no one can make it better than Chef Elliott Sharron, who was my mentor at the Culinary Institute of America at Hyde Park, N.Y. His counsel is reflected in many places in this book.

Chef Sharron's knowledge of and skills with food are quite apparent in this delicious soup. The vegetables are peeled in the order of the time they should be cooked. The rock-hard rutabaga is first and will begin to cook while the carrots are prepared. Next come the celery, the onions, and finally the tender leeks. The lentils are cooked with 2 tablespoons of cider vinegar to cut the bacon grease and help break down the cellulose in the lentils.

INGREDIENTS   ½ **pound lean slab bacon, in ½-inch dice**

I cup *each* finely chopped { rutabaga, carrots, celery, onion, leeks }

Salt, if desired (use sparingly—the meat will contribute saltiness later)

(continued)

½ teaspoon freshly ground black pepper
2 cups (¾ pound) lentils, washed and picked over
2 tablespoons cider vinegar
6 cups chicken stock
6 cups beef stock

Sachet d'épice
1 clove
2 cloves garlic, minced
2 bay leaves, crumbled
½ teaspoon black peppercorns
½ teaspoon thyme
½ teaspoon marjoram
½ teaspoon savory

6 sprigs parsley, tied with string
1 meaty ham bone or 2 ham hocks
½ pound smoked sausage, cut up, to garnish
¼ cup finely chopped fresh chives

SPECIAL EQUIPMENT	Food processor or blender to puree some of the lentils, optional
PREPARATION	Dice the bacon and put into a large (5- to 6-quart) soup pot.
TRY OUT *8 mins.*	Try out the bacon over medium heat to release the fat and crisp the pieces, about 8 minutes. Don't let them burn.
SMOTHER *total of 20 mins.*	Beginning with the rutabaga, peel and chop each vegetable in the order given in the list of ingredients. Add each to the pot when peeled. There will be about a 5-minute interval between vegetables—thus the rutabaga will have cooked 20 minutes by the time the leeks are dropped in. Cover the pot during the process and cook over medium-low heat.
5 mins.	Cook for 5 additional minutes after the leeks have been added. Taste for seasoning.
8 mins.	Add the lentils and cider vinegar to the pot; continue to cook for an additional 8 minutes.
BOIL/SIMMER	Pour in the stocks. Add the sachet and hang the parsley bundle from a handle for easy retrieval later. Drop in the ham bone or ham hocks.

30 mins.	Bring to a boil, reduce the heat, and simmer over medium-low heat for 30 minutes.
	When the soup has cooked, lift out the pork and allow it to cool for a few minutes before picking the meat off the bones. Cut the meat into ⅜-inch cubes and return to the pot. Discard bones, sachet, and parsley.
	If you want a thicker soup, puree 3 or 4 cups of the lentils and vegetables; return to the pot.
TRY OUT	Try out the sausage pieces to release the fat. Pour off and discard the fat. Pat the sausage with paper towels to absorb excess fat.
FINAL STEP	Serve the soup from a heated tureen garnished with sausage pieces and chopped chives.

Chicken Lentil Soup (Sri Lanka)

Serves 6

This chicken lentil soup is doubly blessed with spices. The specially made chicken stock in which the lentils are later cooked is seasoned with chili powder or cayenne. The soup itself then gets a different spiciness from curry powder. Together they blend into an unusual but delicious dish with East Indian overtones.

Red or Persian lentils may be difficult to find in some parts of the country but the Chilean (see page 244) may be substituted. The result will not be as pleasing to the eye but the good taste is about the same.

The recipe was given to me at a picnic of chefs and food writers on a rain-swept beach on Oahu by a charming Sri Lankan woman, Kusuma Cooray, executive chef of Willows, Honolulu's famous restaurant beside the fishponds.

INGREDIENTS	*Stock*
	2- to 3-pound whole chicken
	10 cups water
	2 unpeeled cloves garlic, crushed
	2 tomatoes, chopped
	1 medium onion, sliced
	2 stalks celery, sliced
	2 sprigs fresh dill or ½ teaspoon dried
	1 teaspoon chili powder or cayenne
	1 teaspoon salt, or to taste
	½ teaspoon freshly ground black pepper

(continued)

Soup

Chicken stock (about 6 cups) from above

¾ cup red or other lentils, washed

1 tablespoon curry powder

1 tablespoon clarified butter

1 tablespoon black mustard seeds, if available

2 shallots, finely chopped

1 tablespoon lemon juice, or to taste

2 teaspoons salt, if desired

2 tablespoons cream or coconut milk

2 tablespoons parsley

SPECIAL EQUIPMENT	Chinois or sieve
PREPARATION	*Stock* Skin the chicken. Remove the breast meat, cut into ½-inch cubes, and set aside. Cut the rest of the chicken into joints and put into a large (4-quart) saucepan with water, garlic, tomatoes, onion, celery, dill, chili powder or cayenne, salt, and pepper.
BOIL/SIMMER *1½ hours*	Bring to a boil over high heat, turn heat to low, and simmer for 1½ hours. Strain the stock through a chinois or sieve.
STRAIN/COOL	Cool the stock and skim off the fat. Kusuma's recipe calls for the white breast meat only. As I am fond of dark meat, I pick it off the bones after the stock is made, cube it, and add it to the soup later, along with the white. This also doubles the amount of meat in the soup, which I like.
BOIL/SIMMER *15–20 mins.* *5 mins.*	*Soup* In a large (4-quart) saucepan, combine the chicken stock, lentils, and curry powder. Bring to a boil, cover, reduce heat, and simmer 15 to 20 minutes until the lentils are tender but not mushy. Add the cubed chicken and cook for 5 minutes more.
COOK *Seconds!*	In a skillet, heat the clarified butter until it bubbles. Add the black mustard seeds and turn heat to high. Cover the pan with a lid and allow the mustard seeds to sputter, but only for a few seconds.
SAUTÉ *6–8 mins.*	Turn off the heat immediately, open lid, and add shallots. Turn heat to low and sauté shallots to a golden brown, about 6 to 8 minutes.

Add the seeds and shallots to the soup. Season with lemon juice and more salt if necessary. Add cream or coconut milk.

BOIL

Bring to a fast boil over medium-high heat while stirring. Immediately remove from heat.

FINAL STEP

Serve hot, garnished with parsley.

My Texas Auntie's Lentil Soup

Serves 10 to 12

My Texas Auntie's Lentil Soup came to my kitchen in a mysterious way. She is not my auntie, I hasten to add with regret. The recipe appeared one day, without attribution, among those sent by readers of my books. I thank whoever sent it, as you will when you have prepared it. The dish is big and robust, with Texas overtones.

Note: I discovered much later that she was the aunt of my good friend Fleurette Benckart, who had dropped the recipe on my desk one day without comment or credit.

INGREDIENTS

1 pound lentils, washed and picked over
2 cloves garlic, minced
2 cups finely chopped onions
3½ quarts (14 cups) cold water
1 pound lean ground beef
2 ounces (½ stick) butter
2 teaspoons salt
1 tablespoon dill seed
1 teaspoon freshly ground black pepper
1 15-ounce can tomato sauce
6 ounces spaghetti, broken into 1-inch lengths
Snippets of the white of scallion, to garnish

SPECIAL
EQUIPMENT

None

PREPARATION

Place the lentils, garlic, and onions in a large (4- or 5-quart) kettle or soup pot and cover with the cold water.

BOIL/SIMMER
2 hours

Bring to a boil, then turn down the heat so the liquid only simmers. Partially cover and cook over low heat for 2 hours. Stir frequently.

SAUTÉ *10 mins.*	Sauté the meat in butter until well browned, about 10 minutes. Set aside.
SIMMER	When the soup has cooked 2 hours, add the salt, dill seed, pepper, tomato sauce, and sautéed meat. Return the soup to a simmer; cook for an additional hour.
12–15 mins.	Add the spaghetti pieces, stir to mix through the soup, and cook for 12 to 15 minutes or until the spaghetti is al dente.
FINAL STEP	Ladle the soup into heated bowls. Garnish with the scallion. A red wine and thick slices of country bread go well with the soup.

Cream of Lettuce Soup (German)
Salad Supa, also Salat Suppe
Serves 4 to 6

A dollop of vinegar gives a piquancy to this unusual cream of lettuce soup ladled over small boiled potatoes placed in individual soup dishes. It is equally good cold but should then be served without the potato. Cold or hot, it is a beautiful dish, with green lettuce flakes floating in the creamy soup.

This recipe came to my kitchen from a friend in Kansas whose German forebears came to the Plains states from Russia, where they had colonized choice land along the Volga and Black Sea at the invitation of the German-born Catherine the Great. Later they fled to this country, where their heritage of fine cooking is preserved in recipes of a cookbook, Küche Kuchen, *collected by the American Historical Association of Germans from Russia.*

I adapted the recipe for this delicious soup in a small way by putting the soup in a blender rather than serving the lettuce shreds whole. There is no change in taste but the soup is more delicately presented.

INGREDIENTS	6 slices bacon, cut into ½-inch pieces 6 green onions (½ cup), including tender green stalks, thinly sliced 4 eggs 1 cup heavy or light cream 2 cups milk 1 small head leaf lettuce, shredded 1 cup boiling water 1 teaspoon salt

¼ teaspoon freshly ground black pepper
¼ cup cider vinegar
4 small potatoes (½ pound), peeled and quartered (see below)
Salted water to cover potatoes
3 tablespoons butter, at room temperature
Snippets of chives or parsley, to garnish

SPECIAL EQUIPMENT	Blender or food processor. Melon baller, optional.
PREPARATION TRY OUT 6 mins.	Try out the bacon in a medium (3-quart) saucepan over medium heat until brown and crisp, about 6 minutes. Remove with a slotted spoon and set aside. Discard all but 1 tablespoon of fat.
SAUTÉ 8 mins.	Sauté the onions in the bacon fat over medium heat for about 8 minutes.
BEAT 1 min.	While the onions are cooking, combine the eggs, cream, and milk. Beat for 1 minute with a rotary hand beater or mixer. When the onions are done, add boiling water, salt, and pepper. Pour in the egg/cream mixture and drop in the shredded lettuce.
SIMMER 6–8 mins. 3 mins.	Bring the soup to a simmer over medium-low heat, stirring, while mixture becomes thick and creamy, about 6 to 8 minutes. Do not allow it to boil. Stir in the vinegar and simmer for an additional 3 minutes. Meanwhile prepare the potatoes. For the family, small quartered sections no larger than a small walnut will do. To make a more impressive company dish, cut small balls out of potatoes with a melon baller as you would for potatoes *noisette* or *parisienne*.
BOIL 15–18 mins.	Gently boil the potatoes in salted water for 15 to 18 minutes or until fork-tender. Take care that they do not get mushy.
PUREE	When the soup has cooked, remove from the heat and allow it to cool for a few moments. Put the soup in the work bowl of the blender or food processor and puree until smooth and creamy. Return to pot and reheat.
FINAL STEP	Place 3 or 4 pieces of boiled potato or potato balls in each soup plate and ladle the hot soup over them. Drop a teaspoonful of butter on each, swirl, and sprinkle with chives or parsley. If served cold, don't include the potato or butter. Garnish only with the chives or parsley.

Miso Soup (Japanese)
Miso Shiru

Serves 4 or 5

There are a huge number of miso soups but all have as their chief ingredient a heavy paste that is the fermentation of soybeans, wheat or rice, and salt. It may be red (aka miso) or white (shiro miso) and various shades in between. Miso is seldom a meal in itself; mostly it is part of a dish with other ingredients and seasonings.

Red miso is pungent and quite salty, while white is mellow, with a touch of sweetness. Each has a distinctive taste that sets its mark on other ingredients.

Miso is one of the pillars of the Japanese cuisine, standing alongside tofu (bean curd cake) and shoyu (soy sauce). All are from the soybean, which has become as important to the Japanese diet as rice. A Japanese chef would liken his use of miso to that of a French chef with butter or an Italian cook with olive oil.

While it is served at any meal, miso soup is also a national breakfast dish. It is quick to make and it supplies about one-sixth of the adult protein requirement. When I was writing this book miso soup was on our breakfast menu for a time. We made it first out of curiosity and then because we grew to like it very much.

The soup begins with a stock—dashi, for example, or a clear chicken broth. Miso, which thickens and seasons, is swirled into the stock. To this is added whatever vegetable, meat, or fish strikes one's fancy.

Miso paste can be left at room temperature for a year or more. Since its flavor improves with age, many Japanese will keep a supply of miso in a wooden tub for up to a decade. It should not be frozen.

For those who want miso soup but are unable to find the paste, Kikkoman, the shoyu people, have placed on the market an instant miso soup—one packet spooned into ⅔ cup of boiling water for 1 serving. The choice is red or white.

Here is one of the seemingly limitless varieties of miso soups.

INGREDIENTS   3½ cups Dashi (page 24) or chicken stock
½ cup nameko mushrooms, sliced, or 2 shiitake mushrooms, sliced, or
    5 to 6 small button mushrooms, stems removed, thinly sliced
¼ cup red miso
8 ounces tofu (bean curd)
4 sprigs parsley, finely chopped
Sansho pepper, if available, to garnish

Note: Fresh Japanese mushrooms can often be found in West Coast markets. There is a greater distribution of canned or dried ones. Our domestic mushrooms are a satisfactory substitute.

SPECIAL EQUIPMENT	None
PREPARATION	*Beforehand:* Prepare the stock of your choice as well as the mushrooms. Drain the tofu.
BLEND	Whisk the miso into 2 tablespoons of tepid stock and blend well. Gradually ladle the miso liquid into the stock.

SIMMER	Bring the soup to a simmer. (For a satin-smooth soup, strain from one pot to another.)
	    Add tofu cubes, parsley, and mushrooms. Maintain at a simmer until the mushrooms and tofu are heated.
	    Do not boil or it will become bitter and cloudy.

FINAL STEP	Ladle the soup into individual lacquer bowls and distribute the ingredients equally and attractively. Garnish with a sprinkling of *sansho* pepper. Cover with lids and serve immediately. Other soup bowls will do equally well, of course.

MINESTRONE

We once toured Italy from north to south gathering recipes for bread and pastries. Only twice during that journey did we taste minestrone. A decade later, the search for soup led to a special trip back.

Minestrone is a mellow vegetable soup, and its composition depends on the best vegetables available in the garden or marketplace. In winter I would not use fresh tomatoes, but would choose some of the frozen ones laid by last summer, or canned tomatoes. The taste of minestrone is not of any one ingredient but a blend of all into a rich, zesty dish.

If one or two vegetables of the many called for in a minestrone recipe are not available, substitute freely. If you like more or less of an ingredient called for, adjust the amount to suit yourself and your guests.

Here are five different minestrone recipes.

Minestrone I

Serves 8 to 10

To some, a measure of the character of good minestrone is whether a wooden spoon placed upright in the soup will remain erect or will tilt, the latter indicating a too thin soup. A second measure, of course, is its taste, and this depends much on where it came from in Italy. A beef base, butter, ribbon-shaped pasta, and rice will place it in the north. Tomato, garlic, olive oil, and tubular-shaped pasta indicate the south.

This recipe is from the south.

INGREDIENTS

3 cups dry white beans

Water to cover

2 to 3 pounds meaty beef soup bones

3 quarts water

1 tablespoon salt, if desired

1 15-ounce can tomato puree (or homemade puree)

2 6-ounce cans tomato paste

1 pound tomatoes, fresh, frozen, or canned, coarsely chopped

3 tablespoons olive oil

1 leek, white part only, diced

1½ cups diced onions

2 cloves garlic, finely chopped or mashed

1 cup diced celery

½ cup finely chopped parsley

2 cups finely diced carrots

2 cups (¼ head) finely chopped savoy or other cabbage

1 cup finely chopped zucchini

6 to 8 green beans, diced

½ teaspoon oregano

½ teaspoon basil

2 cloves garlic, peeled and minced

1 teaspoon dried chervil or 1 tablespoon finely chopped fresh chervil

3 tablespoons fatback, finely diced and mashed to a soft pulp

2 ounces broken spaghetti or other small pasta of your choice

¼ teaspoon freshly ground black pepper

1½ cups freshly grated Parmesan cheese

Pesto (see page 364)

SPECIAL EQUIPMENT	None
PREPARATION SOAK *Overnight*	Soak beans overnight in water to cover. Drain and discard water before using the beans in the minestrone.
BOIL/SIMMER *10 mins.*	Place soup bones in a very large pot with enough cold water to cover; bring to a boil. Immediately remove from the heat and drain. Wash meat under cold running water. Rinse out the pot. Put the bones back in the pot, and pour in 3 quarts of water (more to be added later). Add salt, if desired.
1 hour	Bring to a boil; lower heat to simmer for 1 hour. Add tomato puree, tomato paste, and tomatoes.
SMOTHER *15 mins.* SIMMER *1 hour*	While the meat simmers, pour olive oil into a large skillet; cover; and cook the leek, onions, garlic, celery, and parsley over medium heat, stirring occasionally, for about 15 minutes. Add all to soup. Put in the carrots, cabbage, zucchini, and green beans, and season with oregano and basil. Add the reserved beans. Simmer for another hour or until the vegetables are tender and the meat can easily be pulled from the bones. Remove from heat. While the meat and bones cool sufficiently to handle, prepare a paste by mixing garlic, chervil, and fatback. This is best done by mashing the three ingredients against the side of a small bowl with the back of a spoon. Lift the meat from the soup and separate it from the bones. Discard the bones. Dice the meat and return it to the soup. Add the garlic/fatback paste and stir to blend.
BOIL/SIMMER *15 mins.*	Finally add spaghetti or another pasta of choice. Return to a simmer over medium heat and cook for about 15 minutes or until pasta is al dente. Check seasoning, especially pepper.
FINAL STEP	Serve this hearty dish in large heated bowls. Sprinkle liberally with Parmesan cheese. Pass the pesto. Italian country bread is a tasty companion to this dish.

Minestrone II

Serves 8

While there is no pasta in this minestrone from the Piedmont region of northern Italy, it does contain rice and the white cannellini bean.

The tongue will detect a hint of pork, as the leek and onion are cooked in fat rendered from a piece of salt pork. The other vegetables are cooked in butter, another indicator of the soup's northern Italian origin.

Although the traditional pesto can be served with the minestrone, this particular recipe calls for a light garnish of basil, parsley, and garlic. Parmesan cheese is sprinkled separately.

INGREDIENTS

Soup

½ cup dry white cannellini or other similar beans (canned may be substituted—in that case use 1 cup)

4 cups water, to soak beans

4 tablespoons butter

1 cup fresh peas or 1 10-ounce package frozen

1 cup *each* diced (unpeeled) zucchini, carrots, potato

½ cup thinly sliced celery

2 ounces salt pork

½ cup finely chopped onion

1 leek (about ½ cup), white part only, finely chopped

2 cups tomatoes, canned whole-pack, frozen, or fresh

2 quarts chicken stock

1 bay leaf

3 sprigs parsley, tied together

1 teaspoon salt, if desired

Freshly ground black pepper, to taste

½ cup raw white rice

Garnish

1 tablespoon finely cut basil, or 1 teaspoon crumbled dry basil

1 tablespoon finely chopped parsley

½ teaspoon finely chopped garlic

1 cup freshly grated Parmesan cheese, to sprinkle

SPECIAL
EQUIPMENT

None

PREPARATION	*Note:* If cannellini beans are not available, navy, kidney, Great Northern, marrow, or others may be substituted.
	Beans
BOIL *2 mins.* SOAK *1 hour*	In a heavy saucepan, bring 4 cups of water to a boil. Pour in the beans and over high heat boil for *2 minutes* only. Remove pan from heat and allow beans to soak in the water for 1 hour.
SIMMER *1–1½ hours*	Return pan to heat and over low heat simmer uncovered for 1 to 1½ hours, or until the beans are al dente, barely tender. Drain and set aside.
	Soup
SAUTÉ *10–12 mins.*	In a large heavy skillet, melt butter. If the peas are frozen, pour them into the skillet first and allow them to thaw, about 2 minutes. Add the zucchini, carrots, potato, and celery. Allow each to cook 2 or 3 minutes before adding the next. Stir/toss with a wooden spoon until all the vegetables are lightly coated with butter, and cook for about 10 to 12 minutes. Set aside.
SAUTÉ *6 mins.*	Dice the salt pork and render it in a large (5-quart) soup pot (this pot will be the container for all the ingredients) over moderate heat. Stir frequently for about 6 minutes. When the pork pieces are crisp and brown, lift them out with a slotted spoon and put aside to drain on paper towel.
COOK *5 mins.*	Cook onions and leek in the hot fat until they are translucent, about 5 minutes. Add the vegetables from the skillet plus the tomatoes, chicken stock, bay leaf, parsley, salt, and black pepper. Add the reserved beans.
BOIL/SIMMER *30 mins.*	Bring the soup to a boil over high heat, reduce heat, and simmer, partially covered, for half an hour.
COOK *15–20 mins.*	Remove and discard bay leaf and parsley sprigs; add rice and reserved salt pork dice. Cook 15 to 20 minutes, or until rice and beans are tender. If soup is too thick for your taste, add additional stock or water. Season soup with additional salt and pepper, if needed.
FINAL STEP	Mix together the basil, parsley, and garlic to make the garnish. Sprinkle each serving with these. Pass the Parmesan cheese separately.

Minestrone, Peasant Style (Tuscany)
Minestrone alla Contadina

Serves 8

This peasant-style minestrone from Tuscany is assembled and presented in a rather unorthodox way, but the result cannot be challenged.

There are four separate steps in this preparation. First the beans are soaked and cooked. The vegetables are sautéed while the beans cook. The beans are drained; some are pureed to be added to the stock and the others reserved for a last-minute addition. The vegetables and bean puree cook together, and only then is the reserved stock added.

There are two ways to present the minestrone at the table. One is to place croutons in the bottom of each soup bowl and ladle on the soup, followed with Parmesan cheese. The more elaborate way is to use a tureen. Put down a layer of day-old or older bread, then the soup, more layers of bread, and more layers of soup.

Magically it can become a somewhat different soup the day after. Left overnight to thicken even further, the minestrone is brought to a boil and the bread is blended into the soup with a wooden spoon. It is then ribollito, which means, literally, "reboiled."

INGREDIENTS

½ pound cannellini or other dried white beans

2 to 3 quarts water

2 teaspoons salt

1 ounce salt pork and 2 ounces boiled ham or 3 ounces prosciutto, including fat (if you can negotiate a better price for the heel, or end piece, of prosciutto, that is fine for this purpose)

⅓ cup olive oil

1 large red onion, coarsely chopped

1 stalk celery, coarsely chopped

2 cloves garlic, mashed and chopped

1 large carrot, coarsely chopped

12 sprigs parsley, preferably flat-leaf Italian, chopped

½ pound cabbage, savoy preferred, cored and shredded

½ pound kale or collard greens, stripped from stems and shredded

1 large potato, diced

2 small tomatoes, peeled and seeded

½ pound Swiss chard or fresh spinach, stripped from stems and shredded

Salt, if desired, to taste

Freshly ground black pepper, to taste

12 tablespoons croutons or 12 large slices French or Italian bread, several
    days old and quite dry
1 cup freshly grated Parmesan cheese, to garnish

SPECIAL EQUIPMENT	Food processor, blender, or food mill
PREPARATION	Soak beans overnight in water that has been lightly salted.

BOIL/SIMMER
1 hour

Drain beans and cook over medium-low heat in a large (5-quart) covered kettle in 2 to 3 quarts fresh water. Also include pork and ham or
prosciutto (which is quite expensive for this peasant dish). When beans
are tender, remove from heat and allow to stand in their liquid until
needed.

SMOTHER
15 mins.

30 mins.

In a large covered saucepan, heat the olive oil and cook onion, celery,
garlic, carrot, and parsley until the vegetables are soft and translucent,
about 15 minutes. Add the cabbage, kale, potato, tomatoes, and chard
or spinach to the saucepan and cook for another 30 minutes or until the
cabbage and kale are almost done.

    While the vegetables are cooking, lift the meat from the beans. Dis-
card fat and reserve meat.

PUREE
5 mins.

Puree about two-thirds of the beans in a food processor or other equipment and add to the vegetables in the stockpot. (The bean liquid is reserved.)

SIMMER
30 mins.

The mixture will be quite thick, but it will allow the various flavors to
meld. Simmer, covered, for about 30 minutes.

COOK
5 mins.

Add 2 quarts bean broth and reserved lean meat to the pot. Gently stir
to blend together. Add the remaining whole beans. Taste for seasoning
and add salt, if needed (the salt pork and ham will have made their salty
contributions), and pepper. Cook for an additional 5 minutes.

FINAL STEP

If using croutons, place 1½ tablespoons on the *bottom* of each bowl and
fill with minestrone.

    If using the bread slices, place a layer on the bottom of the heated
tureen and pour 2 ladles of soup over them. Add more bread, each time
pouring soup over it, until the bread is used up. Pour remaining soup
into the tureen, cover, and let soup rest for a few minutes before serving.

    Pass freshly grated Parmesan cheese.

FOLLOWING
DAY

Pour leftover minestrone into a stockpot and bring to a boil over medium heat. Cook for about 60 seconds. Remove from the heat. Break up the bread slices with a wooden spoon until the texture of the soup is thick and smooth. Ladle the soup into individual bowls and pour 2 teaspoons of a high-quality olive oil over each serving.

Minestrone freezes well. It can then be made into *ribollito* at some future time.

Le Alpi Minestrone

Serves 6

With the exception of a touch of olive oil, Le Alpi's minestrone is all vegetables—healthful and inexpensive. While many other minestrones are thick (sometimes sufficiently so to hold a spoon erect), this one is lighter and thinner, and each vegetable piece keeps its identity even though the taste is a blend of all.

Le Alpi are the Alps that rise behind the city of Trieste, where this recipe was created.

INGREDIENTS

2 tablespoons olive oil
½ cup finely chopped onion
6 cups water

¾ cup *each* { string beans, cut on bias (French cut)
                diced zucchini, unpeeled
                diced carrots
                diced potato

½ cup thinly sliced celery
¾ cup coarsely chopped cabbage (savoy preferred)
¼ cup chopped green onion
1 tomato, coarsely chopped
6 cups water
Salt, if desired
¼ teaspoon freshly ground black pepper
½ cup finely chopped parsley
1 cup freshly grated Parmesan cheese, to garnish

SPECIAL
EQUIPMENT

None

PREPARATION

Note: On occasion I have cooked this minestrone in a slow cooker for about 8 hours. This is satisfactory if you like your vegetables well cooked, but I prefer the shorter 1-hour method.

SAUTÉ 10 mins.	In a large (5-quart) covered pot, sauté onion in olive oil until soft and glistening, about 10 minutes.

At 2-minute intervals add all the vegetables, one at a time—beans, zucchini, carrots, potato, celery, cabbage, green onion, and tomato.

BOIL/SIMMER
1 hour
Cover the vegetables with about 1½ quarts water and bring to a boil. Cover and reduce to a simmer. Midway into the cooking, add salt, if desired, pepper, and parsley.

FINAL STEP
Serve in heated bowls and sprinkle with Parmesan cheese.

Minestrone (Low-Sodium)

Serves 6

If you have never had soup without salt, this will be a different taste experience—not bland but different. Each vegetable takes on a new dimension.

This soup is also healthful. Sarah Fritschner, a friend and one of the best food writers in the country—she is the food editor of The Courier-Journal *in Louisville, Kentucky—discovered the recipe while writing a story on sodium restriction with the help of the Food and Drug Administration and the Department of Agriculture. She was then with* The Washington Post.

The recipe, which reduces sodium content and increases potassium, calls for lemon, vinegar, mustard, cloves, and other ingredients to substitute for salt.

INGREDIENTS
1 cup dried beans (kidney or other)
4½ cups water
½ green pepper, diced
¼ teaspoon freshly ground black pepper
2 cloves garlic, minced
1 medium onion, chopped
¼ cup minced parsley
½ teaspoon dried mustard
1 tablespoon *each* white cider vinegar and lemon juice
¼ teaspoon sugar
3 whole cloves (tied in small sachet)
½ teaspoon savory
1 teaspoon basil
2 cups finely chopped tomatoes, fresh, home-frozen, or low-sodium canned
1 small zucchini, unpeeled, chopped

(continued)

1 medium potato, cubed (unpeeled, if desired)
Finely chopped parsley, to garnish

SPECIAL EQUIPMENT	None
PREPARATION *Overnight*	*Beforehand:* Soak beans overnight in salted water. Drain.
BOIL/SIMMER *45 mins.*	In a medium (3-quart) saucepan, combine beans, water, and green pepper. Lower heat, cover pan, and simmer until beans are *almost* tender, about 45 minutes.
15 mins.	Add black pepper, garlic, onion, and parsley and continue to simmer for 15 minutes.
20 mins.	Next add mustard, vinegar, lemon juice, sugar, cloves, savory, basil, tomatoes, zucchini, and potato. Simmer, uncovered, until the beans and vegetables are tender, about 20 minutes. Remove clove sachet and discard.
FINAL STEP	Serve in heated bowls. Garnish with chopped parsley. (The addition of salt will, of course, give the soup an entirely different character, which some guests may prefer.)

Mushroom Soup with Parmesan Cheese

Serves 6

After you have made this creamy, light-brown potage, lavish with thin slices of mushroom, you will forever look askance at store-bought mushroom soup or the bland kind served too often in restaurants across the country.

An inspired and unexpected touch is the addition of a blend of Parmesan cheese and egg yolk just before the soup is taken off the stove. The soup is rich-tasting, with the true flavor of mushrooms. It bears no resemblance to the canned.

INGREDIENTS	1½ pounds mushrooms
	3 tablespoons vegetable oil
	2 cups thinly sliced green onions (include some green)
	2 cloves garlic, minced
	3 tablespoons butter
	2 tablespoons flour
	4 cups beef stock

1 tablespoon Worcestershire sauce
1 teaspoon salt, if desired
Freshly ground black pepper
¼ cup Burgundy or Chianti
4 egg yolks
2 tablespoons finely chopped parsley
½ cup grated Parmesan cheese

SPECIAL EQUIPMENT
Food processor or food mill. A blender makes the mushrooms too creamy. Small particles give the soup an interesting texture.

PREPARATION
Clean the mushrooms with a brush or wipe with a damp cloth. Do not wash in water! Snap off the stems and chop them coarsely. Slice the caps thinly and put aside.

SMOTHER
15 mins.
Pour the oil into a medium (3-quart) saucepan, heat, and drop in the chopped mushroom stems, green onions, and garlic. Cover and cook over medium-low heat for about 15 minutes, stirring frequently.

PUREE
Set aside for a few minutes to allow the mixture to cool. Place in a food processor or food mill. Add a tablespoon or two of stock to the work bowl if the mushrooms stick to the glass. Puree into fine particles but not into a cream.

COOK
6 mins.

10 mins.
Return the puree to the heat and add the butter when simmering. When melted, sprinkle in the flour. Blend into a smooth paste. Allow it to cook for 2 or 3 minutes. Add the stock and Worcestershire, whisk until smooth, and simmer for 5 minutes. Add the mushroom slices, return to a simmer, and cook for 10 minutes. Add salt and pepper to taste.

Add the wine.

Meanwhile, blend together the egg yolks, parsley, and Parmesan cheese in a small bowl. Slowly stir the egg mixture into the simmering soup.

FINAL STEP
Serve at once in heated bowls. Pass more grated Parmesan and hot Italian bread.

VARIATION
The Italians serve this soup ladled over 1-inch-thick slices of peasant bread, buttered and grilled under the broiler for 1 minute. Place 1 slice in each bowl.

Pass the Chianti!

Cream of Wild Mushroom Soup (English)

Serves 4

There is an interesting grainy texture in this quick, easy, and delicious soup, made with wild mushrooms, if possible. Wild mushrooms picked in the woods and pastures have a tangy richness that the best store-bought mushrooms cannot match. But don't forgo the pleasure of this soup when only fresh cultivated mushrooms are available.

In Yorkshire, this soup is made with the young field mushroom (Agaricus campestris), which has pale brown gills, blackening as they get older. In my part of the world, the spongelike morel (Morchella esculenta, Morchella vulgaris, and Morchella conica) is used. This soup is one of several ways that these precious morsels are used in my kitchen. (For another morel soup, see next page.)

INGREDIENTS	1 pound wild mushrooms
	4 ounces (1 stick) butter
	3 cups milk or light cream
	2 tablespoons flour
	Salt and freshly ground black pepper
	3 to 4 tablespoons heavy cream, if desired
SPECIAL EQUIPMENT	Food processor or food mill. A blender will chop the mushrooms too finely. Sieve.
PREPARATION CLEAN	If wild mushrooms are used, soak in salted cold water for 3 to 4 minutes to get rid of insects. If domestic, simply brush or wipe with a damp cloth.
	Note: Put aside 2 or 3 small attractive mushrooms to slice for garnish.
SMOTHER *10 mins.*	Slice or chop the mushrooms and cook in 2 ounces of butter in a medium skillet. Cover and cook for about 10 minutes or just until tender.
PROCESS	Chop the cooked mushrooms in a food processor or pass through a food mill. Don't puree. Keep the particles coarse to give the soup an interesting texture.
STRAIN	Strain the mushrooms into a bowl to capture the cooking liquid. Set mushrooms aside. Add milk or cream to the liquid to make a total of 3 cups.
COOK *5 mins.*	Melt the remaining butter in a pan, stir in the flour, and cook gently for a moment or so until it bubbles. Gradually add the milk mixture, stir-

ring over medium heat until the soup is smooth and thick, about 5 minutes.

BOIL/SIMMER
2–3 mins.

Add the mushrooms. Season with salt and pepper to taste and bring just to a boil. Turn down heat and simmer for 2 or 3 minutes, stirring occasionally.

FINAL STEP

Just before serving you may wish to spoon in the heavy cream to give it a marbled effect.

Float the thinly sliced raw mushrooms on the surface of the soup and serve.

Cream of Morel Soup

Serves 6

The triumphant mushroom hunter is home. A brown paper sack bulges with the trophy. Best of all is to discover that the secret gathering place in the old orchard down the road is still a secret.

The morel mushroom is to cooks in my part of the world, the Midwest, what the truffle is to the French. Priceless, almost. These words spring to mind in trying to describe the Morchella—delicate, earthy, slightly musty, leafy, dark brown.

On this spring day the first batch of mushrooms probably will be sautéed, which is the quickest way for the impatient taster to cook them. The succeeding meal will be the morel soup. Morels, frozen just as they are plucked from the earth, can be kept for months and then made into soup for a pleasant out-of-season surprise.

All is manifest in this delicious soup, whose other ingredients are chosen so as not to overpower the fragile taste of these honeycombed beauties.

Store-bought mushrooms may be substituted, but it will be a different soup. I have tried the dried Oriental fungus with some success.

INGREDIENTS

2 cups (about 1 pound) morels, fresh or frozen
4 cups cold water
1 teaspoon salt (for soaking morels)
3 tablespoons butter, approximately
2 green onions, finely chopped
1 cup shredded fresh spinach leaves, ribs removed
¼ cup finely chopped parsley
¼ cup dry white wine
½ teaspoon celery salt

(continued)

2 cups chicken stock
2 cups water
Salt, if desired, to taste
Pepper, to taste
1 cup light cream
2 egg yolks
6 thinly cut lemon slices
Pinch of paprika, to garnish
1 cup croutons, to garnish

SPECIAL
EQUIPMENT

None

PREPARATION
10 mins.

Soak morels in cold water with salt for 3 or 4 minutes. Drain, pat dry on paper towels, and cut into small pieces, about 1 inch in diameter.

SMOTHER
5 mins.

Bring butter to bubbling in medium (3-quart) saucepan. Add the mushroom pieces, cover the saucepan, and cook over medium heat for about 5 minutes.

5 mins.

Add the green onions, spinach, and parsley and continue cooking, covered, for an additional 5 minutes.

SIMMER
15 mins.

Pour in the white wine and celery salt. Add the chicken stock and water and simmer over medium heat for 15 minutes. Don't boil.

Taste for salt and pepper.

BLEND
7 mins.

Blend cream and egg yolks together in a small bowl. Add ½ cup of the hot soup to the cream/egg mixture and then gradually stir this into the larger amount of soup. Heat, stirring constantly. Don't allow the soup to come to a boil, or the eggs will curdle.

FINAL STEP

Ladle into hot soup bowls; top with a slice of lemon and a sprinkling of paprika. Pass a bowl of freshly toasted croutons.

Morel soup may be frozen but do so before the cream and egg yolks are added.

Chanterelle Mushroom Soup under Puff Pastry (Swiss-French)
Soupe de Chanterelles en Croûte

Serves 6

The chanterelle, with its peculiar funnel-shape cap, cannot be mistaken in taste or appearance for any other edible mushroom. It makes a delicious soup.

I had enjoyed chanterelles in France long before I realized that they are to be found over a wide range of forests in the United States as well as on the Continent. In the Midwest this mushroom fruits in the summer; in the Pacific Northwest, in the fall; and in California, in the late fall and early winter.

The chanterelle was the chief ingredient of one of the finest mushroom soups I have ever been served. The place was the Rives Rolle, a lovely hotel on the shores of Lake Geneva in Switzerland, less than an hour's drive north of Geneva. The soup was the spécialité of Jean-Pierre Harnisch, chef de cuisine, *who trained in Lausanne and Paris.*

Presented en croûte—*under flaky layers of puff pastry—it is a handsome and delicious dish.*

INGREDIENTS	3 tablespoons butter
	¼ cup finely chopped carrot
	¼ cup finely chopped celery
	1½ tablespoons minced shallot
	10 ounces chanterelle mushrooms, chopped
	1 cup beef stock or, for a lighter soup, consommé
	3 cups light cream
	1 teaspoon salt, if desired
	Pinch of freshly ground black pepper
	1 pound puff pastry, rolled ¼ inch thick
	1 egg, beaten, with 1 tablespoon cream, to brush pastry

SPECIAL
EQUIPMENT

Food processor, blender, or food mill. Ovenproof bowls in which to serve the soup.

PREPARATION

Note: Each cup of soup will be covered with a lid of puff pastry stuck to the cup rim with beaten egg yolk, then baked.

SWEAT
5 mins.
15 mins.

Melt the butter in a medium (3-quart) saucepan and add the carrot and celery. Cover and cook over low heat for 5 minutes. Add the shallot and continue to cook for an additional 15 minutes or until the vegetables are soft and translucent. Do not brown.

COOK *15 mins.* *20 mins.*	Drop the chopped mushrooms into the saucepan, stir into the vegetables, cover, and cook over medium-low heat for about 15 minutes. Add the beef stock or consommé. Cook at a slow boil over medium heat, uncovered, for about 20 minutes to reduce and strengthen the stock. Add cream, salt, if desired, and pepper. Remove from heat.

PUFF PASTRY	While the soup is cooling, roll out the puff pastry to a thickness of ¼ inch. Let the dough relax completely so that it will not draw back when cut. As a pattern for cutting the puff pastry into circles, trace around the edge of a bowl slightly larger than the bowl or cup to be used in serving.
	    Excess dough is trimmed away before the bowls go into the oven.
	    Ladle the soup into the bowls within ½ inch of the top. Drape the dough over the tops—do not stretch—and trim. Brush the pastry lids with the egg mixture.

BAKE *375° 15 mins.*	Place the bowls on the middle shelf of a 375° oven and bake for 15 minutes.

FINAL STEP	Serve immediately.
	    A disk of puff pastry, slightly smaller than the diameter of the soup bowl, may be floated on the surface of the hot soup at the moment it is brought to the table.
	    The soup is equally good without the puff pastry top, although the presentation is not nearly so glamorous.

Onion Soup Les Halles (French)
Soupe à l'Oignon Les Halles

Serves 10

Onion soup is a national dish in France and fast becoming one in this country despite its travail at the hands of unthinking or uncaring cooks. Served at breakfast, it starts the French farmer's day; and in the early morning hours it tops off the day for a showgirl.

The version I like best is the one made famous in the great produce market at Les Halles, where trucks and hungry truckers converged from all over France. The market has since been moved to the suburbs, but the restaurants that flanked the old cast-iron pavilions remain.

One in particular drew me like a magnet each time we returned to Les Paris—Robert Vattier's, near the Halles metro station. It was the quintessential French restaurant—bottles, not glasses, of red wine; sidewalk tables; checkered tablecloths; and an enthusiastic clientele that embraces financiers, salespersons, clerks, and truckdrivers.

The quality of brown stock is of the utmost importance to soupe à l'oignon *whether to be served* ordinaire *or garnished lavishly with a crouton and cheese, slipped under a broiler, and finally given a tot of cognac spooned under the bubbling brown crust at the moment it is carried to the table. Ambrosia.*

The soup demands the best and richest stock, preferably homemade. It must blend with the onion essence without overpowering the soup with a strong, salty flavor.

INGREDIENTS

2 pounds (about 7 to 10, depending on size) yellow onions, peeled and sliced (see Preparation)

4 tablespoons lard or butter (French cooks traditionally use lard)

2 tablespoons oil, preferably peanut

2 teaspoons salt

¼ to ½ teaspoon sugar

3 cloves garlic, minced

3 tablespoons flour

½ cup red wine to deglaze

3 quarts beef stock, heated

Sachet d'épice

2 bay leaves

8 black peppercorns

½ teaspoon dried thyme

4 or 5 sprigs parsley

1 cup chopped onion, to garnish

10 pieces of bread, cut to fit top of individual bowls

Butter

20 slices Gruyère or Swiss cheese, 4 inches square, ⅛ inch thick

10 tablespoons Cognac or other good brandy, to embellish

SPECIAL
EQUIPMENT

Appropriate tureen or individual ovenproof bowls. The small ovenproof 1½-cup earthenware *petite marmite* is ideal.

PREPARATION
SWEAT
15 mins.

Peel the onions and cut them into quarters lengthwise. Slice across thinly. Heat lard or butter and oil in a large (4-quart) saucepan over medium heat and drop in the onions. Add salt and stir to coat onions with the fat. Cover and sweat for 15 minutes. Stir frequently.

Taste a bit of onion to determine its sweetness. A summer onion, freshly harvested, is full of sugar, but a winter onion has far less and may need help with the addition of a pinch of sugar. The soup needs a touch of sweetness, but use sugar sparingly.

COOK
20–30 mins.

3 mins.

Uncover, add garlic, and cook over medium heat until onions are a deep golden brown. Allow to cook for about 20 to 30 minutes. Stir frequently, scraping the brown residue off the bottom with a wooden spoon.

Sprinkle in the flour, stir, and let it cook for about 3 minutes.

DEGLAZE

Pour the red wine into the pot, scraping up the brown particles with a wooden spoon.

COOK
5 mins.

Cook the onions and wine over medium-high heat to reduce the wine by half, about 5 minutes.

SIMMER
45–50 mins.

Blend in the hot stock, partially cover, and simmer over medium-low heat for 45 to 50 minutes. Add the sachet d'épice. Taste for seasoning and correct. Be aware of the onion's sweetness, or lack of it.

While the soup is simmering prepare the rest of the dish.

Here is how it comes together.

A tablespoon of finely chopped onion will be placed in the bottom of each soup bowl.

Pieces of bread are sliced about ½ inch thick and cut to fit into the soup bowl. Butter and bake the bread in the oven until toasted and brown. Turn the pieces over and brown other side. If bread is not toasted and buttered, it will soak up the soup like a sponge.

Slice the cheese about ⅛ inch thick. Two pieces overlapped should cover the top beyond the edge. The cheese will melt, sealing the soup completely. Guests must break through the crust. If the cheese doesn't fit, patch with small pieces. The soup is just as delicious only partially covered, but it isn't as attractive.

OVEN
375°

Place the rack midway in the oven. Preheat the oven to 375°. Pour hot water into the tureen or bowls to warm them before the soup is ladled in; pour out the hot water.

It is easier to get the bowls into the oven if they are clustered on a cookie sheet or pan and all carried together.

Place the chopped onion in each bowl and fill it almost to the brim with hot soup.

The Cognac may be poured into the soup bowl now or, if there is a break in the crust, spooned in when the bowls come out of the oven.

Place the croutons on top of the soup and lay on the cheese.

10–15 mins.	Place the bowls in the oven and bake for 10 to 15 minutes at 375°, or until cheese has melted.
BROILER *1–2 mins.*	Turn on the broiler. Broil until the cheese is bubbly golden brown—1 to 2 minutes.
FINAL STEP	Serve with chunks of French bread and a robust red wine.

Warn guests that the bowls are very hot.

Variation: The crouton may also be covered with grated Parmesan cheese instead of a large cheese slice. It will not seal the bowl, but no matter. I also like to drop a few slivers of the cheese along into the bottom of the bowl with the onion.

Onion and Almond Soup (Spanish)
Cebollada con Almendras

Serves 6

While this onion soup from Spain shares a number of ingredients with its French counterpart, it differs in a few delicious ways. It is tantalizingly flavored with almonds (almendras). Forty or fifty are finely ground to become part of the soup. The onions are not caramelized as they would be in France, but left pale white.

I had eaten a comparable soup in a small café in Madrid and later found that Penelope Casas, food author and editor, had discovered this recipe in a sixteenth-century cookbook written by the chef to King Fernando, Spanish ruler of Naples. She shared it with me at Craig Claiborne's famous birthday food bash.

INGREDIENTS	2 tablespoons olive oil
	3 large onions, thinly sliced
	6 cups chicken stock
	1 cup dry white wine
	1 bay leaf
	2 sprigs parsley
	Salt to taste, if desired
	Pepper to taste, preferably white
	2 ounces blanched almonds
	¼ teaspoon cumin seeds, roasted and freshly ground (see "Spices, Herbs, and Seasonings," page 372)
	Butter
	6 slices coarse peasant bread, about ¼ inch thick

(continued)

6 or more slices Gruyère cheese, about ⅛ inch thick and large enough to
   cover a *petite marmite* or another ovenproof bowl
   or ½ cup grated Parmesan cheese
¼ cup toasted almonds, sliced, to garnish

SPECIAL EQUIPMENT	Food processor or blender. Sieve or fine chinois. Mortar and pestle, optional. Ideally the soup should be served in *petites marmites,* the small ovenproof bowls, usually with handles, that are traditional for onion soups.
PREPARATION SAUTÉ 10 mins.	In a medium (3½-quart) saucepan, heat the olive oil and sauté the onion slices over medium-low heat until they are translucent and tender but not browned. Add the chicken stock, wine, bay leaf, parsley, salt, and pepper.
BOIL/SIMMER 30 mins.	Bring the stock to a boil, reduce heat, and simmer, covered, for 30 minutes.
GRIND	While the soup is cooking, grind the almonds in a food processor or blender until they are very fine. Add ½ cup of the stock to the almonds in the work bowl and process until the liquid is milky. Strain through a fine sieve or chinois. If many almond particles remain, grind them again. Pour the almond mixture into the simmering soup.
ROAST 2–3 mins.	For a more lively cumin taste, roast the seeds in a small skillet over medium heat for 2 or 3 minutes or until seeds crackle, pop, and brown. Grind in a mortar with pestle. Or use ground cumin. Add cumin to the soup.
30 mins.	Cover and simmer for an additional 30 minutes—1 hour in all.
TOAST 6 mins.	Meanwhile, lightly butter the bread on both sides and place under a broiler for 3 or 4 minutes. If the slices are not buttered, they will absorb the soup and be soggy. Turn the slices over and toast for another 3 minutes. Watch closely. They are inclined to burn.

Remove the bay leaf and parsley sprigs from the stock.

Ladle the hot soup into individual ovenproof bowls (or into a shallow casserole or tureen). Fill to the rim and place a slice of toast over the top. Place cheese slices over the toast to completely cover and seal the top.

Or, if grated Parmesan cheese is used, sprinkle liberally on the toast.

BROIL	Put under the broiler about 6 inches from the flame. (I group my small bowls on a tray or baking sheet that will fit into the oven or

broiler and place them in together rather than trying to handle them one by one.)

5 mins.   The cheese will melt and become golden in about 5 minutes.

FINAL STEP   Serve immediately with a sprinkling of toasted almonds. A coarse peasant bread goes well with this soup.

Green Onion and Forest Mushroom Soup

Serves 6

This soup is a happy marriage of green onions from my garden and black mushrooms picked in a Japanese forest half a world away. While I don't know the name of the hunter who picked and dried the mushrooms in Japan, I do know it is my neighbor with whom I share a garden plot who is responsible for the great number of green onions that I make into this lightly creamed soup each spring of the year.

Since the green part of the onion is as important to the flavor of the soup as the white, it is included, and the resulting soup is a light green with flecks of the darker tops blended throughout. This is a handsome and delicious dish.

There is also a sweetness about the soup that comes naturally from the onions. No sugar is added.

The dried Japanese black mushroom is now sold in many of the specialty food departments of large supermarkets, but if you can't find the ones from Japan, then accept those picked in Poland, which are equally good. While both are sold by the ounce or the fraction of the ounce, remember that this is a dried weight and they will gain both bulk and weight when soaked in water. If substituting fresh shiitake for the dried, eliminate the soaking process.

This soup may be made with either whipping cream (for a rich, velvety taste) or yogurt (less rich but with a pleasant tartness).

INGREDIENTS   8 dried forest mushrooms (Japanese shiitake) or dried Polish mushrooms
6 cups chicken stock
3 or 4 bunches green onions (about 1 pound), including tops
2 large cloves garlic, crushed
$\frac{1}{4}$ cup (4 tablespoons) butter or margarine
3 tablespoons flour
1 cup heavy cream or yogurt
$\frac{1}{4}$ teaspoon salt, or to taste
$\frac{1}{4}$ teaspoon freshly ground black pepper
Parsley sprigs, if desired, to garnish
3 or 4 fresh mushrooms, sliced, if desired, to garnish

SPECIAL EQUIPMENT	Food processor to mince onions; otherwise mince by hand.
PREPARATION SOAK *30 mins.*	In a large bowl soak mushrooms in warm water to cover until puffed and tender, about 30 minutes. Cut off hard stems and discard. Press water out of the mushrooms with the fingers of one hand against the palm of the other. Slice tops into strips about ¼ inch wide and set aside.
SIMMER *25 mins.*	In a large (4½-quart) saucepan, heat chicken stock to a simmer. Drop in the mushroom strips and let simmer while proceeding with onions and garlic.
MINCE	Clean onion stalks, leaving about one third white and two thirds green. Cut in 2-inch lengths if for the food processor. Otherwise mince into pieces no longer than ¼ inch. If in the food processor, take care not to mince the onions too finely. The onions don't need to be uniformly cut. The mixture will be surprisingly moist from its own juices.
SAUTÉ *20 mins.* *2–3 mins.*	Sauté minced green onions and crushed garlic in butter or margarine in covered kettle or large saucepan until softened, about 20 minutes, over medium heat. Add flour; stir until smooth and cook for 2 to 3 minutes more. Stir in hot mushroom stock, a cup or so at a time, or pour very gradually. Bring to a simmer, stirring occasionally; reduce heat.
SIMMER *12 mins.* *10 mins.*	Simmer uncovered until thickened and smooth, about 12 minutes. Pour several tablespoons of hot soup into cream or yogurt (see note below) and mix well before pouring the mixture back into the soup. Add salt and pepper. Return to a simmer. *Note:* Yogurt should be whipped briefly with a fork or whisk beforehand to prevent a curdled look.
FINAL STEP	Remove from the heat and pour into large bowls. Garnish with parsley sprigs and, if desired, mushroom slices to float on the surface when the soup is presented at the table.

Harvest Cream of Onion Soup

Serves 6 to 8

The word harvest *in the name of this soup celebrates not only the gathering of the onions in the gardens and fields but also the restaurant on Cambridge's Harvard Square where the chef created this fine soup.*

The soup is a rich assemblage of two stocks, cream, potato, four herbs, two brandies, one wine, butter, and of course onions.

Chef Bob Kinkead had two versions of the soup for his guests at the Harvest. One came about when someone in the kitchen mistakenly added chopped fresh dill instead of thyme and then went on to replace fresh cream with sour. It was a happy mistake. Both soups are delicious.

Use fresh herbs when available. Calvados (French apple brandy) is quite expensive. However, domestic and less expensive apple brandies may be substituted.

INGREDIENTS	1½ pounds (about 6 to 8) onions
	2 tablespoons butter, clarified
	½ teaspoon freshly ground or cracked black pepper
	4 cups veal stock
	4 cups chicken stock
	1 large potato, coarsely diced
	2 teaspoons thyme (or chopped fresh dill)
	2 bay leaves
	1 teaspoon rosemary
	½ teaspoon marjoram
	1 teaspoon salt
	½ cup brandy
	½ cup white Bordeaux wine
	3 tablespoons Calvados or domestic apple brandy (omit in the dill version)
	1 cup (8 ounces) heavy cream (or sour cream)
	Salt and freshly ground black pepper to taste, if needed
	1 tablespoon grated sapsago cheese and 2 cups unsweetened whipped cream, or fresh dill sprigs and sour cream, to garnish
SPECIAL EQUIPMENT	Blender. Chinois or sieve.
PREPARATION COOK	Peel and slice onions. In a medium (3-quart) saucepan, cook onions in clarified butter over low heat until soft and caramelized, about 20 min-

20 mins.	utes. Add pepper and the 2 stocks, diced potato, thyme (or dill), bay leaves, rosemary, marjoram, salt, brandy, wine, and Calvados (for the heavy sweet cream version).
BOIL/SIMMER *1 hour*	Bring to a boil, reduce heat to medium-low, partially cover, and allow to simmer gently for about 1 hour. Soup will be reduced by 1 or 2 cups. Potato should be soft.
PUREE *10 mins.*	Remove soup from the heat and allow it to cool somewhat so that it can be put through the blender to puree, perhaps in 2 batches.
SIEVE *5 mins.*	For a velvety-smooth soup pour puree through a fine sieve. For a less smooth soup, pour through a chinois (which has larger holes) to ensure that the soup is of an even consistency.
	If the soup is to be held in the refrigerator for 1 or 2 days, or to be frozen, stop at this point.
	Add cream (or sour cream) to soup, if to be served now, and blend thoroughly.
	Add salt and pepper if needed.
FINAL STEP	Bring to a simmer before serving. Garnish with sapsago cheese and whipped cream, or with a sprig of fresh dill only to garnish the dill/sour cream version.

Cream of Scallion Soup with Cheese

Serves 6

A scallion is a close kin of the onion and answers to such names as green onion, spring onion, stone leek, cibal, and Welsh onion. It is similar in appearance to a young onion; its base, however, never forms a large bulb but always keeps a slim profile. It makes a fragrant and appetizing soup.

INGREDIENTS	18 scallions
	1 tablespoon salt
	Water
	4 cups milk
	2 tablespoons butter, melted
	1 tablespoon cornstarch or arrowroot
	Salt, to taste
	¼ teaspoon white pepper

1 teaspoon Hungarian paprika

2 tablespoons grated Cheddar cheese

2 tablespoons finely minced scallion tops, to garnish

SPECIAL EQUIPMENT	Food processor, food mill, blender, or sieve to puree. Whisk.
PREPARATION *10 mins.*	Wash and trim scallions to include an equal amount of green and white bases.
BOIL *10 mins.*	Bring salted water to a boil in a medium (3-quart) saucepan and drop in scallions. Cook over medium heat until fork-tender, about 10 minutes. Drain.
PUREE *5 mins.*	Puree cooked scallions. Return to saucepan and add milk. Heat but do not boil.
BLEND *5 mins.*	In a small bowl, blend melted butter into cornstarch or arrowroot. Add mixture to soup and stir constantly until thickened and smooth, about 5 minutes. Remove from heat. Add salt, if desired, white pepper, and paprika to taste. Blend in cheese and beat with whisk until very smooth.
FINAL STEP	Reheat, if necessary, to serve piping hot. Sprinkle finely chopped green scallion tops over soup and serve. This soup is also delicious chilled.

Scallion Soup with Noodles

Serves 6

Although this soup is named for its principal two ingredients, scallions and noodles, the unsung ingredient, lemon juice, is what gives the delicious broth its special piquancy.

INGREDIENTS	1¾ cups thinly sliced scallions or green onions
	1 clove garlic, minced
	2 tablespoons butter
	4 cups chicken stock
	1 cup fine egg noodles
	2 egg yolks
	1 egg
	3 tablespoons lemon juice

(continued)

1 teaspoon salt, if desired
½ teaspoon freshly ground black pepper
2 tablespoons finely chopped scallion tops or parsley, to garnish

SPECIAL EQUIPMENT	Food processor, blender, or food mill
PREPARATION SMOTHER 8 mins.	Cook scallions and garlic in butter in a covered skillet until soft and translucent, about 8 minutes. Set aside. Don't let the tiny bits burn, because they will then appear in the soup for what they are—tiny burned bits (not attractive).
BOIL 3 mins.	Bring chicken stock to a boil in a medium (3-quart) saucepan. Add egg noodles and boil gently for about 3 minutes, or until al dente.
	Beat egg yolks and whole egg together in a small bowl and add lemon juice in a stream. Add 1 cup of hot chicken stock, whisking until well combined. Pour the mixture into the hot broth and place over low heat. Don't let the mixture boil.
BLEND/HEAT 4 mins.	Add scallions to the broth-egg mixture. Season to taste with salt and pepper. Heat, stirring, until the soup is slightly thickened.
FINAL STEP	Pour into heated bowls and garnish with finely minced green scallion tops or parsley.
	Serve hot.

Curried Parsnip Soup (British)

Serves 4

With parsnip soup, as with the parsnip itself, there seems to be no middle ground as to desirability—you either dote on it or cannot abide it.

The old saw that parsnips must be frozen in the ground to be usable is not true. But the roots can be left in the ground through the winter and dug first thing in the spring. The parsnip is a member of the carrot family with a somewhat spongy character.

This recipe came from one of the manor houses in Herefordshire, England, where a good friend, Mrs. Robert Simpson, is mistress. She told me the recipe originally came from a cookbook put together by Conservative members of Parliament and their spouses. The wife of the minister of agriculture contributed this recipe.

I find parsnips almost too sweet for my taste—as if someone had added a tablespoon of sugar to the dish. Curry, therefore, was an addition that gave it new character and cut the sweetness. I liked it.

INGREDIENTS	2 tablespoons butter
	2 cups chopped onions
	2 cups chopped parsnips
	2 cloves garlic, minced
	1 tablespoon all-purpose flour
	1 teaspoon curry powder
	3 cups chicken stock
	1 teaspoon salt, if desired
	Pinch of freshly ground black pepper
	1 tablespoon freshly toasted coconut or 1 tablespoon toasted slivered almonds, to garnish

SPECIAL EQUIPMENT — Blender or food processor

PREPARATION
COOK
10 mins.
2–3 mins.

In a medium (3-quart) saucepan, with lid, melt the butter until it foams but does not brown. Add the onions, parsnips, and garlic and cook over medium-low heat until parsnips are tender, about 10 minutes.

Sprinkle flour over the vegetables and add the curry powder. Stir to blend and cook for 2 to 3 minutes.

SIMMER
10 mins.

In the meantime, in another vessel, heat the stock to a simmer. Scrape the contents of the saucepan with a wooden spoon to loosen all the particles. Add to the stock and simmer for about 10 minutes. Taste for seasoning. Add salt and pepper, if needed.

PUREE

In blender or food processor, depending on the creaminess wanted, puree contents of saucepan. Taste again for seasoning.

FINAL STEP

Serve in heated bowls. Sprinkle with toasted coconut or almond slivers.

Peanut Soup (Nigeria)

Serves 6

The peanut (sometimes referred to as a groundnut) is a staple in many parts of Africa and from it are derived many good things to eat, including many different kinds of soups. This one is from Nigeria. Crushed red peppers add spicy-hot flavor, while crushed peanuts give it an un-

usual texture that will delight any peanut buff. Nigerians make this soup with fish stock but I find beef stock equally delicious.

INGREDIENTS	1 cup roasted peanuts, hulled
	4 cups fish or beef stock
	1 or 2 small red chili peppers, to taste, or ½ teaspoon cayenne pepper
	½ cup *each* finely chopped green pepper and onion
	Salt to taste, if desired
	½ cup toasted croutons, to garnish

SPECIAL
EQUIPMENT

Food processor. Mortar and pestle.

PREPARATION

Crush peanuts under a rolling pin or spin in a food processor. Don't make the particles too fine—a blender may turn them into peanut butter.

SIMMER
10–15 mins.

Heat the stock in a medium (3-quart) saucepan. If using chili pods, pop open between the fingers and pick out and discard the seeds and ribs. Crush skins in the mortar. Add this pepper or cayenne pepper to the stock along with the green pepper and onion. Bring to a simmer and cook for 10 to 15 minutes or until vegetables are tender.

10 mins.

    Stir in the crushed peanuts. Simmer for an additional 10 minutes, stirring frequently. Add salt to taste, depending on the saltiness of the roasted nuts.

FINAL STEP

Pour soup into hot cups and top with crisp croutons.

Pea Soup with Mint (English)

Serves 8

The sweetness of green peas and the fragrance of fresh mint come together in this soup from Shropshire, England, where the Roman legionnaires introduced peas centuries ago.
    Fresh or frozen garden peas make an exquisite soup—rich green velvet, thickened with egg yolks and cream, flavored with summer mint—that is equally good chilled.
    The final touch—garnish with tiny peas and tiny mint leaves.

INGREDIENTS	1½ pounds shelled fresh (about 3 pounds unshelled) or frozen peas
	4 tablespoons butter
	1 small onion, finely chopped
	1 quart light beef or chicken stock

Salt, if desired
Pinch of freshly ground white pepper
¼ teaspoon sugar
3 or more sprigs fresh mint, to taste
2 egg yolks
I cup thick cream
4 ounces shelled and boiled petits pois, to garnish
Tiny top leaves of mint, to garnish

SPECIAL
EQUIPMENT

Blender, food processor, or food mill. The soup can also be pushed through a fine sieve.

PREPARATION

Shell the peas or thaw frozen peas by pouring boiling water over them only long enough to thaw—not to cook. Drain.

SMOTHER
6 mins.

In a medium (4-quart) saucepan, melt the butter and add the onion. Cover and cook over medium heat until the onion is translucent, about 6 minutes.

3–4 mins.

Pour the peas into the onion/butter mixture. Stir to mix well. Cover and continue to cook for 3 to 4 minutes until the butter has been absorbed.

SIMMER
10 mins.

Add the stock to the saucepan as well as salt, white pepper, sugar, and mint sprigs. Bring to a simmer, cover, and cook for 10 minutes, or until the peas are just tender. Remove from heat and let the peas cool somewhat before proceeding.

PUREE

Puree peas, onions, and mint in the blender, food processor, or food mill until smooth and creamy.

REHEAT

Before serving, reheat the soup, but don't boil. Beat the egg yolks with the cream until smooth, and add to the soup. Heat through, stirring all the time, until the soup has thickened. Do not allow to boil, as the cream may curdle.

Taste again for seasoning.

FINAL STEP

To serve hot, pour into heated soup bowls and garnish with a sprinkling of boiled petits pois. Arrange the mint leaves attractively in the center.

To serve cold, ladle into chilled cups or glass bowls and garnish with mint only.

Curried Green Pea Soup

Serves 6

The tang of curry lifts this pea soup out of the ordinary. In the bowl it is a deceptively cool green, but the spiciness that comes with curry powder and Tabasco is a pleasant surprise.

INGREDIENTS	4 cups water
	2 10-ounce packages frozen peas
	2 tablespoons butter
	1 cup finely diced celery
	1 cup finely diced onions
	1½ cups light cream
	2 teaspoons curry powder
	Salt to taste, if desired
	White pepper to taste
	Dash of Tabasco
	Paprika, to garnish
SPECIAL EQUIPMENT	Food mill, food processor, or blender
PREPARATION	Bring the water to a boil in a medium (3-quart) saucepan.
BOIL/SIMMER *5 mins.*	Add the frozen peas and bring to a simmer. Cook for 5 minutes or until tender.
PUREE	Pour the peas and the water in which they have cooked into the work bowl of a food processor or a blender—depending on how smooth you wish the puree to be. I like the tiny pieces cut by the food processor rather than the creaminess if the blender is used. Return the puree to the saucepan and set aside.
SMOTHER *12 mins.*	Bring the butter to bubbling in a skillet over medium heat and add the diced celery and onions. Cover the skillet and cook the vegetables until they are tender, about 12 minutes.
	Scrape the contents of the skillet into the pea soup and add the cream and curry powder. Add salt, pepper, and Tabasco.
	Taste for seasoning and *texture.* If the diced vegetables in the soup make it too coarse, put the mixture in the food processor for 1 or 2 quick bursts—just enough to cut the dice into finer pieces.

REHEAT	Return to the stove and heat through, but do not boil, or the cream may curdle.
FINAL STEP	Ladle the soup into a heated tureen and sprinkle lightly with paprika.

Hannah Maria's Green Split Pea Soup

Serves 4 to 6

Hawaii seems an unlikely place to find a century-old recipe for a delicious green split pea soup. The Rice family were sugar planters on the island of Kauai in the middle of the nineteenth century, and sixteen-year-old Hannah Maria, the eldest of five children, created this soup.

In her journal, the young girl describes dinner as a noonday meal because in the evening the whale oil that burned in the lamps "smelled awfully" and spoiled appetites.

INGREDIENTS	6 cups beef or chicken stock
	2 cups green split peas, washed and picked over
	3 large onions, finely chopped
	3 tablespoons butter
	4 large ripe tomatoes, peeled, seeded, and chopped, or a 1-pound can
	Salt, if desired
	½ teaspoon freshly ground black pepper
SPECIAL EQUIPMENT	None
PREPARATION	Pour the stock into a medium (3-quart) saucepan and add the split peas.
SIMMER 1½ hours	Simmer, partially covered, over low heat for 1½ hours.
SAUTÉ 10 mins.	Meanwhile, sauté the onions in butter in a medium skillet until tender and just beginning to brown, about 10 minutes.
SIMMER 30 mins. 5 mins.	Add the onions to the soup and continue cooking for an additional 30 minutes. The peas should be tender but not mushy.
	Five minutes before the soup is finished cooking, stir in the tomatoes.
	Season with salt to taste and pepper.
FINAL STEP	Serve in a heated tureen and ladle into heated individual bowls. Aloha!

Green Split Pea Soup with Cheese (Italian)
Zuppa di Piselli Secchi con Formaggio

Serves 6

Green split pea soup is a late fall and wintertime delight that can be reheated time and again, although it is unlikely that much will be left over. This is a recipe by Marcella Hazan from her excellent cookbook The Classic Italian Cookbook.

The peas and potatoes combine to make a thick soup, and it becomes even more so when reheated. If it thickens too much, add stock or water. Use a light—not strong—stock so the delicate flavor of the peas is not overpowered.

INGREDIENTS	½ pound green split peas, washed, picked over, and drained
	¾ pound (about 2 medium) potatoes, peeled and rough cut
	6 cups light beef stock
	2 tablespoons chopped onion
	3 tablespoons olive oil, Italian preferred
	3 tablespoons butter
	3 tablespoons freshly grated Parmesan or Romano cheese
	Salt, if desired
SPECIAL EQUIPMENT	None
PREPARATION BOIL *45 mins.*	Cook the peas and potatoes in 4 cups of stock in a medium (3-quart) saucepan at a gentle boil for 45 minutes.
REST *30 mins.*	Remove from the heat, cover, and set aside to continue to soften for another 30 minutes. The peas should be quite tender. Puree the peas, potatoes, and liquid in a food processor or pass through a food mill. Return to the saucepan.
SAUTÉ *12 mins.*	While the peas are cooking, sauté the onions with the olive oil and butter in a small skillet over medium heat for about 12 minutes. The onions should be a light golden brown.
BOIL *10 mins.*	Scrape the contents of the skillet into the saucepan, add the remaining 2 cups of stock, and bring to a gentle boil. Cook, stirring occasionally, until the oil and butter are well blended into the soup, about 10 minutes.

When the soup has finished cooking, stir in the grated cheese. Turn off the heat, taste, and correct for salt.

FINAL STEP   Serve with additional grated cheese and toasted Italian or French bread.

If the soup is to be eaten later, add the cheese only when you re-heat it.

Green Split Pea Soup with Wine

Serves 8

A hint of mustard and sesame oil and a nip of wine and vinegar give this hearty soup a special character that sets it apart from the dozens of other dishes made with this legume.

There is no meat or meat stock among the ingredients.

INGREDIENTS
- 1 pound green split peas, washed and drained
- 5 or 6 cups water, depending on desired consistency
- 1 bay leaf
- 2 teaspoons salt
- 1 cup minced onions
- 3 cloves garlic, crushed
- 1 cup minced celery
- 1 medium potato, thinly sliced
- 2 cups thinly sliced carrots
- 1 cup chopped tomatoes
- ¼ cup dry red wine
- ¼ teaspoon dry mustard
- ¼ teaspoon thyme
- Several drops of dark sesame oil (very potent)
- 3 tablespoons vinegar
- ¼ cup finely chopped parsley
- Freshly ground black pepper

SPECIAL
EQUIPMENT   None

PREPARATION   Wash and pick over split peas. In a medium (4-quart) saucepan, cover the peas with 5 cups of water. Add the bay leaf and salt.

SIMMER
1 hour   Bring to a simmer over medium-low heat and cook until tender, about 1 hour.

SMOTHER *10 mins.*	While the peas are simmering, cook the onions, garlic, celery, potato, and carrots in a large covered skillet over low heat until the vegetables are soft and translucent, about 10 minutes.
SIMMER *1 hour* *15 mins.*	Add the contents of the skillet to the soup and continue simmering for an additional hour, or a total of 2 hours. Fifteen minutes before serving, add tomatoes, red wine, mustard, thyme, and a few drops of sesame oil. Stir to blend well. If the soup seems thick, add a cup or so of water.
FINAL STEP	Just before serving, add vinegar, parsley, and freshly ground black pepper to taste. Ladle into a heated tureen or warmed soup bowls. Serve with Burgundy wine and peasant bread (page 360).

Cream of Split Pea Soup (Swiss)

Serves 10

The small Swiss village of Guttannen, below Grimsel Pass (elevation 7,103 feet) is so breathtakingly beautiful on a late fall afternoon that it seems only right to discover with equal pleasure a delicious yellow split pea soup at the Hotel Bären. Guttannen is a remote Alpine village where the cows move down the main street from milk rooms under the chalets to pastures across the Aare River. Their comings and goings are announced melodiously by copper bells strapped around their necks.

The hearty and warming soup is the creation of a young chef de cuisine, Peter Rifibach, whose family has been serving good food to travelers in the Alps since 1803. He trained in big hotels in Interlaken and then returned home to take over the family kitchen at the Bären.

The Swiss recipe called for cracklings—cracklings are pieces of pork that have been cooked and rendered of their fat—but because they are sometimes difficult to find except in farm country I have substituted bacon.

INGREDIENTS	½ pound yellow split peas Water to cover ¼ pound bacon, cut into ¼-inch pieces, or cracklings 2 tablespoons butter ½ turnip, chopped ½ cup chopped celery 1 cup leek, washed carefully and sliced 6 to 8 sprigs parsley, tied in a bundle

¾ pound potatoes (about 3 medium), peeled and cut into 1-inch chunks
6 cups beef stock

Sachet d'épice
2 bay leaves, crumbled
2 cloves
6 black peppercorns
1 clove garlic, mashed

1 teaspoon salt, if desired
2 cups light cream
½ cup chopped parsley or chives, to garnish

SPECIAL EQUIPMENT	Food processor or food mill
PREPARATION SOAK *5–6 hours*	Soak the split peas in water to cover 5 to 6 hours or overnight. Drain before using.
SAUTÉ	In a large (4- or 5-quart) saucepan, sauté the bacon pieces until crisp. Pour off and discard the fat.
SWEAT *15 mins.*	Melt the butter in the same saucepan, with the bacon pieces and drop in the turnip, celery, leek, and parsley. Cover and sweat over medium-low heat for about 15 minutes, or until the vegetables are tender and translucent.
BOIL/SIMMER *2–3 hours*	Add the potato pieces and the peas and pour in the beef stock. Cover and bring to a boil; reduce heat to low to simmer for 2 or 3 hours, or until the peas are tender.
SACHET *30 mins.*	Thirty minutes before the soup is done, add the sachet.
PUREE	Remove the saucepan from the heat. Add the salt and cream. Set aside until somewhat cooled, about 10 minutes. Remove the sachet and parsley bundle. Puree the soup.
FINAL STEP	Ladle the soup into heated bowls. Garnish with chopped parsley or chives and serve.

Dhal and Vegetable Soup (Sri Lanka)

Serves 6

Dhal, *a staple of the Indian subcontinent, is the basis for this delicious vegetable soup brought from Sri Lanka to Hawaii by Kusuma Cooray, onetime executive chef of the famous Willows in Honolulu. While* dhal *can be the name for one of more than fifty varieties of leguminous plants, in this recipe it is yellow split peas. It could also be made with lentils.*

Kusuma arrived in the Islands by way of London's Cordon Bleu and La Varenne École de Cuisine, Paris, and for nine years she was the personal chef for Doris Duke in Duke's homes in the Islands and elsewhere.

Her recipe calls for tamarind, the acidic, juicy pulp of the fruit from the tamarind tree. If tamarind is not in your market, the juice of limes may be substituted.

INGREDIENTS	1½ cups yellow split peas
	7 cups water
	2 cloves garlic, grated
	1 teaspoon grated fresh ginger
	1 teaspoon cumin, roasted and ground (see "Spices, Herbs, and Seasonings," page 372)
	1 teaspoon coriander
	1 teaspoon turmeric
	1 teaspoon freshly ground black pepper
	1 medium onion, finely chopped
	2 pounds vegetables—½ pound *each* carrots, string beans, peeled tomatoes, and eggplant (On occasion I have substituted frozen mixed vegetables plus whatever fresh vegetables were at hand.)
	2 cups fresh spinach leaves
	1 tablespoon tamarind pulp or juice of 3 limes
	Salt to taste, if desired
	¾ cup cream
	½ cup slivered almonds, toasted, to garnish
SPECIAL EQUIPMENT	None
PREPARATION	*Note:* Wash peas, pick clean, and soak overnight or use quick-cook method.
	Pour water off the peas, wash under cold running water, and drain.
BOIL/SIMMER *40 mins.*	In a medium (4-quart) saucepan, combine split peas, water, garlic, ginger, cumin, coriander, turmeric, black pepper, and chopped onion.

Place on high heat to bring to a boil. Lower heat, cover, and simmer until the peas are soft, about 40 minutes.

Meanwhile, wash and cut into ½-inch cubes all the vegetables except the spinach. Break the spinach into large pieces, discarding heavy stems. Reserve.

30–40 mins.

When the split peas are soft, add all the cubed vegetables, cover, and cook until they are soft, about 30 to 40 minutes over simmering heat.

The soup can be prepared to this point and set aside in the refrigerator for 1 or 2 days. When needed, reheat and continue.

5 mins.

Add reserved spinach leaves, tamarind or lime juice, and salt to taste, if desired. Stir in cream and remove from the heat.

FINAL STEP

Serve in heated bowls and garnish each with a sprinkling of toasted almonds.

(Almonds may be toasted on a baking sheet in a 300° oven for a few minutes; watch carefully so they don't scorch.)

Red Pepper Soup

Serves 6

This lovely soup is made not with the hot red pepper but with the sweet green pepper, which perversely turns a bright red when it matures. While the pepper gives the soup a lively red color, it is the cool member of an otherwise torrid family. It is known also as a bell or globe pepper, while to my family it is a mango! To others it is simply a sweet pepper.

INGREDIENTS

2 onions, peeled and chopped

3 tablespoons butter

6 cups chicken stock

2 10-ounce jars roasted sweet red peppers, drained and cut into pieces, or 4 to 6 large, fresh sweet red peppers, roasted and peeled (see note below)

1 teaspoon salt, if desired

¼ teaspoon freshly ground white pepper

2 tablespoons chive snippets, to garnish

Note: To remove the skin from a fresh pepper, place it in a 350° oven or under the broiler until the skin is scorched and blistered. The pepper can also be speared with a fork and held over an open flame. Place the charred pepper in a plastic bag for 20 minutes to "steam." The skin can now be peeled away and discarded.

SPECIAL EQUIPMENT	Food processor, blender, or food mill
PREPARATION SMOTHER *8 mins.*	In a medium (3-quart) saucepan, place the onions and butter. Cover and cook over medium-low heat for 8 minutes or until translucent and tender.
BOIL/SIMMER *10 mins.*	Pour the chicken stock into the saucepan and add the roasted red peppers. Bring to a boil, reduce heat, and simmer, covered, for 10 minutes. Season with salt, if desired, and white pepper.
PUREE	When the soup has cooled somewhat, ladle it into the work bowl of a food processor or blender or pour gradually into a food mill. Puree. The job will probably need to be done in batches whichever of the machines you use.
REHEAT	The soup may be prepared in advance and reheated over moderate heat.
FINAL STEP	Pour the hot soup into individual bowls and garnish with snippets of chives.

French Red Pepper Soup
Potage aux Poivrons Rouges
Serves 6 to 8

Potage aux poivrons rouges *is one of the culinary delights awaiting balloonists when they touch down after drifting with the breezes over vineyards, churches, and villages in Burgundy, near Beaune, a small city some 300 kilometers southeast of Paris and the operational base for the fleet of sixteen balloons belonging to the Buddy Bombard Society.*

The French red pepper soup is but one of the delicious creations served to hungry balloonists returned from the Burgundian skies by the society's head chef, Robert Jackson Chambers. It is a beguiling soup because its lovely light red color suggests tomato but its taste is all pepper. The chef describes it as "zingy but sweet."

We arrived at the Bombard château a few days before a major storm system swept into the area from the British Isles and wiped out the balance of our flying schedule. (No ballooning in winds over 10 knots!) We waited out the storm's days in wine cellars, old châteaus, and several ruins and museums, and in addressing the superb food on the Bombard table. The storm didn't abate, but neither did the wine and food, which I enjoyed as much as the flying. French red pepper soup is delicious cold, too.

INGREDIENTS	2 tablespoons butter
	2 large onions, peeled and coarsely chopped
	2 medium carrots, peeled and sliced
	6 cups chicken stock
	6 sweet red peppers (1½ pounds), seeded and coarsely chopped
	1 cup milk
	1 teaspoon salt, if desired
	Pinch of freshly ground black pepper
	Pinch of thyme
	½ cup sour cream or crème fraîche
SPECIAL EQUIPMENT	Food processor or blender; chinois or medium sieve if processor is used
PREPARATION SAUTÉ *15 mins.*	Melt the butter in a medium (3-quart) saucepan; drop in the chopped onions and cook over medium-low heat until they are soft and translucent, about 15 minutes.
COOK *15–20 mins.* *20 mins.* *20 mins.*	Add the carrots, cover, and cook until tender, about 15 to 20 minutes.
	Add the chicken stock; leave uncovered and bring to a boil over medium-high heat for 20 minutes to reduce the stock base in volume and to strengthen its flavor. Skim occasionally.
	Add the red pepper chunks and cook for an additional 20 minutes or until they can be easily pierced with a fork or knife point. Remove from the heat and add milk, salt, pepper, and thyme.
PUREE	When somewhat cool, puree the soup in a food processor or blender. If a food processor is used, then strain and press the soup through a chinois or sieve.
FINAL STEP	If to be served hot, reheat soup over low flame, watching carefully so it does not boil.
	Serve in heated bowls, topped with a dollop of sour cream or crème fraîche.
	If to be served cold, chill in the refrigerator for several hours. It, too, can be topped with the sour cream or crème fraîche.

Potato Soup (Irish)

Serves 6

The potato is to Ireland what rice is to the Japanese, or pasta to the Italians, and one of the best things the Irish make of it is soup. This soup, economical to make, can be put together in less than an hour. It is essentially potatoes and onions cooked lightly over low heat in butter to soften before milk is added. It is then processed or sieved into a creamy soup. A nice final touch is to pour a tablespoon of evaporated milk into each bowl before the soup is ladled in.

Despite tales to the contrary, potatoes are not notably fattening. One medium-size potato totals about 100 calories—the same as a large apple or orange.

More than three centuries ago the potato, a native of South America, was introduced into Ireland, where it became the principal item of food in the Irish diet. It remains so today. In Ireland potatoes have such lyrical names as Aran Banners, Irish Queens, Ulster Chieftains, and Skerry Champions. Irish Cobbers are my favorites when I can get them; otherwise I choose the one at hand.

INGREDIENTS	2 tablespoons butter
	2 pounds potatoes (about 5 or 6 large), peeled and thinly sliced
	2 medium onions, peeled and thinly sliced
	4 cups milk
	1 cup chicken stock
	1 clove garlic, crushed
	Sachet d'épice
	½ teaspoon dried thyme
	2 bay leaves
	8 black peppercorns
	2 blades mace or ½ teaspoon dried
	6 sprigs parsley, tied together
	Salt, to taste (I use about 1 tablespoon)
	White pepper, to taste
	½ cup canned evaporated milk
	Snipped chives, to garnish
SPECIAL EQUIPMENT	Food processor, sieve, or chinois. (A blender whips it too creamy.)
PREPARATION	Melt butter in a medium (3-quart) saucepan until it foams. Drop in the potatoes and onions, toss, and stir to film the pieces with butter.

STEAM
10 mins.

Lay a piece of foil on top of the vegetables and tuck it in around the edges to seal in the steam. This keeps the vegetables from drying out. Cover the pan with a lid and allow the vegetables to soften over low heat for about 10 minutes. Don't let them brown, or the flavor of the soup will be destroyed.

SIMMER
30 mins.

Remove the foil. Add the milk, chicken stock, garlic, sachet, and parsley. Bring to a simmer, partially cover, and cook over medium-low heat for 30 minutes.

PUREE

SEASON

Discard the sachet and parsley. Puree the soup in a food processor or push through a sieve or chinois. Reheat in a clean saucepan. Season with salt, if desired. Although the soup simmered with the black peppercorns in the sachet, it may need an additional sprinkling or two of pepper. Use white pepper, which will not show in the soup. The soup should be thick, the consistency of heavy cream. If too thick, thin with additional milk or chicken stock.

FINAL STEP

Pour a tablespoon of the evaporated milk into each heated soup bowl. Ladle in the soup. Sprinkle snippets of chives over the top. Crisp buttered toast goes well with Irish potato soup, as does Royal Hibernian soda bread.

Russian Potato Soup

Serves 6

A potato soup of many small bits found its way via a daughter-in-law from Russia to my Indiana kitchen, where it was warmly welcomed. It is golden in color, belying its potato origin.

While bacon and ham bits are not to be found in the authentic recipe, some may like to add them to give the soup a slightly different texture and taste.

INGREDIENTS

3 tablespoons butter
2 medium onions, finely chopped
2 stalks celery, finely chopped
½ pound potatoes, peeled and diced
1 carrot, grated
2 cloves garlic, mashed and diced
1 cup water, approximately (to cover vegetables in pan)
1 bay leaf
¼ teaspoon basil

(continued)

1 teaspoon salt, if desired
⅓ cup bacon and ham bits, optional
2 to 3 cups chicken stock, heated
⅛ teaspoon Worcestershire sauce
⅛ teaspoon paprika
1 tablespoon sherry, if desired

SPECIAL
EQUIPMENT

Food processor, optional

PREPARATION
SAUTÉ
15 mins.

In a medium saucepan, sauté in butter the onions, celery, potatoes, carrots, and garlic for about 15 minutes over medium to low heat, taking care that the bits do not burn.

BOIL/SIMMER
20–25 mins.

Cover the vegetables with about 1 cup of water; add bay leaf, basil, and salt, if desired. Bring to a boil, cover, reduce heat, and simmer until all the vegetables are tender. Mash the vegetables into a coarse puree with a potato masher or briefly in a food processor. The mixture should not be pureed into a cream.

FRY
5 mins.

While the vegetables are cooking, fry the bacon or ham bits, if using, until crisp. Drain on paper towels.

  Add the hot chicken stock and meat bits to the blend of vegetables in the saucepan. If the soup becomes too thick as it heats, add more chicken stock.

  Season with Worcestershire sauce, paprika, and sherry, if desired.

FINAL STEP

Serve in hot bowls. Pass coarse chunks of peasant bread and plenty of butter.

Vichyssoise or *Potage Parmentier*
Leek and Potato Soup

Serves 6

Served cold it is vichyssoise; hot it is potage parmentier. *Both are delicious. The cold version was the creation of Louis Diat when he was chef at the Ritz-Carlton Hotel in New York.*

  Although the purist will push the soup through a fine sieve rather than use a machine, my sister in Menton, France, did both to achieve a soup of remarkable smoothness. She first put it in a blender and then through a fine sieve three times. I consider this carrying sieving to an extreme. My vichyssoise is spun once in a blender and for company is sieved as well. At times I use the food mill or food processor.

INGREDIENTS	**4 large potatoes**, about 1½ pounds, peeled and sliced
	4 large leeks
	2 stalks celery, cut into 2-inch pieces
	1 white onion, sliced
	5 cups chicken stock
	1 teaspoon salt, or to taste
	1 cup milk
	½ teaspoon freshly ground white pepper, or to taste
	1 cup heavy cream
	2 tablespoons chopped fresh chives or parsley, to garnish

SPECIAL
EQUIPMENT

Food mill and fine sieve. Optional: blender or food processor.

PREPARATION

Note: Use the white of the leek plus about 2 inches of the green to give the soup a pleasant off-white shading. Split the leeks lengthwise and wash thoroughly to remove all traces of the grit and sand for which leeks are notorious. Slice thinly after washing.

SIMMER
45 mins.

Put the sliced potatoes, leeks, celery, and onion in a heavy 6-quart saucepan or soup kettle. Add chicken stock and simmer, partially covered, until vegetables are tender, about 45 minutes. Remove from the heat and salt to taste. Work the mixture through a food mill and a sieve or puree in an electric blender or food processor. Return to saucepan

5 mins.

over low heat and add the milk. Bring to a simmer for about 5 minutes. Rub the mixture again through the fine sieve. Add pepper and then taste to add salt, if necessary. Blend the cream into the soup.

FINAL STEP

Vichyssoise

Chill thoroughly. Serve very cold, in bowls nested in crushed ice. Pass a small bowl of chopped chives or parsley.

Potage Parmentier

To serve hot, bring the soup to a simmer over low heat. Ladle the soup into a tureen or individual soup bowls. Garnish with chopped fresh chives or parsley.

Potato and Leek Soup
Potage aux Poireaux et Pommes de Terre
Serves 10

Hot potato and leek soup is to be found in almost every working family's kitchen in France, yet it is a near cousin to the elegant vichyssoise.

This is a delicious soup—simple and direct. Few ingredients, no stock—hot water only. It is as simple and forthright in its way as French bread (water, salt, flour, and leavening). For that reason they are admirable table companions. It is a dieter's delight, with the minimum calories for the maximum goodness.

The author Richard Olney, the born-in-Iowa authority on French food, said he would adore to eat this soup every evening of his life. I would join him.

This soup has a certain ruggedness about it that is retained by crushing the potatoes against the side of the saucepan with a spoon or fork. No food mill or food processor, but by hand alone.

INGREDIENTS	2 quarts water
	2 teaspoons salt
	1 pound potatoes, peeled, quartered, and sliced
	1 pound leeks (white part only), split, cleaned, and finely sliced
	3 tablespoons unsalted butter
	1 teaspoon freshly chopped parsley or chives, to garnish
SPECIAL EQUIPMENT	None
PREPARATION BOIL *35–40 mins.* CRUSH *3 mins.*	Bring water to a rapid boil in a large (4-quart) saucepan. Add salt, potatoes, and leeks. Cover and cook at a gentle boil until potatoes begin to fall apart, about 35 to 40 minutes. Crush into small pieces with spoon or fork against the side of the saucepan.
	Remove from heat.
FINAL STEP	Add butter and pour into warmed tureen or individual bowls. Garnish with sprinkling of parsley or chives.
	This soup may be refrigerated, and reheated 2 or 3 days later, or frozen for up to 3 months. If the soup is frozen, do not add butter until it is thawed and reheated.

Iced Cream of Pumpkin Soup
Crème de Potiron Glacée

Serves 6

This is a cool, creamy pumpkin soup that should be served in chilled bowls, kept cold nestled in crushed ice.

Dione Lucas, the distinguished cookbook author, thought so well of this recipe that she called it her "salute to the wonderful pumpkin."

INGREDIENTS	⅓ cup vegetable oil
	6 ounces (1 large) yellow onion, finely chopped
	¼ cup all-purpose flour
	3 cups chicken stock
	1 2-pound can unsweetened pumpkin puree
	or 5 cups fresh pumpkin puree
	2 teaspoons ground ginger
	1 teaspoon salt
	½ teaspoon freshly ground white pepper
	1½ cups light cream or half-and-half
	Crushed ice for serving
	½ cup heavy cream, whipped, to garnish
	½ teaspoon freshly grated nutmeg, to garnish
SPECIAL EQUIPMENT	None
PREPARATION COOK *10 mins.*	Heat the oil in a large (4-quart) saucepan and add the chopped onion. Cook over low heat until the onion is translucent and soft, about 10 minutes.
COOK *15 mins.*	Remove pan from the heat. Stir in flour mixed with small amount of stock, chicken stock, pumpkin, ginger, salt, and pepper. Return to low heat. Cover the pot while the thick pumpkin mixture cooks. Do not uncover, or the pumpkin mixture will bubble and plop all over the stove. (The soup may be prepared up to this point and set aside if desired.)
SIMMER	Pour in the light cream or half-and-half and simmer for about 10 minutes. Taste to correct seasoning.
CHILL *2–3 hours*	Chill soup thoroughly, at least 2 to 3 hours, or overnight.

FINAL STEP
Serve in bowls cupped in crushed ice. Drop a dollop of whipped cream on top of each serving and sprinkle with fresh nutmeg.

Curried Pumpkin Soup

Serves 6

"Your book must have this recipe for the world's best soup," wrote L. L. Waters on the margin of the recipe. I have long respected my friend's judgment on food and other matters for he is a commuter between continents and a critic of several dozen cuisines. His wife remembers that they first had this soup aboard a Singapore Airlines plane bound for an exotic Asian destination.

After preparing it several times, I agree with Waters's final thought: "Forget the rest of the meal when you serve this—nothing can compete!"

Check the age of your curry powder. Fresh is best.

INGREDIENTS
4 tablespoons (½ stick) butter
½ cup chopped onion
I clove garlic, mashed and diced
2 cups pumpkin puree, fresh or canned
4 cups chicken stock
I bay leaf
Pinch of sugar
⅓ teaspoon or more curry powder
Pinch of grated nutmeg
½ teaspoon salt, if desired
¼ teaspoon freshly ground black pepper
2 cups light cream
⅓ cup toasted coconut, to garnish

SPECIAL
EQUIPMENT
None

PREPARATION
SMOTHER
8 mins.
Melt butter in a medium (3-quart) saucepan over medium heat. Add the onion and garlic, cover, and cook until soft and translucent, about 8 minutes.

BOIL/SIMMER
30 mins.
Add the pumpkin puree and stock. Stir well to mix. Add bay leaf, sugar, curry powder, and nutmeg. Bring to a boil, lower to a simmer, and cook for 30 minutes.

While the soup is cooking, taste for seasoning. Add salt, if desired, and pepper.

Remove from heat and add cream. Return to heat only to bring temperature of the soup back to hot. Do not allow to simmer—rising steam only.

FINAL STEP   Serve in hot soup bowls. Garnish with toasted coconut.

Sour-and-Hot Soup (Chinese)
Suan-La-T'ang

Serves 6

The sour comes from wine vinegar and the hot from pepper, which, along with two kinds of dried Chinese mushrooms, creates a piquancy that makes this a favorite Asian soup.

If you cook Chinese dishes frequently you will probably have many of the ingredients on your kitchen shelves already or will know where to get them. If not, try the Chinatown section or specialty food markets in your area.

There are two kinds of dried mushrooms called for; however, this soup will be almost as good even if you have only one. The large dried black ones are sometimes easier to locate than the tree ears or "black fungus."

The meat portion can be either cubes of chicken breast or pieces of shredded pork. The liaison comes from both cornstarch and water and lightly beaten eggs.

This classic soup achieves the ideal in Chinese cookery by so successfully blending its delicious flavors and textures.

INGREDIENTS   4 dried black mushrooms
4 dried tree ears
4 dried tiger lily stems, optional
Boiling water, to cover
¼ cup pork *or* chicken breast
1½ cups canned bamboo shoots
1 3-inch-square cake fresh white bean curd
1 tablespoon cooking oil
1 tablespoon light soy sauce
5 cups chicken stock, heated
Salt, to taste
2 to 3 tablespoons red wine vinegar, to taste
1 tablespoon dark soy sauce, optional

(continued)

2 tablespoons cornstarch
3 tablespoons water
1½ teaspoons sesame oil
1 teaspoon freshly ground white or black pepper
2 eggs, lightly beaten
1 scallion, including green top, finely chopped, optional
1 teaspoon minced fresh coriander, optional

SPECIAL EQUIPMENT

Wok, if available, or deep skillet

PREPARATION SOAKING
20–30 mins.

In a medium bowl, place dried black mushrooms, tree ears, and lily stems and cover with boiling water. Let stand 20 to 30 minutes. Drain. Cut off stems of mushrooms and the hard edges of the tree ears.

CUTTING/ SHREDDING
20 mins.

Cut black mushrooms and tree ears into thin, narrow slices. Shred the long, slender tiger lily stems with your fingers. Cut into 1-inch lengths. Put aside.

Shred the pork with a sharp knife or cleaver into long narrow strips or, if chicken breast meat, cut into cubes. Put aside.

Drain the bamboo shoots and bean curd and slice or shred them as fine as the mushrooms. Set aside.

If more convenient, these steps may be done several hours or the night before making the soup. Put each ingredient in a small bowl, cover tightly with plastic wrap, and hold in the refrigerator.

COOKING
15 mins.

Heat oil in the wok or skillet and add pork or chicken. Stir to separate the meat pieces; add light soy sauce. Add the black mushrooms, tree ears, tiger lily stems, and bamboo shoots.

Stir 1 minute and pour in the hot chicken stock. Taste and season with salt. (Pepper will be added later.) Stir in 2 tablespoons vinegar. Taste before adding additional vinegar. Some may not care for the soup if it is too sour. Add dark soy sauce, if using it.

In a small bowl, mix cornstarch with water into a smooth paste. Stir into the soup. When thickened slightly, add bean curd.

BOILING
3–6 mins.

Bring to a boil. Immediately remove from the heat and allow to cook 3 minutes before adding sesame oil and pepper. Stir to blend.

Heat soup tureen and pour soup into it. Gradually add beaten eggs in a thin stream, stirring as you do so.

FINAL STEP

Sprinkle with scallion and coriander, if desired. Serve immediately.

This soup may be refrigerated for 2 or 3 days and reheated with admirable results or frozen for up to 3 months.

Squash Bisque, Country Style (Jamaica)

Serves 4

There are several varieties of winter squash in the market—banana, butternut, acorn, Hubbard, mammoth, Canada crookneck, and others—and any of these can be used in this Jamaican recipe. Each squash is different, if only slightly, and each gives a slightly different taste to a dish. Experiment to find a favorite.

Acorn and Hubbard squash, which abound in my garden in the summer, are kept in my workshop in winter storage. I have used acorn squash in this recipe with considerable success.

Pickapeppa Sauce, a Jamaican creation, will be a new and unique taste for many. If it is not available, substitute a dash or two of Tabasco sauce.

INGREDIENTS	1 large acorn or other winter squash (to yield about 2 cups of meat)
	1 cup (about ½ pound) fresh tomatoes, peeled and seeded, or 1 cup canned or frozen
	2 tablespoons pearl barley
	1 clove garlic, mashed or minced
	1 bay leaf
	Pinch *each* of marjoram, thyme, and allspice
	1 tablespoon finely chopped scallion tops
	2 teaspoons Pickapeppa Sauce (or more, if desired)
	½ teaspoon sugar
	6 cups beef stock
	Salt, if desired, and freshly ground black pepper, to taste
	⅓ cup dry sherry
	1 slice lean bacon, crisply fried and crumbled (or bacon bits)
	1 tablespoon finely chopped parsley
SPECIAL EQUIPMENT	Blender, food processor, or food mill
PREPARATION BAKE *1 hour*	*Note:* Prepare the squash beforehand. Rather than peel the hard skin of the winter squash, cut the vegetable in half, turn the cut side down on a cookie sheet, and bake it for 1 hour, or until the meat literally falls away from the skin. This method also shortens the cooking time later by 30

minutes. The alternative method is to peel and seed the uncooked squash, cut it into chunks, and cook it for a longer time in the soup.

Place prepared squash in a medium (4-quart) saucepan. Add tomatoes, barley, garlic, bay leaf, marjoram, thyme, allspice, scallion tops, Pickapeppa, and sugar.

Pour in the stock.

COVER/SIMMER
*30 mins. or
1 hour*

Cover, bring to a boil, reduce heat, and simmer for 30 minutes, if squash has been prebaked; or simmer for 1 hour if you are using uncooked squash.

During cooking, add salt, if desired, and pepper. Remove from heat after checking to see if vegetables are done.

BLENDER

Allow to cool somewhat before ladling into blender (my choice because I like this bisque smooth and creamy), food processor, or food mill.

Check seasoning.

FINAL STEP

Pour 2 teaspoons of sherry into each bowl before ladling in the hot soup.

Serve very hot, sprinkled with crumbled bacon and parsley. Offer saltine crackers or freshly toasted croutons on the side.

Creamy Pumpkin Soup

Serves 8

For those who think pumpkin is only for pies or to be carved into Halloween jack-o'-lanterns, this rich, creamy soup will come as a delightful surprise.

It can be made with pumpkin alone or with the addition of uncooked shrimp that have been put through a blender or food processor.

For special occasions, serve in a hollowed-out pumpkin, with individual servings in small squash shells or shells of tiny pumpkins if you can find some.

INGREDIENTS

1 tablespoon butter
¼ cup chopped onion
2 medium leeks, white part only, thinly sliced
2 cups peeled, chopped pumpkin meat or unsweetened canned pumpkin
1 medium potato, diced small
2 medium tomatoes, peeled, seeded, and chopped
4 to 6 cups chicken stock
2 teaspoons salt, if desired
½ teaspoon freshly ground black pepper

2 dashes of Tabasco
½ cup chopped celery leaves
½ cup chopped parsley
½ cup peeled raw shrimp, optional
2 cups light cream
3 tablespoons butter
I cup croutons

SPECIAL EQUIPMENT	Blender, food processor, or fine sieve

PREPARATION SMOTHER *10 mins.* *30 mins.*	In a large (6-quart) saucepan, melt the tablespoon of butter and cook onions and leeks, covered, until translucent and soft, about 10 minutes. Add pumpkin, potato, tomatoes, and stock. Season with salt, pepper, and Tabasco. Add celery leaves and parsley. Cook until the vegetables are tender, about 30 minutes. Remove from the heat.

PUREE *5 mins.*	When the soup has cooled a bit, process it in whichever equipment gives the desired result. *Note:* The food processor leaves tiny particles in the soup. For a truly creamy soup, put it through a blender or fine sieve.

OPTIONAL	*Shrimp:* If shrimp are to be added, peel while the soup cooks. Drop shrimp into the blender or processor along with ½ cup of puree. Blend until smooth and add to the soup pot.

COOK *10 mins.*	Reheat the soup (with or without shrimp) and simmer over low heat for 10 minutes. Add cream and butter and continue heating almost to a simmer, but don't allow to boil. If the soup is too thick, thin with stock or water.

FINAL STEP	Taste for seasoning, garnish with croutons, if desired, and serve hot.

VARIATION	This pumpkin soup is delicious chilled. If you serve the soup cold, omit the croutons and garnish each serving with a thin slice of chilled orange.

Harvest Pumpkin Soup

Serves 6

One of the most famous of all the winter squashes is the pumpkin. And with pumpkin in hand, Wayne Hawrys, a friend and a talented chef in my part of southern Indiana, created this soup to go with a Thanksgiving dinner made by a dozen chefs and cooks who had appeared in my book Cooking Across America. *Each prepared a dish, and the meal was featured in the November 1997 issue of* Eating Well.

Hawrys's dish is a creamy soup served with a yogurt swirl touched with a dusting of pistachio nuts.

An equally delicious soup can be made with butternut squash, the dun-colored one with the long neck and round bottom. A 3½-pound butternut is just right for this recipe.

INGREDIENTS	2 teaspoons vegetable oil (canola preferred)
	1 large onion, chopped
	1 large carrot, peeled and chopped
	1 medium potato, peeled and cut into 1-inch cubes
	4 cups chicken stock
	3½ cups fresh or canned pumpkin or squash
	1 cinnamon stick
	1 bay leaf
	¼ teaspoon dried thyme
	¼ teaspoon grated nutmeg
	½ cup dry sherry
	Salt and freshly ground black pepper
	½ cup vanilla yogurt
	2 tablespoons finely chopped pistachios

SPECIAL EQUIPMENT

Food processor or blender

PREPARATION

To prepare an uncooked pumpkin or butternut squash, cut lengthwise, scrape out and discard the seeds, brush the flesh with oil, and place cut side down on a baking sheet lined with aluminum foil (for an easier cleanup). Place in a 325° oven for 1 hour. When cooled, spoon the flesh out of the shells and mash with a fork for the recipe.

COOK
10–15 mins.

In a large (6½-quart) saucepan, heat the oil over medium heat. Add the onion, carrot, and potato. Cook, stirring occasionally. Don't brown, or it will discolor the lovely gold of the soup.

BOIL/SIMMER
35–45 mins.

Add the chicken stock, pumpkin or squash, cinnamon stick, bay leaf, and thyme. Bring to a boil, reduce the heat, and simmer, uncovered, until vegetables are fork-tender.

PUREE
15 mins.

Discard the bay leaf and cinnamon stick and, when cooled, puree the soup in a blender or food processor, in batches if necessary. The soup should be thick, the consistency of heavy cream. If too thick, thin with additional chicken stock or milk.

WARM
15 mins.

Return to the pot and warm over low heat. Add the nutmeg and sherry and season to taste with salt and pepper.

FINAL STEP

Ladle soup into warmed bowls. Garnish with a swirl of yogurt and a sprinkling of pistachios.

Note: The soup will keep refrigerated for several days. Reheat before serving.

Spinach Soup (Norwegian)
Spinatsuppe

Serves 6 to 8

The mother of the small boy in the New Yorker *cartoon "I say it's spinach, and I say to hell with it!" should have started him on* spinatsuppe. *It is spinach, right enough, but its richly flavored leaves are not overcooked; they are simmered only briefly in a rich chicken stock flavored with freshly grated nutmeg. It is a light summertime soup—green specks suspended in a golden broth.*

The original recipe called for a thickening made with a flour/butter roux. I prefer it not so creamy.

INGREDIENTS

2 pounds fresh spinach or 2 packages frozen chopped
2 quarts chicken stock
3 tablespoons butter
½ teaspoon minced garlic
1 cup finely chopped onion
⅛ teaspoon (approximately) freshly grated nutmeg
1 teaspoon salt, if desired
¼ teaspoon freshly ground black pepper
3 hard-cooked eggs, sliced, chopped, or stuffed, to garnish, or 1 cup sour cream

SPECIAL
EQUIPMENT

Colander. Food processor, optional.

PREPARATION

Note: If the fresh spinach is in a bundle, cut off the stems just below the leaves and discard. Wash under cold running water to remove the grit that seems inherent in the store-bought variety. Snap off the balance of the stems, up to the leaves. Drain through a colander and chop coarsely. If the spinach is frozen, defrost and drain.

BOIL/SIMMER
3 mins.

Bring the chicken stock to a gentle boil in a medium (3-quart) saucepan and add the spinach. Simmer 3 minutes—no longer. The highly nutritious leaves should not be overcooked.

DRAIN

Pour the contents of the saucepan into a colander or sieve set over a bowl. Press down hard on the spinach leaves with a wooden spoon and squeeze out as much liquid as possible. Set the liquid aside in a clean saucepan. Chop the cooked spinach fine by hand or in a food processor but do not allow it to become a puree. Reserve.

SMOTHER
8 mins.

Melt the butter in a skillet, and drop in the garlic and onion. Cover and cook over medium-low heat until soft and translucent, about 8 minutes. Set aside.

SIMMER
4 mins.

Return the saucepan to the heat and bring to a simmer. Scrape contents of the skillet into the stock. Add the chopped spinach and, from that moment, simmer for 4 minutes.

Grate about ⅛ teaspoon of nutmeg into the soup. Season also with salt and pepper. Stir several times.

FINAL STEP

There are several very good garnishes from which to choose. In Norway each bowl is served with a half egg stuffed with a blend of egg yolk and butter floating in the soup.

The soup can also be garnished with egg slices, chopped egg, or a dollop of sour cream.

Leek *Panade* (French)

Serves 6 to 8

A panade *is not an elegant dish. It is a countryman's soup described by such words as "simple," "filling," "tasty," and "delicious."*

A panade *is a rich vegetable broth thickened with bread or a ready-made roux. Its flavor is subtle, reflecting the choice of vegetables available to the cook. Buttermilk is optional in this recipe, but it gives an enticing piquancy to the soup.*

INGREDIENTS

2 cups finely chopped leeks (white part only)
6 tablespoons butter
4 ounces dry white bread, about 6 slices, broken into pieces

2 quarts hot water
1 cup buttermilk, optional
6 egg yolks
2 teaspoons salt, if desired
½ cup finely chopped parsley, to garnish

SPECIAL EQUIPMENT	Food processor, blender, food mill, or heavy whisk to cream *panade*
PREPARATION SMOTHER 10 mins.	Chop the leeks into small pieces. Melt 2 tablespoons of butter in a medium (4-quart) saucepan. Drop in the leeks, cover, and cook over low heat for about 10 minutes. Don't allow them to color.
	Add the pieces of bread, water, and buttermilk, if desired.
BOIL/SIMMER 30–45 mins.	Bring the *panade* to a boil, reduce heat, and simmer gently over low heat for 30 to 45 minutes. Do not stir while it cooks, or the bread will stick to the pan.
	Remove from heat and allow to cool.
PUREE	Puree the *panade* into a creamy smooth mixture in a food processor, blender, or food mill or with a heavy whisk.
	Return the *panade* to the saucepan and slowly whisk in the egg yolks and the remaining 4 tablespoons of butter. Salt to taste.
SIMMER 5 mins.	Over gentle heat, whisk the *panade* until it thickens, about 5 minutes. It will be thick but should not show a furrow when the tip of a spoon is drawn across the surface. If it does, thin with water or additional buttermilk.
FINAL STEP	Ladle into hot serving dishes and sprinkle generously with parsley.
VARIATION	Sorrel leaves can be substituted for leeks in this *panade*.

Sorrel Soup (Israeli)

Serves 4

Sorrel. In Europe it is a cultivated potherb known as garden sorrel and French sorrel (oseille).
In America the genus Rumex, to which it belongs, is mostly wild, and its members (all edible) have such down-home names as sour grass, rabbit's ears, bitter dock, sheep sorrel, spinach dock, and on and on—a big family. It has been characterized as the sour-leaf version of spinach.

There is a unique sourness, pronounced yet pleasant, about sorrel soup, whether hot or cold. This is a chilled version that is richer in appearance than in fact—there is only ½ egg yolk to each serving. The other ingredients, except the sour cream garnish, add almost nothing to the calorie count.

Sorrel (or dock) can be found in the spring in big city markets, where it is quickly snatched up by connoisseurs. The next best thing is to grow your own from a plant bought from a herbalist, or to visit the fields for the wild ones.

INGREDIENTS

½ pound (3 cups) sorrel, tightly packed
4 cups water
I medium onion, peeled and minced (green onions may be substituted)
I teaspoon salt
I teaspoon lemon juice
I tablespoon sugar
2 egg yolks
4 tablespoons sour cream, to garnish
I tablespoon finely chopped fresh basil, marjoram, or lovage, if available

SPECIAL
EQUIPMENT

None

PREPARATION

Rinse sorrel. Strip the leaves from the coarse stems. Hold tightly packed in hand and cut into 3-inch pieces with a knife. Or tear them, if you wish.

BOIL/SIMMER
15 mins.

Pour the water into a medium (3-quart) kettle or pot. Add sorrel, onion, and salt and bring to a boil. Reduce heat and cook slowly, covered, for 15 minutes.

5 mins.

Add lemon juice and sugar. Cook for an additional 5 minutes.

In a small bowl, beat egg yolks until light and creamy. Slowly blend a cup of the hot soup into the yolks, and then pour the tempered egg mixture into the large pot of soup. Stir the soup over low heat until it thick-

5 mins.

ens, 5 to 6 minutes.

CHILL
2 hours or longer

Remove the soup from heat and cool. Refrigerate for 2 hours or longer. Chill the bowls in which the soup is to be served.

FINAL STEP

Whisk sour cream to give it a light and creamy texture; ladle the soup into the chilled bowls and garnish with sour cream. Sprinkle finely chopped herbs of your choice over the tops.

Enjoy.

Tomato and Wild Rice Soup

Serves 4

Summer and fall would be the ideal times to prepare this vegetable-rich soup to be eaten at the moment, or frozen to bring a ray of summer into a cold winter day.

The recipe is the creation of Wendy London, the Mrs. London of Mrs. London's Bakeshop and Restaurant, a onetime landmark establishment in Saratoga Springs, New York. Tomato and wild rice soup is but one of the many good things that earned for the small restaurant a ranking with some of the best in Paris, Vienna, and New York.

Mrs. London suggests that the wild rice be omitted for a lighter soup; or, for a thick soup, use homemade pasta if no wild rice is at hand. Because the soup must simmer for almost an hour to cook the wild rice, some of the liquid will be lost. Replenish with stock or water.

INGREDIENTS	3 tablespoons butter
	3 tablespoons fruity virgin olive oil
	1 medium onion, chopped
	1 medium carrot, chopped
	1 stalk young celery, chopped
	6 large ripe tomatoes, peeled but not seeded, and chopped,
	or 2 16-ounce cans tomatoes, chopped
	2 cups chicken or beef stock (more to replenish, if necessary)
	½ cup wild rice, washed and picked over
	Salt to taste, if desired
	1 grinding of fresh black pepper
	Pinch of sugar
	2 tablespoons chopped fresh basil or ½ teaspoon dried
	½ cup heavy cream or crème fraîche, optional
	Finely chopped parsley, to garnish

SPECIAL
EQUIPMENT

None

PREPARATION
SMOTHER
10 mins.

Place butter and olive oil in a medium (3-quart) saucepan, with lid. Heat until the butter is melted; add onion, carrot, and celery. Cook over medium heat until the vegetables are translucent and partially cooked, about 10 minutes. Stir frequently.

GENTLE BOIL
50–60 mins.

Pour in the tomatoes, stock, and wild rice. Bring to a boil, cover, reduce heat, and boil gently—just above a simmer—until rice opens and fluffs, about 1 hour. Add salt, pepper, sugar, and basil. Stir frequently. If the liquid boils away too much, replenish with additional stock or water. (If you want a thick soup, don't add liquid.)

FINAL STEP
For a richer soup add cream or crème fraîche. Heat after adding.

Serve from a heated tureen into heated soup plates. Sprinkle with chopped parsley to garnish.

Tomato-Dill Soup

Serves 6

Experienced cooks often look askance at box-top recipes, viewing them as self-serving. This tomato-dill soup is an exception.

This recipe came with a jar of Hellmann's mayonnaise, but any good-quality mayonnaise, including one from your own kitchen, will do nicely.

While this was recommended as a cold soup, I find it equally delicious hot.

INGREDIENTS
I cup chopped onion
I clove garlic, minced
2 tablespoons butter or margarine
4 large tomatoes (2 pounds), peeled and chopped
½ cup water
I chicken-flavored bouillon cube
I tablespoon chopped fresh dill weed or ¾ teaspoon dried
¼ teaspoon salt, if desired
¼ teaspoon freshly ground black pepper
½ cup mayonnaise
Fresh dill sprigs, if available, or parsley, to garnish

SPECIAL
EQUIPMENT
Food processor. For a smoother, creamier soup, use a blender.

PREPARATION
SAUTÉ
5 mins.
In a medium (3-quart) saucepan, sauté onions and garlic in butter or margarine over medium heat for about 5 minutes. Add tomatoes, water, bouillon cube, dill weed, salt, if desired, and pepper.

SIMMER
10 mins.
Cover the saucepan and simmer for 10 minutes. Stir to dissolve bouillon cube.

PROCESS
3 mins.
Remove from heat and allow the soup to cool before placing the liquid in the food processor or blender; blend.

Blend in mayonnaise. Reheat the soup gently if it is to be served hot. Cover and chill overnight if it is to be served cold.

FINAL STEP

Serve in heated (or chilled) bowls. Drop a sprig or two of the dill or parsley on each before serving. I like the lacy look of the dill floating on the tomato-red soup.

Sweet and Spicy Tomato Soup

Serves 6

Chunks of ripe tomato floating country style in this delicious, sweet, and spicy brew give this tomato soup a harvest-time touch. It should be made in mid- and late summer, when tomatoes—yours, the neighbors', and the markets'—are bustin' out all over. Fat. Flavorful. And juicy—the tomatoes must be juicy, for they are the only source of liquid in the soup, which still will be quite thick, so save the juice when chopping.

The spiciness comes from celery, onion, green and hot peppers, garlic, cinnamon, and allspice. Spicy, yes. The sweetness comes from a tablespoon of brown sugar.

This soup is good served at all temperatures—chilled, room temperature, or hot. Serve with a dollop of sour cream.

INGREDIENTS

2 tablespoons olive oil
2 stalks celery, coarsely chopped
I small onion, coarsely chopped
I medium green pepper, chopped
I teaspoon minced hot pepper
I large clove garlic, minced
5 or 6 large ripe tomatoes, peeled, cored, and chopped
I tablespoon brown sugar
½ teaspoon cinnamon
¼ teaspoon allspice
Salt and freshly ground black pepper to taste
½ cup sour cream, to garnish

SPECIAL
EQUIPMENT

None

PREPARATION
SMOTHER
8–10 mins.

In a large saucepan, heat olive oil and add celery, onion, peppers, and garlic. Cover pan and cook over medium-low heat until vegetables are tender, about 8 to 10 minutes. Stir frequently. Don't overcook or burn.

BOIL/SIMMER *15 mins.*	Add the tomatoes, brown sugar, cinnamon, and allspice. Bring to a boil. Reduce heat. Correct seasoning with salt and pepper. Cover the saucepan and allow the soup to simmer until the tomato pieces are tender, about 10 minutes.
FINAL STEP	Heat (or chill) bowls. Hot or cold, serve garnished with generous dollops of sour cream.

Iced Tomato and Basil Soup (Italian)

Serves 8

Tomatoes and basil come to fruition in my garden in midsummer, and so begins a pleasant marriage that results in this fine iced italianate soup—light and delicate and fragrant with garlic.

Serve it with hot crostini, butter-saturated slices of French bread baked to crispness with a Parmesan topping. I prefer the soup cold, but some will find it equally delicious hot.

INGREDIENTS	**Soup** 3 pounds ripe tomatoes, peeled, seeded, and finely chopped, or 2½ pounds canned peeled plum tomatoes, seeded and finely chopped 3 tablespoons Italian olive oil 5 cloves garlic, minced 1 cup shredded fresh basil leaves or 1 tablespoon dried 5 cups chicken stock Salt to taste, if desired ¼ teaspoon freshly ground black pepper Pinch of sugar **Crostini** 16 to 20 ¼-inch slices long loaf French bread 1½ sticks butter, melted ½ cup freshly grated Parmesan cheese
SPECIAL EQUIPMENT	None
PREPARATION SCALD	To skin the fresh tomatoes, drop them into boiling water for 10 or 15 seconds, lift out with a slotted spoon, and place under cold running water to stop the cooking process. Slip off the skins. Seed and dice toma-

toes. If canned, cut each tomato in half, carefully press out the seeds, and dice.

COOK
5 mins.
5 mins.

Pour olive oil into a medium (3-quart) saucepan, add the tomatoes, and cook over medium heat for about 5 minutes.

Add the garlic and basil and continue cooking for an additional 5 minutes.

BOIL/SIMMER
5 mins.

Pour in the chicken stock and season with salt and pepper to taste. Add the sugar. Bring to a boil, immediately reduce heat, and simmer for 5 minutes.

CHILL

Chill the soup for several hours or overnight.

Crostini
While the soup is chilling, prepare the cheese crusts. Brush both sides of the bread slices with butter, place on a cookie sheet, and spread with a thick layer of Parmesan cheese. Bake in a 400° oven for 10 to 15 minutes, or until the bread is crisp and the cheese has begun to melt.

BAKE
400°
10–15 mins.

FINAL STEP

Serve the cold soup in chilled cups accompanied by the hot crostini.

Cream of Fresh Tomato Soup with Thyme

Serves 6

When the produce market is glorious with bushels of fresh-picked tomatoes bursting with flavor, the time has come to make this lovely cream of fresh tomato soup with thyme. Or freeze some of those big red tomatoes for later.

The color of the soup is light pink with tiny specks of thyme (also fresh-picked) and bits of onion and carrots and parsley. Because of those tiny particles, it is not velvety smooth, but the sensation of rich smoothness is there.

While it could be made in winter with tomatoes shipped thousands of miles over international and state boundaries, it would not be the same. Good, but just not the same. I do much better with my own frozen tomatoes, picked by me and packaged by my wife. (See Glossary.) In this soup it is difficult to tell the difference between fresh tomatoes and those home-frozen ones.

There is no stock added to this soup, so it depends entirely on the juice of the tomato and the cream.

This soup can be served hot or cold. A sprinkling of 3 or 4 small croutons adds a crisp touch that is pleasant.

INGREDIENTS	5 large red tomatoes, skinned, seeded, and chopped
	2 tablespoons butter
	2 tablespoons olive oil
	1 medium onion, coarsely chopped
	2 medium carrots, coarsely chopped
	2 tablespoons chopped parsley
	2 long sprigs fresh thyme or ¼ teaspoon dried
	1 bay leaf
	Salt and freshly ground black pepper to taste
	1 cup light cream
	1 cup croutons

SPECIAL EQUIPMENT	Food processor, blender, or food mill

PREPARATION SCALD	Drop 2 or 3 of the tomatoes into a saucepan of boiling water. Scald them for no longer than 15 seconds and remove with a slotted spoon. Place them under cold running water while you drop the remaining tomatoes into the hot bath. The skins will slip off with ease. To seed, cut the tomatoes in half and gently squeeze. Then cut them into pieces.

SMOTHER 10 mins.	Heat butter and oil in a large skillet. Add the onion and carrots. Cover and cook over medium-low heat until tender, about 10 minutes. Add the tomatoes, parsley, thyme, bay leaf, and salt and pepper.

BOIL/SIMMER 12–15 mins.	Bring to a boil, lower heat, cover, and simmer until tomatoes are tender, about 12 to 15 minutes.

PUREE 5 mins.	Remove from heat. When the vegetables are somewhat cool, puree in machine. Return to saucepan and set aside until just before serving.

FINAL STEP	When ready to serve, add cream and reheat without boiling. Or refrigerate and serve cold. Garnish with croutons.

Tomato and Pine Nut Soup

Serves 4

Everyone will enjoy this soup—and aside from a bit of olive oil in which to sauté the garlic, it is a dieter's delight. Though the soup is made without stock, a sprinkling of Parmesan cheese would add a calorie or two.

INGREDIENTS
3 tablespoons olive oil
2 cloves garlic, minced
5 to 6 large ripe juicy tomatoes, peeled, seeded, and coarsely chopped
⅓ cup fresh basil leaves
2 tablespoons pine nuts
Salt to taste, if desired
¼ teaspoon freshly ground black pepper
Freshly grated Parmesan cheese, to garnish

SPECIAL
EQUIPMENT
Blender or food processor

PREPARATION
Note: To peel tomatoes, slip them into a pan of boiling water and leave for a slow count of 10. Lift out and place under cold running water for a moment or two. The skins will slip off. Cut tomato in two. Gently squeeze out the seeds.

SAUTÉ
2–3 mins.
Pour olive oil into a medium (3-quart) saucepan and heat gently. Add garlic and sauté, stirring, for 2 or 3 minutes.

SMOTHER
15 mins.
Add tomatoes, cover, and cook over low heat until tomatoes are soft and tender, about 15 minutes.

PUREE
Remove from heat and cool for several minutes before pouring into a blender or food processor work bowl. Add basil leaves and pine nuts. Puree.

Add salt and black pepper to taste. If there are any tomato seeds in the soup, strain it through a chinois or sieve. Return to the saucepan and heat gently over low flame.

FINAL STEP
Serve the soup hot. Sprinkle generously with Parmesan cheese. Freshly baked French bread or another peasant bread is a tasty companion.

Bacon and Tomato Soup

Serves 6

Bacon and tomato soup has the same good flavors that make a bacon and tomato sandwich so outstanding. Bread is served with the soup, to complete the combination.

A special touch is a light sprinkling of freshly grated nutmeg. A slightly different taste will come from substituting yogurt or sour cream for the heavy sweet cream.

INGREDIENTS	1 medium onion, chopped
	2 strips bacon, diced
	2 tablespoons butter
	2 pounds ripe tomatoes, peeled, seeded, and chopped
	1 teaspoon fresh thyme
	2 bay leaves
	4 cups chicken stock
	Salt and freshly ground black pepper
	½ cup heavy cream, sour cream, or yogurt
	Freshly grated nutmeg, to garnish

SPECIAL
EQUIPMENT

Food processor, food mill, or blender (although the blender whips the soup too velvety for my taste)

PREPARATION
SAUTÉ
15 mins.

Chop the onion and bacon into small pieces and sauté in butter in a medium (3-quart) saucepan until the onion is soft and the bacon cooked.

Peel the tomatoes by placing them in boiling water for about 10 or 15 seconds; remove and let cold water run over them for a moment or so. Slip the skins free. Cut tomatoes in half and gently squeeze out the seeds. A stream of water will help wash away the seeds. Chop tomatoes.

SAUTÉ
6 mins.

Add tomatoes, thyme, and bay leaves to the saucepan. Sauté for 6 minutes.

SIMMER
20 mins.

Add stock and salt and pepper to taste. Bring to a boil and turn the heat down to low to simmer soup for about 20 minutes.

PROCESS
5 mins.

Remove bay leaves and put the soup through food processor or food mill—or blender if you like a very smooth texture. Taste to correct seasoning.

FINAL STEP

Serve hot or cold with a dab of whipped heavy cream, sour cream, or yogurt in each serving. Sprinkle with the freshly grated nutmeg.

Turnip Stew (French)
Navets en Ragout

Serves 6

My love affair with turnips came late in life, and it began in a small French restaurant with navets en ragout. *My mother was an outstanding cook, but for some reason her cookery did not embrace turnips, although I know they were available in the markets where she shopped. Perhaps my father didn't like them.*

The turnip deserves better treatment than it gets in most kitchens. It is one of our oldest vegetables, cultivated by man for its edible leaves and root for more than 4,000 years. It is popular in France, where it is often part of elegant dishes and cooked in many inventive fashions, yet its versatility is little known or appreciated in the United States.

The first and finest turnips come to the market during the first cool weather. Winter turnips are older and larger and should be blanched to remove the slight bitterness that is often present.

This stew is distinctive because the turnips are cut into small balls with a melon baller; hence they cook faster than the whole turnips. They also make an attractive pattern in the soup bowls when served. If a melon baller isn't readily available, the turnips can be cubed.

INGREDIENTS	2 pounds white turnips
	4 cups salted hot water to blanch turnips
	4 cups chicken stock
	1½ teaspoons sugar
	2 tablespoons butter
	3 egg yolks
	2 teaspoons finely chopped onion
	Salt, if desired, and freshly ground black pepper to taste
	Grated nutmeg, to garnish, optional

SPECIAL EQUIPMENT

Melon baller

PREPARATION

Peel turnips and cut sufficient balls or cubes to fill 4 cups.

BLANCH
5 mins.

Heat the salted water to boiling in a medium (3-quart) saucepan. Drop in the turnips; immediately remove the saucepan from the heat. Cover and let the turnips stand in the water for 5 minutes. Pour off the water; rinse the turnips under cold running water.

COOK
15 mins.

Return the turnips to the saucepan and add chicken stock. Add sugar and cook over low heat until tender, about 15 minutes. Stir in the butter.

Drop the egg yolks into a small bowl and add ¼ cup of the hot liquid from the saucepan. Beat vigorously until the mixture is smooth. Gradually pour the egg mixture over the turnips, stirring with a large spoon to bring the liquid up from the bottom of the pot.

SIMMER *10 mins.*	Bring the stew *almost* to a boil, stirring constantly, and add the finely chopped onion. Taste for seasoning. Simmer over low heat for 10 minutes.
FINAL STEP	Serve at once in heated soup bowls. Sprinkle with grated nutmeg, if desired.

White Turnip Soup (French)
Potage aux Navets Blancs
Serves 6 to 8

All turnips may look alike, but they are not. The best turnips for the table grow in cool weather when the sugar that makes the roots sweet accumulates there rather than respiring through the leaves when the nights are warm.

Always choose the smallest and most tender turnips available. This soup, which is made without a prepared stock, is thickened with bread slices.

The turnip is a member of the family that includes collard greens, broccoli, kohlrabi, and rutabaga. In China it is known as mu-ching; *in Japan,* kubura *or* kabura.

INGREDIENTS	1 tablespoon butter 8 small turnips (about 1½ pounds), peeled and coarsely chopped 1 large onion, finely chopped 6 to 8 cups boiling water 4 to 5 slices firm, good-quality white bread, such as peasant-type or French 2 teaspoons salt, if desired 2 to 3 grinds of black pepper (about ½ teaspoon) 4 egg yolks 1 cup light cream ½ cup chopped parsley or chives, to garnish
SPECIAL EQUIPMENT	Food processor, blender, or sieve
PREPARATION SAUTÉ *5 mins.*	Melt butter in a medium (3-quart) kettle and add chopped turnips and onion. Sauté over medium heat for about 5 minutes, or until onions are translucent. Stir frequently. Bring 6 to 8 cups of water to a boil—the amount depending on how much soup you wish to make, as well as its desired strength. Pour the

boiling water into the turnip/onion mixture. Break the bread slices into the kettle.

BOIL/SIMMER
15 mins.
Heat the soup to a boil, reduce heat, and simmer for about 15 minutes, or until turnips are tender when pierced with a fork.

COOL
Set the soup aside to cool. Season with salt, if desired, and pepper.

PROCESS
When the soup has cooled sufficiently, pour into a food processor or blender or press through a sieve with a wooden spoon.

Note: At this point the soup can be refrigerated for a day or two, or frozen for several weeks. Later the egg, cream, and garnish will be added.

BLEND
Before serving, reheat the soup—but do not boil—and add the egg yolks beaten with the cream. Stir constantly until the mixture is blended and creamy.

Check seasoning.

FINAL STEP
Serve in heated soup bowls and garnish with parsley or chives.

Turnip Soup with Green Peas (French)

Serves 4

A rich homemade chicken consommé brings out the best in a turnip. Add shelled fresh or frozen young peas and you will have made the renowned soup created by Antonin Carême, the great French chef and author. There are two parts to the soup that come together at the last moment when the hot turnip broth is poured over the green peas in a warmed tureen.

INGREDIENTS
6 small turnips (12 ounces), peeled and diced
2 tablespoons butter
4 cups chicken consommé
Pinch of sugar
½ teaspoon salt, if desired
⅛ teaspoon freshly ground black pepper
1 10-ounce package frozen peas, thawed, or 2 cups shelled fresh young peas, blanched
½ cup croutons, to garnish

SPECIAL EQUIPMENT
None

PREPARATION
SMOTHER
10–12 mins.

Peel and dice turnips. Melt the butter in a large skillet, add turnips, cover, and cook over medium heat for about 10 to 12 minutes, or until they begin to color—changing from white to a light yellow. Set them aside.

SIMMER
10–15 mins.

Bring the consommé to a simmer in a medium (3-quart) saucepan. Add the turnips and a pinch of sugar. Add the salt, if desired. Simmer, skimming if necessary, until the turnips are cooked and soft when pierced with a fork, about 10 to 15 minutes.

If the peas are frozen, pour boiling water over them and let stand for 3 minutes. Drain.

If the peas are fresh, blanch in boiling water until bright green, about 1 minute. Drain.

FINAL STEP

Place the peas and croutons in a warmed soup tureen and cover with the hot turnip soup. Serve immediately in heated individual soup bowls.

Vegetable Cheese Chowder with Beer

Serves 6

Vegetables and an aged sharp Cheddar or Cheshire cheese are combined in this easy-to-make chowder that can be prepared quickly and economically. It is a time-saver because frozen mixed vegetables are used. As a midday dish it is a fine meal in itself.

I have made this soup with several members of the Cheddar family, which includes Cantal, Lancashire, Scotch Dunlop, Leicester, Greek kaseri, and Caerphilly, and all versions were successful. No processed cheese, please!

INGREDIENTS

10 ounces frozen mixed vegetables

4 tablespoons butter or margarine

¼ cup flour

1 teaspoon salt, if desired

1 teaspoon dry mustard

2 cups milk

1 teaspoon Worcestershire sauce

2 cups shredded Cheddar, Cheshire, or another cheese of the Cheddar family

1 cup beer (or additional milk)

1 cup croutons

SPECIAL EQUIPMENT	None
PREPARATION	*Note:* Prepare the frozen vegetables according to package directions, drain, and set aside.
COOK *4 mins.*	In a large saucepan, melt butter or margarine; stir in flour, salt, and mustard. Cook over low heat, stirring constantly, until mixture is smooth and bubbly. Remove from heat. Stir in the milk and Worcestershire sauce.
4 mins.	Heat the milk mixture, stirring constantly until it boils and thickens enough to coat a spoon. Stir in the cheese.
5 mins.	Cook and continue to stir over medium heat until the cheese is melted, about 5 minutes. Stir in the vegetables and beer, and bring the soup back to a simmer.
FINAL STEP	Serve in heated tureen and bowls. Pass the croutons for garnish.

A Garden Vegetable Chowder

Serves 10

At my house this chowder is often made exclusively with home-grown ingredients. It is a joy to the cook, and also to the gardener, who may be overwhelmed by the cornucopia his labors in the soil have produced.

Produce stands also groan with a surplus of vegetables (at a good price) beginning in early summer and on into the autumn. A vegetable chowder, robust as it is, may have greater appeal in the winter when the garden or the roadside stand is but a memory. Frozen, the chowder will last into spring.

This is a meatless chowder, save for a cup of chicken stock or instant bouillon. Although milk is among the ingredients, I often leave it out (especially if the chowder is to be frozen).

The ingredient that gives the chowder an unexpected turn is the cheese. It quickly melts into the chowder and adds to its creaminess.

The list of vegetables is not sacred. Almost any product of the garden, your own or the farmer's, may be used—turnips, peas, potatoes, celery, carrots, lima beans, cabbage, eggplant, leeks, okra, parsnips, peppers (sweet or hot), and rutabaga. The following are my favorites.

INGREDIENTS	1½ pounds zucchini 3 tablespoons butter 1 medium onion, chopped (1 cup)

(continued)

1 clove garlic, minced

2 tablespoons freshly snipped parsley

1 tablespoon fresh basil or 1 teaspoon dried

1 cup green beans, cut into 1-inch pieces

⅓ cup all-purpose flour

1½ teaspoons salt, if desired

¼ teaspoon freshly ground black pepper

1 cup chicken stock or 1 tablespoon instant chicken bouillon granules

1 teaspoon lemon juice

2 cups hot water if stock is used; 3 cups for the bouillon granules

1½ cups corn, freshly cut off the cob, or 1 10-ounce package frozen whole-kernel corn

1 14½-ounce can evaporated milk, optional

6 medium tomatoes (about 1½ pounds), peeled, seeded, and finely chopped

1 cup shredded fontina cheese

½ cup grated Romano cheese

Chopped parsley, to garnish

SPECIAL EQUIPMENT	None
PREPARATION	*Note:* If possible use 8-inch or smaller zucchini. The larger ones get seedy.
COOK 8 mins.	Cut the zucchini lengthwise in half, then cut into ⅜-inch dice. Melt butter in a large (6-quart) saucepan or Dutch oven. Stir zucchini, onion, garlic, parsley, basil, and beans into butter. Add flour and cook for 8 minutes, or until the vegetables are tender. Stir salt and pepper into the vegetable mixture. Cook over low heat, stirring constantly, until bubbly, about 3 minutes.
3 mins.	
BOIL/SIMMER 5 mins. 8 mins. 6 mins.	Stir in the stock or bouillon, lemon juice, and hot water. Heat, stirring, to boiling. Add corn and return to boiling. Turn down the heat and simmer until the corn is cooked—about 8 minutes. Stir in milk and tomatoes. Heat just to boiling. Stir in cheeses. Cook and stir until cheeses are melted, but do not let the chowder heat above a simmer.
FINAL STEP	Serve in bowls from heated tureen. Garnish with parsley.

Mrs. London's Vegetable Soup

Serves 6

This soup is a gathering in of garden vegetables at their prime and cooked together for a matter of only minutes. The cabbage is cooked for 60 seconds. All the vegetables retain their fresh garden color and crispness.

The soup was served at Mrs. London's Bakeshop and Restaurant, once an important part of the scene at Saratoga Springs, New York, a summer resort town known for its racetrack, ballet, bottled water, and symphony orchestra.

INGREDIENTS

2 leeks, sliced (about 3 cups)—white stalks plus 1 inch of green

4 tablespoons butter

1 cup broccoli, cut or broken into florets

1 cup cauliflower, cut or broken into florets

1 cup small brussels sprouts

1 small carrot, thinly sliced

3 to 4 cups rich chicken or beef stock, depending on thickness desired

1 cup cabbage, thinly sliced into 3-inch lengths

Salt, if desired, to taste

¼ teaspoon freshly ground black pepper

1 tablespoon finely chopped fresh chervil or savory, or 1 tablespoon chopped fresh parsley

SPECIAL
EQUIPMENT

None

PREPARATION
SAUTÉ
5 mins.

Sauté sliced leeks in butter in a medium (3-quart) saucepan until soft and translucent. Add broccoli, cauliflower, brussels sprouts, carrot, and stock.

BOIL
5 mins.
1 min.

Bring to a gentle boil and cook for 5 minutes until vegetables are almost cooked. Do not overcook—vegetables should remain crisp and not lose their color. Add cabbage and cook for 1 additional minute—no more. Season to taste and stir in fresh chervil, savory, or parsley.

FINAL STEP

Bring the pot to the table and ladle into heated soup plates. Pass saltines or a coarse peasant bread.

Doubly Rich Country Vegetable Soup

Serves 8

There are two levels of richness to be achieved in this soup. First the meat, the soup bones, and a mirepoix of vegetables are cooked together to make a rich stock. The meat is set aside, the stock is strained, and the soup bones and cooked vegetables are discarded. A new harvest of vegetables is added to the vegetable-rich stock and cooked for a relatively brief period to retain crispness. The meat is either sliced and served as a seperate dish, or cut into bite-size pieces and left in the soup.

There is nothing inviolate about the list of vegetables. The season and weather will dictate which fresh vegetables will be included. The freezer, of course, has greatly extended the vegetable season. Nevertheless, it is more economical (and more timely) to shop for vegetables in season when the low price reflects their abundance.

This recipe calls for a great number of vegetables, but an excellent soup can be made with only half the number.

My mother, Lenora Clayton, used only the minimum of salt, pepper, and other seasonings to ensure that the flavor of the vegetables would come through clear, clean, and true.

INGREDIENTS

Meat and Stock
2 to 3 pounds beef rump in one piece
3 pounds veal and/or beef bones
Water to cover (and discard)
3 quarts water
3 carrots, unpeeled and coarsely chopped
3 onions, peeled and chopped
4 stalks celery, chopped
2 cloves garlic, minced
2 cloves
2 tomatoes, peeled, seeded, and chopped, or canned or frozen
3 tablespoons tomato paste
2 sprigs parsley
2 bay leaves
2 teaspoons salt, if desired
1 teaspoon freshly ground black pepper

Soup
Note: The vegetables that follow may be cut *paysanne* style (¼ inch by ¼ inch by ⅛ inch); *fermiere* (disks of vegetables), or *brunoise* (small dice).

10 cups stock from above

¾ cup *each* peeled, sliced carrots and sliced celery

½ small head cabbage, finely shredded, large center ribs discarded

I cup cut green beans

¼ green pepper, thinly sliced

I cup whole kernel corn, fresh or frozen

I½ cups finely chopped onions

2 leeks, thinly sliced

4 ripe tomatoes, seeded and coarsely chopped, or canned tomatoes

I cup asparagus tips

SPECIAL
EQUIPMENT

Fine chinois or sieve

PREPARATION
BOIL
15 mins.

Meat and Stock

In a large (6- to 8-quart) saucepan, place the meat and bones and cover with water. Bring to a boil; then pour off the water and the sediment it will carry with it.

BOIL/SIMMER
2 hours
2 hours

Again cover the meat with about 3 quarts water; bring to a boil, reduce heat, and simmer, partially covered, for 2 hours.

Add all the roughly cut or chopped vegetables and the herbs and spices indicated for the stock, stir, and return stock to a simmer. Partially cover and cook for an additional 2 hours or a total of 4 hours.

During the final hour, season with salt and pepper to taste.

STRAIN

Take the meat from the pot, and set aside on a plate to cool before cutting all or part of it into small pieces, if the meat is to be served in the soup. Pour the stock through a chinois or sieve and reserve the liquid. Discard the soup bones and cooked vegetables. Skim off the fat and discard.

The stock and meat may be prepared to this point and held for 1 or 2 days before completing the soup. Keep refrigerated.

REHEAT

Soup

Reheat the stock to a boil and add the thinly cut and sliced vegetables in the order listed.

SIMMER
45 mins.

Return the soup to a boil, reduce heat, and simmer over low heat for 45 minutes, or until the various vegetables are cooked but not mushy. Add the meat to be heated before serving.

Taste for seasoning and add if needed.

FINAL STEP　　If the meat is in one piece, remove it to a warm platter and slice as one would a pot roast.

　　Pour the soup and vegetables into a heated tureen. Bring the tureen to the table and ladle soup into large bowls. Pass the sliced beef.

　　Serve a crispy bread and a green salad for a complete meal.

Sweet Corn Soup

Serves 6

The true sweet corn aficionado, with a dozen ears in hand, will race, not walk, from the patch where the corn was picked and into the kitchen where the water is boiling to cook the ears at the very peak of their sweetness.

There is another way to achieve this sublime taste of fresh sweet corn without the athleticism that harvesting and running requires.

It is a delicious soup of corn cut off the cob and cooked just a few moments in milk flavored with bacon bits, onion, and perhaps a touch of cayenne. Half the soup is pureed to give the soup its creaminess and then returned to the pot.

I like yellow sweet corn rather than white for the golden color it gives the soup.

INGREDIENTS
6 ears fresh corn, husked
4 strips bacon, cut into ½-inch pieces
1 medium onion, finely chopped
3 cloves garlic, mashed and chopped
4 cups milk
Cayenne, to taste
Salt and freshly ground black pepper to taste
Butter, at room temperature, to garnish
Paprika, to garnish

SPECIAL
EQUIPMENT
Food processor or blender

PREPARATION
8 mins.
With a sharp knife, cut the kernels from the ears. I hold the ear vertically and slice down top to bottom. You can also place a large box grater on its side in a glass baking dish and grate the corn off the cob horizontally. Set aside for the moment.

FRY
5 mins.
In a large (1½-quart) saucepan, fry the bacon pieces over medium heat. Stir to keep the bacon from sticking to the bottom.

SMOTHER *6 mins.*	Add the onion and garlic and cook for 6 minutes. Stir occasionally.
BOIL/SIMMER *10 mins.* *6 mins.*	Add the cut corn and milk to the saucepan. Add the cayenne and salt and pepper to taste. When the milk comes to a boil, reduce the heat and simmer for about 6 minutes.
COOL *20 mins.*	Remove from the heat and allow the soup to cool somewhat before pureeing.
PUREE *8 mins.*	Place about half the soup in a food processor or blender and puree until creamy, then return it to the saucepan.
REHEAT	Reheat the soup and taste again for seasoning.
FINAL STEP	Ladle the soup into warmed bowls and top each with a dollop (a teaspoon) of butter and a sprinkling of paprika.

Watercress and Green Onion Soup

Serves 6

This is a recipe for a delicious and forthright soup that allows the full flavor of watercress to prevail, tempered with green onions. Some watercress recipes are complicated and confuse the search for the true taste of watercress with too many other ingredients.

This recipe, from the fine kitchen of Chef Kusumu Cooray in Honolulu, gets to the heart of the matter.

It is equally good hot or chilled.

There is a secret place about a mile from my home, across two fields and several hills, where I find watercress growing in a stream whose source of cold rushing water is a large rock-lined break in the hillside a few yards away. I suppose others visit this cool, shaded spot to pick the plant, but I have never seen another soul near the place—that is why I consider it secret.

Cultivated watercress appears frequently in our markets and it is sold in tight bunches of crisp succulent stems set with crunchy little leaves that have a pungent, peppery taste.

INGREDIENTS	2 bunches (about 12 ounces) fresh watercress, coarsely chopped 1 bunch (6 ounces) green onions, coarsely chopped 4 leeks, whites only, well cleaned and chopped 3 tablespoons butter 4 cups milk 1 tablespoon flour Pinch of nutmeg

(continued)

Pinch of white pepper
Salt to taste, if desired
1 cup light cream or milk
2 egg yolks
½ cup watercress "petals" or leaves, to garnish

SPECIAL
EQUIPMENT

Food processor, blender, or food mill

PREPARATION

Note: Before chopping the watercress reserve some attractive leaves for garnishing.

Carefully rinse leeks to remove all sand.

SMOTHER
10 mins.

Chop the watercress, onions, and leeks into 1-inch pieces. Melt the butter in a medium (3-quart) saucepan and add the chopped vegetables. Cover and steam at low heat for about 10 minutes, or until the vegetables are tender.

Bring the milk to just below a boil in a separate pan. When the vegetables are cooked, sprinkle with flour and stir in milk. Add nutmeg, white pepper, and salt. Blend well.

SIMMER
30–35 mins.

Simmer for 30 to 35 minutes. Beat the cream (or milk) and the egg yolks together in a small bowl. Temper with 1 cup of hot broth from the soup and return this to the saucepan. Stir over low heat until the soup thickens, about 3 to 4 minutes.

PUREE
3 mins.

Allow the soup to cool a few moments before putting it into the work bowl of a food processor or blender, or through a food mill or sieve.

FINAL STEP

This soup may be served hot or cold, and it is delicious either way. Drop watercress leaves over the surface of the soup before serving.

Basil and Zucchini Soup

Serves 6

Green . . . green . . . cool . . . cool.

These words spring immediately to mind when the dark green basil leaves are blended with the light green zucchini slices. This soup is low in calories, as there is no stock, only the juice of the zucchini and a bit of water. The soup is decidedly basilish; if it is too much for your taste reduce the leaves to ¼ cup. This is an excellent soup for a luncheon or a first course, served with a dollop of yogurt or sour cream.

INGREDIENTS	6 cups sliced zucchini
	½ cup fresh basil leaves, about 20
	3 cups water
	1 teaspoon salt
	2 tablespoons lemon juice
	½ cup yogurt or sour cream, to garnish
SPECIAL EQUIPMENT	Blender, food processor, food mill, or sieve
PREPARATION BOIL/SIMMER *10 mins.*	Place zucchini and basil leaves in a medium (3-quart) saucepan with water. Add salt. Bring to a boil, reduce heat, and simmer for 10 minutes.
PUREE	Remove the saucepan from the heat, add lemon juice, and allow the vegetables to cool before placing in a machine to puree, or putting through a food mill or sieve.
CHILL *1 hour or longer*	Chill well—at least 1 hour.
FINAL STEP	Chill the serving bowls. Garnish each cup of soup with a dollop of yogurt or sour cream.

One-Can-Plus-Five Soup
Cream of Vegetable with Crab

Serves 8

Cans of five different condensed soups plus a can of lobster or crabmeat are for the occasion when time is fleeting and you want to produce a masterpiece. This is your soup!

Five soup flavors blend with the seafood to give an entirely new taste.

One-Can-Plus-Five Soup came from Esther Shelburne's Indiana kitchen, where I have been eating delicious meals for more decades than either of us cares to remember.

The recipe has been changed slightly to conform with a caveat laid down by my friend Chef Elliott Sharron. If canned soups are used, lift them out of the ordinary by adding something. In this soup that something is a soup maker's standby—sautéed onions, garlic, and a dash of Tabasco.

If you find its name more amusing than descriptive, tell your guests they are having Cream of Vegetable Soup with Crab.

INGREDIENTS

1 cup finely chopped onions

2 cloves garlic, finely diced

2 tablespoons butter

1 10¾-ounce can of *each*
{
tomato soup
green pea soup
chicken with rice soup
cream of chicken soup
cream of mushroom soup
}

1 6-ounce can lobster or crab pieces

2 cups water, approximately (depending on thickness desired)

Salt carefully, if at all (canned soup carries a heavy load of salt)

½ teaspoon freshly ground black pepper

Dash of Tabasco (or more if needed)

½ cup light cream

2 tablespoons sherry

1 cup croutons, to garnish

SPECIAL
EQUIPMENT

None

PREPARATION
10–12 mins.
SAUTÉ

In a covered medium (4-quart) saucepan, sauté onions and garlic in butter over medium-high heat until tender and glossy, about 10 to 12 minutes.

Note: Do not dilute condensed soup as directed on the can. Liquid will be added later. Use the soups from the cans full-strength at this stage.

BOIL/SIMMER

10 mins.

Pour contents of the 5 cans of soup and 1 can of seafood over the sautéed onions and garlic. At this point the mixture will be very thick. Add 2 or more cups of water and blend well. Bring to a gentle boil, reduce heat, and simmer for 10 minutes. Remove from heat.

Season with salt, pepper, and Tabasco to taste. Add cream and sherry.

The soup can be made several hours before serving. Refrigerate until ready to use.

FINAL STEP

Reheat the soup until it steams but does not boil. Pour into heated tureen and bowls. Garnish with croutons.

Famous Full-Meal Soups and Stews

THERE ARE SEVERAL RICH and delicious soups and stews that are so famous as to be legendary and are known by names that transcend their ingredients, however exotic. Brunswick stew, for instance, is a hunter's dish, although ingredients vary widely from one hunt to the next. What is put in the pot depends entirely on the hunter's skill and luck. There are several gumbos (the name *gumbo* comes from the African word for okra). All rely on either okra or filé, a sassafras powder, for thickening. Gumbos are complete meals unto themselves. At the table it remains only to praise the hunter, the butcher, and the cook.

Brunswick Stew

Serves 12 to 14

Brunswick stew—a hunter's stew of squirrel and rabbit—is a large dish for a number of robust eaters. Skimpy eaters need not apply, nor is it worthwhile to make this stew in reduced quantities.

James Beard calls Brunswick stew "one of the most famous of American dishes." Lillian Marshall, a Kentucky author and food authority, describes it as "that imperishable Southern favorite." Marion Harland, a cookbook author, wrote in 1889 that "it is named for Brunswick County, Virginia, and is a famous dish at the political and social pic-nics known as barbeques."

A friend in the hunting fraternity is an absolute must if it is to be the authentic stew—

how else do you come by two or three squirrels? But if game is in short supply, the stew can also be made in combination with chicken and/or store-bought fresh or frozen domesticated rabbit.

John Gallman is my hunter as well as my friend. A former director of the Indiana University Press, he is as meticulous about his game as he was about his books. He gave me two dressed squirrels with this note attached: "Fox squirrels (Sciurus niger), larger than Gray squirrels, taken in the forenoon December 24 along White River, very fat, prime and corn-fed (from nearby fields)."

This traditional Brunswick stew is made with potatoes, but Beth Gallman, a discerning cook familiar with all game, uses rice with squirrel and potato with rabbit (and chicken). She says the rice does not overpower the delicate flavor of the squirrel.

Some cooks leave the meat on the bone. I find that guests prefer to have the meat already cut into bite-size chunks.

INGREDIENTS	3 squirrels
	or 2 rabbits, or both
	or 1 4-pound stewing chicken
	or a combination of the three
	⅓ cup flour
	3 tablespoons butter
	½ pound salt pork, in ¼-inch dice
	3 medium onions, minced
	10 cups water
	6 cups finely chopped tomatoes, fresh or canned
	1 6-ounce can tomato paste
	2 cups lima beans, fresh or frozen
	2 cups whole kernel corn (fresh off the cob is best)
	2 cups chopped red bell peppers (for color)
	3 cups potatoes (if for rabbit and/or chicken), peeled and cut into ½-inch cubes, or ½ cup raw rice (if for squirrel)
	Salt to taste, if desired
	½ teaspoon freshly ground black pepper, or to taste
	2 teaspoons red pepper, or to taste
	2 teaspoons Worcestershire sauce
	½ teaspoon Tabasco
	1 cup red wine
SPECIAL EQUIPMENT	None

PREPARATION	*Game:* Care should be taken with game that has been shot. Clean out all shot or as many as possible. Cut away and discard meat in which blood has collected, or it will make the stew bitter. Cut up as for fricassee.
SAUTÉ 10–12 mins.	Shake the pieces of game in flour in a plastic bag until they are well covered. In a large, deep skillet melt butter until foaming. Lay down the game pieces in one layer without crowding. Over high heat brown the pieces until nicely browned, about 10 to 12 minutes. Lift out the pieces and set aside.
TRY OUT 6 mins.	In the same skillet try out the salt pork until the fat is rendered and the dice are crisp.
COOK 10 mins.	Add the onions and cook over medium heat for about 10 minutes or until translucent and tender.
BOIL/SIMMER 1½ hours approximately	(The time for cooking the game will vary according to the age of the squirrel and rabbit. Young require less time; old and tough, longer. One and a half hours is an approximation. Test for doneness with a fork.) Into a large (6-quart) stew pot, pour the water and scrape in the onions and pork bits from the skillet. Add the game pieces, tomatoes, and tomato paste. Bring to a boil, reduce heat, and simmer for 1½ hours.
30 mins.	Add lima beans, corn, peppers, and potatoes or rice. Taste for seasoning and add salt, if needed, black pepper, and red pepper as desired. Pour in Worcestershire sauce, Tabasco, and red wine. After 2 hours of cooking, the meat should pull easily from the bone. The meat pieces may be left intact (since they are quite small) or cut off the bone and into bite-size pieces. The stew should be moist, yet somewhat firm. If too thick, thin with water or chicken stock. When I have found I had too much liquid in the stew, rather than boil it down in the big pot and overcook the game, I have ladled out several cups of the stock, boiled it down over high heat, and returned the concentrated liquid to the pot.
FINAL STEP	Ladle into a large heated tureen and serve in heated dishes. For a different presentation, cool the stew to room temperature, turn it into an earthenware dish, and top with a rich ⅜-inch-thick pastry crust brushed with beaten egg yolk and cream. Cut a vent in the pastry to let steam and juices escape. Bake at 375° till the crust is browned and the stew thoroughly reheated.

Burgoo

4 gallons, enough for a small army

One of the great regional soup/stews in this country is burgoo, found at its finest in Kentucky and southern Indiana. It peaks in the Bluegrass State at Derby time when gallons of it are eaten by natives and happy visitors.

Burgoo needs to be made in quantity if it is to attain the taste first discovered by frontiersmen, who dropped portions of every meat and vegetable at hand into a big iron pot. Squirrel and rabbit were common ingredients when every household had a hunter, but now domesticated animals provide the meat.

Burgoo is served at country festivals, racing meets, and social affairs of every kind. Traditionally it is ladled into tin cups, but it is equally good in regular soup bowls. Chunks of corn bread or corn dodgers—and a quantity of beer—fill out the menu, and the dinner! Not to be overlooked are coleslaw and, for dessert, fruit cobbler.

Obviously 4 gallons is for a large, 50-guest gathering, but the burgoo can be frozen and brought out over the months ahead whenever the fancy or hunger strikes. It also makes great gifts—jarred in small quantities and appropriately wrapped.

Yet, despite what old-timers say, burgoo can be made in smaller quantities. For example, only half of this recipe can be made successfully by reducing all ingredients by half. So if 4 gallons is too much, reduce by half or even two-thirds—but not further, for then it will not be worth the bother to assemble the ingredients (regardless of their quantity) nor the time to make it.

Burgoo is what you want it to be just as long as you include a variety of meats (two or more) and a number of vegetables and herbs and spices. This Bluegrass country recipe comes from the St. James Court kitchen of Lillian Marshall, Louisville's highly acclaimed cook, teacher, and author.

There are so many ingredients in burgoo that it is wise to keep a check of each as you go.

The meats for burgoo can be cooked in one large pot, but the assembled burgoo will demand more—one 18-quart container or two small ones. The burgoo may be cooked in one or more covered kettles on the top of the stove for 7 or 8 hours or in a slow oven (250°) for 12 to 14 hours. The latter method requires little attention and no stirring, and I like the resulting texture better.

INGREDIENTS   (separated into first and second days)

First Day
1 fat hen, 4 to 5 pounds
3 pounds beef chuck
2 pounds pork shank

2 pounds veal chuck
2 pounds breast of lamb
I rabbit, if desired
I ½ pounds venison, if available
(If game meat is not used, substitute an equal quantity of other meats.)
Water, to cover the above

Second Day
4 pounds potatoes, peeled and diced
2 pounds onions, finely chopped
I pound carrots, diced
I cup diced celery
2 green bell peppers, seeds and ribs removed, chopped
2 pods hot red chili peppers, soaked and cut into bits
I pound dry white beans
2 cloves garlic, mashed
2 cups red wine
⅓ cup Worcestershire sauce
Tabasco to taste (several dashes)
I pound tomatoes, seeded and chopped
I quart tomato puree
2 cups whole kernel corn, fresh, canned, or frozen
I cup white vinegar
2 tablespoons salt (or more after tasting) and freshly ground black pepper
     to taste
2 10-ounce packages frozen okra or I pound fresh okra, cut into
     1-inch pieces
2 quarts beef stock
I tablespoon thyme

SPECIAL EQUIPMENT	A selection of large pots or other large receptacles. A food processor or meat grinder. (A blender will cut the meat too fine and leave it with no personality.)
PREPARATION	*Note:* Take heart, for there are more ingredients in burgoo than instructions.
BOIL/SIMMER *2 hours approximately*	Choose a large kettle that will hold all the meat and water to cover. Bring to a boil. Skim frequently. Turn down the heat and simmer, covered with lid, until the meat is tender enough to fall from the bones, about 2 hours.

COOL *Overnight*	Remove meats, cool, and discard bones and pieces of fat. Put meat through a food processor or meat grinder (coarse blade). The result should be coarse-grained particles not unlike meat cut for chili or used in hamburger. Refrigerate and reserve.
DEGREASE	Degrease the broth by skimming well, or refrigerate overnight; the following morning skim off hardened fat. In a large cooking vessel combine ground meat with potatoes, onions, carrots, celery, peppers, beans, garlic, red wine, Worcestershire, Tabasco, tomatoes, tomato puree, and corn.
BOIL	Bring the broth to a boil in a separate pot. Pour enough of the broth over the meat and vegetables to within an inch of covering the mixture—not quite enough to cover it. Add vinegar, salt and pepper, okra, beef stock, and thyme. Cover the cooking vessel.
COOK (VARIES) *8–14 hours*	The burgoo may be cooked in either of two ways: in a covered kettle on top of the stove (7 to 8 hours), stirring occasionally; or in a 250° oven (12 to 14 hours). The oven method requires no stirring and results in a homogeneous mass, whereas the liquid often separates from the meat and vegetables on the stove top. For the oven method a large casserole or roaster is in order—or two smaller pots, with lids, if more convenient. Burgoo should be very thick but still soupy. Add broth (or water) if burgoo needs thinning.
FINAL STEP	Ladle into big bowls or tin cups, pass the corn bread—and enjoy!

GUMBO

Gumbo, one of the South's great regional dishes, is a thick savory stew made with fish or fowl and served on a bed of steaming hot white rice.

Three ingredients are used in thickening gumbo, and from them it also gets much of its good flavor. The first is a roux of oil and flour, cooked until nut-brown; the second is okra; and the third is filé.

Roux is a constant in making gumbo, but the choice of the other two thickeners—okra or filé—lies with the cook. Okra, a green vegetable conical in shape, has considerable thickening powers and is widely used in savory stews and to thicken such things as ketchup. Some find its mucilaginous quality somewhat objectionable, but this is well hidden in gumbo.

The word *gumbo* stems from the African word for okra, *quingumbo,* the seeds for which were brought to America by West African slaves.

Filé, the other gumbo thickening ingredient, is powdered sassafras leaves. It both thickens and flavors. (The bark and roots of the sassafras tree are brewed into a fragrant, rose-colored tea.)

The choice between okra or filé must be made before the gumbo is cooked. If it is to be okra, the vegetable is cooked along with the other ingredients. The unique quality of filé is that it is stirred in *after* the gumbo has cooked, not before. Filé, which adds so much to the finished dish, becomes stringy and unpalatable if cooked with it. As a consequence, filé is stirred into only the amount of soup to be served at one time, or into individual servings, so that any leftover gumbo can be reheated later.

There are those who love the taste of filé and will sprinkle a bit on a gumbo already thickened with okra, as a condiment. (But most true Creole cooks insist that no authentic gumbo includes both.) The tangy nature of filé has been described as "the taste of pine needles."

Roux, which has the consistency of a thick sauce or gravy, is a mixture of equal parts of fat—oil, bacon drippings, shortening, butter, or margarine—and flour, deeply browned (in Creole cooking) in a heavy saucepan or skillet over low heat for a long time, about a half hour or more.

Roux can have many flavors, depending on what the cook is making and which liquids are added. White roux is commonly used as a base for white sauces and soufflés and is cooked for a relatively short time. Brown roux, also used in sauces, is cooked a little longer until the flour turns a light toasty color.

The longer a roux is cooked, the darker it becomes and the more flavor it develops. The cooking pot should be of heavy metal to lessen the chance that it will scorch. If the roux is burned it will not thicken the stew and will impart an unpleasant taste—the trick is to cook the roux as long as possible to maximize its flavor without burning. It demands constant attention.

A few gumbos are made without a roux and depend entirely on okra or filé for thickening. Those gumbos are light, not the usual dark brown, and, frankly, not highly favored by gumbo lovers.

Three gumbo recipes follow.

One is prepared with shellfish and/or finfish. The second gumbo is a good one to have as a standby in the freezer; it can be made into either a fish or a fowl dish. The third is made with chicken and sausage.

Seafood Gumbo

Serves 8

The Stone Crabber, a restaurant perched on the banks of Purify Creek where it flows into the Gulf at Panacea, Florida, had a superb seafood gumbo prepared along classic lines.

The Stone Crabber was the only business in the small town of Panacea. In the early 1900s Panacea was a prosperous resort that attracted people from all over to drink and bathe in the sulfur waters. The waters were believed to be a "cure-all" or panacea for their ills. Today all of this is gone and even the artesian wells have been filled in or ditched.

Julia Damon Hanway, the owner of the Stone Crabber, gave me this recipe for which her restaurant was noted.

The gumbo may be made with either okra or filé. It may also be made with almost any combination of shellfish and finfish that's available. Rice may be added to the gumbo as it is cooking or it may be boiled or steamed and served separately. Or the gumbo can be ladled over the rice to serve.

INGREDIENTS

Roux

1 cup oil or bacon drippings
1 cup all-purpose flour

Gumbo

1 pound fresh okra or 1 10-ounce box frozen okra (if chosen rather than filé)
1/4 pound butter or margarine
2 cups *each* finely chopped celery and onions
1 cup *each* finely chopped green bell pepper and fresh parsley
2 cloves garlic, minced
10 cups water or lightly flavored fish or chicken stock
1 pound whole tomatoes, fresh or canned
1 6-ounce can tomato paste
1 cup uncooked rice, optional (see above)
2 bay leaves
1/4 cup Worcestershire sauce
Dash of Tabasco
1 teaspoon cumin seeds, roasted and crushed (see "Spices, Herbs, and Seasonings," page 372)
1/4 teaspoon *each* cayenne and thyme
2 teaspoons salt, or to taste
1/2 teaspoon freshly ground black pepper

1 cup dry white wine

1 large crab body, cleaned and quartered, if available

2 pounds uncooked shrimp, shelled and deveined

1 pint oysters

½ pound crabmeat

(If some of the shellfish items are not available in the market,
substitute finfish in the same amount, such as catfish, scrod,
red snapper, sea bass, etc.)

2 tablespoons filé (if chosen as thickener)

Hot white rice, optional (see above)

½ cup chopped parsley, to garnish

SPECIAL
EQUIPMENT

None

PREPARATION
COOK
45 mins.

Roux

In a heavy saucepan or skillet, heat the oil or bacon drippings over medium heat. Add the flour, a tablespoon at a time, and blend into the fat.

The roux should cook slowly over low heat for 45 minutes or until it becomes a deep chocolate brown. Allow small bubbles to rise through the roux, and stir constantly with a whisk or wooden spoon. Be careful not to scorch.

When the roux has cooked, set the skillet aside.

Okra (optional)

Thaw frozen okra in boiling water according to instructions on the package. If fresh, wash, stem, and break okra pods into ½-inch pieces. Blanch either thawed or fresh pods 3 to 5 minutes in lightly salted boiling water to firm the texture. Drain.

COOK
20 mins.

In a large (6- to 8-quart) saucepan or kettle, melt the butter to bubbling and add the okra. Cook over medium heat for 20 minutes or until the okra is slightly browned and its ropy texture has disappeared.

SMOTHER
15 mins.

(If okra is not used, move directly to this step.)

Add celery, onions, green pepper, parsley, and garlic. Cover and cook over medium-low heat for 15 minutes. The vegetables should be translucent and slightly tender. Stir occasionally.

Pour the roux into the saucepan with the vegetables. Stir to blend well.

Note: The liquid to be added can be either water or a stock. The gumbo will be richer if made with fish or chicken stock (see Stock). The stock should be a lightly flavored one, however.

BOIL/SIMMER
1½ hours

Add the water or stock to the saucepan and place over medium-high heat to bring to a boil.

While the liquid is heating, add the whole tomatoes, tomato paste, rice (if wanted here), bay leaves, Worcestershire sauce, Tabasco, cumin, cayenne, thyme, salt, if desired, and pepper. Add the wine.

The crab body is added to the gumbo now; the other shellfish and/or finfish will be added later.

Bring the gumbo to a gentle boil, partially cover, and simmer over low heat for 1½ hours.

The gumbo may be prepared to this stage and held in the refrigerator for 2 or 3 days before adding the shellfish. Putting the gumbo aside for a day or so will enhance its flavor.

In the meantime prepare the seafood and/or finfish. If the shrimp are frozen, drop them into cold water for a moment to separate the pieces. Set aside. Cut the fish into 2-inch pieces. If the gumbo has been refrigerated, bring to room temperature.

SIMMER
30 mins.

Drop the shellfish (and/or finfish) into the gumbo and return the soup to a simmer. Let it cook for an additional 30 minutes or until the shellfish are cooked. Skim off any oil on the surface and discard.

If the gumbo seems too thick, add water to desired consistency. It should be quite thick.

Gumbo thickened and flavored with filé should not be reheated; therefore, add filé only to the portion that is to be served at this time.

FINAL STEP

Ladle the gumbo over a bed of hot white rice for each serving. Pass the filé as a condiment. Garnish with parsley.

Two-Way Gumbo

Serves 8

Two-way gumbo is a basic preparation that can be made into either a chicken or a seafood gumbo. The gumbo base is easy to make and quite economical. It can be stored in the refrigerator for several days or indefinitely frozen at 0°F.

When okra and other vegetables are plentiful, cook up a big potful and put aside for a spe-

cial day when the urge to have gumbo comes over you and there is chicken or seafood to spare.

The roux is optional in this recipe. Without it, the gumbo will be lighter in color and not so thick. However, if a roux is desired, use one of the recipes on pages 338 or 342.

INGREDIENTS

Gumbo Base
2 pounds fresh or frozen chopped okra
2 onions, chopped
2 stalks celery, chopped
2 cloves garlic, minced
1 pound fresh tomatoes, skinned, seeded, and chopped, or
    1 16-ounce can whole tomatoes
3 ounces tomato paste
Salt, if desired
½ teaspoon freshly ground black pepper
1 tablespoon Worcestershire sauce
¼ teaspoon Tabasco sauce

Chicken
1 3-pound chicken, disjointed
3 tablespoons flour
Salt, pepper, and garlic powder to season flour
3 tablespoons butter
4 cups water
1 cup red wine
Salt, if desired
¼ teaspoon freshly ground black pepper

Seafood
2 quarts water
1 pound raw, peeled, and deveined shrimp, fresh or frozen, or 6 cleaned
    crabs
Salt, if desired
¼ tablespoon freshly ground black pepper
White rice (to serve with either gumbo)
1 tablespoon filé for either chicken or seafood gumbo
    (if used to thicken instead of okra)

SPECIAL
EQUIPMENT

None

PREPARATION	*Gumbo Base*
BAKE	Preheat oven to 250°. Place all the ingredients through the tomato paste
250°	in a heavy Dutch oven or covered casserole and bake in the oven for
3 hours	3 hours. Stir occasionally.

Stir in salt, black pepper, Worcestershire sauce, and Tabasco sauce. Remove cover for the last 30 minutes in the oven.

Put aside. Refrigerate or freeze if not to be used immediately.

Chicken

FRY
30 mins.

Shake chicken pieces with seasoned flour in a paper bag to coat completely. Fry in a heavy skillet in butter until golden brown. Lift out and set aside.

BOIL
45 mins.

In a medium (4-quart) saucepan, bring 2 cups of water and the wine to a boil and drop in the chicken pieces. Cook over medium heat until tender, about 45 minutes.

30 mins.

Add roux and gumbo base mixture and blend well. Cook gently over medium-low heat for 30 additional minutes. Season with salt and pepper, if needed.

Either pick the meat off the chicken bones and cut into bite-size pieces or serve the larger pieces.

Seafood

BOIL/SIMMER

30 mins.
15 mins.

Place the gumbo mixture (and roux if used) in 2 quarts of water in a medium (4-quart) saucepan. Bring to a boil and cook together for 30 minutes. Add seafood and simmer for 15 minutes. Add salt and pepper to taste.

Prepare white rice.

(The filé may be used for thickening *after* the gumbo is taken off the stove.)

FINAL STEP

Mound hot rice in each soup dish and ladle on the gumbo—either chicken or seafood. Serve with corn bread.

Chicken and Sausage Gumbo

Serves 8

The chicken in this delicious gumbo is doubly useful. The meat is cut into bite-size pieces to become the principal ingredient. The carcass is simmered to produce the rich stock with which the gumbo is made.

Meats chosen to go with gumbo in secondary roles range from ham to a variety of smoked sausages including the garlicky and darkly flavored boudins and andouilles. The latter two are difficult to find away from Cajun and Creole sources. Nearly as good are Polish kielbasa and other good-quality smoked sausages.

INGREDIENTS

Chicken
1 4-pound *whole* chicken, disjointed to fry
Liberal sprinkles of salt, pepper, garlic powder, and cayenne
1 cup flour, to coat chicken
½ cup bacon drippings or oil

Stock
Chicken carcass
10 cups water
1 cup *each* chopped onions, carrots, and celery
2 bay leaves
½ teaspoon salt
¼ teaspoon freshly ground black pepper

Roux
1 cup oil (after frying chicken—supplement, if necessary)
1 cup all-purpose flour

Okra (if chosen rather than filé)
2 cups sliced okra, fresh or thawed, if frozen
¼ cup vegetable oil

Gumbo
2 cups *each* finely chopped green peppers, onions, and celery
1 cup finely chopped parsley
2 cloves garlic, minced
2 quarts chicken stock (from above)
½ teaspoon cumin seed, roasted and crushed
    (see "Spices, Herbs, and Seasonings," page 372)
1 teaspoon freshly ground black pepper
1 teaspoon salt, if desired
2 bay leaves
½ cup tomato paste
8 drops Tabasco sauce

(continued)

I pound smoked spiced sausage, thinly sliced on the diagonal
(see text above)
I tablespoon filé (if chosen as thickener)
Hot cooked white rice

SPECIAL
EQUIPMENT

None

PREPARATION

Chicken
Disjoint the chicken and put aside the bony carcass, neck, wing tips, and giblets for the stock (see below).

SEASON
30 mins.

Place the choice chicken pieces on a baking sheet and season with salt, pepper, garlic powder, and cayenne. Leave undisturbed for 30 minutes. Place the pieces in a paper sack and add 1 cup of flour. Shake thoroughly to coat.

FRY
45 mins.

Heat the fat in a large skillet over medium heat until just smoking. Fry the chicken until golden brown and tender enough to be taken off the bones, about 45 minutes. Debone. Reserve deboned meat and add bones to stockpot.

Stock

BOIL/SIMMER
2½–3 hours

At the same time, place the raw chicken carcass, including neck, wing tips, and giblets, in a large (5-quart) saucepan or kettle and cover with 10 cups of water. Add the onions, carrots, celery, and seasonings. Bring to a boil, reduce heat, partially cover, and simmer for 2½ to 3 hours, until the bones have given up all their flavor.

Roux
There should be about ½ cup of hot oil in the skillet in which the chicken was fried. Scrape loose the particles from the bottom. Add more oil to make 1 cup.

COOK
30–45 mins.

Over medium-low heat slowly stir the 1 cup of flour into the oil. The roux will be an off-white color and gradually change to a dark nut-brown. It must be stirred during the entire cooking period to prevent scorching or burning. Use a whisk or wooden spoon.

The darker the roux becomes, the more taste it will impart.

Okra (optional)
Wash, stem, and slice fresh okra into ½-inch pieces, or thaw frozen okra.

COOK
45 mins.

Place ¼ cup of oil in a skillet and cook okra over medium heat for 45 minutes or until slightly browned. It will be added to the gumbo in progress.

Gumbo
When the roux has cooked, stir in the green peppers, onions, celery, parsley, and garlic. Blend well.

SMOTHER
1 hour

Cover and cook over low heat—barely bubbling—for 1 hour. Stir frequently. When the okra has cooked, lift it with a slotted spoon and add it to this mixture.

STRAIN

Strain the chicken stock and discard carcass and vegetables. If any meat is clinging to the bones pick it off and add to the reserved pieces.

Return the stock to the large saucepan in which the chicken cooked and add the contents of the skillet. Stir to blend. Add the cumin, pepper, salt, bay leaves, tomato paste, and Tabasco sauce.

SIMMER
1 hour

Partially cover and simmer over low heat for 1 hour.

TRY OUT
20 mins.

While the gumbo is cooking, try out the sausage slices in a skillet to remove excess fat, about 20 minutes. Lift the pieces out of the skillet with a slotted spoon and add to the gumbo. Discard the fat.

30 mins.

Thirty minutes before the gumbo is completely cooked, add the chicken.

Taste for seasoning.

Prepare hot white rice.

If gumbo is to be thickened with filé, remove from the heat and add filé to whatever portion you will be serving at this meal.

FINAL STEP

Ladle the gumbo over a bed of hot rice. Pass the filé. Serve with corn bread and wine. Delicious!

Goulash (Hungarian)
Gulyás

Serves 10 to 12

In Hungary it is gulyás. In other kitchens it is goulash. This is a herdsman's stew—pork or beef, a garden of vegetables, sauerkraut—and all brought to spicy life with paprika, Hungary's favorite seasoning.

The finest paprika, sometimes called "rose" paprika, is imported from Hungary. If of high quality, it is a vibrant red, and varies in strength from mild to hot. Use enough in goulash to give a real bite, as it will be cooled somewhat when the sour cream is added. Goulash should not be bland.

Lard is suggested in the recipe because in Hungary, where the pig is the major meat animal, it is the commonest shortening.

Rather than being thickened with flour or another thickening agent, this goulash is given more body with pureed vegetables.

INGREDIENTS

1 tablespoon lard or cooking oil

2½ to 3 pounds lean pork, cut into ½-inch chunks

3 tablespoons lard or butter

4 medium onions (about 1 pound), finely chopped

4 large carrots (about 2 cups), finely chopped

3 stalks celery (about 1 cup), finely chopped

2 cloves garlic, minced

3 to 4 tablespoons imported sweet Hungarian paprika,
   depending on strength

½ teaspoon dried thyme or 1½ teaspoons fresh

½ teaspoon dried savory or 1½ teaspoons fresh

½ teaspoon caraway seeds

3 quarts beef stock

2 cups tomato puree

2 cups chopped cabbage (½ small head)

4 ounces green beans, cut in 1½-inch lengths, optional

1 pound sauerkraut, rinsed and drained

2 large potatoes (about 2 cups), peeled and cut into ½-inch cubes

2 cups sour cream

Salt, if desired, to taste

½ teaspoon freshly ground black pepper

Chopped parsley or chives, to garnish

SPECIAL EQUIPMENT	Food processor or blender
PREPARATION SEAR *12 mins.*	In a medium (3-quart) saucepan, heat 1 tablespoon lard over high heat until it begins to smoke. Drop in the pieces of meat. Stir to sear and brown on all sides, about 12 minutes. Lift the meat out with a slotted spoon and set aside for the moment.
SWEAT *12 mins.*	Drop 3 tablespoons lard or butter into the hot pot and add onions, carrots, celery, and garlic. Cover and sweat over medium heat until the onions are soft and begin to brown, about 12 minutes. Stir in the paprika, thyme, savory, and caraway seeds. Add stock, tomato puree, and chopped cabbage.
SIMMER *1½ hours*	Reduce heat, partially cover, and simmer over medium heat for 1½ hours.
BLANCH *5 mins.*	If the beans are to be included, cut them into 1½-inch lengths; blanch in a quart of boiling salted water. Drain; rinse under cold water to stop the cooking. Reserve.
THICKEN	During the last half hour of simmering, dip 1½ cups of vegetables from the pot and puree them in a food processor or blender. Return the puree to the goulash to thicken.
SIMMER *15 mins.* *20 mins.*	Add sauerkraut and simmer for an additional 15 minutes. Drop in the potatoes and green beans and simmer for another 20 minutes or until the potatoes are just tender. When the stew is done, stir all but a few spoonfuls of sour cream into the goulash and turn off heat. Taste for seasoning and adjust.
FINAL STEP	Serve stew in heated bowls. Top each serving with a dollop of the reserved sour cream; sprinkle with parsley or chives. Serve with a full-bodied red wine such as Hungarian Egri Bikavér or a tart, dark beer.

Garbure (French)

Serves 10

Garbure: *My French dictionary calls it simply a soup of cabbage, ham, bacon, and pickled goose. It is so far beneath the notice of Escoffier that it isn't mentioned once in his classic compendium of 2,984 recipes. The authoritative Larousse Gastronomique describes it in passing as a "peasant-type soup," but gives no recipe.*

But in rural France, especially in the Pyrenees, it is a traditional soup that is really a stew. The Basques believe a garbure is the proper thickness when a spoon will stand upright in a bowl all by itself.

Each season dictates what goes into the soup, for it should be garden-fresh. The classic garbure contains, along with the vegetables, confit, which is meat, such as goose or duck, cooked and preserved in its own fat. Confit had been omitted from this recipe because it is difficult to find (though not difficult to make) in this country. Use confit d'oie or canard if you are fortunate enough to have a supply of either.

INGREDIENTS

Note: While the ideal is to use freshly picked beans, the recipe here calls for dried or frozen beans, as they are always available. By all means, use fresh ones if you have them.

1 pound dried Great Northern or other white beans
Water, as necessary
½ pound smoked slab bacon
½ pound smoked pork butt
1 ham bone, if available
½ pound Polish kielbasa
1 medium cabbage (about 2 pounds), trimmed, cored, and finely shredded (chiffonade)
3 leeks (about 1 pound), washed and sliced, including 2 inches of green
1 head garlic (8 to 10 cloves)
2 carrots, peeled and cut into 1-inch pieces
1 10-ounce package frozen lima beans, defrosted, or 1 pound fresh, if available, shelled
3 medium potatoes, peeled, cut in half, and sliced ½ inch thick
2 medium turnips, cut into ½-inch cubes
1 pound chestnuts, if available, roasted and peeled
1 pound confit, if available

Sachet d'épice
2 bay leaves
1 teaspoon dried thyme or 1½ teaspoons fresh
1 teaspoon dried marjoram or 1½ teaspoons fresh
½ teaspoon cayenne
10 black peppercorns

12 slices dry rye bread or other dark bread

SPECIAL EQUIPMENT	Large 8- to 10-quart stockpot or two smaller ones
PREPARATION	*Note:* There are two basic steps to begin the *garbure*. The dried beans are cooked to soften, and the meats are parboiled to remove excess saltiness.
BOIL 5 mins.	Place the dried beans in a medium (3-quart) saucepan; add cold water to cover to the depth of 2 inches. Bring to a boil over medium heat and cook for 5 minutes. Remove from heat and let stand for 1 hour. Drain and set aside.
PARBOIL	Cover the meats in a saucepan with cold water and bring to a boil. Immediately remove from heat, drain, and set aside.
BOIL	Place the reserved meats in a large (8- to 10-quart) stockpot or 2 smaller ones; add 4 quarts of cold water. Bring to a boil over medium-high heat. Skim off foam or fat and bone particles as they rise. Stir once so meat does not stick to the bottom.
SIMMER 1½–2 hours	When the pot boils, in about 15 or 20 minutes, reduce heat and simmer while the vegetables are prepared. As each vegetable is finished add it to the pot.

Note: The whole garlic head, unpeeled, is dropped into the pot. It will not break apart during the cooking but later the cloves will be separated and the hulls squeezed lightly to push out the soft garlic pulp, which will be added to the *garbure*.

Add the chestnuts and the confit if you have them.

Partially cover the pot and reduce heat to a gentle simmer. Continue to simmer for a total period of 1½ hours. Half an hour before the *garbure* is finished cooking, drop in the sachet. Test the vegetables for doneness. If done, remove from the heat; if not, continue cooking as needed, up to 20 or 30 minutes.

When cooked, lift out the meats and cut into 1½-inch pieces. Discard the bones. Return the meat to the soup. Remove and discard the garlic and sachet.

FINAL STEP   Bring the *garbure* to a simmer before serving. Place a slice of dry bread in each soup plate and ladle the soup over it.

Red wine and a mixed green salad are excellent companions to this one-dish meal.

Garbure will keep well in the refrigerator, although it will have more vegetable and herb flavor when eaten immediately. It freezes well.

Seafood Jambalaya

Serves 12 or more

Many hold that jambalaya got its name from jambon, French for ham. It has come to mean a variety of wonderful stews that are made with whatever seafood or meat or poultry is available. Try a combination, as in the following recipe, of shrimp, oysters, crab, ham, and sausage.

While this recipe calls for kielbasa, the Polish sausage found in most American meat departments, the authentic jambalaya is made with one of the spicy, dark-flavored Creole-Cajun sausages—boudin blanc (a white pork sausage), boudin rouge (blood sausage), and andouille (smoked sausage made with meat from the neck and stomach of the pig). Any of these will be a praiseworthy substitute for the kielbasa.

Jambalaya has moved far beyond Cajun boundaries in southern Louisiana and is a welcome dish on tables across the country.

I watched Paul Prudhomme, the celebrated New Orleans chef, make jambalaya in the kitchen of his motor home pulled into the driveway of Craig Claiborne's Long Island home in celebration of the latter's birthday. This is Prudhomme's basic recipe, with a shortcut or two suggested by Pierre Franey, cohost of the celebration as well as coauthor with Claiborne of food columns and books.

Prudhomme makes jambalaya with a long-simmered fish stock, whereas Franey takes a shortcut by cooking the shrimp shells into a light, tasty broth. If the shrimp have been preshelled and there is no fish stock, use a chicken stock or a light beef stock.

This recipe is true to its jambon antecedents—ham as well as sausage. It can easily become shrimp jambalaya by not adding the oysters and crab.

INGREDIENTS   *Broth*
Shells from 2 pounds raw shrimp
6 cups water
6 peppercorns
½ cup chopped onion

1 stalk celery, chopped

1 bay leaf

(Salt will be added to the finished jambalaya.)

Stew

1 pound Creole-Cajun sausage (see above), in 1-inch pieces, or 1 pound
    kielbasa, in 1-inch pieces

1 pound smoked ham, in ½-inch cubes

1 cup finely chopped green peppers

1 cup finely chopped celery

2 cups finely chopped onions

1 clove garlic, minced

½ cup tomato puree

1 16-ounce can tomatoes or 2 cups ripe tomatoes, peeled, seeded,
    and chopped

1 recipe shrimp broth (see above) or 7 cups fish stock

½ teaspoon dried thyme

1 bay leaf

1 teaspoon crushed dried oregano

1 teaspoon red pepper, or to taste

½ teaspoon dried basil

1 teaspoon freshly ground black pepper

1½ cups raw rice

2 cups shucked oysters

1 pound crabmeat, picked over

1 cup finely chopped green onions

SPECIAL
EQUIPMENT

Chinois or heavy sieve

PREPARATION
BOIL/SIMMER
20 mins.
STRAIN

Broth

Peel and devein the shrimp and set the meat aside. Put the shells and
other ingredients into a medium (3-quart) saucepan and bring to a boil.
Reduce heat and simmer 20 minutes. Strain the broth through a chinois
or sieve. Much of the flavor is in the shells, so press and pound with a
heavy spoon or pestle until all the moisture has been extracted. Discard
shell residue and reserve broth.

Stew

COOK
10 mins.

Drop the sausage pieces into a large heated saucepan or casserole and
sear over medium-high heat. Stir frequently. Cook for about 10 min-

10 mins.

15 mins.

3 mins.

BOIL/SIMMER
1 hour
15 mins.
5 mins.

FINAL STEP

utes. The sausage will render considerable fat as it cooks. Pour off and discard all but 1 tablespoon of the fat.

Add the ham pieces and continue cooking, stirring often, for an additional 10 minutes.

Add the peppers, celery, onions, and garlic. Scrape the bottom with a wooden spoon or spatula as the mixture cooks to loosen and incorporate the brown particles stuck to the bottom of the pan. Cook about 15 minutes.

Add tomato puree and tomatoes. Stir to blend and cook together for about 3 minutes.

Pour in the broth and bring to a boil. Add thyme, bay leaf, oregano, red pepper, basil, and black pepper. Cook over low heat for 1 hour.

Add rice, cover, and cook for 15 minutes.

Add reserved shrimp, oysters, and crab and cook 5 minutes more. Stir in the green onions.

Taste for salt.

Ladle from the pot or heated tureen into heated large but shallow soup bowls.

Pot-au-Feu (French)

Serves 10

Pot-au-feu, as delicious and famous as it is in France and elsewhere, is simply a meat-and-vegetable stew. It is easy to make although the making extends over 5 hours from first simmer to table.

Pot-au-feu (literally "pot on the fire") is a bountiful dish that can be served in two courses—a superb broth first, as well as a full dinner of meat and vegetables. Or it can be combined in a large soup plate as one dish. At our house, guests are served the broth first. Then soup plates are used again for the meat and vegetables. This allows everyone to have more of the rich broth ladled over the meat and vegetables. Slightly bourgeois, but after all, it is a bourgeois dish.

Pot-au-feu begins with a gallon of rich beef stock or bouillon in which the meats are simmered for several hours, then removed from the pot and set aside. Next the vegetables are simmered in the bouillon but for a much shorter period of time. The marriage of all parts is the final simmering and blending together of flavors just before serving.

The cabbage is cooked separately, but in a portion of the same broth, as are the potatoes. Cabbage greatly enriches the garnish, but it is best kept apart in the beginning so that its distinctive flavor does not overpower the delicacy of the soup. And potato cooked for a long period in the pot would tend to cloud the broth.

There is no denying that making a pot-au-feu is an all-day affair. True, most of the time pots are simmering quietly on the back of the stove, but there must be a watchful eye to make sure a surge of gas or electricity does not turn a simmer into a raging boil.

INGREDIENTS

Meats and Bouillon
4 pounds beef brisket, rolled and tied in a bundle
2 cloves garlic, peeled and cut into slices
4 quarts beef stock
2 medium onions, peeled and spiked with 2 cloves each
2 medium carrots, unpeeled, washed, chopped into 2-inch pieces
3 stalks celery, chopped into 2-inch pieces
6 to 8 sprigs parsley
Additional stock or water, if needed, to barely cover meat
1 4-pound chicken

Vegetable Garnish
2 small cabbages (about 2 pounds each)
1½ pounds leeks
1 pound small turnips, peeled, trimmed, and quartered
12 to 14 long, thin carrots (about 1 pound), peeled

Sachet d'épice
2 bay leaves
12 black peppercorns
½ teaspoon thyme

2 small apples, peeled, left whole
4 or 5 medium potatoes, peeled and quartered
Salt
Freshly ground black pepper
12 slices dry bread, preferably French, sliced ⅜ inch thick
1 cup grated Parmesan cheese

Accompaniments
Coarse salt
Small dill pickles or sour gherkins

(continued)

Dijon-type mustard
Horseradish

SPECIAL EQUIPMENT	Large 10- or 12-quart soup pot plus assortment of smaller pots and bowls. Chinois or colander.
PREPARATION	Be certain meat is tied in a tight bundle that won't pull apart during cooking. With a sharp knife, make random gashes on all sides of the meat and tuck in the garlic slivers. Set aside. Do not put meat into the stock until stock is bubbling hot, in order to seal in the juices rather than dissipate them as starting with cold broth would do.
BOIL	Pour the beef stock into the large pot. Bring to a medium boil and add the onions spiked with cloves. Add one of the other vegetables—carrots, celery, and parsley—each time the stock returns to a boil.

When the stock is boiling again, lower the meat into the pot. Add additional stock or water, if necessary, to cover. |
| **SIMMER** *1½ hours* | Partially cover and lower heat so the pot gently simmers for about 1½ hours.

Cut off the wing tips of the chicken, truss the chicken, and set aside. Add the wing tips, neck, and giblets to the simmering stock. |
| **PARBOIL** *12–15 mins.* | Strip off the outer leaves of the cabbages. Cut each cabbage into quarters. Cut out the core, leaving just enough of the end to hold the leaves together. Fit the quarters snugly into a saucepan so they will not lose their shape or come apart during cooking. Cover with salted water. Parboil for about 12 to 15 minutes. This will remove the excess water in the leaves and diminish their aggressive flavor somewhat. Drain the cabbage, press to force out the water, and return to the saucepan, again arranging to fit tightly. As a precaution, I place a pie pan on top of the cabbage quarters and lightly weigh it down. Set aside for the moment. Also prepare the leeks by cutting off the green tops, leaving only the white cylinders. Cut each leek lengthwise but do not cut through the root end, so that the leek will not come apart. Carefully wash the leeks. Tie the leeks in 1 or 2 bundles, depending on their size. Set aside for later. |
| **SIMMER** *1½ hours* | When the bouillon has cooked for 1 hour, ladle some of it over the cabbage to barely cover. Heat to simmer, covered, over very low heat and continue to simmer until ready to serve—a good 1½ hours. |

SIMMER *1½ hours*	Lower the trussed chicken into the pot with the beef. The liquid should barely cover it. If not, add stock or water. Cover partially and simmer for 1½ hours until tender when pierced with the point of a sharp knife. *Review:* When finished, the beef will have cooked 3 hours and the chicken 1½ hours. *Note:* The bird can be stuffed—before cooking—with an easy-to-make dressing of bread crumbs; the minced heart, liver, and gizzard of the chicken; 1 beaten egg; 1 crushed clove garlic; and allspice moistened with milk and seasoned with salt and pepper to taste.
LIFT OUT	After a total of 3 hours' cooking, lift out both the beef and the chicken and place in another pot or casserole, moisten with a cup of broth, cover with foil, and keep warm until the final assembly. Strain the broth through a chinois or colander. Rinse the pot and return the broth to it.
BOIL/SIMMER *30 mins.* *30 mins.* *15 mins.*	There are three things left to do in the final hour. Bring the broth to a gentle boil and add turnips, carrots, sachet, and apples. Simmer gently for 30 minutes. Add the leek package(s) to the broth. Continue to simmer for an additional 30 minutes. During the last half hour boil the potatoes in a small saucepan in stock taken from the large pot. Add salt and pepper to taste. Cook for about 15 minutes or until fork-tender. With a slotted spoon lift out the potatoes, and keep them warm in a dish towel. Save the bouillon in which the potatoes were cooked to augment the other broth if necessary.
KEEP HOT	Lift out the vegetables in the large pot and carefully place them in a saucepan with a cup of broth and keep hot during the soup course. Remove the sachet and apples and discard.
REHEAT	If the beef and chicken have cooled in the interim, put them back into the hot stock for 5 or 6 minutes. Remove them again, and, as with the vegetables, keep them hot while the guests enjoy the first course.

Soup

Place a bread slice in each bowl and ladle soup over it. Pass Parmesan cheese to sprinkle on top.

Meat

Cut the strings off the meat and carve into attractive ½-inch slices. Carve the chicken and place it on a serving platter.

Vegetables

Lift out several of the cabbage pieces and place down the center of another large serving platter. Cut the strings from the leek bundle(s) and place the leeks down one side of the platter. Arrange carrots, turnips, and potatoes along each of the other sides.

Pass the two platters. The meat and vegetables may be put in the soup bowls (as we do at our house) or the bowls can be removed and plates used.

A tureen of the rich bouillon should be kept on the table throughout the dinner to moisten meat and vegetables.

Pass the accompaniments.

Crusty French bread is an absolute must to be served with pot-au-feu. So is a simple young red wine such as a Beaujolais nouveau or a Côtes du Rhône.

Shabu-Shabu (Japanese)

Serves 6 to 8

Shabu-Shabu is a Japanese communal dish that directly involves the diners in the preparation of the meal. Each person dips pieces of tissue-thin beef and freshly cut vegetables into a shared pot of boiling broth in the center of the table.

The meat cooks quickly in the steaming broth and is done in seconds. With practice and some luck the chopsticks will keep a grip on the meat during the brief interval of cooking, while the vegetables, which take a little longer, are dropped into the broth to be retrieved at will by the guests.

As the morsels are lifted out of the bowl they are dipped into a seasoned sauce in individual dipping bowls. Each guest has his own rice bowl where he may rest his bite en route to his lips or gather up a bit of rice as well.

The broth is enriched by the brief cooking of the meat and vegetables, and it is later ladled into small bowls and served, lightly salted, with a bit of chopped onion.

Traditionally the stock in which the cooking takes place is water flavored by a 4-inch square of kombu (giant kelp). If kombu is not available in stores of your city that specialize in Asian foods, court bouillon (see Stock) or a light chicken broth may be substituted. The broth must be light, with little body, so that it doesn't intrude on the natural flavors of the meat and vegetables.

If there is one thing difficult about shabu-shabu, it is to get a piece of well-marbled beef cut paper-thin by the butcher. Markets in big cities catering to Japanese cuisine regularly carry shabu-shabu slices in their meat cases, but not all of us are fortunate enough to live near such a market. Ask the butcher for paper-thin slices, thinner even than for sukiyaki—they should be about 3 by 8 inches, cut from best-quality sirloin. It is difficult to do this slicing at home, even if meat is held in the freezer for a half hour or so to stiffen it and make it easier to cut. I have done the slicing on my electric slicer, but it is tedious work.

Equally important in preparing a shabu-shabu meal is the presentation at the table of beef and vegetables beautifully arranged on a platter with the same artistic care that one would give a flower arrangement. The vegetables should be cut into pieces of uniform size so that their overall cooking time is equal. For nutritional as well as aesthetic reasons, twice the volume of vegetables as of meat is used.

The traditional Japanese cooking vessel for shabu-shabu is a donabe, a flameproof earthenware casserole. If a donabe is not among your kitchen vessels, use a flameproof ceramic casserole or a wok.

To provide a heat source in the middle of the dining-room table, with a vessel of bubbling broth on top, may seem to be a problem, but there are a number of ways to surmount it. You may have what the Japanese use—a portable gas or electric burner, or a charcoal brazier. An electric skillet is a good substitute, especially one with recessed handles. Slow cookers often have an outer shell in which to do deep frying—these are very good.

It is easy to prepare ahead for shabu-shabu, and certainly there is no greater way to involve guests than to arm them with chopsticks, or fondue forks for the less dexterous, and let them pick and choose their way through a delicious meal.

The first time I was served shabu-shabu was not in Asia but in Studio City, California, where Kiyo Sharp, née Miyake, prepared the dish as her mother was taught to make it in her Japanese village.

INGREDIENTS

Meat and Vegetables

1½ pounds choice sirloin, cut for shabu-shabu, above

1 head napa cabbage (Chinese cabbage)

10 to 12 green onions

1 large white onion

3 clusters enoki mushrooms

12 fresh or dried shiitake mushrooms or ½ pound cultivated mushrooms

1 cake tofu (bean curd)

½ pound *shirataki* filaments or ½ pound Chinese bean thread or "cellophane" noodles (transparent noodles)

Broth

4-inch square kombu (giant kelp) or 4 to 5 cups light chicken broth, to fill cooking vessel ⅔ full

4 to 5 cups water—to fill cooking vessel ⅔ full

(continued)

Sauce
½ cup sesame seeds
¾ cup each water and soy sauce
½ cup vinegar
6 tablespoons lemon juice
¼ teaspoon Ajinomoto or Ac'cent or monosodium glutamate (MSG),
    optional

Rice
1 cup Japanese short-grain rice (Botan or Japan Rose)

SPECIAL
EQUIPMENT

See discussion of traditional Japanese equipment in text above.

PREPARATION

Meat and Vegetables

Meat: Cut paper-thin. As they are stacked, offset the slices in the pile so they can be picked up easily one at a time with chopsticks later on. If slices persist in clinging together, clump each piece into a loose ball and arrange.

Vegetables: As each vegetable variety is cut, it should be placed on the serving platter, covered with plastic wrap, and refrigerated until used.

Napa: Remove coarse outer leaves, trim bottom, and cut crosswise into ½-inch strips.

Green onions: Trim off most of the green, and cut white portion diagonally into 1-inch lengths.

Large white onion: Peel and cut in half lengthwise. Cut across to make ¼-inch slices.

Enoki mushrooms: Cut off the root cluster 1 inch and gently separate stalks so they can be picked up by chopsticks.

Fresh cultivated mushrooms: Brush clean, trim stems, and cut into thin slices.

Fresh shiitake: Clean if necessary, cut off and discard stems and slice as above, or

Dried shiitake: Soak according to instructions on package, drain, discard stems, and slice as above.

Bean curd: Rinse under cold water and blot dry; cut into 1½-inch cubes and arrange on platter.

Shirataki filaments: Rinse in hot water several times and finally once in cold water, or

Bean thread: Soak in warm water to soften. Drain. Later they will absorb the flavor of the broth and become quite tasty.

Rice: At the same time prepare the rice according to package instructions. Japanese short-grain rice must first be washed under running water.

SIMMER
3–4 mins.

Broth

If using kombu, wipe it off with a moist cloth and place it in the cooking vessel. Fill the vessel two-thirds full of cool water. Bring to a boil, remove kombu just *before* boiling point is reached, and simmer gently 3 to 4 minutes. This can be done in the kitchen and the broth brought to the table already prepared. If using chicken stock heat to a simmer in the vessel.

TOAST
5 mins.

Sauce

Toast the sesame seeds in a skillet for about 5 minutes over medium heat until 1 or 2 of the seeds pop. Place the seeds in a blender or a Japanese *suribachi* (grinding bowl, or use a mortar and pestle) and process until powdery.

Place the powdered sesame seeds in a medium bowl and mix together with water, soy sauce, vinegar, lemon juice, and Ajinomoto, if using it. The sauce can be refrigerated for 2 or 3 days but it is better made fresh. When ready to serve, pour a portion of the sauce into individual cups or bowls, one for each guest.

FINAL STEP

Each guest is served a portion of rice in a small bowl, which is usually held under the piece of meat or vegetable as it travels from *donabe* to mouth. With chopsticks or fondue fork in the other hand, the diner picks up a piece of meat from the serving platter and swishes it to and fro in the simmering broth until the red meat turns pink. Next, it is dipped into the sauce. Diners alternate between meat and vegetables.

When the meat and vegetables have been finished, the broth is ladled into individual bowls and seasoned with salt if necessary, and chopped onion is added.

VARIATION

Other one-pot dishes *(nabemono)* include *chirinabe,* fish chunks and vegetables; *mizutaki,* vegetables and chicken pieces; and sukiyaki, one of the best-known of Japanese dishes, a beef creation that became popular in Japan only at the turn of the century and after Western diplomats and traders had introduced beef eating to a nation of Buddhists.

Two Breads

A Peasant Loaf

Good soup deserves good bread. To give the loaf taste and texture the dough should be put together with simple ingredients and allowed to mature before it is baked. Such a loaf will not overpower a delicate soup, yet it will do justice to a robust chowder.

The ingredients of a good peasant loaf are flour, water, yeast, and salt. The dough is left for hours, not minutes, to rise and slowly develop full flavor before it is shaped into loaves and baked.

Many of the recipes for soups in this book call for a peasant-type bread to accompany the meal or to be used to thicken a soup or stew. This versatile loaf can be trimmed of its crispy crust and cut into rounds to be covered with cheese and toasted, or made into croutons or whatever.

The peasant loaf is made with bread flour milled from hard wheat to give the dough the ability to withstand the expansion it undergoes when it more than triples its original volume. It is baked at high heat to provide the quick oven spring that makes possible the open formation of the cellular structure common to country bread.

INGREDIENTS   2 packages dry yeast
2 cups water (70°)
6 cups bread flour, approximately
2 teaspoons salt

2 teaspoons water
Butter or shortening

BAKING
EQUIPMENT

One nonstick baking sheet or long baguette pans, if available. If your pans are not nonstick, be sure to grease them.

PREPARATION
3 mins.
4 hours

Sprinkle yeast over the 2 cups of water in a mixing bowl. Let stand for a moment or two; stir to dissolve the yeast particles.

Add 3 cups of flour and stir into a thick batter. Cover the bowl with plastic wrap and let stand for 4 to 6 hours to develop flavor while it puffs to double its size. Salt will be added later.

DOUGH

Mix the salt in 2 teaspoons of water and pour into the batter. Add flour, ½ cup at a time, stirring first with a wooden spatula or spoon and then working by hand as it gets less sticky. When the dough is shaggy but a solid ball, turn out onto the work table. Begin kneading aggressively—push down with the fingers of both hands, turn the dough a quarter turn, and fold over—and continue this rhythm. Sprinkle on flour as needed to give the dough additional body—it should not slump when formed into a ball. Occasionally slam the dough down hard against the work surface to speed the formation of the gluten. Dough should be elastic, firm but not hard.

FIRST RISING
1½ hours

Lightly film a bowl with butter or shortening and place the lump of dough in it. Cover tightly with plastic wrap and leave at room temperature to more than double in volume, about 1½ hours.

SHAPING
10 mins.

Punch down the puffy dough and put it on the lightly floured work surface. Shape into 1 loaf or divide the ball into as many pieces as you want loaves (or rolls). For round loaves, *boules,* shape the pieces into balls and place them on the baking sheet. For baguettes roll the dough under the palms to extend each piece to 16 to 20 inches in length. Place it in a special baguette pan or on a baking sheet.

SECOND RISING
1½ hours

Cover the loaves with wax paper or with a wool cloth (dough won't stick to it). (Nonstick sheets of silicone are marvelous for covering rising dough, among their many other uses.) Leave loaves at room temperature until they have risen to more than double in volume.

PREHEAT
450°

Place 1 cup of hot water in a shallow pan in the bottom of the oven to provide steam during the first few minutes of baking. Preheat oven to 450°.

BAKING *450°* *25–30 mins.*	This is a very hot oven—filled with steam—so be careful when opening door. 　　With a razor blade, make diagonal cuts down the length of long loaves or a tic-tac-toe design on the *boules.* Place the loaves on the middle shelf of the oven. 　　Loaves are done when they are golden brown and are hard on the bottom and hollow-sounding when thumped.
FINAL STEP	Place on a rack to cool—and listen to the wonderful crackle of the crust as it cools.

Rich Corn Bread

There are certain soups and stews that cry out for corn bread to accompany them. Burgoo (page 334) is one, for example, and Catfish Chowder (page 91) another. Stone Crabber Oyster Stew (page 175) is thickened with crumbled corn bread.

*　　The ingredients for this butter-and-egg-rich corn bread can be juggled to accommodate a southerner's preference for white cornmeal and no sugar. Here it is (northern style) made with yellow cornmeal and some sugar.*

INGREDIENTS	1½ cups yellow cornmeal ½ cup all-purpose flour 1 teaspoon *each* salt and sugar 2 tablespoons baking powder 1 cup milk 3 eggs, at room temperature ¼ cup heavy cream, at room temperature ⅓ cup butter, melted
BAKING PAN	1 (for thick) or 2 (for thin) 9-by-9-inch baking pans, greased or lined with parchment paper if not made of Teflon or other nonstick material
PREPARATION *10 mins.*	Preheat oven to 400°. 　　In a mixing bowl, measure cornmeal, flour, salt, sugar, and baking powder. In a small bowl beat together the milk and eggs and pour into the dry ingredients. Beat until thoroughly blended. Pour in the cream and stir in the butter. Blend the mixture.
FORMING *2 mins.*	Divide the batter into 2 baking pans to the depth of ½ inch for thin breads or pour all the batter to a depth of 1½ inches into 1 pan for one thicker bread.

BAKING
400°
20–25 mins.

Bake in the oven until bread is nicely browned. Insert a toothpick or cake-testing pin in the bread—it will come out clean and dry if bread is done.

FINAL STEP

Remove bread from the oven. Serve hot. Cut in squares or rectangles.

Sauces

MANY SOUPS, such as minestrone and bouillabaisse, benefit greatly with the addition of flavors concentrated in a thick sauce spooned into the soup when it is served. Three are presented here—the traditional Italian pesto; an herbed cheese sauce; and rouille, which is so satisfying with fish soups and stews.

Pesto

Makes 1½ cups

Pesto, created by the Italians for their soups and pastas, is simply—and literally—a paste of fresh basil, garlic, cheese, nuts, olive oil, and sometimes butter. A really fine pesto will enhance the plainest soup.

The finest pesto is made with freshly picked basil leaves. If they are in short supply, substitute a mixture of dried basil and fresh parsley or fresh spinach. Fresh basil leaves can be frozen for later use. Or the pesto itself can be frozen for future use.

Marcella Hazan, in her book The Classic Italian Cook Book, *suggests a proportion of four parts Parmesan to one part Romano cheese to keep the flavors of pesto in balance. A well-rounded pesto, she says, is never made only with Parmesan.*

Two ways to prepare pesto are given below—by machine and by hand. The sequence in adding ingredients varies between the two.

INGREDIENTS

2 cups fresh basil leaves, chopped, or 2 cups chopped fresh spinach leaves or flat-leaf parsley, and 3 tablespoons dried basil

¾ cup olive oil

2 tablespoons pine nuts or walnuts

2 cloves garlic, crushed

1 teaspoon salt, if desired

1⅓ cups freshly grated Parmesan cheese and ⅓ cup freshly grated Romano cheese

2 tablespoons butter, softened to room temperature

SPECIAL EQUIPMENT

Food processor or blender, or, for the hand method, a mortar and pestle

PREPARATION PROCESS
45 secs.

Machine

Put the leaves, olive oil, nuts, garlic, and salt in food processor or blender, and process at high speed for about 45 seconds. Scrape down the sides of the work bowl from time to time.

The mixture at this point should be thin enough to run off the spatula easily. If it appears too thick, blend in additional olive oil.

Pour the sauce into a bowl and stir in the grated cheeses and butter. While the cheese can be added to the mixture in the machine, the texture will be too fine for an authentic pesto.

Mortar and Pestle

The ingredients are added in this order: basil leaves (or other leaves), nuts, garlic, salt, cheeses, olive oil, and butter.

10 mins.

Place the basil, nuts, garlic, and salt in a large mortar. Use a rotary motion to grind and crush the ingredients against the side of the mortar. (The Japanese *suribachi* is excellent for this.) When the mixture becomes a paste, add the grated cheese and continue to grind with the pestle until a perfect blend is achieved. Put aside the pestle.

4 mins.

Begin to add the olive oil, a few drops at a time. Beat it into the mixture with a wooden spoon. When all of the oil has been added, beat in the butter.

FINAL STEP

Spoon 1 or 2 tablespoons of a hot soup into the pesto before serving. One tablespoon of pesto swirled on top of a soup in the tureen, with additional pesto to be passed, is a Genoese tradition.

Note: In summertime, when basil is plentiful in the markets, make extra pesto to hold in the freezer for later use.

Herbed Cheese Sauce

Makes 1 cup

Pesto, of course, is traditional for Italian dishes; but there are other sauces made with different ingredients that are equally delicious. This one is made with butter, a little olive oil, and parsley instead of basil (the basic ingredient of pesto).

INGREDIENTS	1 cup freshly grated Parmesan cheese
	⅓ cup butter, at room temperature
	1 tablespoon olive oil
	¼ cup finely ground walnuts
	1 clove garlic, minced
	1½ teaspoons minced parsley
	½ teaspoon *each* chervil, basil, and marjoram
SPECIAL EQUIPMENT	None
PREPARATION	Thoroughly mix together all the ingredients in a bowl. The mixture will be stiff.
FINAL STEP	Place a dollop of the sauce in each serving of soup. Leftover sauce will keep for days in the refrigerator, or months if frozen.

Rouille

Makes 1½ cups

Rouille, the fiery red pepper sauce from the Mediterranean, adds a new and delightful dimension to fish soups and stews, especially bouillabaisse. Some cooks mix a spoonful or two of the hot soup into the rouille before it is served; others thin it with a bit of olive oil. At the table, the guests help themselves to the rouille and swirl it into their own soup.

INGREDIENTS	½ sweet bell pepper (red preferred), ribs removed, seeded, then chopped, or 1 4-ounce can pimiento, chopped
	1 slice firm white bread, 2 inches thick, crust removed
	2 small dried red peppers, stemmed but not seeded, or 1 teaspoon Tabasco sauce
	8 to 10 fresh basil leaves, chopped, or 1 tablespoon dried
	3 cloves garlic, peeled and diced
	½ teaspoon salt (sea or kosher preferred)

¼ teaspoon freshly ground black pepper
6 tablespoons good-quality fruity French or Italian olive oil

SPECIAL
EQUIPMENT

Blender, food processor, or mortar and pestle

PREPARATION

Blanch the bell pepper pieces in water for 5 minutes over medium-low heat. Drain. Dip the bread in water and squeeze dry.

To make by hand, first grind the dried red pepper in mortar and then add sweet peppers (or pimiento), chopped basil leaves, and garlic. Grind with pestle until blended. Add bread, salt, and pepper and continue blending until the mixture is a fairly smooth puree. It will not be as smooth as rouille done in a blender, but I like the coarseness. Stir in the olive oil in a thin stream. The consistency should be that of mayonnaise.

To make in a blender or food processor, place all the ingredients in the work bowl and puree.

FINAL STEP

The rouille may be used immediately or refrigerated for 2 or 3 weeks. Frozen, it can be stored indefinitely.

To Garnish

THE PURPOSE OF A GARNISH is to provide style as well as substance. It may be simple, such as a pinch of chopped parsley or chives, or complicated, such as quenelles or almond balls.

The challenge is to provide each soup or stew with a garnish that offers a clear but complementary contrast, taste, or color without overwhelming the dish. Flavor is the primary consideration. Chopped herbs add little in the way of texture or body, and are used to provide color and flavor.

When a soup or stew is finished and about to be served, look at it critically. Is it lacking color? Texture? Be restrained, however. Many times the small but delicate touch is the right touch—a tiny dollop of cream swirled into the soup, or just a hint of sherry. Understate rather than overstate.

While most recipes in the book suggest the garnish, here is a guide that includes others.

CROUTONS, CRACKERS, AND CRISPS

Croutons, small cubes of buttered bread, fried or baked, are best served on thick and cream soups, where they do not absorb the liquid as quickly as in a broth. Souffléed crackers (soaked in water and baked) or Parmesan crackers (dipped in butter, sprinkled with cheese, and baked) are especially good with iced soups, the latter with tomato soup. Crisps are cut from thinly rolled dough made with flour and grated cheese, and baked.

PROFITEROLES

These tiny baked puff shells made from *pâte à chou* or puff paste may be floated on soups as they come from the oven or first filled with a pâté, or a vegetable, chicken, or fish puree. Puff paste is also used to make soup peas or soup nuts, but these are fried, not baked.

CREAM TOPPINGS

These can be a swirl of heavy cream across a pureed soup or cream whipped to a stiff frothiness with herbs or spices, mustard, or horseradish. A swirl of sour cream or yogurt is equally good.

DUMPLINGS

These are small pieces of dough or batter, steamed, boiled, or fried, and served in the soup or stew. They can be dropped into thin soups during the cooking process or cooked separately if they are to be used in a thick or cream soup. The flavor of some dumplings is enhanced with the addition of herbs or spices or freshly grated cheeses.

MEATS

Most meat garnishes are diced small or cut into julienne strips. Fish, veal, or chicken may be ground into a paste and made into quenelles.

SEAFOOD

Seafood garnishes are diced or flaked; the pieces should be large enough to be distinguishable.

PASTA

Fine noodles, vermicelli, spaghetti, and other macaroni products are used as garnishes in many soups. These include filled types of pasta such as wonton and kreplach.

CEREALS

Rice or barley, cooked.

EGGS

Eggs are a versatile garnish for soups—among various forms are a slice of hard-cooked egg floating on the surface, a sprinkling of cooked and grated yolk, and a raw egg beaten and swirled into hot soup to cook into lacy threads throughout the soup.

VEGETABLES

- Small vegetables such as peas or young snow peas may be left whole.
- Green and wax beans should be cut into small cross sections.
- Asparagus tips may be left whole.
- Divide broccoli heads into tiny florets.
- Slice leafy vegetables such as lettuce, spinach, and sorrel into thin ribbons known as chiffonade.
- Cut large vegetables—carrots, turnips, and potatoes—into narrow julienne strips or into *brunoise* (fine dice).
- Parboil raw vegetables to soften them slightly without losing their crispness. Do not parboil tomatoes.

FRUIT

Thin slices of lemon or mint leaves complement consommé beautifully—both visually and on the palate. Four or five small fruits such as raspberries or blueberries or slices of luscious ripe strawberries add color and flavor to iced fruit soups.

Spices, Herbs, and Seasonings Important to Soups and Stews

HERBS AND SPICES ENHANCE flavor and add aroma as well as pungency and piquancy.

Herbs, which are the leaves and stalks of aromatic plants, supply an attractive taste and aroma to all dishes, especially soups and stews. Most herbs are more pungent when fresh than dried. The fresh ones are preferred to dried, which are less aromatic. To store dried herbs, whether commercially or home-dried, place them in airtight containers away from strong light. This will help preserve their aroma.

As a rule, use about half as much of a dried herb as a fresh one. This varies according to the age and strength of the dried herb.

Spices are the seeds, berries, or bark of aromatic tropical plants. Buy them in small quantities, as they tend to lose their flavor quickly.

Basil or Sweet basil Pungent and robust, belongs to the mint family and is one of the best-known herbs.

Bay leaves Dried leaves of edible laurel. Imported varieties from Portugal and Turkey are preferred to the California variety, which is quite strong.

Cayenne Spicy-hot red pepper, dried and ground.

Chervil Aromatic herb of carrot family, similar to parsley but more delicate.

Chili pepper A fine red pepper with a satiny surface.

Chili powder A blend of chili peppers, cumin seed, oregano, and garlic powder.

Chive Slender green grassy-looking stalk that grows from onionlike bulb. Has delicate onion flavor. Fresh is preferred but it is available freeze-dried.

Clove Nail-shaped dried flower bud of the clove tree. Rich and pungent in flavor.

Coriander or Cilantro (Chinese parsley) Aromatic herb and spice of carrot family known and used since biblical times. Seeds have flavor like lemon peel and sage. Leaves have parsleylike flavor, but more exotic; taste for the leaf is acquired.

Cumin or Comino seed Aromatic seeds with bitter, warm flavor, especially when freshly roasted in small skillet and ground. Pungent.

Curry powder Blend of spices from India. By varying proportions of four to forty spices, different curries are produced. Curry powder generally contains cumin, turmeric, ginger, red pepper, and coriander.

Dill Aromatic foliage, seed, and stem. Its flavor is enticing and mild, but use a light hand.

Filé A powder obtained from pounded sassafras leaves and used to thicken gumbo. One tablespoon of filé has the thickening power of 1 pound of okra.

Garlic Potent flavored bulb of onion family. Wildly popular with some, less with others, but generally enjoyable if used with discretion. Also available as a powder, a salt, and instant minced and chopped. Fresh is highly recommended.

Ginger Warm in flavor, it is the dried root of a subtropical plant grown in China, Japan, India, and British West Indies.

Marjoram One of the best-known herbs; belongs to mint family. Very pungent, especially when fresh. Dried, it loses its flavor quickly.

Mint A widely grown herb with delightful cool, pungent flavor. Fresh leaves or dried flakes.

Nutmeg Kernel of fruit of nutmeg tree. Ground nutmeg loses its flavor quickly, so grate the whole kernel, if possible. One of the oldest known spices.

Onion Onions are available fresh or as onion powder, onion salt, instant minced onion, etc.

Oregano Has a pleasant, pungent fragrance, which intensifies when dried. Don't keep long; it changes color and character as it grows stale.

Paprika A red pepper grown in Spain and Hungary. Method of grinding determines ultimate flavor. Spanish is milder than Hungarian. Buy choice paprika—many ordinary paprikas have more color than flavor.

Parsley Curly parsley is decorative and tasty; Italian parsley has a flat leaf and a more pronounced flavor. Dried flakes are tasteless.

Pepper Buy whole peppercorns for finest flavor. When whole peppercorns are called for in soups or stews, crush them slightly so they will release flavor. Black pepper is a dried immature berry; white pepper is the mature berry with hull removed.

Pimiento Ripe fleshy fruit of a type of sweet pepper, most commonly found packed in jars in its own viscous juice.

Red pepper Whole ground or crushed pods of hot red peppers, including cayenne.

Rosemary Spiky leaves of this fragrant member of the mint family with a strong pungent flavor.

Saffron Dried stigmas of purple crocus grown in Mediterranean regions. Expensive, but gives a beautiful yellow color and a distinctive flavor to dishes. Buy in threads rather than ground, for fresher flavor. Must be steeped in hot liquid to bring out flavor.

Sage Very pungent dried leaf of shrub belonging to the mint family.

Savory Summer savory is more common and aromatic than winter savory. Has clean balsam fragrance. Good in fish soups and stews.

Shallot Small lavender-pink onion that produces large clusters of small bulbs with delicate onion flavor.

Sorrel Long slender leaves, used fresh, have pleasant acid and sour flavor. A sour grass, it is easy to grow as a perennial.

Soy sauce A pungent, brown salty sauce fermented from soybeans that is one of the primary seasonings of Asian cooking. Chinese soy sauces, in general, are quite salty and have a dense flavor. Japanese soy sauces have a relatively bright taste and aroma, and are less salty. Japanese soy sauces are graded "light" or "dark." The popular Kikkoman brand, one of the few big commercial brands that are naturally fermented, is dark.

Tabasco sauce A commercial liquid pepper seasoning made with fresh-picked, hot tabasco peppers, salted and cured for 3 years and blended with vinegar. Produced on privately owned Avery Island, Louisiana.

Tarragon Related to the wormwood family, it is available fresh or dried and has a delicate subtle, lemon-and-licorice flavor. The fresh is much preferred.

Thyme Essential to many soups and stews, it is number two (after parsley) among America's favorite herbs. The dried is available as whole leaf or powdered.

Turmeric Bright yellow, with a rich appetizing aroma, turmeric has a rather sharp mustardy flavor. An ingredient of curry powder.

Standard Weights and Measures

American Measure Equivalents

Make certain all measurements are level.

Dash	= 8 drops
1 tablespoon	= 3 teaspoons
4 tablespoons	= ¼ cup
5⅓ tablespoons	= ⅓ cup
8 tablespoons	= ½ cup
16 tablespoons	= 1 cup (dry)
1 fluid ounce	= 2 tablespoons
1 cup (liquid)	= ½ pint
2 cups (16 ounces)	= 1 pint
2 pints (4 cups)	= 1 quart
4 quarts	= 1 gallon
8 quarts	= 1 peck (dry)
4 pecks	= 1 bushel
16 ounces (dry measure)	= 1 pound

Fluid Measure Equivalents

AMERICAN	BRITISH	METRIC
4½ cups or 1 quart 2 ounces	1¾ pints	1 liter
2 cups (generous) or 1 pint (generous)	¾ pint (generous)	1 demiliter (½ liter)
½ cup (scant) or ¼ pint (scant)	3 to 4 ounces	1 deciliter (⅒ liter)

Weight Equivalents

BRITISH AND AMERICAN	METRIC
0.035 ounce	1 gram
1 ounce	28.35 grams
3½ ounces	100 grams
4 ounces (approximately)	114 grams
8 ounces	226.78 grams
1 pound 1½ ounces (approximately)	500 grams
2.21 pounds	1 kilogram

Approximate Weights and Measures of Some Common Foods

	1 TABLESPOON	1 CUP	1 PINT	1 QUART
Barley, pearl		8 ounces	1 pound	2 pounds
Butter		8 ounces	1 pound	2 pounds
Cabbage, shredded or chopped				12 ounces
Carrots, diced raw				1 pound 3 ounces
Celery, chopped raw			8 ounces	1 pound
Curry powder	¼ ounce	3½ ounces		
Legumes:				
Beans, kidney, dry			12½ ounces	1 pound 9 ounces
Beans, lima, dry			13 ounces	1 pound 10 ounces
Beans, white, dry			14 ounces	1 pound 12 ounces
Lettuce, shredded				8 ounces

	1 Tablespoon	1 Cup	1 Pint	1 Quart
Milk, liquid, whole		8½ ounces	1 pound 1 ounce	2 pounds 2 ounces
Mushrooms (medium-size), sliced or chopped		3 ounces	6 ounces	
Oils, cooking or salad		8 ounces	16 ounces	2 pounds
Onions, dehydrated flakes		2½ ounces	5 ounces	10 ounces
Onions, chopped		4 ounces	8 ounces	1 pound
Paprika	¼ ounce	4 ounces		
Parsley, chopped		3 ounces	6 ounces	
Pepper, ground	¼ ounce			
Peppers, green, chopped		4 ounces	8 ounces	1 pound
Pimientos, drained, chopped		7 ounces	14 ounces	
Potatoes, cooked, diced			12½ ounces	1 pound 9 ounces
Rice, raw		8 ounces	1 pound	2 pounds
Salt	½ ounce	8 ounces		

Courtesy The Culinary Institute of America

Can Sizes and Their Approximate Equivalents

Size of Can	Number of Ounces	Number of Cups	Number of Servings
8 ounces	8	1	2
Picnic (also called No. 1 Eastern)	11	1⅓	2–3
No. 1 tall	16	2	3–4
No. 2	20	2½	4–5
No. 2½	28	3½	5–6
No. 3	33	4	6–8
No. 10	6 pounds 10 ounces	13	25–26

Comparative U.S., British, and Metric Weights and Measures for Ingredients Important to Soups and Stews

	UNITED STATES	BRITISH	METRIC
Butter	1 tablespoon	½ ounce	15 grams
	½ cup	4 ounces	125 grams
	2 cups	1 pound (generous)	500 grams
Cheese	1 pound (generous)	1 pound (generous)	500 grams
Cheese, grated			
Parmesan	1 cup (scant)	4 ounces (scant)	100 grams
Cornstarch	1 tablespoon	⅓ ounce	10 grams
Fish	1 pound (generous)	1 pound (generous)	500 grams
Fruit, fresh	1 pound (generous)	1 pound (generous)	500 grams
Fruit, dried	2 cups	1 pound (generous)	500 grams
Meats	1 pound (generous)	1 pound (generous)	500 grams
Meats, diced	1 cup	8 ounces	226 grams
Pepper, whole black	4½ tablespoons	1 ounce	30 grams
Pepper, whole white	3⅝ tablespoons	1 ounce (generous)	30 grams
Pepper, ground	4 tablespoons	1 ounce (generous)	30 grams
Rice	1 cup	8 ounces	240 grams
Salt	1 tablespoon	½ ounce	15 grams
Spices, ground	1 teaspoon	¹⁄₁₂ ounce	2½ grams
	2 tablespoons	½ ounce	15 grams
Vegetables, fresh	1 pound (generous)	1 pound (generous)	500 grams
Vegetables, dried (lentils, peas, etc.)	2 cups	1 pound (generous)	500 grams

Glossary

Aftertaste Flavor sensations remaining in mouth after food is eaten.

Al dente Firm to the bite, as with pasta.

Arrowroot Starchy white powder used to thicken delicate soups and sauces. Available in the spice section of markets.

Bain-marie A vessel containing hot water in which delicate dishes can be cooked, and also kept warm until served. Similar to a double boiler.

Barley, pearl Polished barley.

Base See *Food base.*

Beat To stir and lift while mixing to a smooth texture.

Bisque Thick cream soup or puree, especially of shellfish, bivalves, and crustaceans. (Classic bisques included the flavor drawn from the shells.) To a lesser extent, also of vegetables.

Blanch To cook or partially cook very briefly in boiling water to remove surface impurities, or to aid in removing skin, or to facilitate later cooking.

Blend To combine a number of ingredients so that all are distributed equally, often inseparably. Also, to process in a blender.

Boil To heat or cook in a liquid whose temperature reaches 212°F (at sea level). The surface will be broken by a steady bubbling action. In a rapid boil, the bubbles will be vigorous and rolling; in a medium boil the bubbles are gentle. A very slow boil, in which the liquid hardly moves, is also called a simmer.

Bouillon Consommé with pronounced beef flavor.

Bouillon cup China cup with two handles used for clear and cream soups.

Bouquet garni See *Sachet d'épice* below.

Break Occurs when ingredients separate and lose emulsification, usually when heat is too high or after standing. Many soups that break can simply be reheated and blended again with a wire whip or spatula. Others that appear curdled can be put through a fine-mesh strainer or blended in a food processor or blender.

Brown stock The liquid made by the simmering in water of previously browned and caramelized bones and vegetables.

Brunoise Cut into fine dice; usually refers to vegetables.

Casserole A covered vessel of metal or earthenware with small handles, for use both on the stove burner and in the oven. When made of metal, a good backup pot for making soups and stews.

Chiffonade Shredded vegetables or meats used in soups or as garnish.

Chili powder A blend of chili peppers, cumin seed, oregano, and garlic powder.

China cap See *Chinois* below.

Chinois Cone-shaped strainer of metal with long handle and hook to fasten to edge of pot. Made in various sizes with mesh or holes from fine to coarse. Semisolids can be forced through perforations with special roller made for the purpose.

Clam broth Liquid obtained from fresh clams when steamed open.

Clarify To make a liquid clear by adding egg whites and shells and removing solids in suspension, as in the preparation of consommé. Also, to treat butter by melting over low heat and straining off residue so it can be heated to a higher temperature without smoking.

Colander Wide strainer with coarse mesh or holes for draining liquids from solid foods.

Consommé A clear, strong, sparkling broth clarified and enriched by the addition of lean chopped meat, egg whites, and aromatics.

Court bouillon A stock made with vegetables used in soups and various fish dishes.

Cube To cut into small equal-sized squares or dice, generally ½ by ½ inch.

Curry powder A mixture of roasted pungent spices traditionally including cumin, turmeric, ginger, red pepper, and coriander.

Deglaze To loosen cooked particles and dissolve the caramelized drippings in the bottom of a pan so they may be incorporated into the stock, soup, or stew.

Dice To cut into tiny pieces smaller than cubes; also, the tiny cubes themselves.

Drippings Fats and liquids that collect in bottom of pan or skillet and become concentrated.

Emincé Cut fine.

Filé A powder obtained from pounded sassafras leaves and used to thicken gumbo. One tablespoon filé has the thickening power of 1 pound of okra, which is also a thickener for gumbos.

Fines herbes Finely chopped mixed herbs. The traditional fines herbes combination is parsley, chervil, tarragon, and sometimes chives.

Food base Concentrated food product used to make stocks, broths, sauces, and gravies, and used as a seasoner and flavor booster. Principally beef, chicken, and seafood.

Fumet Stock with intensified flavor, usually fish, made by boiling down or reducing normal stock.

Garnish To decorate and enhance food by adding other attractive foodstuffs before serving.

Herb bouquet See *Sachet d'épice.*

Julienne Cut into thin matchstick-size pieces.

Kettle Large metal pot, usually of cast iron, with lid and wire loop handle (bail). Unexcelled for holding heat and for slow cooking.

Leek Resembles a large green onion (scallion) but is much larger, and is used as a seasoning vegetable in soups and stews.

Legumes Vegetables of the pea or pulse family such as beans, peas, and lentils, including dried.

Marmite Cooking or serving vessel resembling a round pot with short or stub handles. Individual earthenware marmites are traditionally used for onion soup and a rich clear beef soup called *petite marmite.*

Minced Chopped or ground fine.

Mirepoix Mixture of vegetables, usually onions, celery, and carrots, to season stocks, soups, and stews.

Monosodium glutamate Abbreviated MSG. A concentrated form of sodium extracted from grains or beets. While it has no pronounced flavor of its own, it will enhance certain dishes such as frozen meats and vegetables. Seldom needed with high-quality and fresh ingredients. Marketed also as Ac'cent and Ajinomoto.

Okra Long green vegetable pod often used in gumbos and soups, which also serves as a thickener.

Paysanne Peasant-type vegetable soup; also a term describing vegetables cut into small flat shape.

Petite marmite Rich beef broth usually served in an individual earthenware casserole (the latter also sometimes referred to as a *petite marmite*).

Pinch As much as can be held between the thumb and forefinger. Example: a pinch of paprika.

Poach To cook just below the boiling point—205°F.

Potage Soup, usually quite thick.

Puree A pulp or paste of vegetable or fruit pushed through a sieve or food mill or put into blender or food processor.

Quahog or *quahaug* Round hard-shell Atlantic coast clam.

Raft Floating layer consisting of ground meat, vegetables, and egg whites, which forms in cooking consommé.

Ragout A thick savory stew.

Reduce To reduce volume through evaporation by cooking or simmering, to concentrate and intensify the flavor.

Roux Cooked mixture of melted fat and flour used for thickening.

Sachet d'épice A bundle of herbs and spices in a metal tea ball or tied in a cloth or cheese-cloth bag to flavor stocks, soups, and stews. Tied to the handle of a pot, it can be removed easily when the cooking is completed. Known also as bouquet garni, herb bouquet, or fagot.

Saucepan Small- or large-size saucepot; may have loop handles or one long handle and one loop handle. See also *Saucepot* below.

Saucepot Round deep vessel with loop handles and cover; larger in diameter than depth.

Sauté To fry rapidly in a small amount of fat until evenly browned.

Scum Extraneous matter that rises to the top of liquids being cooked. Should be carefully and continually lifted off with skimmer, especially in making clear stocks and broths.

Shallot Small flavoring vegetable of onion family, less pungent than garlic and more aromatic than onion.

Simmer Slow cooking just below, or at, boiling point—205° to 210°F. The French call it "making the pot smile."

Skim To remove matter rising to the top of liquids as they cook.

Slow cooker A covered electrical pot for long, gentle cooking at low temperatures.

Smother See *Sweat* below.

Stew Small pieces of meat cooked in liquid that combines with the juices to form a gravy. Also, seafood dish cooked quickly in milk or cream and seasonings. All-vegetable stews are also possible. Also said of the cooking process involved.

Stock The liquid in which meat, poultry, fish, or vegetables have been cooked, to be used in making many soups and stews. Stocks fall into two general categories, brown and white.

Stockpot Large pot for cooking stock, with straight sides and relatively small diameter so that the liquid bubbles up through the maximum amount of meat and vegetables to extract their flavor. The larger stockpots are fitted with spigot and strainer near the bottom to facilitate drawing off clear stocks.

Strain To put liquid through a sieve or filter to separate solids from liquids.

Sweat To sauté food under a cover so that it will release its own juices as it cooks.

Synthetic stock Stock made with dehydrated vegetable proteins resembling natural stocks such as beef or chicken.

Tofu (bean curd) A pure-white, custardlike loaf made from soybeans. Tofu is widely used in Asian cooking and is gaining popularity in the United States as a diet food because of its low ratio of calories to protein.

Tomato paste Tomato puree reduced to a solid content of 20 percent to 25 percent.

Tomato puree The flesh of tomatoes cooked, strained, and reduced to a heavy sauce.

Tomatoes, frozen Tomatoes are slipped into boiling water for a count of 10, lifted out and skin pulled off. They are immediately dropped into pint- or quart-size plastic bags and frozen. Tomatoes may be held in the freezer at 0°F for a year.

Try out To sauté until the fat is cooked out.

Tureen Deep vessel for serving soup.

Vichyssoise Potato-and-leek cream soup created by chef Louis Diat, of New York's Ritz-Carlton Hotel, and named for Vichy, France.

White stock The liquid made by a long simmering of fresh meat, poultry, fish, or vegetables that have not previously been caramelized, as with brown stock.

Index

ABOUT THE AUTHOR

BERNARD CLAYTON, Jr., began his career as a reporter and foreign correspondent; baking and cooking were his hobbies. He has been writing cookbooks for more than thirty years. When Clayton travels, he investigates historical and regional recipes, conversing with cooks and bakers around the world. He is the author of numerous cookbooks, including the definitive *Bernard Clayton's New Complete Book of Breads, Bernard Clayton's Cooking Across America, The Complete Book of Pastry,* and *The Breads of France.* He lives with his wife in Bloomington, Indiana.